THE MURDER OF SERGEI KIROV

History, Scholarship and the Anti-Stalin Paradigm

Grover Furr

AAKAR

THE MURDER OF SERGEI KIROV
History, Scholarship and the Anti-Stalin Paradigm
Grover Furr

First Published in India 2015

ISBN 978-93-5002-303-7

Published in agreement with Erythros Press and Media, LLC, Ohio, USA for publication and sale only in the Indian Subcontinent.

Published by
AAKAR BOOKS
28 E Pocket IV, Mayur Vihar Phase I, Delhi 110 091
Phone : 011 2279 5505 Telefax : 011 2279 5641
aakarbooks@gmail.com; www.aakarbooks.com

Printed at
Mudrak, 30 A Patparganj, Delhi 110 091

Table of Contents

Acknowledgements and Dedication

Once again, I would like to express my continuing gratitude to Kevin Prendergast and Arthur Hudson, Inter-Library Loan librarians at Harry S. Sprague Library, Montclair State University.

Their tireless efforts to obtain hard-to-find articles and books in many languages make my research possible.

*****

I dedicate this book to Susana Magdalena Sotillo, Ph.D., dedicated scholar and teacher, incisive and supportive critic, *mi compañera y mi camarada*, with all my love and respect.

Without your encouragement and support this work would never have been undertaken.

List of Abbreviations

Egge: Egge, Osmund. *Zagadka Kirova. Ubiystvo, razviazavshee stalinskii terror.* Moscow: ROSSPEN, 2011.

Kirilina: Kirilina, Alla. *Neizvestnyi Kirov.* St Petersburg: "Neva"; Moscow: "Olma-Press", 2001.

Lenoe: Lenoe, Matthew. *The Kirov Murder and Soviet History.* New Haven: Yale U.P. 2010.

Lubianka 1922-1936: *Lubianka. Stalin i VChK-GPU-OGPU-NKVD. IAnvar' 1922 - dekabr' 1936.* Moscow: IDF, 2003

Lubianka 1937-1938: *Lubianka. Stalin i Glavnoe Upravlenie Gosbezopasnosti NKVD.* 1937-1938. Moscow: "Materik", 2004.

RKEB 1: *Reabilitatsiia: Kak Eto Bylo. Mart 1953 - Fevral' 1956 gg. Dokumenty Prezidiuma TsK KPSS i Drugie Materialy.* Moscow: Mezhdunarodniy Fond "Demokratiia", 2000.

RKEB 2: *Reabilitatsiia. Kak Eto Bylo. Febral' 1956 - nachalo 80-kh godov. T. 2.* Moscow: "Materik", 2003.

RKEB 3: *Reabilitatsiia. Kak Eto Bylo. Seredina 80-kh godov - 1991. Dokumenty. T. 3.* Moscow: "Materik", 2004.

R-PP: *Reabilitatsia: Politicheskie Protsessy 30-x - 50-x gg.* Moscow: Izdatel'stvo politicheskoi literatury, 1991.

Introduction.

The basic facts have never been seriously disputed. At about 4:30 p.m. on December 1, 1934 Sergei Mironovich Kirov, First Secretary of the All-Union Communist Party (Bolshevik)[1] of Leningrad *oblast'* (province) and city, entered the Smolny Institute, headquarters of the Bolshevik Party. Kirov mounted the stairs and walked along the corridor of the third floor towards his office. Leonid Vasil'evich Nikolaev, an unemployed Party member, was standing in the hallway. Nikolaev allowed Kirov to pass by and then rushed towards him from behind, took out a pistol, and shot Kirov in the back of the skull. Nikolaev then tried to shoot himself in the head but missed and fell in a faint on the floor a few feet from Kirov's body.

Nikolaev was seized on the spot. From this point on there is little agreement.

Either late that night or sometime the next day his interrogations began. At first Nikolaev seems to have claimed that he had killed Kirov on his own, without any accomplices, in order to draw attention to what he felt was unfair treatment of himself. Within two or three days he began to hint that others were involved. Before a week was out Nikolaev had admitted that he was part of a conspiracy by a clandestine group of Party members opposed to Joseph Stalin and favoring Grigorii Zinoviev, Leningrad First Secretary before Kirov.

NKVD investigators now turned their attention on this group. Interrogations of those Nikolaev had named, and then of the persons named by those men, led to a number of partial and a few fuller confessions. Three weeks after the murder fourteen men were indicted for conspiracy to kill Kirov. They were tried on December 28-29, convicted, and executed immediately. Meanwhile, Nikolaev's brother Piotr and wife Mil'da Draule

---

[1] In Russian the Party's title was "VKP(b)" (Vsesoiuznaia Kommunisticheskaia Partiia (bolshevikov), or "All-Union Communist Party (bolshevik)"; informally, it was still referred to as the "Bolshevik Party", "Bolsheviks", etc.

had made more and more self-incriminating confessions. In March 1935 Draule was tried, convicted, and executed.

*****

The larger significance of the Kirov murder unfolded only gradually during the next three years. The threads that bound the Kirov conspirators to Zinoviev and Kamenev, followed up by NKVD investigators, led to the three Moscow "Show Trials" of 1936, 1937 and 1938, and to the trial of the military commanders known as the "Tukhachevsky Affair" of 1937. This last led in turn to the "Ezhovshchina", also known as the "Great Terror" of 1937-1938, during which some hundreds of thousands of Soviet citizens, most certainly innocent, were arrested and executed, with many others being imprisoned.

On March 5, 1953 Joseph Stalin died. Within months Nikita Khrushchev had become the most powerful leader of the Soviet Union. Before Stalin had been dead many months Khrushchev began organizing a campaign to attack Stalin. A major part of this effort was to declare that Stalin had fabricated false cases against all the defendants of the Moscow Trials and Tukhachevsky Affair.

Khrushchev hinted at these things in his famous "Secret Speech" of February 25, 1956. In the same speech he also cast doubt on the official version of the Kirov assassination. Within the party leadership Khrushchev and his men promoted the "rehabilitations" of a great many persons who had been executed during the 1930s, including some of the Moscow Trial defendants. Khrushchev and his men tried hard to find any evidence they could to prove that Stalin had been behind Kirov's murder. But they were unable to do so, and so at length settled for a story that Nikolaev had acted on his own.

The version that Stalin had caused Kirov to be killed continued to circulate, becoming widely believed both inside and outside the Soviet Union. Outside Russia the "Stalin did it" version continued for a while thanks to books by two well-known anticommunist writers: Robert Conquest, who wrote *Stalin and the Kirov Murder* in 1989, and Amy Knight, author of *Who Killed Kirov?* (1997). Both these works rely heavily on rumors and hearsay.

During the Gorbachev period another attempt was made by highly-placed Party officials to promote the view that Stalin had killed Kirov. This attempt also failed due to the utter lack of evidence to support it. Since 1990 the view officially accepted in Russia has been that Nikolaev acted alone, and that Stalin "used" Kirov's murder to frame former or putative rivals, forcing them to admit to crimes they had never committed, and executing them and, ultimately, many thousands more.

In 1993 Alla Kirilina's book *Rikoshet* appeared. Kirilina was long the head of the Kirov Museum in Leningrad, an official government position that gave her great familiarity with Kirov, his life and his death. This study contains references to a modest number of primary sources and even reprints a few of them. In 2001 this book was republished as the third part of Kirilina's much longer study *Neizvestnyi Kirov* ("The Unknown Kirov").

In the Fall of 2010 American historian Matthew Lenoe published *The Kirov Murder and Soviet History*, a mammoth 800-page work under the aegis of the prestigious Yale University Press series "Annals of Communism." While Lenoe acknowledges his debt to Kirilina's work, his book is much longer, with many more references to primary sources. While Kirilina's book is more discursive in nature Lenoe's is, or appears to be, evidence-based. It contains translations, complete or partial, of 127 documents. A number of these are primary sources for the Kirov murder investigation.

The Problem

Both Kirilina's and Lenoe's books contain evidence – the texts of many primary documents and references to yet others. Both arrive at the same conclusion: that Kirov's assassin Nikolaev was a "lone gunman" and that everyone else accused of complicity in the murder was "framed", falsely accused, forced to give false confessions incriminating themselves and others.

If Kirilina's book, or the more recent and much more detailed work by Lenoe, had solved the Kirov murder the present study would be largely superfluous. But any attentive reader will notice immediately that neither Kirilina nor Lenoe proves this case at all. Though they cite a large number of primary sources only two of those documents in any way support the hypothesis that Nikolaev was a "lone gunman". There are serious problems with both of these documents. All of the other primary documents support the original conclusion reached at the time by the Soviet investigators of the NKVD, the Soviet prosecution, and the court: that Nikolaev was part of a clandestine Zinovievite terrorist conspiracy linked with other similar conspiratorial groups.

In the present study our goal has been to solve the Kirov murder case. Towards this end we review all the evidence as objectively as possible, with appropriate skepticism, and without any preconceived conclusion in mind. The main conclusion of our study is that Nikolaev was not a "lone gunman" at all. The Soviet investigators and prosecution got it right in December 1934. A clandestine Zinovievite conspiratorial organization, of which Nikolaev was a member, killed Kirov.

The only sensible way to approach the Kirov murder is to begin with Kirilina's and Lenoe's studies. These two books set forth the present state of research on this question. Each contains much valuable evidentiary material that any future student must take fully into account. We study each of these works with great care, Kirilina's in one chapter, Lenoe's far longer and more ambitious work in several chapters. We expose in detail the very considerable – ultimately, fatal – flaws in each of them.

It is our conclusion that both authors began with the preconceived idea that is also the official position of the Russian government today, as it was of the Gorbachev regime that preceded it: that Nikolaev alone was guilty and everyone else was "framed." This conclusion is contradicted by virtually all the evidence, as our careful study of that evidence shows. We examine and reveal the errors Kirilina and Lenoe make in reaching their erroneous conclusion, exposing their faulty reasoning and use of primary sources.

We also draw upon much evidence that is directly relevant to the Kirov case but that neither Kirilina nor Lenoe used. It may not be coincidental that all of this evidence supports the hypothesis that Nikolaev was part of a Zinovievite conspiracy – that is, the conclusion drawn by the Soviet prosecution and courts in the 1930s.

We do not try to account for the fact that Kirilina and Lenoe make a large number of faulty suppositions, errors of reasoning and argumentation, and omissions in their consideration of relevant evidence. It is hard to imagine that these scholars made so many flagrant errors without noticing them – that is, it is hard to believe that some of them were not made deliberately to attempt to force their conclusions to "fit" the preconceived "official" conclusion that only Nikolaev was guilty.

However, it is easy to underestimate the power of a well-established, privileged preconceived framework of analysis on the minds of any researcher who is himself seriously biased. The pressures, both psychological and academic, to reach a conclusion acceptable to leading figures in the field of Soviet history, as well as to officials in Russia who control access to archives, are considerable indeed. Consequently, the disadvantages, professionally and otherwise, of reaching a conclusion that, no matter how well demonstrated, will be displeasing to powerful forces in the archival, political, and academic communities, are clear to anyone who is familiar with the highly politicized nature of the field of Soviet and indeed of all of communist history.

We devote a great deal of attention to analyzing and detailing the defects in Kirilina's and Lenoe's research. We devote special attention to the crucial parts of Kirilina's and Lenoe's arguments – to Nikolaev's "first confession" and, in the case of Lenoe, to Genrikh Liushkov's article in the Japanese magazine *Kaizo* of 1939. This is essential in order to "clear the field" – to establish that these, the most authoritative works on this problem, have failed to solve the question of Kirov's murder. Our task is similar to that of an architect who, called to inspect a structure, discovers that its construction down to the very foundation is so faulty that the entire edifice must be razed and a sound structure erected in its stead. Once we establish that neither Kirilina's nor Lenoe's studies are adequate and that any objective study of the Kirov murder must begin again from the beginning, we proceed to do so.

A problem that confronts everyone interested in the Kirov assassination is that the Russian government continues to keep top-secret many, perhaps most, of the investigative materials for the Kirov murder, as well as for the subsequent and related investigations into the Kremlin Affair, the three Moscow "show trials", and the Tukhachevsky Affair. In Russia there is a statutory 75-year limit upon the expiration of which documents are supposed to be declassified and made public. Many documents from the 1930s have indeed been made public. But most of the investigative materials related to all of these alleged conspiracies are still classified, unavailable even to trusted scholars. Nevertheless, so many primary sources have been published over the past 20 years that, we argue, we have enough evidence to resolve the matter of the Kirov murder in a definitive manner.

Implications

In his informative discussion of Khrushchev's campaign to "rehabilitate" those convicted of complicity in Kirov's murder Lenoe correctly situates the Kirov case at the foundation of the conspiracy trials of the 1930s in the Soviet Union as follows:

> If the official charges in the first two trials – that former Zinoviev supporters had conspired to murder Kirov – were entirely bogus, then the indictments in all of the succeeding show trials collapsed. … But if there was some truth to the charge that Zinovievites conspired to kill Kirov, then that preserved the possibility of arguing that the latter charges were also valid, at least in part. (591-2)

Lenoe understands the implications of the Kirov case. Khrushchev aimed to debunk the then-canonical narrative of Soviet history during the 1930s and create a new one out of whole cloth, one in which Stalin was the criminal who had framed and executed a great many innocent Party members. In order to construct this new narrative he had to begin by completely rewriting the Kirov case.

Lenoe goes on to cite some of the falsehoods invented by Khrushchev and his men in order to persuade the more pro-Stalin members of the Party Presidium that all those convicted of guilt in Kirov's murder save Nikolaev had been innocent, "framed." But as we shall show Lenoe is still far too credulous of Khrushchev's lies. According to Lenoe even though Khrushchev and his men had concealed much evidence, destroyed other evidence, and generally lied in their study, they were basically correct in concluding in a secret report that Nikolaev had acted alone.

Khrushchev realized that the complete rewriting of Soviet history he wanted necessitated a reversal of verdicts in the Kirov case. And the reverse is also true. To reinstate the original verdict against the defendants in the December 1934 Kirov trial implies that the defendants in the conspiracy cases that followed it: the Moscow Center trial of January 1935, the Kremlin Affair of 1935, the three Moscow "show" trials of 1936, 1937, and 1938, and the Tukhachevsky Affair trial of June 1937, might well have been guilty. Since the testimony in all three "show" trials and in the Tukhachevsky Affair trial implicated Leon Trotsky, it raises the possibility that Trotsky might have been guilty too. Likewise it suggests that other party leaders tried and executed in non-public trials might be guilty as well.

In short, the whole post-Khrushchev paradigm of Soviet history that we have called, for short, the "anti-Stalin" paradigm[2], is in play in the Kirov murder, many of its mainstay "facts" uncertain, questionable, or bogus. This would entail a reassessment of one of the major historical figures of the 20th century, Joseph Stalin, and consequently of the entire history of the Soviet Union, in which Stalin and the period of his sway is pivotal.

A "paradigm shift" of this magnitude would disturb any academic discipline. Arguably, it would be especially threatening in such an overtly politically-charged field as the study of communism, of which Soviet history is inevitably a vital part. Perhaps it is not surprising that few scholars wish to squarely face the prospect of coming down on the side of such a change. As we discuss in this study Lenoe spends several pages of his Introduction assuring his readers that he is steadfastly anticommunist and anti-Stalin even though he concludes that Stalin "didn't do it" – did not have Kirov assassinated.

The fact that Lenoe felt the need to publish what might be called a statement of his "political reliability" just because he has concluded that the evidence shows Stalin did *not* commit a certain crime of which others had suspected him, and despite the fact that both the Gorbachev-led Soviet regime and the Russian government since then had long concurred in this assessment, attests to the charged political and moral aura surrounding virtually every question of Soviet history during the Stalin period.

The Kirov murder case is one of a small number of cardinal and therefore "hot-button" issues in Soviet history. Others include the Moscow

---

[2] See Grover Furr and Vladimir L. Bobrov, "Stephen Cohen's Biography of Bukharin: A Study in the Falsehood of Khrushchev-Era 'Revelations'". *Cultural Logic* 2010, page 5. At http://clogic.eserver.org/2010/Furr.pdf

Trials, the *Ezhovshchina*, or "bad time of Ezhov" of 1937-1938 (also known, in Cold-War terminology, as "the Great Terror"), and Nikita Khrushchev's "Secret Speech" to the 20th Party Congress in 1956. All of these events are crucially linked to the Kirov affair. Of course there are other pivotal events in the Soviet history of this period too, such as collectivization, the famine of 1932-33, the Molotov-Ribbentrop Pact, and the Katyn Forest massacre, that are not immediately linked to the Kirov Affair except insofar as they all involve the Stalin leadership. Nevertheless the Kirov murder is fundamental to our understanding of both elite and mass politics of the 1930s in the USSR, and in fact to the fate of socialism itself.

The notion that Kirov was killed by a "lone gunman" and hence that Stalin framed all the rest of those accused of complicity and conspiracy is a foundational part of the anti-Stalin paradigm. This in turn means that many people – some of them powerful in academia and even in politics and the media – will be displeased at any research that calls this paradigm into serious question, regardless of the evidentiary basis of that research. The historical legitimacy not only of Russia but of the other post-Soviet states is constructed upon the demonization of the Stalin period and upon certain foundational events that are referenced to justify that demonization. Ideological anticommunism, always avidly promoted for obvious reasons by powerful capitalist forces, is also tied to a very negative interpretation of all communist movements, and especially that of Stalin.

It should surprise no one that scholars are wary of reaching conclusions that will prove unpopular in important circles. Powerful academic, economic, media, and other influential elites are strongly predisposed to favor negative historical portrayals of Stalin and the Soviet Union of his day. Meanwhile, there are no corresponding powerful interests that might look with equanimity, much less with favor, upon more positive interpretations. Nor do any powerful institutions exist to promote objective research to discover the truth by the best methods "and let the chips fall where they may."

Viewed from this perspective it is perhaps less surprising than it might otherwise be that until the present study no researcher has ever approached the primary source evidence in the Kirov murder case in a spirit of objectivity and decided the matter as though it were just another historical problem, albeit a fascinating one. Whatever their reasons, however, neither Kirilina nor Lenoe have done so. The evidence they themselves cite – to say nothing of the very large amount of primary source evidence that they unquestionably know about but have simply omitted – is sufficient to prove that their conclusions are incorrect. *On the evidence* there can simply be no doubt that Kirov was killed as a result of a conspiracy of clandestine terrorist Zinovievites.

Our Analysis

This study begins by reviewing in detail the three most recent scholarly studies of the Kirov affair: by Kirilina, Lenoe, and the Norwegian historian Åsmund Egge. These are the only books whose authors gained access to and drew upon many primary sources. No study of the Kirov affair before Kirilina's was able to use the primary sources that have been made public since the end of the Soviet Union in 1991. Kirilina's study, titled *Rikoshet* ("ricochet") was republished in 2001 as the final part of her much longer book *Neizvestnyi Kirov.* (As the head for many years of the Kirov museum in Leningrad – St. Petersburg Kirilina resisted the attempt to reduce Kirov to the question of his murder.) We will use this edition rather than the first 1993 version because it is the more recent one.

We devote much more attention to Lenoe's 2010 study because it is far more recent still and, in addition, much fuller. Lenoe translates either in whole or, usually, in part, a number of important primary documents. Lenoe also explicitly draws upon Kirilina's book. His is both the most recent and the most authoritative study of the Kirov murder to date. As we shall show, Lenoe's study is also very seriously flawed. Nevertheless, because of Lenoe's unprecedented access to primary source materials and the sheer length of his study, any reconsideration of the Kirov murder has to begin with a detailed critique of Lenoe's account. We devote several chapters to it.

Egge's book, published in Norway in 2009 and in Russia in 2011, has been anointed by the Boris Eltsin Foundation's "History of Stalinism" series. In many respects the most disappointing of the three, it does cite documents not mentioned by either Kirilina or Lenoe, a fact whose implications we explore. We devote a separate chapter to it as well.[3]

---

[3] Egge and Lenoe were apparently unaware of each other's work and do not reference each other. Both cite Kirilina.

We also devote several chapters to a detailed study of a number of especially crucial primary sources. Some, like Nikolaev's first interrogation, are also examined by both Kirilina and Lenoe. Others, such as Genrikh Liushkov's article in the March 1939 issue of the Japanese magazine *Kaizo*, are studied only by Lenoe. We also examine a large third group of very important evidentiary documents that constitute critical evidence in the Kirov murder and yet were ignored by Kirilina, Lenoe, and Egge.

In a concluding chapter we outline what we see as the major conclusion and its implications: that the version of the Kirov murder gradually uncovered by Soviet investigators in the December 1934 and January 1935 trials, the Kremlin Affair interrogations (we do not have any trial records in this case), and the pretrial and trial materials of the 1936, 1937, and 1938 Moscow "show trials", is basically accurate. The conspiracies alleged at these trials did exist, and Kirov was murdered as a part of them. We explore, as space permits, some of the implications of our conclusions, which contradicts – indeed, overturns – the scholarly consensus since Khrushchev's day both inside and outside the USSR and post-Soviet Russia.

We fully realize that this conclusion will be deeply displeasing, even unacceptable, to some scholars in the highly-politicized fields of Soviet and communist history. Nevertheless, given the evidence we have it is the only objective conclusion possible. This study of the Kirov murder is one of a number of recent studies that tend to dismantle the "anti-Stalin" paradigm on purely evidentiary bases. We conclude that a new history of the Soviet Union during Stalin's time, one dramatically different from the version current since Khrushchev's day, is in the process of replacing the "anti-Stalin" paradigm.

Chapter 1.

Kirilina.

In his introductory chapter Lenoe states that his "greatest debt is to Alla Kirilina, the most knowledgeable scholar in the world on Kirov's killing." (Lenoe 15) The long-time head of the Kirov Museum in Leningrad / St. Petersburg, Kirilina's most recent work on the Kirov murder is *Neizvestnyi Kirov* ("The Unknown Kirov") (2001). The third part of this work, "Rikoshet" (also the title of an earlier book by Kirilina) is Kirilina's discussion of the assassination, investigation, trial, and aftermath. In it Kirilina expounds the view of the murder implied in her clever title: that Nikolaev was a "lone gunman" and the bullet that killed Kirov "ricocheted" to kill many others.

Kirilina wrote her study before the release of many of the evidentiary materials that we now have and that Lenoe and Egge cite. Apparently even her position as director of the Kirov Museum did not gain her access to these materials, let alone to those that have still not been declassified. For our present purposes Kirilina's study of Kirov's murder and its aftermath is important mainly because Egge and, especially, Lenoe admit they drew heavily on it. We will examine Kirilina's "Rikoshet" in two respects. First we will demonstrate that Kirilina has not solved – indeed, it seems she has not even attempted to solve – Kirov's murder. We will then point out some important facts that Kirilina reveals and that Lenoe has omitted or suppressed, matters missing from Lenoe's much longer study.

Since Khrushchev's day, and especially since the later Gorbachev period, the official Soviet and Russian view of the Kirov assassination is that the assassin, Leonid Nikolaev, was a "lone gunman". Kirilina, Lenoe, Egge, and virtually all other "mainstream" scholars of Soviet history have adopted this "official" position, the implication of which is that the Moscow Trials were fabrications or falsifications and the defendants innocent, unjustly executed by Stalin. In the present study we show that there is no evidence at all for this position, and a huge amount of evidence against it. It would appear that anticommunist scholars have embraced it for ideological reasons alone.

Kirilina begins with the assumption, all but universal among mainstream historians of the Soviet period, that the Moscow trials were frameups, "falsifications." (205) The problem with this assumption is that it basically predetermines the rest of Kirilina's study. The Kirov murder figured prominently in all three of the public Moscow "show" trials of 1936, 1937 and 1938. If the Moscow Trials are declared to have been frameups of innocent men, no one remains as an accomplice or accessory to Nikolaev's act. Since no one seriously believes any longer that Stalin had Kirov killed, the only remaining possibility permitted by the assumption that the trials were falsifications is that Nikolaev must have acted alone.

In short Kirilina "begs the question" of Kirov's assassination. She does not pose a hypothesis and then set out to determine whether the available evidence supports that hypothesis or another one. Rather, she assumes from the outset that Nikolaev acted alone. As we shall demonstrate, Lenoe and Egge do this as well. Like them Kirilina cites a lot of evidence to which she was the first scholar to have access. This evidence is very interesting and important. Moreover, it does not at all support her preconceived conclusion.

We will briefly examine some examples of what appears to be incompetence in Kirilina's book. We will also identify some statements that appear to be intentionally false. Of course, some form of prevarication is essential in a work such as Kirilina's – one that presents itself to its readers as an attempt to discover the truth, to "solve the crime", but instead presents a biased argument in favor of a preconceived conclusion.

Moreover, when that preconceived conclusion runs counter to virtually all the evidence we have – and we have a great deal of evidence concerning Kirov's death – an author determined to deny this fact and to promote instead a version of events which is contradicted by the evidence at every turn may be compelled to employ transparent means in her attempt to disguise the truth. What appears to the objective reader as incompetence may well be instead (or also), like the deliberate falsehoods, an attempt to persuade and deceive rather than genuine ignorance or incompetence.

Incompetence

Like Lenoe, whose work we shall examine later, Kirilina makes a number of careless errors:

* She reports a newspaper account that claims Andrei YA. Vyshinskii, prosecutor in the Moscow Trials and assistant prosecutor in the Kirov trial of December 1934, believed that "confession is the queen of evidence" (219):

> The newspaper "Moskovskii Komsomolets in St. Petersburg", in its issue of 6-13 December 2000, published a short notice on the Kirov murder. It questions whether it was Nikolaev who murdered Kirov and argues that at the foundation of Nikolaev's confession is the incorrect conceptual position of A. Ia. Vyshinski, at that time Prosecutor General of the USSR, who considered that "confession is the queen of all evidence"...

This canard has long since been refuted. Vyshinskii's speech to the February-March 1937 Central Committee Plenum, published in 1995 (*Voprosy Istorii* №.2, 1995, p. 11), specifically *attacks* the notion of relying upon confessions instead of other evidence. In his later work, *The Theory of Trial Evidence in Soviet Law* (Moscow 1946) Vyshinskii *criticizes* the fact that confession, even when obtained under "torture" (*pytki*), was considered "queen of proofs" in the 15th and 16th centuries in Europe.

> The methods of "proof" were also extremely simple and unique. The most reliable means of "proving" was the use of physical suffering, torture, under the blows of which it was easy to obtain the defendant's own confession, which was considered to be "the best evidence in the world", "the queen of evidence." [4]

Though Kirilina is critical of the other assertions in this article she never points out the author's (Bastrykin's) error in falsely attributing to Vyshinskii what in fact he strongly opposed.

* On p. 342 Kirilina states:

---

[4] Vyshinsky, A. IA. *Teoriia sudebnykh dokazatel'stv v sovetskom prave* ("Theory of Trial Evidence in Soviet Law"), Section 3. At http://scilib.narod.ru/Other/Vyshinsky/v.htm#1_3

> I note that it was Iagoda who first uttered these words at the trial of the Bloc of Rights and Trotskyites in 1938: "*Zaporozhets released Nikolaev at my direction.*"

The text of the trial not only shows that Iagoda never uttered these words but that, on the contrary, Iagoda specifically denied doing any such thing! Iagoda stated in pre-trial interrogations available to Kirilina that he was informed of Nikolaev's release only after the fact. We discuss this issue in detail in another chapter of the present work.

* On pp. 342-3 Kirilina again insists:

> Zaporozhets had no connection at all to the release of Nikolaev on October 15 [1934].

citing as her evidence Khrushchev-era witness Anshukov, who testified that Zaporozhets was in the hospital in a cast.

But Iagoda had never claimed that Zaporozhets was in Leningrad at the time of Nikolaev's detention on October 15, 1934. On the contrary, in his pretrial interrogation of May 19, 1937 Iagoda stated "I personally did not give any directives about getting rid of Borisov. Zaporozhets was not in Leningrad at all at that time."[5] In this same interrogation Iagoda testified that he learned about the upcoming attempt to assassinate Kirov from Enukidze after a conference of the conspiracy, the Right-Trotskyite-Zinovievite bloc, in the summer of 1934. Then, in Iagoda's words:

> Answer: I summoned Zaporozhets (assistant head of the Political Division) from Leningrad, informed him about the possibility of an attempt on Kirov's life, and instructed him not to stand in its way. (181)
>
> [...]
>
> Answer: Zaporozhets told me about this a little while after Nikolaev had been released.
>
> Question: What did he tell you?

---

[5] *Genrikh Iagoda. Narkom vnytrennikh del SSR. General'nyi komissar gosudarstvennoi bezopasnosti. Sbornik dokumentov*. Kazan', 1997, p. 184.

> Answer: Zaporozhets was in Moscow, came to see me, and related how in Leningrad a certain Nikolaev, who had been watching Kirov's automobile, had been detained by personnel of the Operations Division. He was brought to the Political Division and upon being searched in the presence of Gubin there were found materials that constituted evidence of terrorist intent. Gubin reported this to him and Zaporozhets released Nikolaev. (183)

So Iagoda never claimed that Zaporozhets was in Leningrad when Nikolaev was detained on October 15. The volume *Genrikh Iagoda* was published in 1997; Kirilina's book *Neizvestnyi Kirov* was published four years later, in 2001. Kirilina had ample time to consult the former volume and see that Anshukov's statement did not contradict Iagoda's testimony. But she failed to do so.

* Kirilina notes that under the law of December 1, 1934, terrorist cases were to be tried without defense attorneys or the right of appeal. She then notes that at the August 1936 Moscow Trial defense attorneys were indeed permitted, but appeals were not allowed.

> By order of the CEC of December 1, 1934 cases involving terrorists were to be conducted without defense attorneys, behind closed doors, and without the right of appeal. At the 1936 Moscow trial there were both defense attorneys and a public. Perhaps this departure from the order and providing the defendants with the right to appeal the sentence were a "guarantee" of Stalin's in collusion with the defendants?
>
> In this case they did not allow the defendants this right. On the night of August 23-24 1936 the court announced its sentence and that same night they were taken straight from the courtroom to be shot. (Kirilina 369)

This is false. The post-trial appeals of a number of the 1936 trial defendants, including Zinoviev, Kamenev, I.N. Smirnov, and Natan Lur'e, were published on page three of the newspaper *Izvestiia* of September 2, 1992, years before Kirilina's book was published. Kirilina had no excuse for stating that the right of appeal was denied to these defendants. Either

Kirilina invented this "fact" or copied it uncritically from some other source.

Falsehoods

In addition to errors such as those above that might plausibly be laid to carelessness Kirilina makes many statements that are more accurately described as "deliberately deceptive" or "falsehoods". All are attempts to de-emphasize or discount evidence that supports the existence of a conspiracy involving Nikolaev.

Kirilina notes that in his interrogation of December 6, 1934 Nikolaev

> ...at first confessed that Kotolynov and Shatskii were participants in the "Terrorist act", but failed to cite a single bit of specific evidence in confirmation of this statement. (Kirilina 277)

By "specific (literally, "concrete") evidence" Kirilina evidently means "material evidence" of some kind. In support of this statement she cites IU. Sedov's article "Wrongfully executed" ("Bezvinno kaznennye") in the journal *Trud* of December 4 1990. But even Sedov did not demand "specific evidence" from a person giving a jailhouse confession.

Kirilina's demand for "concrete evidence" (*konkretnoe dokazatel'stva*) is dishonest. Does she really expect that Nikolaev would have carried around a piece of paper signed by Kotolynov and Shatskii in which they agreed to take part in Kirov's assassination? The phrase

> ... but failed to cite a single bit of specific evidence in confirmation of this statement

is a "tell" – a sign that Kirilina is all too conscious of the weakness of her case, an attempt to dismiss evidence that disproves her own hypothesis.[6]

A few pages later Kirilina refers to an interrogation of Nikolaev of December 20, 1934, during which Nikolaev claimed he had approached the

[6] A "tell" (short for "telegraph") is an unconscious gesture or expression by which a poker player gives a sign to other players whether his hand is good or bad. This makes it impossible to "bluff" his opponents, an essential skill in poker.

the Latvian consul in Leningrad both for money and to ask him to make contact with Trotsky on behalf of their group. Kirilina says that this is "not supported by any documents." This is yet another "tell" – as though the imprisoned Nikolaev would have documents either on his person or, anywhere at all attesting to this. (280) However, this statement of Nikolaev's is an interesting one and begs further consideration. We will examine it in a later chapter.

* According to Kirilina Nikolaev stated in a confession of December 4 1934 that

> "he was a member of an underground counterrevolutionary organization", that its "participants adhered to the platform of the Trotskyist-Zinovievist bloc". "The former opposition had their own specific accounts to settle with Kirov in connection with the struggle which he had organized against the Leningrad oppositionists." (281)

We have known since the early 1980s from Trotsky's own pen that a real "Right-Trotskyist bloc" involving Zinoviev and Kamenev did in fact exist.

Kirilina states:

> By the way, none of those who confessed about the "Leningrad center" named with Nikolaev or Shatski among its members. (283)

This is simply false. In the text of the December 12 interrogation of Zvezdov in Lenoe's book we read:

> Question: Lay out for us the membership of the Center and the other branches of the Leningrad organization.
>
> Answer: The membership is as follows:
>
> 1. The Leningrad Center:
>
>   a. Rumiantsev, Vladimir – head of the organization.
>
>   b. Kotolynov, Ivan.
>
>   c. Tsarkov, Nikolai.
>
>   [...]

h. Nikolaev, Leonid. (Lenoe 310)

Three of those arrested and tried alongside Nikolaev for Kirov's murder – Levin, Sositskii, and Miasnikov – were Trotskyites. (Kirilina 290). Lenoe admits as much in his treatment of the incident, even pointing out that there is some evidence the Latvian consul, Bissenieks, did in fact give some money to Nikolaev. Bissenieks never denied meeting with Nikolaev. (Lenoe 382-3) Moreover, Nikolaev talked the language of the opposition. We know that some others arrested in connection with the case, like Evdokimov and Gorshenin, did as well. Kotolynov and others in the Zinovievite group were briefly expelled from the Party in 1927 for "Trotskyite" activity.[7] It would have been natural for lower-level conspirators to seek a connection with Trotsky.

As Kirilina notes, the NKVD also did not consider the evidence of a "Trotsky connection" firm at that time (291). But Nikolaev's claiming to have asked to be connected with Trotsky would naturally have appeared to them as worth pursuing. Investigators are trained to follow up every possible avenue of inquiry. And it is certainly not evidence *against* the existence of a conspiracy!

Concerning the August 1936 "Zinoviev-Kamenev" trial Kirilina states that there was no material evidence:

> Once again, not a single document, not a single piece of material evidence, not a single outside witness was brought forward at the trial. The whole indictment was built exclusively on the self-incrimination of the accused... (367)

Then on pages 368-9 Kirilina juxtaposes passages from the January 1935 trial of Zinoviev and Kamenev to some passages from the transcript of the August 1936 trial. Although Kirilina does not acknowledged it this section of her book is taken directly from Trotsky's "Bulletin of the Opposition" No. 52 of October, 1936! Kirilina even copies word for word Trotsky's claim that

---

[7] We will return to this point in the chapter "Bukharin and Kotolynov."

> ...not a single document, not a single piece of material evidence, was brought forward at the trial. (367)

However, Trotsky proceeded to admit that the Honduran passport of V. Ol'berg, with which he entered the USSR illegally and which was, in his testimony, obtained with the aid of German Trotskyists, did constitute a piece of "material evidence." Kirilina conceals this part of Trotsky's statement from her readers, thereby deceiving them, for at least this one piece of "material evidence" was presented at the trial.

Furthermore, we know that Trotsky himself was deceiving his readership in this discussion of the August 1936 Moscow Trial, as he had done in his discussion of the Kirov murder in No. 41 of the "Bulletin of the Opposition". For Trotsky and his son Leon Sedov discussed between themselves the "bloc" of Trotskyites, Zinovievites and others. This bloc was indeed formed in 1932, just as stated in the testimony in the August 1936 Moscow Trial. Sedov informed his father that Zinoviev and Kamenev were indeed a part of the bloc. We will discuss this issue in another chapter.

All this Trotsky and his son denied in public. This was natural enough – in fact necessary, if they were to preserve their underground conspiracy within the USSR. But this information about the bloc was discovered and published by Trotsky historian Pierre Broué in 1980. Then in 1991 it was discussed again in an article in the Soviet journal "Voprosy Istorii KPSS" ("Questions of History of the CPSU") by American historian Arch Getty. It was publicized in Russia again in a work published in 1995 by Vadim Rogovin, who quoted it. Kirilina's book was published in 2001. She either did, or should have, known about the bloc and informed her readers.

As a final example of Kirilina's dishonesty consider the following:

> In the Japanese magazine "Kiitso" of April 1939 Liushkov published materials in which he categorically rejects any involvement by Iagoda in the conspiracy against Kirov. Liushkov was at 4 Liteinyi pereulok (lane), in the NKVD, near Agranov, when Stalin phoned the latter and ordered him to send Borisov to the Smolny for questioning. Agranov immediately gave the appropriate instructions. It was only 30 minutes from the moment of

> Stalin's call to the moment of the auto accident with Borisov, as Liushkov pointed out. And we can agree with Liushkov's opinion that this amount of time was simply insufficient to organize the murder of Borisov. (353)

This can only be a deliberately deceptive statement.

> * In both pretrial interrogations and at trial Iagoda repeatedly insisted that he had had nothing to do with Borisov's death while at the same time also insisting that he was, indeed, involved in the conspiracy to murder Kirov. Kirilina cites Iagoda's lack of participation in the first as evidence against Iagoda's confession to the second.
>
> * Kirilina has clearly never read Liushkov's article in the journal *Kaizo* ("Reconstruction") of April 1939. If she had she would have seen that Liushkov insisted that Iagoda was indeed involved in a conspiracy – to force Zinoviev and Kamenev to falsely confess to Kirov's murder at their August 1936 trial.[8] Liushkov also claimed that Shatskii was Nikolaev's sole co-conspirator in the assassination of Kirov. Kirilina would certainly not have omitted these important details of Liushkov's article had she actually read it. Therefore, she gave her readers the false impression that she had read Liushkov's article but in reality she never did.

In his book Lenoe cites Liushkov's *Kaizo* article at length, setting it forward as the strongest evidence now available that Nikolaev was a "lone gunman." In a later chapter of the present work we too examine the *Kaizo* article and demonstrate that Lenoe's interpretation of it is incorrect. Lenoe, however, has clearly read Liushkov's article. It is just as clear that Kirilina has never read it.

Materials In Kirilina's Book But Omitted By Lenoe

Kirilina and Lenoe share the same goal: to present Nikolaev as a lone assassin. Perhaps the most powerful method of arguing a preconceived

[8] Liushkov was lying in this article, which was written for propaganda purposes, as we shall show.

idea is to suppress evidence that fails to support it. In the case of the Kirov murder there is so much evidence of a conspiracy that, were it all to be simply suppressed, almost nothing would remain. Therefore, in addition to the omission of evidence inconvenient to the preconceived conclusion, other techniques of misdirection must be employed.

Lenoe has told us that he considers Kirilina to be the greatest expert on Kirov's murder. He cites Kirilina's book many times, and ought to have cited it in some places where he did not. But Lenoe has also omitted some evidence that Kirilina presents. Lenoe has tailored his argument in a somewhat different and, arguably, more careful manner. Usually there is a discernable method to his omission of Kirilina evidence.

Nikolaev's Finances

Kirilina frankly acknowledges the evidence that Nikolaev was not in financial difficulties in 1934. She quotes from December 11, 1934 interrogation of Nikolaev's mother, Maria Tikhonovna:

> As far as its material situation the family of my son Leonid Nikolaevich did not experience any hardships. … The children were also fully provided with all the necessities, including milk, butter, eggs, clothing and footwear. (238)

Kirilina quotes this passage from the article by historian IUrii Zhukov, where it is somewhat fuller.

> As far as its material situation the family of my son Leonid Nikolaevich did not experience any hardships. They occupied a separate three-room apartment in a cooperative house, which he received in return for payment of the cooperative unit. The children were also fully provided with all the necessities, including milk, butter, eggs, clothing and footwear. During the last 3-4 months Leonid was unemployed, which somewhat worsened the provisioning of his family, but even then they did not experience any special hardship.[9]

---

[9] IU. N. Zhukov. "Sledstvie I sudebnye protsessy po delu ob ubiystve Kirova." *Voprosy istorii* 2, 2000, p. 40. (Zhukov 2000)

Lenoe does not even mention this interrogation and passage. Perhaps he has omitted it because he argues that deprivation was a primary factor motivating Nikolaev's supposedly "lone assassination." This passage would constitute strong evidence against Lenoe's theory.

Lenoe writes "Nikolaev was desperate for money in the fall of 1934" (299). Even if he was – and the testimony just cited casts serious doubt on that statement – desperation for money does not necessarily entail neediness. Lenoe also quotes the indictment against Nikolaev:

> Through the confessions of a series of persons who were interrogated in the present case as witnesses, including Nikolaev's mother T. Nikolaeva and his wife, Milda Draule, the investigation has established that the accused Nikolaev did not suffer from material need during this period of time, and neither did his family. (Lenoe 350)

Anyone reading Lenoe's book alone would have no idea where this testimony came from, and might assume it was fabricated by the NKVD instead of his mother's testimony and in fact represents Kirilina's viewpoint as well.

Kirilina continues:

> Unmistakeable signs of the family's good material circumstances are the fact that L.V. Nikolaev himself possessed a bicycle (that was a sign in those years of a certain level of income), and in 1933-1934 the Nikolaevs rented a private dacha in the prestigious area of Sestroretsk. (238)

Nikolaev was even fined 25 rubles and ordered to pay an additional 19 rubles by the Party for hitting a pedestrian with his bicycle. (Kirilina 242-3) Kirilina cites evidence that Nikolaev always had had good jobs, even easy work, and was never unemployed until his dismissal from a job at the Institute for Party History in April 1934. She speculates that Nikolaev must have had good connections to be recommended for such jobs. (Kirilina 244-5) Neither Kirilina nor Lenoe try to account for these "good connections" as any good investigator would be sure to do. Perhaps they do not wish to suggest that these good connections were, most likely, the Zinovievites who were later tried and convicted of Kirov's murder along with Nikolaev. Nikolaev's wife Mil'da Draule also had a relatively well-paying job. (Kirilina 246)

If Nikolaev did indeed feel he was in need of money this "lack" was only a subjective one. He and his family still rented a private country house during the summer he was unemployed. Had they suffered genuine want they could simply not have done so. No one facing eviction or hunger rents a summer cottage. Lenoe never informs his readers that Kirilina acknowledged that Nikolaev was not in any real financial need.

We also know that Nikolaev chose not to take another job while he prepared to assassinate Kirov, a fact stated in the Prosecutor's Indictment ("Obvinitel'noe zakliuchenie", p. 20) as follows:

> In one of his confessions the accused Nikolaev directly states:
>
> "I informed him (Kotolynov) that I had decided not to go back to work during the period when I was preparing the [terrorist] act in order to have enough free time to carry out the murder of Kirov. Kotolynov approved my decision.
>
> (vol. 2, l.d. 85)
>
> The wife of the accused L. Nikolaev – Milda Draule, confirms this. She states:
>
> "...From the end of March 1934 right up to his (i.e. L. Nikolaev's) arrest he did not work anywhere. The reason for this is not Nikolaev's inability to find work, but his stubborn refusal to accept any kind of work. Having devoted himself fully to the preparation of the terrorist act, I presume that he did not want to tie himself to work anywhere..."
>
> (vol. 3, l.d. 201).

Kirilina never mentions this fact. Lenoe quotes at length from the indictment but omits this part of it here – a point we will consider in another chapter of the present work.

Nikolaev's Interrogation of "After December 4"

In a passage we have already quoted above Kirilina says that Nikolaev made the following admission "after December 4":

> ...[H]e was a member of an underground counterrevolutionary organization", that its "participants adhered to the platform of the Trotskyist-Zinovievist bloc". "The former opposition had their own specific accounts to settle with Kirov in connection with the struggle which he had organized against the Leningrad oppositionists. (281)

We do not know at what point "after December 4" Nikolaev made this statement. Without citing any evidence or reasoning Kirilina simply declares it "fabricated" – as indeed both she and Lenoe do with all the evidence that does not fit their predetermined schema:

> That is why the investigation steadily fabricated the 'conspiracy' version (281)

But at least Kirilina does record this statement, thus allowing others to view it in a different light. Lenoe does not clarify or even cite this important quotation. He does quote parts of a December 13 interrogation of Nikolaev in which some wording appears similar to some of what is in Kirilina's quote, but suppresses the passage in which Nikolaev cites the supposed motive of the Leningrad Trotskyite-Zinovievite group in killing Kirov – that "the former oppositionists had their own accounts to settle with Kirov in relation to the struggle that he had organized against the Leningrad oppositionists."

Nikolaev's Confession of *circa* December 8

Kirilina quotes the following important remarks from Nikolaev without a precise date but implying December 8 or shortly afterwards:

> The Kotolynov group was preparing a terrorist act against Kirov, and its direct implementation was entrusted to me personally. I was aware from Shatskii that the same task had been given to his group too, and also that this work was being conducted by them independently of our own preparation for a terrorist act.

> …I first met Shatskii in 1933. Our next meeting was during the summer of 1934 at 28 Krasnye Zaria Street [Kirov's home address – GF], where Shatskii was conducting surveillance on the apartment and ascertaining all of Kirov's movements. He did this in order to prepare a terrorist act."
>
> "Kotolynov said that … getting rid of Kirov would weaken the leadership of the Party [literally, the ACP(b), or "All-Russian Communist Party (Bolshevik)"] … Kotolynov worked out directly with me the technical details of carrying out the act, approved them, specially determined how accurately I could shoot. He was my immediate leader in carrying out the act. Sokolov determined the suitability of this or another point in Kirov's normal route, thus facilitating my work. … Iuskin was informed about the preparation for the attempt against Kirov and worked out with me the variant of an attack in the Smolny.
>
> Zvezdov and Antonov knew about the preparations for the act… They were directly tied to Kotolynov… (Kirilina 281-2)

Lenoe does not reproduce this text or refer to it. He does summarize an interrogation of December 6 that contradicts this text in some places:

> Eventually Nikolaev "confessed" that he had recruited Shatsky to watch Kirov's apartment for him, and strongly implied that Kotolynov had masterminded a conspiracy to murder Kirov. Moreover, he said that Kotolynov was planning to go to Moscow to assassinate Stalin. (Lenoe 288)

Though he relies heavily on Kirilina's book Lenoe does not clarify the relationship between the direct quotes cited by Kirilina of *circa* December 8 or shortly thereafter, and his own summary of part of a long interrogation of December 6.

On top of that Lenoe indulges in a favorite practice of his: to put quotation marks around any words or phrases that do not fit his preconceived conclusions, as he does here around the word "confessed". Lenoe acts as though using these "scare quotes" constituted some kind of argument that the confession was not genuine! This is one manifestation of the fallacy of "assuming that which is to be proven," a common error which Lenoe frequently commits. We will consider Lenoe's practice of "begging the question" and of "argument by scare quotes" in a separate chapter.

Kirov's Learning

On pages 325-327 Kirilina discusses Kirov's broad reading, especially in philosophy, and his involvement in education. Indeed Kirilina seems to have some respect for Kirov! She was, after all, head of the Kirov Museum for many years. Lenoe omits all this in his introductory chapters on Kirov's life.

In contrast to Kirilina, Lenoe strives to insult Kirov at every turn. He says that Kirov is "generally perceived as one of the despot's thuggish henchmen." (119). By whom? Lenoe never tells us. Evidently he has invented this "fact". However, Kirov is not so "perceived" by Kirilina, Lenoe's major source, so this "perception" is not "general." The best Lenoe can do is to quote the British consul in Leningrad, who said that Kirov was "brutal looking", whatever that means. British imperialists were "generally" regarded as "thuggish" by millions of people around the world. Perhaps Lenoe never mentions the evidence of Kirov's learning because it might contradict Lenoe's attempt to portray Kirov as "thuggish" and "brutal."[10]

An Earlier Attempt To Kill Kirov?

Kirilina writes:

> In one of his interrogations L.V. Nikolaev confessed that he had first planned to kill S.M. Kirov on November 14, 1934. And with this goal in mind he met him at the Moscow Station in Leningrad. But he did not shoot since a large number of people met Sergei Mironovich there.

[10] We consider Lenoe's anticommunist bias in another chapter.

> And so he mingled with the crowd of those people and went away. (341)

This event is also recorded in his diary under the date of November 14, where Nikolaev also seems to say that he had only tried to meet with Kirov on October 15. Yet in a diary entry of a few days beforehand, November 9, Nikolaev had written:

> If on 10/15 and 11/5 I was not able to do this … however now I am ready – that I am going to my execution is nothing – only it is easy to say it. (259)

This diary selection is quoted by Lenoe on page 242, along with a further section that appears to make it clear that he had intended to kill Kirov on November 5 as well. Since November 5 is in the past, it sounds as though Nikolaev is ready for yet another attempt – perhaps that of November 14, mentioned above.

It would have been useful to put this passage in Nikolaev's diary alongside the text from the undated interrogation quoted by Kirilina. From what we can see, the interrogation appears to confirm the notes in the diary that Nikolaev had made not one, but several aborted attempts to kill Kirov earlier. Lenoe omits this.

In any case pages 18-19 of the indictment contain a quotation from Nikolaev's confessions in which he plainly states that his diary accounts were faked:

> Here it should be noted that in order to conceal the traces of the crime and to hide my co-conspirators, and also to disguise the true motives for the murder of comrade Kirov, the accused L. Nikolaev prepared a number of documents (a diary, statements addressed to various institutions, etc.) in which he tried to portray his crime as an act of personal despair and frustration due to his supposedly serious material situation, and as a protest against the "unfair treatment of a living human being by some government officials."
>
> (vol. 1, l.d. 6).
>
> The accused L. Nikolaev himself admitted the falsity and fictional nature of this version, and explained that he had created this version by prior agreement with the members of the terrorist

group, which had decided to portray the murder of comrade Kirov as a personal act and thus conceal the real motives of this crime.

In his confessions of December 13 of this year L. Nikolaev directly stated:

"...I was supposed to portray the murder of Kirov as the act of an individual, in order to hide the participation in it of the Zinovievist group."

(vol. 1, l.d. 266).

Zinoviev's Oppositional Activity

Kirilina transcribes a short passage from one interrogation of Grigory Evdokimov, a Zinovievite and former Leningrad official accused as a member of the Moscow Center of the bloc of Trotskyites, Zinovievites, and Rightists:

> At interrogation on December 24 G.E. Evdokimov stated: "In November 1934 he [Zinoviev] criticized the work of forming a united front [in France] and blamed the French Communist Party and also the leadership of the Comintern for striving for a united front in France." (Kirilina 365)

Another arrested Zinovievite, I.S. Gorshenin, went even further:

> I.S. Gorshenin went even further in his criticism of the foreign policy of the USSR. At interrogation on December 25 he stated: "Com. Stalin is consciously not activating the Comintern and is transferring the center of all attention onto the official diplomacy of the Commissariat of Foreign Affairs and in essence sacrificing the interests of world revolution to the idea of building socialism in one country." (Kirilina 365)

Kirilina explains these statements in the following manner:

> I should note that it was towards the end of 1934. The Opposition, or rather its leaders, had voted for Stalin's political program – the building of socialism in one

> country – at the 17th Party Congress. However, they did not agree with it and continued the line of world proletarian revolution, carrying on a covert struggle against the Stalin leadership. (Kirilina 365)

Kirilina takes it for granted that the oppositionists were guilty of "double-dealing" (*dvurushnichestvo* – "two-facedness", deliberate deception) in that they had rejoined the Party dishonestly. By contrast Lenoe blames Stalin for suspecting "double-dealing", implying that Stalin had imagined this out of paranoia. We discuss this issue elsewhere in the present work.

Lenoe never mentions these statements. On the contrary, he chooses to reproduce large parts of an interrogation of Zinoviev from December 22, 1934 in which Zinoviev denies any oppositional activity, and denies even oppositional thoughts after 1932. (Lenoe 328-333) This facilitates Lenoe's portrayal of Zinoviev as the innocent victim of a frameup – something that would be harder if he had juxtaposed Evdokimov's and Gorshenin's statements against Zinoviev's professions. In short, Kirilina admits that a "covert struggle" by Zinovievites and others against the Party line did in fact continue, while Lenoe ignores it, in effect denying it.

In his confession of January 13, 1935, to which neither Kirilina nor Lenoe refers, Zinoviev went further and agreed that a Moscow centre of former Zinovievites, hostile to the Party line, still existed. We will discuss this document when we set to resolving the Kirov murder ourselves.

So Kirilina's work is disingenuous in the same general way that Lenoe's is. Both of them proceed from the *idée fixe*, the preconceived conclusion that Nikolaev was a "lone gunman" and, therefore, everybody else must have been "framed." But despite his acknowledged indebtedness to Kirilina's work Lenoe ignores it when he finds it convenient for his argument to do so.

Chapter 2.

Lenoe's Introduction.

Lenoe organizes his Introduction as follows:

* He briefly summarizes the circumstances of Nikolaev's murder of Kirov at Smolny Institute in Leningrad on December 1, 1934.

* He outlines the thesis of his book.

* He briefly outlines the Khrushchev-era investigations and accounts of the murder.

* He discusses the evidentiary problems with testimony given long after the event and the reasons why accounts based on memories of past events are not to be trusted.

* Lenoe admits he had limited access to the former Soviet archives, so he has not seen all the evidence there is.

* He cites his debts to previous scholars.

* He makes a declaration of his anticommunist bias.

Much of what Lenoe writes in this chapter is useful. For example, he points out that the Khrushchev-era investigations of Kirov's murder had the ulterior motive of trying to inculpate Stalin. This meant that these so-called "studies" were not really studies at all. Rather the Khrushchev investigators, evidently led by Petr Pospelov[11] and Ivan Serov, Khrushchev's head of the KGB, pretended to carry out an objective study while cherry-picking the documents they chose to present to the "Molotov Commission", the high-level group formed to reinvestigate the repres-

---

[11] Pospelov was an early supporter of Khrushchev, who promoted him to Secretary of the Central Committee and then Candidate Member of the Presidium of the CPSU (formerly named the "Politburo"). Like Khrushchev himself Pospelov had been an enthusiastic promoter of the "cult of personality" around Stalin.

sions. Lenoe also points out that Serov had other important files concerning the Kirov murder destroyed altogether.

Lenoe's discussion of the unreliability of accounts that rely on memories of events long past is sensible. Although these remarks are made in a general way, in reality they constitute a criticism of the work of Conquest, Tucker, Knight, and all writers who have concluded that Stalin had Kirov killed. All such works have to rely on rumor and hearsay, since there is no real evidence whatsoever of any involvement by Stalin in Kirov's death.

Lenoe frankly admits that he was refused complete access to all of the evidence that still exists. This is refreshing – though it would have been better if he had discussed what this withholding of evidence strongly implies: that the evidence withheld by the Russian government must contradict the official version that Kirov's killer was a "lone gunman," or why would they withhold it? But this is Lenoe's version too, a fact that perhaps explains why he does not draw the logical conclusion from the fact that much evidence is withheld. Lenoe also neglects to point out that Kirilina, to whose work Lenoe acknowledges his "greatest debt", failed to acknowledge that she too did not have access to all the evidence.

Nor does Lenoe point out the obvious conclusion: if Khrushchev was determined from the outset to prove either that Stalin had Kirov killed or that Nikolaev was a "lone gunman" – that is, that no conspiracy existed – then the evidence he and Kirilina were permitted to see has been carefully tailored to "fit" that conclusion and is as biased as Khrushchev's men could make it. That in turn means that anyone who, on the basis of this evidence, concludes that no conspiracy existed needs to reconsider that conclusion very carefully. By contrast if – as the present study demonstrates – despite all the attempts to expurgate, withhold, and distort it the available evidence should nevertheless point strongly towards the conclusion that a conspiracy did in fact exist, that itself is a powerful argument in favor of a conspiracy.

Lenoe's Introduction contains a number of weaknesses that characterize the remainder of his study: false statements; deliberate deceptions; "begging the question" or assuming the truth of statements that need to be proven; and anticommunist bias. Any one of these would prove fatal to any historical investigation.

Factual Inaccuracies and False Statements

Lenoe describes the cohort of party members to which Leonid Nikolaev, Kirov's assassin, belonged as follows:

> To bridge the distance between themselves – the avant-garde – and the masses, Communist officials in the 1920s and early 1930s recruited factory workers into the party in large numbers. As Communists these "promotes" (*vydvizhentsy*) benefited from access to white-collar jobs, as well as better apartments, better rations, and superior educational opportunities. ... Hundreds of thousands of others got an education and made professional or bureaucratic careers, becoming the backbone of the Soviet state by the 1940s. Yet others, thrust into positions for which they had little or no training, failed.

Then Lenoe describes Nikolaev as "one of these failures",

> an unemployed communist named Leonid Nikolaev, ... had held about a dozen jobs since he joined the party in 1924, during the recruitment campaign that followed Lenin's death. Since his most recent firing in April 1934 he had been unemployed. (2)

Lenoe is mistaken; Nikolaev was anything but a "failure." Nikolaev had managed to get away from regular blue-collar work. He had one higher-paying, non-production job after another until his firing in April 1934. That suggests that he almost certainly had "friends in high places", influential persons who were able to get him these kinds of jobs. Dismissed from a comfortable job with a good salary because he refused to leave Leningrad on a Party assignment, Nikolaev decided not to look for any more work. This is consistent with his being part of a Zinovievite conspiracy, though of course it does not prove it. (From 1917 to 1926 Zinoviev had been Chairman of the Petrograd, and then the Leningrad, Soviet – the political leader of the Leningrad Party. He was replaced by Kirov.)

According to the testimony of his family members Nikolaev and his family suffered no material difficulties despite the fact that only his wife, Mil'da Draule, was employed after April 1934. Entries in his diary record worries over finances. But that could be explained by evidence cited by Lenoe and Kirilina that suggests Nikolaev used this diary to create a "cover story" to make it look as though the assassination was an act of individual protest. We study this question fully in the present work.

Nikolaev planned to shoot himself to death on the spot after killing Kirov. After he failed to do that and was questioned by NKVD investigators his story of "individual protest" quickly broke down. Before long he confessed that its purpose was to shield the other members of the conspiracy from suspicion.

Lenoe writes:

> For the Communist leadership, the murder in Smolny was traumatic, not just because the victim was one of them but also because the murderer was a Communist and a worker. Something had gone badly wrong, for the party and the proletariat were supposed to be pillars of the regime. (2-3)

Lenoe returns repeatedly to this notion that Stalin and Party leaders would have felt especially chagrined by the fact that Nikolaev was a worker. (274; 344) But he gives no evidence to support this repeated assertion, which is certainly false. During the 1920s and early '30s virtually all the opposition groups in the Bolshevik Party had working-class members. Some were made up primarily of workers, or at least of people from working-class backgrounds. This was particularly true of the Zinovievites, followers of Grigory Zinoviev who had been First Secretary of the Leningrad Party until 1926. Leningrad was the most industrialized city, with the largest number of workers and working-class Party members, in the country.

After listing some of the Bolsheviks' successes during the 1920s and early 30s Lenoe writes:

> · They had also ruled with police terror, which increased greatly in the late 1920s…

Lenoe does not say what he means by "police terror" or give any examples of it. I can identify nothing that could accurately be so described during this period.

> …suppressed all open political dissent…

In reality "open political dissent" was permitted and in fact was commonly expressed, for example at factory and union meetings. However, it is true that *organized* political dissent was not permitted. And factions within the Bolshevik Party had not been permitted since 1921, a ban suggested by Lenin. Opposition political parties were not permitted – but neither had they been since before 1920.

In making the three statements above Lenoe is guilty of a double standard. No one would accuse a Western capitalist country of such acts without citing specific examples. In the case of the Bolsheviks Lenoe acts as though evidence is not necessary.

> ...confiscated private property, banned most private businesses...

Here Lenoe tacitly assumes that private property is somehow "sacred." Communism of course opposes "private property" and "private businesses" on principle. (Under President Lincoln the United States "confiscated private property" by freeing the slaves.) Such confiscations characterized Bolshevik policy from before the Revolution of 1917 when they advocated "land to the tiller" – that is, the confiscation of landlord property, and the nationalization of major industries. After the end of the Soviet Union authorities "confiscated public property" – that is, privatized it.

> ...and forced the peasants who still made up the majority of the population to work for very little on collective farms managed by the party/state apparatus. (3)

This statement is, to put it politely, highly misleading. *Most* peasants had always "worked for very little". Lenoe appears to imply here that most peasants had earned more than "very little." The real situation was very different. Most peasants in Russia were poor. About a quarter of them, the *batraki*, or farm laborers, had no land at all. About half of the rest were poor peasants, unable or barely able to sustain themselves even in the best years by farming a very small parcel of land with the most primitive means.

Whenever famines broke out many of the *batraki* and the *bedniaki* or poor peasants simply starved to death or died of malnutrition-related diseases. Considerable starvation occurred even in non-famine years when rich peasants (called *kulaks*) or middlemen who bought and resold grain, withheld grain from the markets to await higher prices.

Lenoe writes:

> As a direct result of forced collectivization more than five million country people died of starvation in 1932-1933. (3)

Lenoe does not attempt to provide any evidence in defense of this statement, much less to prove it. He simply states this as a "fact". But it is false. There is no evidence that collectivization caused the famine of 1932-33. In reality it was due to crop failure. Professor Mark Tauger, the leading expert on the famine, points out that famines had wracked Russia, including the Ukraine, every 2-3 years for at least a millennium.[12] The famine of 1932-33 was yet another one in this seemingly endless series. Undoubtedly, had collectivization taken place during years when no crop failure occurred, a great many fewer people would have died. But this could not be known in advance, and in fact there were few such years.

Every researcher knows these facts. We must assume that Lenoe knows them too. But he fails to engage them and their evidence, or even to refer to them. Therefore, this statement appears to be a "declaration of loyalty". In it Lenoe self-consciously puts himself into what we may call the Cold-War anticommunist camp, one tenet of which is that collectivization was somehow immoral.

Lenoe further writes:

> In the months following the murder, Stalin did all he could to heighten the atmosphere of suspicion and dread that accompanied the killing. (3)

If, as Lenoe tries to argue, Kirov's murder really had been the act of a "lone gunman", if there was no underground terrorist conspiracy and

---

12 For a brief overview of this question see Mark Tauger. "Famine in Russian History". *Modern Encyclopedia of Russian and Soviet History, Volume 10: Supplement.* (Gulf Breeze, FL: Academic International Press, 2011), 79-92. Tauger's own works on the famine are cited at page 92. Tauger cites E.P. Borisenkov and V.M. Pasketskii. *Tysiachtletniaia letopis' neobychainykh iavlenii prirody.* ("Thousand-year Chronicle of Extraordinary Natural Events"). Moscow: "Mysl'", 1988. Wheatcroft argues that the 1946-1947 famine was due to factors beyond the Soviet government's control: poor weather conditions worldwide and the terrible destruction of the war. Wheatcroft, Stephen G. "The Soviet Famine of 1946–1947, the Weather and Human Agency in Historical Perspective." *Europe-Asia Studies*, 64:6, 987-1005

Stalin knew it, then there would be much truth to this statement. However, the present study argues that, on the evidence, such a conspiracy did exist and went much farther than just the men convicted and executed for conspiring to kill Kirov. We now have a great many primary sources from this period of Soviet history. None of it suggests that Stalin and other Soviet leaders did not believe there was a conspiracy and were only cynically spreading this idea. But if they really did believe such an underground terrorist conspiracy existed, it would follow that the "atmosphere of suspicion" created was understandable.

> He warned of terrorist plots to assassinate the entire Soviet leadership… (3)

Lenoe implies that such plots did not exist. But there is a great deal of evidence that they did exist – including pretrial and trial confessions by Moscow Trial defendants, but much other evidence as well, including evidence from outside the Soviet Union – and no evidence that these confessions were "scripted", forced on the defendants by the NKVD, or otherwise faked. We will review some of this evidence in the present book.

> …and proclaimed that no one could be trusted because "enemies" had penetrated the party itself. (3)

This is a false statement. Lenoe cites no evidence that Stalin ever said "no one can be trusted", nor can I find any such quotation by Stalin. Stalin did state that former oppositionists could not be taken at their word – i.e., simply believed when they claimed they had ceased their oppositional activity. But this was no more than an acknowledgement that conspirators lie in the service of their conspiracy.

Lenoe claims:

> In Leningrad thirteen men, mostly former Left sympathizers, were framed, charged with plotting a terrorist attack on Kirov, and executed together with the actual assassin, Leonid Nikolaev. (3-4)

Here Lenoe anticipates the central hypothesis of his book. The present study argues that this hypothesis and statement of Lenoe's is wrong. As we shall show Lenoe fails to present any evidence whatsoever that these men were "framed." On the contrary: all the evidence we have points towards their guilt.

Lenoe continues:

> Two of Stalin's most prominent former rivals, Grigory Zinoviev and Lev Kamenev, were tried in January 1935 for "moral complicity" in the assassination and sentenced to long prison terms. (4)

This statement is false. There is no mention of "moral complicity" in the charges or sentence handed down against Zinoviev, Kamenev and others.

Zinoviev was sentenced to 10 years imprisonment for leading an underground conspiratorial group of his supporters whose members, with his knowledge, not only spread hatred of the party leadership but travelled to Leningrad and met with the leadership of the "Leningrad center" which carried out the murder of Kirov. One part of the sentence statement reads as follows:

> As a result of the counterrevolutionary activities of the "Moscow Center" in specific links of the Zinovievist counterrevolutionary underground there arose purely fascist methods of struggle, and there appeared and strengthened terrorist sentiment directed against the leaders of the Party and government, which had as its result the murder of comrade S.M. Kirov, prepared and organized by the "Leningrad Center" of the same counterrevolutionary group.
>
> All of the defendants in the present case have fully admitted their guilt.[13]

As leader of the group Zinoviev was sentenced to ten years imprisonment. Kamenev received the lightest sentence, five years, because the court found as follows:

> 11. KAMENEV, Lev Borisovich

[13] "Prigovor" (Sentence), undated (January 16, 1935), p. 6. In Volkogonov Archive, LOC. I have put a facsimile online at http://msuweb.montclair.edu/~furrg/research/prigovor011635.pdf

> As one of the leading members of the "Moscow Center", but who had not taken any active part in its activities during the recent period. (8)

We deal with other of Lenoe's falsehoods in his Introduction in a separate chapter.

Begging the Question

Lenoe refers to:

> false accounts of the assassination in the Soviet press during the 1930s (10)

…and…

> They [Khrushchev-era investigators] made extensive use of the layer of falsified evidence from the Great Terror. (9)

These statements commit the fallacy of "begging the question." They "assume that which should be proven" – in fact, they assume away the problem that Lenoe supposedly did his research, and wrote his book, to solve.

That would not be so if, later in his book, Lenoe were to prove that the accounts of the Kirov assassination related in the Moscow Trials testimony (the source of the Soviet press accounts) were false. But he never does that. Moreover, he does not examine any of these accounts. He does not even identify them – say, in an appendix, or in a footnote to inform his readers where they can find this evidence should they want to examine it themselves.

Much less does Lenoe argue that the canonical version of Kirov's assassination, as it was gradually revealed in the various trials between December 1934 and March 1938, is false in any way. In fact, Lenoe conceals the existence of these accounts from his readers. Lenoe simply *asserts* that they were false without any evidence or, indeed, any argument at all. Yet this is the central thesis of his book. The principal result of the present study is that the much-maligned Soviet or "Stalin" account of the Kirov murder is, in fact, the correct one.

Torture

In his Introduction Lenoe makes frequent reference to torture. He speaks of

> ...[d]ocuments from the renewed "investigation" of the Great Terror years (1936-1939), many of which are witness statements given under torture or the threat of same. (8)
>
> NKVD officers tortured witnesses until they provided testimony supporting fantastic charges of conspiracy against former party leaders. (9)
>
> ...the use of torture by Stalin and his secret police to extract false but politically useful 'confessions' of terrorist conspiracies. (17)

Lenoe fails to demonstrate even a single example of torture against a witness or defendant in any of the trials concerning the Kirov murder: those of December, 1934; January, 1935; the first Moscow public, or "show", trial of August 1936; the second Moscow trial of January 1937; the third Moscow trial of March 1938. He alleges, though he does not prove, that some former NKVD officials once involved in the case were tortured in the later 1930s. But even if Lenoe could prove that these men really were tortured and their confessions scripted and false, it would not affect this central issue. Their testimony was peripheral at best to the basic question: Was there a conspiracy to murder Kirov?

Nor does Lenoe prove torture in any other instances. He merely cites allegations made in the 1950s. But by his own admission Khrushchev and his men were busy destroying documents and falsifying charges against Stalin in the '50s and '60s. The truthfulness of these, or any, allegations must be demonstrated, not taken for granted. Lenoe makes no attempt to do so.

In any case "allegations" are not evidence. The fact that someone alleges that he, or a third party, was tortured does not mean that he really was – especially when, as during the Khrushchev years, investigators were under pressure to try to prove the trials of the 1930s were fabricated and that torture had been employed. We devote a part of the present study to the fallacy of appeals to "torture" used as a rhetorical device of persuasion to conceal Lenoe's lack of evidence.

Even if it could be established – and it has not been – that one or more of the central defendants were in fact tortured, that would not mean that this testimony was false. A person may be tortured to induce him to tell what he knows, as well as to induce him to sign a false or "scripted" confession. Tortured people can either lie or tell the truth. Likewise, defendants who are not tortured may either lie or tell the truth. Therefore, even if Lenoe could establish that one or more of the main defendants who testified about the Kirov murder had been "tortured" (whatever that means), that would not establish that his testimony was false.

By ignoring the Moscow Trial testimony Lenoe is again positioning himself with respect to this historical question. All the Moscow Trial testimony supports the hypothesis that Nikolaev, Kirov's assassin, was a part of a network of clandestine Opposition terrorist conspiracies. It is considered unacceptable by some persons in the highly politicized field of Soviet history to reach the conclusion that the Moscow Trials were not "scripted" and that Opposition conspiracies existed – even though on the evidence there is no doubt at all that such a conspiracy did in fact exist.

Anticommunism

A researcher needs to be as objective as possible so that his preconceived ideas and biases do not fatally prejudice his investigation. By contrast, Lenoe takes pains to express his anticommunist bias in the strongest terms. He admits that he believes communism is "evil", a "cruel failure with millions of victims". (16) Statements of this kind serve no research or investigative purpose. They only serve to warn the reader that the writer who advertises his bias so blatantly cannot be trusted to be objective when gathering, examining, interpreting, and drawing conclusions from the evidence.

Imagine that Lenoe, instead of declaring that he believes communism to be "evil" and "a cruel failure with millions of victims", made the same statement but about capitalism! The impropriety for a scholar of even thinking in such terms, much less in parading these opinions before his readers, would become apparent to the most anticommunist reader.

Lenoe calls Stalin "one of the greatest mass murderers of modern world history" (3) as though it is a proven fact. So serious a charge requires strong evidence to justify it. Lenoe cites no evidence to support this statement. In reality, no study has ever proven such an accusation.[14]

Lenoe asserts that "[i]n Leningrad thirteen men, mostly former Left sympathizers, were framed" [for Kirov's murder]. (4) It will astonish readers to learn, as we will demonstrate in the present study, that Lenoe has virtually *no evidence at all* to support his thesis that even a single one of the defendants was innocent. This declaration of Lenoe's does put him squarely in support of the official Soviet / Russian government position and is consistent with the only "acceptable" and "mainstream" view that the Moscow Trials were frameups. But it is not in the least supported by the evidence – on the contrary, all the evidence we now have refutes it.

Lenoe asserts that:

> ...the end of constructing Communism justified means that included mass violence, summary trials, and the starvation of millions. (13)

As Lenoe makes no effort to prove any of these grave charges, we may conclude that he thinks they are "obvious". They are an obligatory component of anticommunist propaganda. All revolutions cause "mass violence" – but nothing compared to that of the First World War, believed "justified" by the leaders of all the major countries of Europe, Japan, the United States, and the Ottoman Empire. "Summary trials" characterized all sides during the World War. (We have dealt briefly with "the starvation of millions" above.)

Lenoe refers to "Stalin's use of Kirov's death to justify terror" and claims Stalin "presided over the execution of thousands of senior party officials who had no record of political opposition" "in an apparent attempt to eliminate any possible source of resistance to his rule." (4) Neither of

---

[14] We cannot discuss this question exhaustively in the present study. However, far from killing millions collectivization arguably saved millions of lives by sparing the USSR future famines. As for the NKVD's killing of a little fewer than 700,000 people in 1937-1938, the evidence shows that in fact Nikolai Ezhov did it without Stalin's knowledge. See the beginning of the next chapter for a little more on this question.

these statements are supported by any evidence. Lenoe provides not even a footnote for these statements.

Moreover, we question Lenoe's use of elusive language here. What does "presided over" mean in this context? It could mean no more than that Stalin was the de facto leader of the country at the time. Would we say that President Franklin D. Roosevelt "presided over" the Jim Crow system in the Southern United States? He certainly chose not to stop it and reaped political benefits from it. Yet historians would never say he "presided over it" even though his title was "president" – "one who presides."

As for "senior party officials who had no record of political opposition," Lenoe cannot possibly know this since even he admits that much evidence from the 1930s remains top secret in Russia today. But the main point is surely this: what is pertinent is not whether a person, "senior party official" or not, had "a prior record" but whether they were guilty of the crimes they were charged with – i.e., whether they were convicted on the basis of credible evidence. To raise the question of executions without any context is to do what Khrushchev did. Khrushchev had reason to think his 1956 audience, all of them "senior party officials", would agree with him. But scholars must consider matters of evidence.[15]

Lenoe claims that Stalin "insisted that NKVD investigators build a case against former party oppositionists". (9) By "build a case" Lenoe must mean "fabricate a case", for otherwise investigators are acting correctly in pursuing their investigations where the evidence leads them. It is the job of prosecutors everywhere to "build cases". But Lenoe gives no evidence that Stalin ordered the NKVD to *fabricate* any case against anyone. To our knowledge no such evidence exists.[16]

---

[15] We discuss a little of the evidence against those senior Party officials whom Khrushchev mentioned in his "Secret Speech" to the 20th Party Congress in Grover Furr. *Khrushchev Lied: The Evidence That Every "Revelation" of Stalin's (and Beria's) Crimes in Nikita Khrushchev's Infamous "Secret Speech" to the 20th Party Congress of the Communist Party of the Soviet Union on February 25, 1956, is Provably False.* Kettering, OH: Erythrós Press & Media LLC, 2011.

[16] We know that Ezhov fabricated cases against a great many persons during 1937-1938, but no evidence connects Stalin with such fabrications.

Some of the statements Lenoe makes in his Introduction are clearly ideological rather than historical. For example, he writes:

> Stalin's Communist denouncers were in the right, and the cause of de-Stalinization was just. (11)

A few pages later Lenoe is more explicit about why he feels that he needs to proclaim his anticommunist *bona fides* in strident tones.

> Some may be tempted to accuse me of apologizing for Stalin because I do not take on faith the received narrative that he ordered Kirov's murder. (16)

It should be obvious that no historian ever has to explain or give reasons for *not* taking some historical conclusion "on faith." But Lenoe knows that the field of Soviet history has rules of its own, for he proceeds to compose a virtual credo of the faithful anticommunist:

> To prevent misunderstandings, I want to make my position clear. I have an immense, personal contempt for despots and authoritarians of all stripes, from Stalin to Mao, from Hitler to Franco, from Rios Montt to Pinochet, Pol Pot, and King Leopold II, Belgian ruler of the "Congo Free State."...
>
> Stalin was one of the deadliest tyrants of world history, and Communism as a system of government was a cruel failure with millions of victims. (16)

Lenoe then criticizes the Bush administration for its policies restricting civil liberties and use of torture in the wake of 9-11. (16-17)

What does any of this have to do with whether Kirov was murdered by a conspiracy of clandestine Oppositionists, as alleged by the Soviet government at the time; by Stalin; or by a "lone gunman"? Perhaps only this: Lenoe knows that Soviet history, particularly of the Stalin period, is a discipline in which ideological conformity is considered all-important in powerful circles.

To arrive at a conclusion that Stalin did *not* commit some crime of which he has been widely accused by famous anticommunist historians is to run the risk of being labelled "pro-Stalin", "pro-communist", or at least "insufficiently anticommunist." In fact, the present study will undoubtedly be called "an apology for Stalin" because it "does not take on faith the received narrative", though that "received narrative has, since 1990, not been that Stalin killed Kirov, but that Nikolaev was a "lone gunman" and because we prove that Stalin did not "frame" any of the Kirov defendants, any of the Moscow Trials defendants, any of the defendants in the Tukhachevsky Affair. In fact, there is no evidence anywhere that Stalin ever "framed" even a single person.

The thesis Lenoe attempts to prove throughout this book is the same, in the end, as that of Soviet anti-Stalinists. Despite their attempts to "frame" Stalin for Kirov's murder, the government-sponsored researchers of both Khrushchev and Gorbachev eras were forced to conclude that there was no evidence to support this conclusion. This position is also supported by Alla Kirilina, the main Russian scholar of the Kirov assassination. Few of Lenoe's readers will know this. But the best-known books on the Kirov assassination outside of Russia – those by Robert Conquest and Amy Knight – both argue that Stalin had Kirov killed.

Lenoe does point out that Russian authorities still keep important documents of the Kirov assassination investigation top-secret, unavailable to him or to any other researchers. (14-15) It did not occur to Lenoe to ask why this might be. A logical hypothesis would be that the still-secret documents contradict the "orthodox" or "mainstream" position of today's Russian authorities that Nikolaev was a "lone gunman" and that no clandestine Opposition conspiracies really existed during the 1930s.

We know this position is false. We shall discuss the fact that letters exchanged between Leon Trotsky and his son Leon Sedov revealed to researchers in the 1980s that a "bloc" of Trotskyites, Zinovievites, Rightists and others did in fact exist. Lenoe never refers to this bloc or to the implications for his thesis of the official Russian denial of its existence.

Chapter 3.

Lenoe's Errors.

In order to demonstrate that Lenoe's book contains serious lapses of objectivity it is perhaps sufficient to enumerate some of the large number of outright falsehoods it contains. This section will identify and analyze those we think are the most noteworthy. We will not attempt to "psychologize" Lenoe as he attempts to do with Stalin. Unlike Lenoe, we admit that we have no way of knowing what was going on in his consciousness when he wrote these false statements. Perhaps he really thinks they are true! If so, he should have investigated them more carefully before printing them as fact.

> As a direct result of forced collectivization more than 5 million died of starvation in 1932-33. (3)

This is false, unsupported by the best research. Excellent research has shown that there was a secular famine in 1932-33 as there had been every 2-4 years in Russia for at least the past thousand years. But the famine of 1932-33 was the last famine in Russian / Soviet history (except for the terrible 1946-7 famine caused by the huge destruction of the war and weather problems).[17]

Stalin was:

> One of the greatest mass murderers of modern history… (3)

---

[17] Much of the scholarship on the famine of 1932-33 is highly tendentious and even deliberately falsified. For the best, most objective and qualified research see Davies, R.W. and Stephen G. Wheatcroft. *The Years of Hunger. Soviet Agriculture, 1931-1933.* Palgrave Macmillan 2009 (2004) and Tauger, Mark. Review of R. W. Davies and Stephen G. Wheatcroft, *The Years of Hunger: Soviet Agriculture, 1931-1933.* New York: Palgrave Macmillan, 2004. At http://eh.net/book_reviews/years-hunger-soviet-agriculture-1931-1933 Wheatcroft and Davies believe that bad weather was "a further major factor" in the famines. Tauger believes the poor weather was the single most important factor. Borisenkov and Pasketskii., previously cited, have shown that serious crop failures and famines had occurred every 2-4 years with frightening regularity for at least a millennium.

This too is a "declaration of loyalty" rather than the conclusion of scholarly research. In reality no mass murders, either by Stalin or that he was responsible for, have ever been demonstrated. Lenoe does not tell us what events he has in mind. Perhaps the following:

- The "Great Terror". Several hundred thousand persons were convicted falsely and / simply shot by the NKVD under Ezhov. Stalin never ordered or condoned these murders, which Ezhov and his accomplices committed under the guise of fighting active counterrevolutionary rebellions.[18] After Beria replaced Ezhov as head of the NKVD hundreds of thousands were freed from prisons and camps, while Ezhov and his accomplices in the NKVD were investigated, arrested, tried, convicted, and punished, often by execution.
- The Moscow Trials and Tukhachevsky Affair. ALL the evidence we have – and there is a great deal of evidence public now – support the guilt of these men.
- The "Katyn Massacre." Likewise, there exists much evidence that the Soviets tried and shot some Poles – not just prisoners of war but others – and the Germans later shot many more of them.[19]

---

[18] Apparently Robert Eikhe, and then a number of other First Secretaries, approached Stalin and the Politburo after the June 1937 Central Committee Plenum and asked for these special powers to deal with conspiracies, rebellions, and revolts in their areas. This led to the Politburo Decree "On Anti-Soviet elements" of July 2, 1937 which authorized all First Secretaries to arrest "kulaks and criminals" who had returned to their areas, shoot the "most dangerous" of them, and exile the rest to other areas. For the next year or more Stalin was flooded with reports of conspiracies and revolts from all over the USSR, some of which have been published.

According to Khaustov, a very anti-Stalin researcher and one of the compilers of several of these invaluable document collections, Stalin believed these reports: "The most terrible thing was that Stalin made decisions on the basis of confessions that were inventions of certain NKVD workers. Stalin's reactions showed that he took these confessions completely seriously." *Lubianka. Sovetskaia elita na stalinskoi golgofe. 1937-1938*. Ed. V.N. Khaustov (Moscow: MDF, 2011, p. 6. Now online at http://www.k2x2.info/politika/lubjanka_sovetskaja_yelita_na_stalinskoi_golgofe_1937_1938/p4.php

[19] See Grover Furr, "The "Official" Version of the Katyn Massacre Disproven?" *Socialism and Democracy* 2 (2) August 2013, 96-129 for a report on discoveries that refute the "official" version.

Once again, it is considered "beyond the Pale" in anticommunist circles, academic and otherwise, to state these facts.

According to Lenoe, Stalin:

> insisted that NKVD investigators build a case against former party oppositionists in the days after the killing. (9)

In a later chapter of this study we demonstrate that this statement is false, another classic example of Lenoe's "begging the question" by assuming that which he ought to have proven.

Likewise, Lenoe refers to "false accounts of the [Kirov] assassination in the Soviet press during the 1930s. (10) Lenoe never even discusses these accounts, much less establish that they were "false". He is in no position to do so since he failed to examine the testimony presented before and during the 1936, 1937, and 1938 Moscow Trials. In reality, judging from the evidence available at the time and what we have today, the accounts of the Kirov assassination in the Soviet press during the 1930s were and conform far more closely to the evidence we now have than does Lenoe's own version.

Lenoe states:

> I have consciously striven to include all plausible evidence contradicting my case. (16)

This is perhaps the most blatant falsehood in Lenoe's long book. As we will demonstrate, in reality Lenoe ignores virtually all the evidence presented after the trial of the Leningrad defendants in December 1934 until the end of the March 1938 Moscow trial. This is a huge amount of evidence – in fact, it is most of the evidence now available to us. But Lenoe never studies any of it. In the present study we conclude that all this evidence, plus all the evidence Lenoe does discuss, demonstrates that Lenoe's hypothesis that Nikolaev was a "lone gunman" is groundless, without any foundation in the evidence.

Lenoe writes of:

> ...the use of torture by Stalin and his secret police to extract false but politically useful "confessions" of terrorist conspiracies. (17)

There is no evidence whatsoever that torture was used to extract false confessions, and Lenoe cites none here. NKVD men, particularly under Ezhov's direction during 1937-1938, did use torture and fake confessions widely. In 1939 Ezhov and a number of his closest assistants were arrested and confessed to doing this. Though much still remains secret in Russia we now have enough of these confession statements to make it clear that Ezhov, not Stalin, was responsible for these faked confessions based in many cases on torture.[20]

Kirov "stuck with" Stalin:

> …whatever his private doubts or fears may have been. (63)

Lenoe presents no evidence whatsoever that Kirov had any "private doubts." This allegation appears to be a relic of earlier propagandistic accounts of Kirov's murder in which the killing was attributed to Stalin. Lenoe rejects these versions but retains a component part of them: that Kirov had some kind of "doubts" or "fears" of Stalin.

Lenoe states:

> Molotov was a mass murderer, one of the two or three men closest to Stalin in the 1930s. (266)

This is an astounding statement. Lenoe cites no evidence that Molotov ever ordered anyone at all, much less "masses", to be murdered (nor, of course, did Molotov ever murder anyone himself). No doubt Lenoe could have made some sort of case to support this claim. After all, virtually all high-ranking Bolsheviks of the Stalin period and even before and afterwards have been called "murderers" by some anticommunist or other at some time. Such statements mean nothing unless accompanied by evidence – nothing, that is, except for proof that the author of such statements has strong biases. But Lenoe does not justify this statement in any way.

Concerning the Nakhaev case, about which little is known, Lenoe states

---

[20] See Grover Furr, "The Moscow Trials and the "Great Terror" of 1937-1938: What the Evidence Shows." July 31, 2010. At http://msuweb.montclair.edu/~furrg/research/trials_ezhovshchina_update0710.html

> He [Nakhaev] was shot in short order.[44]

Lenoe's note 44, on page 772, reads as follows:

> Khlevniuk, *Stalin i Kaganovich*, 432, 459, 411-412.
> Agranov telegram to Stalin in Khaustov et al., *Lubianka, 1922-1936*, 565.

Agranov's telegram to Stalin makes no reference whatsoever to Nakhaev's trial or execution. The only one of these references that says anything about Nakhaev's fate is Khlevniuk, who states:

> Nakhaev was probably shot.[21] (412)

Even Khlevniuk admits that he does not know even whether Nakhaev was shot, let alone "in short order." Lenoe turns Khlevniuk's surmise into a statement of fact – a falsehood that appears to be deliberate. What's more, this issue is irrelevant to proving Lenoe's case about Kirov's murder.

Lenoe states the following about a confession by Nikolaev of December 5, 1934:

> In Nikolaev's quite plausible account Shatsky expressed anger at Stalin's Seventeenth Party Congress speech calling for the firing of former oppositionists… (287)

The problem is that this never occurred. Stalin did not call for firing former oppositionists. Neither of the two speeches Stalin gave at the 17th Party Congress says anything remotely resembling this. On the contrary: a number of prominent oppositionists who had renounced their opposition – dishonestly, as it turned out – and been readmitted to Party membership, had been promoted again to very high positions and addressed the Party Congress in January 1934, Bukharin, Piatakov, Zinov'ev, and Kamenev among them.[22] This seems to have been in-

---

21 "Skoree vsego, Nakhaev byl rasstrelian."

22 The rough draft of the Politburo resolution proposing that Zinov'ev and Kamenev be reinstated in the Party and not have to pass through the "purge", or review of membership, then taking place, may be seen at http://www.rusarchives.ru/evants/exhibitions/xviiexp/217.shtml It appears that the handwriting is Stalin's. The resolution was passed on December 12, 1933, one month before the 17th Party Congress.

tended as a signal to all that former oppositionists would be readmitted once they renounced their opposition.

It's possible that Lenoe simply failed to check Stalin's speeches at the Congress to verify whether Nikolaev was telling the truth. If that is so, then this is a serious lapse on Lenoe's part. But the NKVD investigators would not have failed to check it. Assuming Nikolaev actually made such a statement, his doing so would have been strong evidence to the investigators that Nikolaev was lying. And in turn that would have signaled to the investigators that his story was beginning to fall apart. It would have encouraged them to press Nikolaev even harder on the falsehoods and inconsistencies in his statements. Sure enough, the very next day, December 6, Nikolaev first stated that Kotolynov and Shatskii were participants with him in the "terrorist act". (Kirilina 277)

On page 289 Lenoe writes:

> To get him to interrogations the guards had to put him into a straitjacket and carry him down the hall while he struggled and shouted, "It is I, Nikolaev, they're torturing me, remember me!"[19]

Note 19 to this passage (289) reads as follows:

> See Kirilina, *Neizvestnyi Kirov*, 277.

The Kirilina reference states that Nikolaev declared a hunger strike but gives no evidence or source for this statement. The "Reply to Iakovlev" (June 1990) quotes the claim about torture but gives no source at all for it. We will examine the "Reply to Iakovlev" in a future chapter.

The actual source is the article by IUrii Sedov, "Wrongfully Executed" ("Bezvinno kaznennye") in the journal *Trud* of December 4, 1990. But Sedov gives no source for this statement either! Elsewhere in this review we have shown that Sedov himself has told deliberate falsehoods, including in this very article.

The lack of a source strongly suggests that this statement is no more than a rumor – unless Sedov or one of his staff simply invented it themselves. In either case it is of no value. It hardly needs to be said that rumors are not evidence. Lenoe himself never refers again to this allegation that Nikolaev was tortured.[23] He should not have included it – at a minimum, not without tracing its provenance, as we have easily done here.

On pages 312-3 Lenoe states:

> Zvezdov gave the interrogators almost everything they needed. He placed Nikolaev inside a tightly organized "counterrevolutionary group" that aimed to replace Stalin. The group was made up of former Trotskyites and Zinovievites. It had strict rules of secrecy, so that the following Alice in Wonderland reasoning could be applied – the lack of evidence of a conspiratorial organization could serve to demonstrate just how top secret, insidious, and widespread the organization really was.

On one level this is nonsense. There was no "lack of evidence of a conspiratorial organization". Zvezdov had confessed that there really was a secret Trotskyite-Zinovievite group. As we shall discuss and as Lenoe himself admits, many others among the accused, including Kotolynov and Nikolaev, also agreed such a group existed. Again as we discuss elsewhere in the present work Trotsky and his son Sedov agreed that it existed too.

Logically, Lenoe could only refer to "lack of evidence of a conspiratorial organization" if he were to state up front that he did not "count" confessions or interrogations as evidence. That is, if he were to take the position that only written agreements among the conspirators confirming their conspiracy constituted evidence of the existence of a conspiracy. Of course this would be absurd. The whole point of conspiracy is secrecy: to leave *no* evidence. A conspiracy that left written evidence of its existence would hardly be a conspiracy at all. Furthermore, even the existence of written evidence of such a conspiracy would not constitute more reliable evidence than the testimony of its participants, for documentary evidence can be fabricated just as easily as can confessions, if not more so.

---

[23] Moreover, the fact that Nikolaev *may* have claimed he was being tortured does not prove that he was in fact tortured, much less that what he testified was false. We discuss the issue of "torture as smokescreen" elsewhere in the present book.

Not once in his whole book does Lenoe argue that any of those who confessed did so because of torture or threats. He suggests this as a possibility, but never states it as a fact in even a single case. Presumably he would have done so if he had the slightest grounds. Therefore, Lenoe's reference here to "Alice in Wonderland" is disingenuous. There is plenty of evidence of a conspiracy.

Lenoe is so eager to deny that any counterrevolutionary organization existed that he makes absurd statements like the following:

> At the trial … Kotolynov testified that he had belonged to a "counterrevolutionary Zinovievite organization," but that all the members did was stay in contact with one another. They had no specific agenda or division of responsibilities. (314)

Lenoe does not trouble to examine this statement. And it is incredible. For one thing, if Kotolynov were correct, that "all the members did was stay in contact with one another", then why did he agree it was "counterrevolutionary"? For another thing, a number of other defendants testified that the Zinovievites were indeed involved in political activity. (We examine this statement by Kotolynov further on.)

On page 321 Lenoe writes of "the accelerating campaign to rewrite Soviet history … to exaggerate Stalin's role…" His footnote to this passage (note 52 on p. 776) refers to Lavrentii Beria's book on the Bolshevik movement in the Caucasus and specifically refers to pages 54-62 of Amy Knight's book on Beria. But Knight's book says nothing about any such "campaign". Therefore this is a false reference, the only result of which can be to mislead the reader into believing that such a "campaign" existed.

On the same page Lenoe writes:

> One important remaining hole in the case was that Nikolaev could not or would not provide convincing evidence that he'd actually belonged to the Zinovievite organization anytime during the 1920s. (321)

As we have shown elsewhere, Tsar'kov confirmed that Nikolaev was a member of the Zinovievite organization during the 1920s. What other "convincing evidence" of Nikolaev's, or anyone's, membership does

Lenoe want – a membership card dated sometime during the 1920s? Of course illegal conspiratorial communist organizations do not have membership cards, lists, or other paraphernalia. Moreover, Nikolaev's membership during the 1920s is irrelevant to the question of whether he was a member in 1934! This kind of remark is a "tell", as we explain more fully elsewhere: a signal, no doubt unconscious, to the attentive reader that Lenoe has no evidence and is trying to disguise this lack with specious verbiage.

In an attempt to discredit the NKVD investigation Lenoe writes that, in order to inform Party leaders about the results of the investigation:

> [m]oving with remarkable speed, the TsK executives called plenary sessions of the regional party committees in Moscow and Leningrad for December 15-16...

Lenoe implies that 15-16 days after the assassination was "remarkably" fast. That, one presumes, is intended to suggest to the reader that a "rush to judgment", some kind of phony procedure and trial, went on. But there was nothing "remarkable" about the "speed" in which the case against Nikolaev and the underground Zinovievite center in Leningrad was prosecuted. For the sake of comparison: in the USA in 1901 there were only 9 days between President McKinley's death on September 14, 1901 and the beginning of the trial of his assassin, Leon Czolgosz, on September 23. In the Kirov case there were 27 days between the assassination and the trial.

Lenoe states:

> The Stalinist leadership drove the mass operations onward by issuing mandatory quotas for arrests and executions to provincial NKVD organizations. (468)

This is false. Ezhov did indeed call for arrest and execution quotas. This was in violation of the notes coming from Stalin and the central Party leadership, who always used the term "limits" of arrests and executions requested by local Party and NKVD leadership. "Limit" means "no more than, but it can be less than", while "quota" means "no less than" – an enormous difference.[24] In any case, there is no reference or citation of evidence at all for this serious accusation.

Lenoe states:

> Tukhachevsky and his fellows were tortured and shot. (468)

This is a false statement. There has never been any evidence that Tukhachevsky was tortured. Lenoe's note to this statement (note 48, p. 787) reads as follows:

> Getty, *Road to Terror*, 437-453; Jansen and Petrov, *Stalin's Loyal Executioner*, 69-78.

Getty's text does not claim Tukhachevsky was tortured. However, Jansen and Petrov do claim that "They [Tukhachevsky and other officers] were tortured until they confessed." (69) Jansen's and Petrov's source (note 74, p. 230) reads:

> S. IU. Ushakov, A.A. Stukalov. *Front voennykh prokurorov.* M[oscow], 2001, p. 71.

This is the supposed memoirs of a prosecutor, Afanas'ev, who claims he was present while Ezhov, Stalin, Molotov and others discussed Tukhachevskii and decided to have him tortured. But there is no evidence that any of this is true. There is no reason to think Afanas'ev was present during any of these discussions, which he reproduces verbatim. None of the biographers of Tukhachevsky, including the recent and extremely anti-Stalin books by Iulia Kantor, even mentions Afanas'ev's account at all.

Concerning Trotsky, Lenoe states with indignation:

> It was not Trotsky who collaborated with foreign imperialist powers… it wasn't Trotsky who ordered Kirov's murder, but it might well have been Stalin. (513)

---

24 Ezhov might be considered part of "the Stalinist leadership" – but so was Stalin, of course. Lenoe's use of this evasive term suggests he may be aware of this contradiction and concealing it from his readers.

Lenoe has no evidence for these statements. But there exists a great deal of evidence to support both of these accusations against Trotsky. Specifically, there is a great deal of evidence to implicate Trotsky in collaboration with both Germany and Japan.[25] There is also a great deal of testimony that Trotsky had a role in the Kirov assassination. We will explore that in the present book as a part of our examination of the Moscow Trials. For now, we should recall that the group tried, convicted, and executed for the Kirov assassination in December 1934 – Nikolaev, Kotolynov, and the rest – were members of a Trotskyite-Zinovievite bloc that, thanks to Trotsky's own admission, we know really did exist and that we know was indeed in touch with the exiled Trotsky.

Other false statements:

> Beria...accumulated in his safe materials incriminating other party leaders. (555)

There is no evidence whatsoever to support this allegation. Beria was charged with something like this, but all writers including Amy Knight, whom Lenoe cites elsewhere, make it clear that the charges against Beria were untrustworthy and unsupported by any evidence.

> Khrushchev and many of his allies genuinely did want to end mass terror... (555)

The problem with this statement is that there was no "mass terror" in 1953, nor had there been for many years before that. The only period in Soviet history that might be described as one of "mass terror" was the "Ezhovshchina" of 1937-1938. Khrushchev himself was in the thick of it, one of the worst perpetrators, while it was Stalin and Beria who had put an end to it.[26] In the three months he was Minister of the combined MGB and MVD after Stalin's death it was Beria who pushed reforms of the legal system.[27]

---

[25] Grover Furr, "Evidence of Leon Trotsky's Collaboration with Germany and Japan." *Cultural Logic* (2009), at http://clogic.eserver.org/2009/Furr.pdf

[26] There is a great deal of documentation for these statements. See, for example, Furr, *Khrushchev Lied* 250-257.

[27] For a short discussion of this in English see Knight, *Beria*, Chapter 9. There are now many discussions of Beria and his reform activities in his "100 days" from March to June 1953. A list of Russian-language books available in 2005 is at the end of Furr, "Stalin and

Ivan Serov and "Katyn"

Lenoe writes:

> Ivan A. Serov…participated in the execution of nearly 15,000 Polish prisoners of war in the Katyn forest in 1940. (560)

This statement is false. Lenoe's footnote is to an article by Nikita Petrov, an investigator with the anticommunist "Memorial Society", in the Russian journal *Otechestvennaia Istoriia* in 1997. No doubt few people will check this article. There Petrov says:

> In 1940 Serov was a participant in one of the most disgusting Stalinist crimes – the mass murder of Polish prisoners of war and civilians, which later became known as the "Katyn affair" after the name of the locality near Smolensk where the remains of those executed were first discovered.
>
> Executions also took place in the Ukraine. Serov was responsible for them. In the 1940s and 1950s the blame for these crimes was consistently laid to the Hitlerites. Serov, who was then the Chairman of the KGB, exposed himself by expressing dissatisfaction with the security officers who failed to cover up their crime. "They couldn't cope with such a small matter," – in anger Serov let the cat out of the bag. "There was a lot more of them (executed Poles – N.P.) in the Ukraine when I was there. But not a thing was said about it[28], nobody found even a trace…"

Below we will analyze the source Petrov cites. Here we note several matters.

---

the Struggle for Democratic Reform. Part Two." *Cultural Logic* 2005, at http://clogic.eserver.org/2005/furr2.html

[28] This saying, "Komar nosa ne podtochil", means "Nobody found fault with the job."

> * Serov does not at all claim he "participated in" the Katyn massacre. On the contrary: Serov makes it clear that he had nothing to do with "Katyn". He refers only to his time in the Ukraine.

According to this statement by Petrov, what Serov said is that those who did participate in Katyn had acted incompetently, while he himself had been more careful and no one had found any sign of those he had had executed.

> * Serov did not admit to shooting any Poles at all. He refers to his victims as "them", a word that appears simply to mean *rasstreliannykh*, "people who were executed". There's no suggestion that it means "Polish prisoners of war and civilians", or even just "Poles." It is Petrov – "N.P." – not Serov, who inserted the reference to "executed Poles."

Petrov's source is page 204 of the first volume of Sergei Khrushchev's work *Nikita Khrushchev: krizisy i rakety; vgliad iznutri* (Moscow: Novosti, 1994). This passage is in the abbreviated English translation, as follows:

> In Poland Stalin's name was associated with many bitter memories. These included the Ribbentrop-Molotov Pact, signed on the eve of the invasion of Poland, the anonymous graves of Katyn … In those years I heard about Katyn for the first time. I was staggered by the monstrous accusations, and of course I didn't believe them. However, I soon realized they were true.
>
> I happened to hear confirmation of them from General Serov, an authoritative source who had very vehemently denied the accusations. It was a topic he didn't mention in Father's presence, but for some reason he dropped in one day while Father was away.
>
> At the time everyone was disturbed about Katyn. Rada's husband, Aleksei, in some connection I no longer recall, asked the general how they could have missed it.
>
> Ivan Aleksandrovich reacted angrily, I would even say painfully, to the question. He started to make caustic remarks about the Belorussian Chekists, who in his opinion, had been unforgivably careless. "They couldn't cope with such a small matter" – in a fit of anger Serov

> let the cat out of the bag. "There was a lot more in the Ukraine when I was there. But not a thing was said about it, nobody found even a trace."[29]

This passage reveals yet more important points.

> * The words that Sergei Khrushchev attributes to Serov here do not confirm that the Soviets had carried out the Katyn massacre or that he even knew about it, much less that he participated in it. Rather, they are an angry outburst against the incompetence of whoever shot the Poles buried at Katyn.
>
> * Serov could not have been referring to any supposed participation by himself in killings at Katyn. Serov's sphere of activity had been the Ukraine.

There were allegedly executions at Khar'kov prison of Polish POWs from the Starobel'sk camp. These executions are indeed considered to be a part of the "Katyn' massacre." But Serov could not have been referring to these executions. He says "There was a lot more in the Ukraine when I was there," meaning people – it was Petrov who added "Poles" – executed, in the Ukraine. The alleged "Katyn'" executions in the Ukraine, in Khar'kov prison of prisoners from the Starobel'sk camp, were approximately 4,000. This is several thousand *fewer*, not more, than the Germans claimed were found in the mass graves at Katyn'.

There were plenty of executions in the Ukraine during the late 1930s, including many of Ukrainian nationalists. Serov must have been involved in those – Khrushchev himself certainly was, as First Secretary of the Communist Party of the Ukraine, and Serov was Khrushchev's man.

Sergei Khrushchev supposedly heard these words when he was present at a conversation between Serov and Aleksei Adzhubei, Nikita Khrushchev's son-in-law. It is further evidence that either (a) Sergei Khrushchev's memory of this conversation is faulty; or (b) that it never took place at all, and he fabricated it.

---

[29] Sergei N. Khrushchev. *Nikita Khrushchev and the Creation of a Superpower.* Tr. Shirley Benton. (University Park, PA: Penn State University Press, 2000), 165-6. In the original, unabbreviated Russian language text it is on pp. 203-4.

Sergei Khrushchev writes that "At the time everyone was disturbed about Katyn." But it is impossible that Adzhubei, much less Serov, would have made the error of thinking that Katyn' was in Belorussia rather than where it actually is, in the Smolensk oblast' of Russia. Therefore, it is Sergei Khrushchev who has made this error.

Assuming that Sergei Khrushchev was, as he claims, present at a conversation between Aleksei Adzhubei and Serov during the period shortly after the 20th Party Congress (February 1956), he has not remembered it correctly – he could not have heard "Belorussia". Moreover, even Sergei Khrushchev does not claim that Serov referred directly to Katyn' – this is his own interpretation. And that interpretation is incorrect, as we have shown above.

The history of the executions of Polish prisoners of war and other Poles, called the "Katyn massacre", is hotly contested. Belief that the Soviets were the culprits is a kind of shibboleth of respectability in some Cold-War oriented circles, where it is indeed considered improper even to acknowledge the existence of the important and fascinating historical controversy around this topic. One possibility is that the Soviets shot all the Poles, as the Nazis claimed in their 1943 propaganda report. But Serov's account above does not confirm that.

In the Russian original Sergei Khrushchev said Serov "v serdtsakh progovorilsia." The translator renders this accurately with the phrase "in a fit of anger Serov let the cat out of the bag". But "letting the cat out of the bag" is exactly what Serov did *not* do. Much less did he admit that he had played a role in it.

Why would Sergei Khrushchev have claimed unequivocally that Serov had "let the cat out of the bag"? Only because he realized that the words he attributes to Serov do *not* do this. But Sergei Khrushchev *wanted* the text to confirm Soviet guilt in Katyn, and the only way to accomplish that was to invent it.

There is a more fundamental issue here. Petrov's, and therefore Jansen and Petrov's, and thence Lenoe's, analysis tacitly assumes that the passage in Sergei Khrushchev's book is genuine: not only that Serov actually said something like this in S. Khrushchev's presence but that Khrushchev's son accurately recalled the precise words Serov spoke in 1956. But Lenoe's own book contains a good, brief summary of research

> …that human memory is highly malleable and oral transmission of narratives unreliable. (9)

No one else heard Serov say the words Sergei Khrushchev attributes to him. Under the principle "testis unus testis nullus" this fact alone disqualifies the statement as evidence.[30] In addition, Khrushchev evidently did not write them down until decades later. Moreover, by the time he did write them down Gorbachev and El'tsin had already claimed that the USSR did shoot the Poles at Katyn and this fact was very widely publicized. Lenoe's discussion of the fallibility of memory includes examples of memories being contaminated by statements made later on. No one has claimed that Aleksei Adzhubei, who Sergei Khrushchev claims was also present, recorded these words by Serov.

Lenoe should have checked this, as we have done here. He should have examined Petrov's words with care and compare them to Petrov's source, Sergei Khrushchev's account. After all, what else are scholars for if not to hunt for sources and evidence, and verify or disprove fact-claims? Had he done so he would have discovered what we have pointed out here – that even in Sergei Khrushchev's dubious account it is very clear that Serov did *not* claim that he had "participated" in the Katyn massacre.[31]

Shatunovskaia

> Shatunovskaya…again appealed to Mikoyan, and Mikoyan supposedly appealed to Stalin for clemency. Stalin refused. (563)

There is no evidence to support the claim that "Stalin refused" to liberate Shatunovskaia. Lenoe's footnote is to somewhere in Shatunovskaia's rambling memoirs – "passim", he writes – and to the second volume of the "rehabilitation" volumes (*Reabilitatsiia. Kak Eto Bylo*, vol. 2, p. 904).

This latter reference of Lenoe's is pure bluff. Page 904 of the volume in question contains the thumbnail biographical sketch of Shatunovskaia. It says nothing about any appeal or any refusal by Stalin. In Shatunovskaia's

---

[30] For example, see the discussion at http://www.livius.org/th/theory/theory-testis.html

[31] In addition, it is far from certain that the Soviets were in fact guilty of the "Katyn massacre". See the materials I have gathered in my page devoted to this question: "The Katyn Forest Whodunnit", http://www.tinyurl.com/katyn-the-truth

memoir the passage in question is narrated not by Shatunovskaia herself but by her daughter.[32] But the real point is this: neither Shatunovskaia herself nor her daughter could have known what Stalin did and did not want to do. Mikoian mentions Shatunovskaia several times in his own memoir but has nothing like this. Shatunovskaia's book is full of such rumors and we will have occasion in this book to examine untruthful statements by her again.

In any case Lenoe himself has found her to be thoroughly unreliable. Evidently he included this rumor simply because it makes Stalin "look bad."

"Torture"

> Pospelov...chose to rely on "evidence" that was extracted under torture in the process of fabricating a case against arrested NKVD chief Yagoda. (573)

This claim itself is a fabrication. Anyone who reads the transcript of the March 1938 Moscow Trial will see that Iagoda was convicted not on the basis of evidence from others but on his own confessions. Other defendants testified about Iagoda's activities too, but we have no evidence whatsoever that any of this testimony was "fabricated", much less that any of those who gave this evidence were "tortured."

In another section of the present book we show that Iagoda himself confessed to involvement in the Kirov assassination but strongly disagreed with Prosecutor Vyshinskii's charge that he had been an "accomplice" in the murder. Iagoda also vigorously rejected other accusations against him. This is good evidence that he had not been tortured and did not fear torture in the future (say, as revenge for rejecting a number of Vyshinskii's charges). Moreover, Iagoda's testimony at trial agrees with his pretrial testimony in interrogations published in 1997, which we also examine elsewhere in this book.

Lenoe repeats this same falsehood a page later:

---

32 O.G. Shatunovskaia. *Ob ushedshem veke.* La Jolla, CA: DAA Books, 2001, 228-9. At the Sakharov Center site, http://www.sakharov-center.ru/asfcd/auth/auth_book27b5.html?id=86374&aid=1175

> Yakushev was a perpetrator, a torturer, and a collaborator in Stalin's fabrication of false cases against Yagoda and dozens of others. (574-5)

Lenoe avoids any examination of the Moscow Trials generally or the 1938 Moscow Trial in which Iagoda was a defendant, so he has no basis at all to declare the case against Iagoda "false." Lenoe cites no evidence that Iakushev was a torturer so he has no business claiming that he was. As for Lenoe's accusation that Iakushev was a "perpetrator", this is simply incoherent: "perpetrator" of what? It sounds "bad" – which is the point, no doubt – but doesn't mean anything at all.

In fact we know that Iakushev lied when interrogated by Khrushchev's men. In March 1956 Iakushev, former Leningrad NKVD man, claimed in a letter to Frol Kozlov, one of Khrushchev's most trusted aides, that Borisov had been murdered as part of NKVD involvement in Kirov's murder.[33] But Borisov was not murdered at all, as everyone – Gorbachev's investigators, Kirilina, Lenoe, Egge, and our own research too – agrees. Therefore Iakushev was lying about this, no doubt as instructed by Khrushchev's men. So nothing that Iakushev testified can be trusted. Lenoe fails to point this out.

Serov again

> A second memorandum added substantially to the picture of a lone gunman and a fabricated criminal case against the Zinovievites. (581)

The memorandum in question (582 ff.) gives a "picture" – the word Lenoe uses here – but it provides no evidence whatsoever to sustain the charge of fabrication. On the contrary, the memorandum is yet another part of the Khrushchev-era campaign to try to prove Stalin had Kirov killed. In pursuit of this goal the authors of the memorandum disregarded any evidence that points towards any other conclusions. In fact the memo is good evidence that Serov and his men, who wrote the memorandum, had no evidence that could discredit the Moscow Trial verdicts.

---

[33] Reabilitatsiia. Kak Eto Bylo. Febral' 1956 – nachalo 80-kh godov. Moskva: "Materik", 2003. (RKEB 2), 36-37.

Note the distinction between this statement and the logical fallacy that "absence of evidence is not evidence of absence", a form of the argument from ignorance. We are not claiming here that it is the "lack of evidence" that Nikolaev was a "lone gunman" that proves he was not. Rather, we assert that Khrushchev's men would have brought forth any evidence they could find that Nikolaev was a "lone gunman" since they very much wanted to prove he was, and went on to claim that he was anyway.

If Khrushchev's men had been able to find evidence to support their conclusions they would certainly have cited it. Therefore we can be certain that Khrushchev's men, Serov & Co., could not find any such evidence. But they had total access to everything, including evidence they destroyed (592) and all the evidence that, Kirilina, Lenoe, and Egge were not allowed to see. This itself is the best possible indication that no such evidence exists. Meanwhile we have a huge amount of evidence that Nikolaev was a participant in a conspiracy.

Lenoe recognizes that Serov's word is not to be trusted:

> Serov was Khrushchev's man throughout this period.
> (591)

Lenoe is sporadically skeptical about Serov's actions. But Lenoe's whole analysis is fundamentally based on the materials of Serov's reports on the Kirov assassination, all of which were aimed at framing Stalin and refuting any notion that Nikolaev was part of any conspiracy. Lenoe fails to add that this fatally compromises anything Serov had to say, whether about the Kirov assassination or about anything else. This is hardly surprising, since Lenoe comes to the same preconceived conclusion that Sedov & Co. came to. In fact Lenoe admits that it was Khrushchev's men who in April 1956 invented the notion that Nikolaev was a "lone gunman" (578-579)

Therefore despite his words of wisdom in cautioning his readers that Serov and Khrushchev were striving not to discover the truth but to implicate Stalin in Kirov's murder, Lenoe proves to be very credulous of what Serov says.

For example, Serov is the only source for the Khrushchev-era contention, still solemnly repeated today, that Beria and/or Stalin had Radek and Sokol'nikov murdered in their prison camp. There's no reason to accept this story.[34] Even if the NKVD men whom Serov named as having confessed to these murders did make the statements Serov attributes to them – and we do not have those statements, only Serov's claim –, that would not mean that those statements are true. As Lenoe himself admits Serov and Khrushchev were fabricating a great deal during this period to try to exculpate all of those who had been repressed in the 1930s and to blame Stalin. Lenoe has a good discussion of the ways in which memories of past events can be reconstructed. (9-11)

But Lenoe does accept it. (486) Only a little checking is required to prove that Serov was lying here too. An article of our own examining this question is awaiting publication. Lenoe could have done this checking just as easily.

Since Lenoe chose not to check Serov's claim he should at least have reasoned that, absent corroboration and given his practice, which Lenoe does document, of discrediting Stalin whenever possible, Serov's credibility is nil. Perhaps Lenoe's failure to exercise skepticism in this particular case is a reflection of the fact that, like Serov, Lenoe is devoted to a preconceived notion that there were no conspiracies and thus that Nikolaev was a "lone gunman."

> They [authors of Serov report, below] demonstrate[ed] that the defendants, including Yagoda, were almost certainly innocent of any conspiracy. (595)

This statement of Lenoe's too is false. The text of the report that follows (595-599) contains demonstrable lies that Lenoe's book itself disproves. For example, the following statement from Serov's August 31 1956 report is disproven by Lenoe himself.

> …it is worth noting that even on the eve of trial the investigators had no evidence of any interest on Nikolaev's part in any of the former oppositionists, much less of [closer] connections between him and Kotolynov, Rumiantsev, or others among the accused. (596)

[34] We have an article pending in which we demonstrate that Serov fabricated this story.

Lenoe's own book proves that this statement of Serov's is a deliberate lie, as we show in other chapters of the present study. Nikolaev wrote about Kotolynov in his diary; directly implicated him as early as December 4 1934; and went on to describe Kotolynov's role in training himself (Nikolaev) for the assassination. We have this information today, and Lenoe himself records some of it. Serov simply withheld it from the Molotov Commission (to which his report was directed in 1956). Lenoe also points out that Serov withheld other materials from the Molotov Commission, and had yet other materials destroyed. So even had Molotov wanted to study the primary documents of the Kirov case himself, Serov could have hidden the evidence from him.

The rest of Serov's report deals with the Kirov-related testimony after 1934 which we will consider in a separate part of this study. For the present we simply note that Lenoe's remark above is incorrect. In reality Serov's report is highly dishonest. It contains numerous deliberate falsifications. We will identify some of the more important lies later. But there are so many lies in it that to identify them all would unduly lengthen this study to no purpose.

Most important for our purposes, Serov's report contains no evidence at all that Iagoda and the other Moscow Trial defendants were innocent of Kirov's murder, and nothing that might impeach any of the evidence that they were guilty. We will examine this question in detail in the section on the Moscow Trials. It is central to understanding how utterly bankrupt Lenoe's argument is.

Lenoe claims:

> No one was "covering" for Stalin at this moment – the Khrushchevites revealed many of his most heinous crimes. (604)

This statement is false. In reality Khrushchev and his men did not reveal a single "crime" of Stalin. To this date, every single supposed "revelation" of "crimes" alleged by Khrushchev & Co. against Stalin has been proven false.[35]

---

[35] See Grover Furr, *Khrushchev Lied: The Evidence That Every "Revelation" of Stalin's (and Beria's) Crimes in Nikita Khrushchev's Infamous "Secret Speech" to the 20th Party Congress of the Communist Party of the Soviet Union on February 25, 1956, is Provably False.* Kettering, OH:

Lenoe mentions "…Zhukov apparently reading aloud from archival documents" at the 1957 Central Committee Plenum. But Lenoe fails to tell his readers that Zhukov read from a falsified copy of Iakir's June 9, 1937 letter to Stalin, omitting Iakir's frank admission of guilt in treason. Lenoe (635) refers to A.N. Shelepin's speech to the 22nd Party Congress in 1961 and quotes Khrushchev's reference to Shelepin's speech as well (636). Lenoe fails to note that Shelepin's speech is also comprised of falsifications from beginning to end. Shelepin also quoted a falsified copy of the letter of Iakir's to Stalin, again omitting Iakir's confession to treason.[36]

Lenoe quotes Aleksandr Iakovlev's 1990 letter about the Kirov murder, including the following line:

> Yagoda was falsely placed among the members of the nonexistent "Right-Trotskyite Bloc." (639)

Lenoe has to know from Getty's and Broué's studies of the 1980s that the Right-Trotstkyite Bloc did indeed exist. He cannot be ignorant of this work, since he states that he received help from Getty. But he fails to inform his readers that Iakovlev was either lying or just incompetent here. We will take a closer look at this matter in another chapter.

Lenoe claims:

> It was a fairly common practice for senior Bolsheviks officials to have partners identified as "housekeepers" – Stalin in his later years did. (672)

Lenoe gives no evidence to support this statement.

We could give more examples of false statements in Lenoe's book. But the general point should be clear now. Lenoe frequently makes assertions without evidence when those assertions are either demonstrably false or when there is no evidence to support them.

Erythrós Press & Media LLC, 2011, *passim*. Russian edition: Ferr, *Teni XX-go S"ezda, ili Antistalinskaia Podlost'*. Moscow: Eksmo-Algoritm, 2010.

[36] For a more detailed study of Iakir's letter and Zhukov's and Shelepin's falsifications of it see Furr, Khrushchev Lied, 209-211.

More Errors

In the course of his long book Lenoe makes a number of statements that are false and have been disproven by scholarly research. Of course every scholar makes errors. But Lenoe does not make his mistakes at random. Each and every one of these false statements has the same political tendentiousness: they can all be usefully termed "anti-Stalin". In this long book I have not been able to find a single example of an erroneous statement that tends to make Stalin look "good." All of Lenoe's errors tend towards making Stalin appear "bad."

This cannot be explained as the usual occurrence of some errors or mistakes that may be expected to appear in any lengthy and complex scholarly work. Errors made by chance would vary in their political tendencies. Nor can it be set down to carelessness, for the same reason. Therefore Lenoe's errors constitute further evidence of his lack of objectivity, his *a priori* anticommunist and anti-Stalin bias.

The Famine of 1932-33

Lenoe writes:

> As a direct result of forced collectivization more than five million people died of starvation in 1932-1933. (3)

This is a false statement. No scholarship on the 1932-33 famine proves anything remotely like this. Anticommunists have been searching for such evidence for many years. The reality is that famines had occurred every 2-4 years in Russian history, going back at least a thousand years. The work of American scholar Mark Tauger, who has devoted his life to the study of these famines, demonstrates this decisively. We have discussed this issue, with appropriate references, in an earlier chapter.

In reality, collectivization was necessary in order to stop the endless cycle of famines and increase agricultural production at least to the point at which people did not starve or die of starvation-related diseases. It was thanks to collectivization that the famine of 1932-33 was the last famine in Soviet history except for the 1946-47 famine, caused by the confluence of the terrible destruction of the war with harsh climactic conditions. Whether the 1946-47 famine was handled well or poorly by the Soviet government is a debatable point, but no one claims it was deliberate.[37] After that, the USSR never again suffered a famine.

Dr. Lidia Timashuk

Lenoe writes:

> Nikita Khrushchev recalled two other "hysterical" female denouncers endorsed by Stalin, the history graduate student Nikolaenko in Kiev and a Komsomol official in Moscow, Mishakova….In the prosecution of the so-called Doctors' Plot just before his death, Stalin again used a woman pushed around by her male superiors, the doctor Lidiya Timashuk, although Timashuk was probably not psychologically ill in the clinical sense, as Volkova and Nikolaenko seem to have been.
>
> Stalin's cynical use of exploited, desperate, and sometimes psychologically ill women was a particularly vicious instance of a basic practice of Soviet governance… (278)

This is all wrong. Khrushchev lied in his account of Timashuk and the "Doctors' Plot" in his "Secret Speech." Evidently Lenoe is ignorant of the fact that Timashuk had nothing to do with the "Doctors' Plot". She had tried to inform Party officials about the mistreatment of Politburo member Andrei Zhdanov in August 1948. Timashuk was awarded the Lenin Prize in January 1953 but had it taken away in April 1953, when Lavrentii Beria examined the "Doctors' Plot" charges, found them baseless, and persuaded the Presidium to release all the arrested doctors.

---

[37] The most recent study is by Stephen G. Wheatcroft, "The Soviet Famine of 1946–1947, the Weather and Human Agency in Historical Perspective." Europe-Asia Studies, 64:6, 987-1005. Wheatcroft concludes that this famine was part of "the World Food Crisis of 1946-1947" which "was the most serious global food shortage of modern history, when famine simultaneously threatened Central and Eastern Europe, India, Indo-China and China, and bread rationing was introduced in Britain for the first time ever" (1004) That is, the policies of the Soviet government had nothing to do with it.

All of Timashuk's letters to various officials about all these events were published with commentary in the Russian historical journal *Istochnik* in 1997, long before Lenoe began to write his book. It appears that Lenoe may have "believed" – relied upon – Jonathan Brent and Vladimir Naumov, *Stalin's Last Crime,* a terrible, dishonest book that mangles the details of the "Doctors' Plot" while deliberately omitting the evidence that fails to support their thesis – something that, unfortunately, Lenoe also does. The Brent-Naumov book received a devastatingly negative review by prominent anticommunist researcher Gennadii Kostyrchenko in the Russian Zionist journal *Lekhaim* in October 2004 and another just as negative by Fedor Liass in *Zametki po evreiskoi istorii* 2 (51), February 2005.

So Stalin did not "use" Timashuk. But the main issue for our purposes is this: Lenoe made this accusation not just despite the fact that he had no evidence to support it, but despite the fact that there is a lot of evidence to disprove it. Once again it appears to be a method to Lenoe's mistakes: make any statement as long as the result is a "fact" that reflects badly upon Stalin.

Lenoe evidently "believed" Khrushchev's stories about Nikolaenko and Mishakova as well. Yet a major theme of his book is to show how Khrushchev and his men tried to "frame" Stalin as Kirov's murderer by withholding and destroying evidence, before they finally had to abandon the attempt as hopeless. Why, then, would Lenoe "believe" Khrushchev here? Once again: evidently because it makes a good "anti-Stalin" tale.

Sergo Ordzhonikidze's Death

Lenoe writes:

> ...a number of specialists and administrators in Ordzhonikidze's commissariat were charged with sabotage, and some were arrested. Ordzhonikidze made an effort to defend some of these men, which culminated in a private conflict with Stalin on the eve of the February 1937 TsK plenum, and Ordzhonikidze's death, probably by suicide. (466)

Once again, this is false. Ordzhonikidze made no such attempt "to defend" his subordinates. Moreover, there was no "private conflict with Stalin" – quite simply, it never happened. There is no evidence of this.

Not only that – there is no evidence that Ordzhonikidze committed suicide, either!

Lenoe's only source here is the book by Oleg Khevniuk, *Stalin i Ordzhonikidze* (1993 – there is an English version as well). Khlevniuk asserts that Ordzhonikidze opposed Stalin, had an argument with him, and shot himself. But Khlevniuk has no evidence for any of this. He evidently based his version on a Khrushchev-era introduction to a biography of Ordzhonikidze in which these allegations were made, also without any evidence. When this biography was reissued a few years later, after Khrushchev's ouster, this unattributed information was cut out. Lenoe had no business using a secondary source as evidence. He should have checked.[38]

Zhukov's Reading at the June 1957 Central Committee Plenum

Lenoe states:

> On the afternoon of April 25 [1957] the Presidium met to discuss the rehabilitation of Tukhachevsky, Yakir, and Uborevich, the three leading generals executed for treason in 1937… Khrushchev challenged, "Let the old members of the Politburo tell us how they decided the question of bringing Yakir to trial, how this first step was prepared." Marshal Zhukov seconded Khrushchev with "we've got to get to the bottom of this." (601)

On the following page Lenoe discusses the June 1957 Central Committee Plenum at which this question arose again:

> Zhukov and Shvernik denounced Molotov's, Kaganovich's, and Malenkov's prominent roles in the Terror, with Zhukov apparently reading aloud from archival documents. (602)

---

[38] See Furr, Khrushchev Lied, 114-6, where I give more details.

Lenoe cites the transcript of this Plenum, published in 1999, in which Zhukov read the text of a letter from Iakir to Stalin of June 9, 1937. The relevant section of the transcript reads as follows:

> You all know Iakir, he was a well-known developing and very strong worker. He was arrested for nothing. On June 29 1937 [sic] on the eve of his own death he [Iakir – GF] wrote a letter to Stalin in which he says:
>
> 'Dear, close comrade Stalin! I dare address you in this way because I have told everything and it seems to me that I am that honorable warrior, devoted to Party, state and people, that I was for many years. All my conscious life has been passed in selfless, honorable work in the sight of the Party and its leaders. I die with words of love to you, the Party, the country, with a fervent belief in the victory of communism.'
>
> - Molotov, Malenkov, Kaganovich. 1957. Moscow, 1990, p. 39.

In 1994 the text of the 1963-4 "Shvernik report" to Khrushchev concerning these military men was published, containing a fuller text of Iakir's letter. Here is that text; the part omitted by Zhukov in 1957 is in boldface:

> "Dear, close com. Stalin. I dare address you in this way because I have told everything and it seems to me that I am once more that honorable warrior, devoted to Party, state and people, that I was for many years. All my conscious life has been passed in selfless, honorable work in the sight of the Party and its leaders. – **then I fell into a nightmare, into the irreparable horror of treason… The investigation is finished. The indictment of treason to the state has been presented to me, I have admitted my guilt, I have repented completely. I have unlimited faith in the justice and appropriateness of the decision of the court and the government. Now each of my words is honest**, I die with words of love to you, the Party, the country, with a fervent belief in the victory of communism.'

This fuller text was published in 1994 in *Voennyi Arkhivy Rossii* (1993), p. 50; in "Tragediia RKKA", *Voenno-Istoricheskii Arkhiv* 1 (1994), p. 194. Finally, it was publish in the authoritative volume *Reabilitatsiia. Kak Eto Bylo.* Vol. 2 (2003), p. 688.

This document is strong evidence that Iakir and, by extension, the other commanders tried and executed with him, were guilty. Their guilt suggests that Bukharin's confessions at the March 1938 Moscow Show Trial were truthful, since Bukharin incriminated Tukhachevsky. They are of capital importance for the subject he is studying. But there is no trace of them in his book.[39]

We know that Lenoe is aware of the Shvernik report because he examines the part of it concerned with the Kirov assassination and concludes "the ongoing investigation appears to have been impartial." (630-637; 638) It is possible, of course, that Lenoe did not read the whole report, but only that part dealing with Kirov; if so, this was a grave error on Lenoe's part.

This passage is also further proof that Khrushchev and his men are never to be trusted. It's not clear whether Marshal Zhukov knew that he was reading a letter that had been faked through expurgation. Nor did this happen only one time. At the 22nd Party Congress in October 1961 Aleksandr Shelepin, Khrushchev's head of the KGB (after Serov), read the same Iakir letter in his address to the Congress, and also omitted Iakir's admission of guilt![40] Lenoe warns his readers about Khrushchev's attempt to "frame" Stalin, but then fails to take his own counsel.

Khrushchev's "Secret Speech"

Lenoe discusses Khrushchev's secret report to the 20th Party Congress of February 25, 1956 (571 ff.). It is important for his purposes as it marks the beginning of the official inquiry into the Kirov assassination, the documentation of which comprises the second half of Lenoe's massive book. Yet Lenoe never mentions the fact that every "revelation" made by

---

[39] See Furr, Khrushchev Lied, 209-212.

[40] "Speech of Com. Shelepin", in XXII s"ezd kommunisticheskogo partii Sovetskogo Soiuza. 17-31 oktiabria 1961 goda. Stenograficheskii otchiot. (Moscow: Gos. Izdat. Politicheskoi Literatury, 1962), II, 403.

Khrushchev of alleged crimes and misdeeds by Stalin and Lavrentii Beria was false. This fact has been well known since at least early 2008.[41] Some of these falsehoods had long been recognized. But, unaccountably, Lenoe takes Khrushchev's speech at face value.

Khrushchevites "Revealed Many Of Stalin's Most Heinous Crimes"

Later, in connection with the June 1957 Plenum, Lenoe states "the Khrushchevites revealed many of his [Stalin's] most heinous crimes". (604) But Lenoe does not mention a single one of them.

It is hard to believe that this is an accident; for in reality there is no evidence that Khrushchev "revealed" even a single "crime"- not just at the June 1957 Plenum, but ever! Every single allegation Khrushchev made of a "crime" by Stalin that has been checked has proven to be a falsification. The Russian edition of the present author's book on this subject, *Antistalinskaia podlost'*, was published and widely publicized in Russia long before Lenoe's book was completed. But even had it not been, or if Lenoe had not heard of it, neither Lenoe nor any historian has any business taking Khrushchev's word, or anyone's word, as "true" without looking for evidence. That is the case with any fact-claim by anyone. But it should be especially true for Khrushchev since Lenoe knows that Khrushchev and his men were falsifying and questions Khrushchev's motives in trying to pin the Kirov assassination on Stalin.

Post of General Secretary

In a section titled "Was There a Move to Replace Stalin with Kirov?" Lenoe notes that a 1963 report states that "a number of delegates to the Seventeenth Party Congress [held in January 1934 – GF] wished to abolish the office of general secretary and return the party to 'collective leadership'… (614). Lenoe is evidently unaware that Stalin himself had already tried three times to resign from the post of General Secretary: on August 19, 1924, December 27, 1926, and December 19, 1927. On the latter date, when his request to be permitted to resign was not accepted by the Central Committee, Stalin made the suggestion to "annihilate"

---

41 Ferr, Grover (Furr). *Antistalinskaia Podlost'*. Moskva: Algoritm, 2007. (Antistalinskaia) This is the Russian original. *Khrushchev Lied* is an updated version (2011).

(*unichtozhit'*) the post of General Secretary. This suggestion was also rejected. (For details see Furr, *Khrushchev Lied* 245-250)

However, after the 17th Party Congress the term "General Secretary" was no longer used. Stalin was elected simply to the secretariat and his name was among those of the other Secretaries. For example, in the relevant section from the transcript of the 18th Party Congress in March 1939 the secretaries are all listed alphabetically, i.e. as equals. On March 18, 1946 a Plenum of the Central Committee passed a resolution concerning the composition of the Politburo, Secretariat, and Orgburo of the party. Here Stalin was indeed listed before the other secretaries, out of alphabetical order. But Georgii Malenkov is also listed out of alphabetical order. Once again, there is no mention of the post of "General Secretary." Once again Stalin was elected simply as a member of the Secretariat at the Central Committee Plenum after the 19th Party Congress in October, 1952. Even the official notice of Stalin's death on March 5, 1953 stated simply that his posts were Chairman of the Soviet of Ministers of the USSR and Secretary of the CC of the CPSU.

That is, Stalin was not General Secretary of the Party after 1934. Furthermore, he had wanted to resign from the position and abolish the position. Lenoe is either ignorant of these facts or does not share them with his readers.

Khrushchev, however, acted differently. At the September 1953 Central Committee Plenum Khrushchev got himself elected "First Secretary of the Central Committee of the CPSU", a post that did not exist before. In 1964 Leonid Brezhnev succeeded Khrushchev as First Secretary and in 1966 was elected to the new post of General Secretary of the Party, which was the title of all the Soviet leaders through Mikhail Gorbachev.

Chapter 4.

Fallacies and Errors in Lenoe's Argumentation.

Lenoe writes:

> With the arrests of Antonov, Tolmazov, and Zvezdov, Agranov's men began to accumulate substantial evidence about continuing social ties between former Zinoviev supporters. These were treated as threads in an extended web of political conspiracy. Stalin and the central NKVD officers were extraordinarily suspicious of *dvurushnichestvo* ("two-facedness") among the former Zinovievites. In particular they were concerned about a directive Zinoviev supposedly issued his followers in 1928 to recant their views and rejoin the party. Stalin and Agranov chose to view this directive as a sign that Zinoviev sought to undermine the party from within. (306)

A party member who rejoined the Party not out of commitment to its line but for some other reason, be it simple careerism or – as alleged here – a plan to "bore from within" in concert with others, to use Party membership in an attempt to gain privileged access to Party positions and members in pursuit of the goal of getting rid of the Party and government leadership – was said, understandably, to be guilty of "two-facedness", an expression that also exists in English meaning "deceitful, insincere". "Hypocrisy" is also a good translation of *dvurushnichestvo.* Such a person professed loyalty to the Party while in fact undermining it; vowing to follow Party discipline but in reality following the discipline of their own fraction. If the former Zinovievites were still loyal to Zinoviev then they were members of a secret Party fraction, and such fractions had been banned at Lenin's urging at the Tenth Party Congress in 1921.[42]

If the "ties between former Zinoviev supporters" were "social" rather than political then they would not be evidence of a conspiracy. However, Lenoe has no evidence that these ties were only "social" or that they were only "former" Zinovievites – i.e. no longer part of an active fraction, illegal under Party rules. No evidence, that is, other than the initial testimony of these men after their arrests. But this is not good evidence. For one thing, *all* suspects, the innocent as well as the guilty, can be expected to deny guilt when first questioned. For another, the suspects soon changed their stories and confessed to still being part of an underground Zinovievite group. For a third, we have evidence from other sources that these conspiracies were still persisting.

So Lenoe does not decide this question on the basis of the evidence available but instead simply asserts that these suspects were only "former" Zinovievites. Lenoe's thesis is that Nikolaev was a "lone gunman". It is essential for his thesis that these men did not have a political formation separate from that of their Party organizations.

There was nothing "extraordinary" in Stalin's suspiciousness about "two-facedness." If the men in question were sincere supporters of the Party's line, then all was well and Nikolaev was indeed only a "lone gunman." But if they were not sincere supporters of the Party line, then Nikolaev was a participant in a secret terrorist conspiratorial group within the Party. The question is not one of Stalin's psychology ("extraordinarily suspicious") but one of fact: Did such a conspiracy exist or not?

In 1928 Zinoviev had written his supporters to urge them to rejoin the Party as he had done. On December 10 1934 Antonov said:

---

[42] After the successful consolidation of power by the Communist Party following the Russian Revolution of 1917 and the Russian Civil War, the Bolshevik leadership, including Lenin, instituted a ban on fractions within the party as Resolution No. 12 of the 10th Party Congress in 1921. It was passed in the morning session on March 16, 1921 (Protokoly 585-7). Supporters of Trotsky sometimes claim that this ban was intended to be temporary. But there is no language in the discussion at the 10th Party Congress suggesting that it was intended to be temporary (*Protokoly* 523-548). See *10-i s"ezd RKP(b) (8-16 marta 1921 goda). Protokoly* (Moscow: Partizdat, 1933).

> Rumiantsev was…dissatisfied with the position taken by Zinoviev, who advocated return to the party under particular conditions. (307)

The only condition permissible for a person to join or rejoin the Party was that he pledge to support the Party's line. Antonov's phrase, "particular conditions", are suspicious precisely because they mean Zinoviev had other reasons in mind. On December 11, one day later, Zvezdov confessed that he knew that an underground anti-Party organization did exist:

> I am aware that in the course of 1933-1934 the former leaders of the Zinovievite opposition, Bakaev, Kharitonov, Gertik, and Zinoviev himself, renewed their efforts to revive their organization.
>
> The former leaders of the Zinovievite opposition who were in Moscow and were [also] tightly connected with Leningrad hoped to drag our old Komsomol group of former Zinovievites into a battle with the party and the party leadership. Antonov, Nikolai, with whom I study at the Institute, told me about this. … Antonov heard about this from Kotolynov.… [Antonov] said that now the old ties were being activated and a new attack on the party leadership was being prepared. (309)

In the following pages of his book Lenoe cites a lot of evidence that the erstwhile Zinovievites had indeed formed an underground anti-leadership group and, therefore, had rejoined the Party in a duplicitous or "two-faced" manner. Lenoe's Document 55 is a confession by Zvezdov of December 12 in which he details the membership of the Leningrad groups. It begins with a reference to a December 11 interrogation in which Zvezdov had already "assert[ed] the existence in Moscow of a counterrevolutionary organization, founded on the base of the old Trotsky-Zinoviev bloc." (310)

After a lengthy excerpt from Zvezdov's December 12 confession Lenoe asks: "Why did Zvezdov and other purported members of the 'Leningrad Center' confess?" Thereupon Lenoe proceeds to suggest every reason –

threats, torture, the "Rubashov" phenomenon[43] – except one: that they confessed because it was the truth. Lenoe does not even raise this as a possibility! This glaring omission exposes the fact that Lenoe simply *assumes* the confessions were false, untruthful and "scripted". And the fact that Lenoe feels compelled to make such an assumption, even tacitly, exposes another fact: Lenoe has no evidence whatever to support his assumption – because if he did have any he would certainly have cited it.

Lenoe reproduces parts of a confession by Tolmazov of December 12 (Document 56, 314-6). Tolmazov confirms the existence of the underground Moscow and Leningrad groups of Zinovievites. According to Lenoe's translation Tolmazov even used the word "center" to describe these groups.

On page 316 Lenoe concedes that Kotolynov admitted that the Zinovievites had rejoined the Party dishonestly and maintained their own organization. However, Lenoe does not give the text of this interrogation and conceals from his readers the fact that this text has been published elsewhere. We discuss this document in another chapter. In it Kotolynov admits that Zinoviev's letter of 1928 was "a written instruction to deceive the Party". (Lubianka 1922-1936, 577) Lenoe fails to inform his readers of this statement of Kotolynov's. Whatever Lenoe's reason for omitting it, this document is devastating to his argument.

To sum up: there is a great deal of evidence from the interrogations that the Zinovievites in Leningrad and Moscow did indeed rejoin the Party in a "two-faced" manner. There is no evidence at all to suggest that these confessions were "scripted."

The late Pierre Broué was a champion of Trotsky's and fiercely hostile to Stalin. According to him it was simply taken for granted by informed people that when Oppositionists in general rejoined the Party they were doing so "two-facedly:"

> Lev Sedov called the Smirnov group either the "former capitulators" or the "Trotskyite capitulators." Everybody had known, from 1929 on, that people in the Smirnov

---

[43] Rubashov, a character in Arthur Koestler's 1940 novel *Darkness at Noon*, confesses to crimes of which he is innocent out of a mixture of guilt and loyalty to the party.

> group had not really capitulated but were trying to fool the apparatus, and were capable of organizing themselves as an Opposition within the party: the fact was so universally known that Andrés Nin, the Spaniard deported from the Soviet Union in August 1930, explained it openly to his German comrades of *Die permanente Revolution* who printed his declaration without apparent problem.
>
> "Young Turks," "Left Stalinists," they [Ian E. Sten and V.V. Lominadze] had already begun to organize and act as an opposition in 1929, had been unmasked in 1930 and were continuing their oppositionist activities despite public confession of mistakes and self-criticism, which induced the apparatus to call them "double dealers."[44]

With "two-facedness" as brazen as this Stalin would have been foolish ***not*** to suspect it! In any event, he was correct in this case. Any competent, honest examination of the evidence must conclude that the underground Zinovievite groups did exist.

Anticommunist Bias

It is the duty of scholars to train themselves in the ability to be objective in the interpretation of evidence. As scholars we should distrust our own preconceived ideas more than anyone else's. After all, it is our own ideas that are most likely to mislead us.

In the criminal justice system jurors are enjoined to judge the guilt or innocence of a defendant based solely on the evidence, reasonably interpreted. Judges and lawyers query jurors about anything that might prevent them from deciding a case purely on the basis of evidence. If a juror's biases or preconceived ideas are so strong that they would prevent him or her from deciding purely on the basis of the evidence, that juror is supposed to be excused from that case. His (or her) biases, prejudices, and/or preconceived ideas, will prevent the juror from studying the evidence objectively.

---

[44] Pierre Broué, "Party Opposition to Stalin (1930-1932) and the First Moscow Trial." In John W. Strong, ed. *Essays on Revolutionary Culture and Stalinism*, (Columbus, OH: Slavica, 1990), at p. 104

Everyone, historians included, has biases, prejudices, and preconceived ideas. The scholar in any field of study is obliged to be aware of them, distrust them, and make allowances for them. This is as true, and as important, for the historian as it is for the physicist or chemist.

Overt, open, admitted, and obvious bias and prejudice is the easiest to identify. But, of course, it is possible to pretend objectivity while in reality permitting one's prejudices and biases to predetermine the results of one's study. This kind of covert bias is more insidious, harder to discern. It is more likely to lead astray those readers who are unwary or lack sufficient knowledge of the subject matter.

Lenoe makes no attempt to control or even to conceal his strong anticommunist bias. He gives it free rein. It is impossible not to be struck by Lenoe's frequent and vehement expression of his anticommunist views. It is as though Lenoe were unaware that any kind of bias fatally compromises objectivity and therefore makes the discovery of the truth impossible.

What follows is an examination of some of the more flagrant examples of overt expressions of bias in Lenoe's book. I make no claim to completeness, which would be otiose anyway, a mere catalog. Further examples of anticommunist bias are treated in other sections of this study. I also omit discussion of Lenoe's "Introduction" (1-18) here since I deal with it separately.

In Chapter 1 Lenoe calls Lenin "intolerant" and Stalin "vengeful". He gives no evidence for either statement. This lack of evidence reduces these remarks to the status of mere insult, nothing more than an expression of Lenoe's own personal bias. Moreover, Lenoe himself later cites evidence against Stalin's "vengefulness" by pointing out that Stalin "signed off on or even initiated the rehabilitations" of former Oppositionists who spoke at the 17th Party Congress in January, 1934 (127).

Lenoe says Kirov "stuck with" Stalin "whatever his private doubts or fears may have been" (63), but cites no evidence that Kirov had any "doubts or fears" at all. Lenoe calls Stalin's "Dizzy with Success" article of March 2 1930 "in all probability a deliberate attempt to scapegoat local officials." (108) This is a good example of the anticommunist double standard. When a communist – let alone Stalin – issues a call for moderation, it is assumed that he has a sinister, ulterior motive in mind. Normally, no such assumption would be made in the case of a non-communist – certainly not without evidence.

Lenoe calls Andrei Zhdanov a "hard-bitten Stalinist." (111) The word "hard-bitten" means "tough in a fight" – but Lenoe has cited no fights in which Zhdanov had proven his toughness. As used here it seems to be a kind of throw-away, generalized negative comment. Again, according to Lenoe, Kirov was "generally perceived as one of the despot's thuggish henchmen." (119) But his evidence for this "general" perception is Bullard, the British Consul in Leningrad, someone who can hardly represent a spokesperson for the "general" viewpoint. Lenoe has ample space to demonstrate how Kirov acted like a "thug" but does not do so.

As for "henchman" – a word that anciently had a positive connotation – Lenoe evidently uses it for its negative overtones alone. Like "hard-bitten", "henchman" tells us about Lenoe's biases but conveys no information about Kirov. This may be why he uses these terms: to assure the authorities in the anticommunist field of Soviet history that he has the appropriate anticommunist attitudes and values.

Lenoe calls penal labor "slave labor." (125) Yet inmates of American or other prisons who are required to work are never referred to as "slaves." The correct term is "penal labor", which has been employed in the United States and other capitalist countries, where it is never referred to as "slave labor." This is another example of the anticommunist double standard.[45]

Lenoe claims "Stalin admired Zakovsky for his scorched-earth approach to policing." (145) He cites no evidence for this claim. How can Lenoe "channel" Stalin – know what he was thinking? What does "scorched-earth approach to policing" mean? The answer seems to be: nothing – but it "sounds bad." Once again, it is just an insult. Lenoe is again reassuring his readers that he is "politically correct" in that he despises communists and never misses an opportunity to insult or belittle them. This passage simply represents Lenoe's prejudices on display.

---

[45] The anticommunist double standard in historiography is discussed in, e.g. James Prickett, "Anti-Communism and Labor History," *Industrial Relations* 13 (October, 1974), 219-227. Online at http://tinyurl.com/prickettindrel74

In transcribing Nikolaev's "Plan" to murder Kirov Lenoe annotates Nikolaev's remark "Us and Them" as follows:

> [note the contraposition of the general population to the Communist elite] (241)

This is an example of what could be termed "ventriloquism". These are Lenoe's words which he would like us to believe Nikolaev "meant to say." Lenoe would like Nikolaev to have said them. Alas for Lenoe, Nikolaev didn't say them, so Lenoe puts those words into his mouth. In reality there's no indication Nikolaev meant anything like this. In view of the rest of the evidence, by "us" Nikolaev almost certainly meant "we, the Zinovievites" or "we, the clandestine Zinovievite-Trotskyite bloc" and by "them" the Stalin leadership. But Lenoe's preconceived idea that Nikolaev was a "lone gunman" precludes his considering this possibility. Lenoe is eager to identify evidence of anti-Bolshevik sentiment among workers generally.

Moreover, it is impossible that Nikolaev meant "the general population." In the excerpts from Nikolaev's diary, letters, and interrogations that have been made public Nikolaev never refers to "the general population" at all. The discourse of communists at that time was very class-conscious. Nikolaev would never have assumed that the Soviet population was one "general" interest group. If he had meant "the working class" or "the peasantry" he would have said so.

Lenoe describes the special law passed in early December 1934 stipulating expedited and abbreviated trials and executions for terrorism as follows:

> In a genuine emergency – Kirov was the first senior party leader to take a bullet since Lenin in 1918 – party leaders still claimed the right of resort to state terror. (255)

The December 1 1934 law describes a procedure similar to a military trial. This has nothing in common with "state terror" no matter how this vague term is understood. This is the anticommunist double-standard again. In his introduction Lenoe expresses criticism of the Bush Administration's "Patriot Act" and indefinite detention without trial at Guantanamo Bay, Cuba of terror suspects – something he does not even accuse the Stalin-era USSR of doing. But Lenoe does not call the American administration's action "state terror." Moreover, this accelerated and simplified trial procedure was not applied in any of the three public Moscow trials of 1936, 1937 and 1938, at which the defendants did have the right of appeal. Some of their appeals have been published.[46]

Lenoe states:

> ...Nikolaev's real identity, a working-class Communist who had turned against the regime, was potentially devastating for official versions of reality. It needed to be kept quiet. (274)

On page 344 Lenoe repeats the notion that it would be a "disaster for Soviet propaganda" if Nikolaev turned out to be a worker. But nowhere does Lenoe cite any evidence to support this statement. No wonder! There could hardly be any. Many Oppositionists were workers or former workers. In the 1920s there had even been a "Workers' Opposition" group. The fact that yet another Oppositionist was from a working-class background was nothing new and by itself could have no special significance.[47]

Moreover, though working class in his origins, in practice Nikolaev was well on his way out of the working class. He had enjoyed privileged blue-collar or white-collar work for a number of years. Nikolaev's own career was thus vastly different from that of most other workers in Leningrad or in the USSR generally. Lenoe shows no curiosity about how this could have happened. One obvious possibility is that he obtained these privileged positions by virtue of his membership in the underground Zinovievite group. Some of the Zinovievites had medium-level Party posts and were in a position to exert influence.

Lenoe accuses Sinel'nikov, a Khrushchev-era biographer of Kirov, of ignoring Kirov's role in what Lenoe terms "the brutal pacification of the Azerbaijani countryside" during the Civil War (524). But he does not tell us what "brutality" allegedly occurred and what Kirov allegedly had to do

---

[46] "Rasskaz o desiati rasstreliannykh" ("Story of ten who were shot"), *Izvestiia* September 2 1992, p. 3.

[47] Wendy Z. Goldman *Terror and Democracy in the Age of Stalin* (Cambridge University Press, 2007) discusses the political struggles and opposition within the industrial working class in the 1920s and 1930s.

with it. Lenoe's own summary of Kirov's time in Azerbaijan during the Civil War contains no such allegations (50-1; 57-63). Like Sinel'nikov, therefore, Lenoe himself "ignores" whatever happened during this period.

Later in the book Lenoe permits himself the following tirade:

> The author of this report unwittingly reveals a great deal about the nature of the "truth" in Bolshevik rhetoric by the middle 1930s. The officer treats the centrally controlled show trial of August 1936 as establishing a "true" revolutionary narrative, while dismissing Yenukidze's alternative narrative as 'counterrevolutionary." Evidence for the competing narratives is irrelevant – the sole criterion for truth is now the declarations of the central authorities or the story-lines presented in the mass spectacles organized by them. Moreover, believers in the Stalinist "truth" care far less about whether it corresponds to the real world that whether they can demonstrate their power by forcing others to reiterate its tenets. For Stalin and his loyalists the ability to get the entire populace to repeat their "true" narrative of events both indexed and reproduced their power. (503-4)

Once again Lenoe cites no evidence for this sweeping generalization. This anticommunist rant also has the appearance of a coverup. The August 1936 Moscow Trial in fact presented a great deal of evidence concerning the Kirov assassination. Lenoe ignores all of it – and then has the temerity to claim that it was the communists who considered "evidence" irrelevant! Anyone who troubles to read those pretrial investigative materials now available – the published transcript of the August 1936 Moscow Trial, and the materials from the Harvard Trotsky Archive where the "bloc" of Trotskyites and Zinovievites, including its membership, is acknowledged by Trotsky himself, to mention but a few – can see that the Soviet authorities were very concerned indeed about evidence.

It is Lenoe, not the report's author or the Bolsheviks generally, for whom "evidence ... is irrelevant". We devote a part of the present study to an examination of the pretrial interrogations of Genrikh S. Iagoda, Commissar of Internal Affairs and thus head of the NKVD until August 1936 and a defendant at the March 1938 Moscow Trial. In those confessions Iagoda directly implicates Enukidze as an accessory in Kirov's murder. These confessions are cited unproblematically as evidence by prominent anticommunist scholars. Enukidze's involvement in Kirov's assassination would fully explain his attempt to frame the murder in terms of personal revenge rather than political terrorism. In that chapter we demonstrate that Lenoe is aware of these materials but conceals them from his readers. There can be little doubt that he does this because the evidence they contain thoroughly disproves Lenoe's "lone gunman" hypothesis.

"Argument By Scare Quotes"

Lenoe has frequent recourse what we may call "argument by scare quotes." Lenoe puts scare quotes around certain statements and assertions without explaining to his readers what this means or why he does so. Evidently these are statements, such as confessions, and assertions that Lenoe believes to be false or that he wishes his readers to consider as false. But he never explains what makes him think they are false. Nor does Lenoe ever cite any evidence that they are false. We are forced to guess, to surmise that the scare quotes are intended to signal to the reader that s/he too ought to look upon these statements and assertions with suspicion, if not with outright disbelief. However, Lenoe does not explain just how his readers' should alter their own opinions as a result of this use of scare quotes.

Principled researchers try to account for the evidence by formulating hypotheses. Broadly speaking, two hypotheses are relevant in the case of the Kirov murder:

Hypothesis #1: In murdering Kirov Nikolaev acted as a participant in a clandestine Opposition group.

Hypothesis #2: All the evidence that points to the existence of this clandestine Opposition group was falsified by "Stalin" – Stalin himself, the NKVD and/or Prosecutor's office acting under his instructions, etc.

Late in his book Lenoe surveys the Khrushchev-era attempts to invalidate the 1930s testimony concerning the Kirov murder. We will examine Lenoe's survey later on. But Lenoe realizes that Khrushchev and his men were trying to pin the Kirov murder on Stalin and also trying to prove that no conspiracies at all existed. Lenoe acknowledges that the Khrushchevites had recourse to falsifications. In any case, his study of Khrushchev's machinations is no excuse for not studying the available evidence himself.

As employed by Lenoe this practice of using scare quotes is another form of "begging the question" – of assuming the falsehood of certain statements and assertions without citing any evidence that they are false, of "assuming that which is to be proven." Like any researcher Lenoe is obligated to prove that these statements are false. Since Lenoe never explains his use of scare quotes, it appears as though he is attempting to convey to his readers that he has proven, or disproven, something that he has not. We will cite some examples here.

Properly understood, this practice of "argument by scare quotes" is one type of "tell". By using scare quotes Lenoe is tacitly – and, no doubt, unintentionally – admitting to his attentive readers that he cannot prove what he claims he has proven, but that he is unwilling to honestly admit this fact. This type of argument, then, is one more example of the textual or rhetorical strategies Lenoe evidently feels he must employ in order to convince his readers he has proven his hypothesis while disguising the fact that in reality he has done nothing of the kind For a researcher who had evidence would set it forth clearly, and Lenoe does not do this.

Lenoe writes:

> Eventually Nikolaev "confessed" that he had recruited Shatsky to watch Kirov's apartment for him, and strongly implied that Kotolynov had masterminded a conspiracy to murder Kirov. (288)

All researchers need to be prepared to find evidence that does not support their hypotheses and to deal with such evidence honestly and with objectivity. Since Lenoe does not explain his use of scare quotes here, we may conclude that he doubts this confession is genuine solely because it contradicts his hypothesis that no conspiracy existed and Nikolaev acted alone. Lenoe owes his readers an explanation for the scare quotes and the doubts or suspicions they imply.

Two pages later Lenoe does this again:

> In the Nikolaev case, Agranov had made progress with Pyotr Nikolaev's "confession" of his participation in the plot to murder Kirov. … There was the putative

> "counterrevolutionary group" consisting of former oppositionists from the Vyborg Ward Komsomol and other acquaintances of Nikolaev …
>
> In the case of the "counterrevolutionary group" that would eventually become the so-called "Leningrad Center" Sokolov had so far proved the one really productive arrest (other than Nikolaev himself). … [H]e named a large number of former oppositionists who supposedly constituted a group still opposed to the party, and he placed Nikolaev inside the group. This was progress towards "proving" the kind of conspiracy that Agranov had to create for Stalin. (290-1)

On page 304 the words "Leningrad Center" and "Moscow Center" occur six times, and "center" once by itself. Lenoe puts scare quotes around them every time.

Lenoe's reasoning seems to be as follows:

* Lenoe's thesis is that Nikolaev acted alone.

* Therefore, there could have been no group and, consequently, no Leningrad and Moscow centers.

* Therefore any confession in which they appeared must be false and any proof or evidence fabricated.

It is, of course, fallacious to reason in this manner.

Then Lenoe states:

> On December 9 Vladimir Rumiantsev, arrested on December 6, provided interrogators with the first "evidence" of what might be interpreted as conspiratorial activity by Zinoviev and Kamenev. (304)

Why the scare quotes around "evidence"? Lenoe is devoted to the hypothesis that everybody except Nikolaev was falsely accused and convicted. But if this were so, then any evidence that contradicts his preconceived ideas has to be a fabrication – therefore, not really evidence, but "evidence". Lenoe, that is, sticks to his preconceived hypothesis no matter what the evidence says.

On page 308 Lenoe uses scare quotes four times, twice around "Leningrad Center." The other two concern Zvezdov's confessions:

> It appears to have been Vasily Zvezdov who provided Agranov with breakthrough "evidence" about the existence of a well-organized "Leningrad Center" conspiring against the party leadership...Two days later ...he did "confirm" the existence of an underground Zinovievite organization dedicated to fighting the party leadership. (308)

This passage does, in fact, convey useful information, however indirectly, to the reader: *namely, that there is no evidence that would persuade Lenoe such an underground Zinovievite organization did in fact exist!* For in the case of a secret, conspiratorial group there can scarcely be any other evidence for its existence than evidence – testimony – from its members. Those who, like Lenoe, discount all such evidence in advance ought to be forthright and admit directly that they have made up their mind to ignore all the evidence that does – or could reasonably be expected to – exist.

On the following page Lenoe puts scare quotes around "Leningrad Center", "Moscow Center", "groups", and "centers." Then he states:

> Zvezdov was following their script.

What "script"? I use scare quotes advisedly here, since Lenoe gives no evidence at all that such a "script" existed. He imputes a "script" to the investigators but fails to inform us how they managed to get the suspects to utter confessions following this so-called "script". Absent any evidence of it, however, the "script" remains an invention of Lenoe's mind – hence my own use of scare quotes here. So Lenoe puts scare quotes around evidence that does not fit his preconceived hypothesis, but *no* scare quotes around evidence that does not exist at all, evidence that he, Lenoe, has invented – this "script."

Lenoe's bias dictates his conclusions throughout. On page 313 he writes:

> Why did Zvezdov and other purported members of the "Leningrad Center" confess?

Lenoe goes on to discuss "physical abuse", "other forms of torture", and other putative reasons why prisoners might give false confessions. But he cites no evidence that any means of coercing false confessions were used in this case, or in any of the Kirov investigation.

The possibility that Zvezdov and/or other defendants were coerced to give false confession is a hypothesis. Like all hypotheses it must fail if there is insufficient evidence to support it. A hypothesis that is not supported by any evidence does not have to be refuted; it "falls of its own weight." In the case of this hypothesis of Lenoe's – that those who, like Zvezdov, confessed that there was a conspiracy, that Nikolaev was in it, etc., because they were persuaded or coerced to follow a "script" composed by the investigators – Lenoe cites no evidence at all.

This fact – lack of evidence – would oblige any honest investigator to discard it in favor of hypotheses that better account for the existing evidence. But Lenoe never considers the possibility that the confessions might have been genuine, despite the fact that they are mutually confirmative and that he can find no evidence at all that they were false. Any competent and honest investigator considers all possible explanations that satisfy the evidence, including those that contradict his preliminary hypothesis. Lenoe consistently fails to act in this manner.

On page 324 Lenoe writes:

> Also on the thirteenth Genrikh Liushkov took a damning "confession" from Rumiantsev, who detailed supposed connections between the Moscow and Leningrad "Centers." (324)

Later on the same page Lenoe uses scare quotes around "counterrevolutionary group", noting that "Kotolynov evidently did not contest the label." Correct! The only one "contesting the label" is Lenoe himself – and he gives no reason for doing so.

When Lenoe discusses Nikolaev's early confessions, during which the defendant claimed he acted on his own, he does not use scare quotes around the word "confession." Undoubtedly this may be explained by the fact that Lenoe's own hypothesis is that Nikolaev acted alone. Therefore he does not wish to convey to his readers that these early confessions might be false.

Nikolaev later explicitly admitted that part of his assignment was to pretend that he was a "lone gunman":

> "…I was supposed to describe the murder of KIROV as an individual act in order to conceal the participation in it of the Zinovievite group."
>
> (vol. 1 p. 266).

This passage is taken from the Prosecutor's indictment. This document is reprinted by Lenoe in his book, but with some significant omissions. This passage is one of those that Lenoe omitted. We will discuss it in more detail in a later chapter on the documents Lenoe omits.

A moment's reflection is enough to make anyone realize that the earliest confessions of a defendant are normally those likely to contain the most falsehoods. Nikolaev could not deny his own role in murdering Kirov – he was caught red-handed. But he could deny any role by others, and this he did for at least a day or two.

On page 327 Lenoe writes:

> The time had come for the press to reveal the "true" perpetrators of the crime.

On page 343 Lenoe writes:

> …NKVD officials were concerned with demonstrating at trial that Nikolaev … had belonged to the "counterrevolutionary Zinovievite-Trotsky organization" in 1934.

In this case we know that Lenoe is wrong. We have known since the early 1980s that a bloc of Zinovievites and Trotskyites did indeed exist. Sedov and Trotsky wrote each other about it. It is simply not possible that Lenoe was ignorant of this fact, published in major journals a quarter-century before his own book was published. Furthermore, Lenoe acknowledges the help of Arch Getty (15), one of the researchers who, along with Pierre Broué, discovered Sedov's and Trotsky's correspondence about the bloc. Lenoe fails in his responsibility to inform his readers of this fact. Instead he tries to cast doubt on its existence through scare quotes.

Psychologizing; or, "When You Have No Evidence, Attack The Person"

An old adage advises courtroom lawyers: "When you have no evidence, attack the person." Lenoe often permits himself to comment upon Stalin's character. These comments are always derogatory and never accompanied by any evidence.

What could possibly motivate an historian to so abandon any pretense at objectivity? Perhaps Lenoe feels it necessary to prove over and over again that he is "on the right side" – that although he is arguing that Stalin did *not* connive at Kirov's murder, that does not mean he is "pro-Stalin". After all, very early in his book Lenoe does make a big point of assuring and re-assuring his readers of his impeccable anti-Stalin and anticommunist leanings. (16)

Whatever the reasons for it, the fact remains that *ad hominem* argumentation is a logical and rhetorical fallacy. Moreover, the careful reader understands that the *ad hominem* argument is a tacit admission that the person who uses it has only weak evidence to support his case, or no evidence at all. Whatever Lenoe's reasons for employing it, there is simply no legitimate defense for it. We will give some examples of this warrantless psychologizing as further evidence of the basic weakness of Lenoe's argumentation in this book.

Lenoe describes Stalin's friendship with Kirov, the fact that Kirov stayed at Stalin's apartment on his trips to Moscow, the evidence that Stalin "loved" Kirov, and Stalin's modest lifestyle. (138-139) Perhaps reluctant to be painting what could be construed as a positive picture of Stalin Lenoe continues:

> At one level, the question of Kirov's and Stalin's personal friendship is irrelevant. Many people who knew Stalin have commented that he was a great actor, expert at concealing his real feelings and thoughts. He was undoubtedly capable of greeting someone warmly while plotting against them. (140)

Lenoe cites no evidence to support this claim. Nor does he even deign to name a single one of those "many people." Much less does he stop to ask himself how they could possibly "know" this about Stalin, or anybody. How did they know Stalin's "real feelings", so that they could know when he was "concealing" them? Conversely, if Stalin was so "expert at concealing his real feelings", how did these people "know" them?

This remark appears to be an example of the well-documented anticommunist double-standard. Under this double-standard when a non-communist is warm and friendly, this shows his true nature. When a communist acts the same way he is being duplicitous, "concealing his real feelings and thoughts" which must, of course, be "bad" ones – because he is a communist. Famed press critic A.J. Liebling mocked this knee-jerk anticommunism in the last edition of his book *The Press*:

> The formulas most newspapers have fallen back on for foreign news are few. One is, "Man go to church, good, man, no lie. Man not go to church, bad, lie." Ergo "Franco, Salazar, Adenauer, Christian Democrats, good truthful. Communists, bad, whatever they say lie."

Liebling then usefully demonstrates how this bias affects reporting:

> Thus, as an example of formula thinking, if Sicilians riot because living conditions are ghastly, and a Communist leader says, later, "Look at Sicily, living conditions are ghastly," then *living conditions cease to be ghastly*. By agreeing with *any* charge the Communist takes the truth out of it, first, because he is trying to turn it to his own advantage – which, to revert for a moment to nonformula sanity, has not one thing to do with whether it is true or not – second, because even if it were not true it would be to his advantage, so he would invent it. It is therefore a lie, because (a) Communists and liars, they do not go to church, and (b) they invented it. And the Sicilians themselves are liars, because they allowed the Communists to agree with them, thus putting themselves in the position of people who agree with liars.[48]

Lenoe's thesis reflects this "formula": Stalin claimed Kirov was murdered by an oppositionist conspiracy; Stalin was a bad man; therefore Stalin was a liar; therefore Kirov was not killed by an oppositionist conspiracy; therefore all the evidence that points to an oppositionist conspiracy was fabricated by Stalin!

Lenoe follows up these sentences quoted above with an anecdote that is supposed to illustrate the duplicity he alleges.

---

[48] A.J. Liebling. *The Press*. New York: Pantheon, 1975 (1961), 261.

> Also, surface civility among top leaders and their families in the Stalinist elite often concealed bitter political rivalries. In December 1934, for example, Maria Svanidze's husband Aleksandr would denounce Avel Yenukidze to the NKVD for supposedly plotting a coup against the Soviet leadership.[90] Svanidze and Yenukidze saw Stalin regularly together in cordial home circumstances.

This passage is revealing, though not in the way Lenoe apparently intends. His footnote 90 is to the book by IUrii Zhukov, *Inoi Stalin* (759). Although Zhukov's book is a work over 500 pages in length Lenoe gives no page reference. We have taken the trouble to locate the passage, which is on page 176 of Zhukov's book. Zhukov actually dates Svanidze's denunciation of Enukidze not to December 1934 but to "the first days of January 1935". Lenoe omits to inform his readers that in the very next paragraph Zhukov cites the confessions of both Enukidze and Peterson, both made within minutes of their respective arrests in cities far away from each other, that they had indeed been plotting such a coup.

One would never guess from any of Lenoe's numerous citations to Zhukov's book or to the same author's important article on the 1935 "Kremlin Affair" in *Voprosy Istorii* (2000) that IUrii Zhukov concluded, on the basis of the evidence, that Enukidze was indeed plotting against Stalin, or that Zhukov was able to cite a great deal of evidence in support of that hypothesis, which he arrives at only reluctantly and towards the end of his article. Much less does Lenoe inform his readers that, if Zhukov is correct, Lenoe's own hypothesis that Nikolaev was a "lone gunman" is exploded, since Enukidze confessed to being a major player in the conspiracy by the Rights, Trotskyites and Zinovievites to assassinate Kirov.

It was, of course, Svanidze's duty, as it was that of any Party member or, indeed, of any Soviet citizen, to report information about such a plot. The fact that Enukidze was a highly-place and long-trusted person would have made such a conspiracy all the more dangerous. Therefore the passage Lenoe quotes to illustrate "bitter political rivalries" among "the Stalinist elite" does so – but in a very different manner than that intended by Lenoe. It corroborates a great deal of other evidence now available to us that the opposition conspiracies of the 1930s were genuine and serious,

ous, thus helping indirectly to disprove Lenoe's thesis about Kirov's murder.

After outlining an attempt by Stalin to investigate possible fabrication of cases by the OGPU (about to be changed, in mid-1934, to the NKVD) and his concern to get qualified prosecutors Lenoe asserts:

> For Stalin the emphasis on "revolutionary legality" had to do with establishing order and riding herd on the NKVD and not necessarily with any concern for reducing state violence. (143)

One might object that "riding herd on the NKVD" is precisely an attempt to "reduce state violence". In addition we need to ask: How can Lenoe possibly know what Stalin's motives were? Lenoe assumes Stalin must have had authoritarian, manipulative, or bureaucratic motives rather than any motives, such as reducing violence, that Lenoe's readers could sympathize with. This shows Lenoe's anticommunist double standard at work again. A non-communist politician who showed concern to obtain qualified prosecutors and to investigate faking of cases by the police would presumably be praised. But Stalin "communist, bad man, lie", so he must be up to something nefarious.

Another example of this psychologizing – really, name-calling – from Lenoe:

> The Soviet leader was suspicious and held grudges. (256)

How does Lenoe know this? Don't ask! This is a minor example compared to many others, such as the following:

> It is clear that Stalin in the early 1930s was bent on monitoring ex-oppositionists closely and crushing any hint of recalcitrance on their part. (277)

But according to the source Lenoe cites this has nothing to do with "monitoring ex-oppositionists." The editorial board of *Bol'shevik*, the Party's leading journal, had proposed publishing a letter by Engels. Stalin wrote an argument critical of Engels' letter and proposing that it not be published, and his document was subsequently ratified by the Central Committee. The Engels article itself was not published but instead Zinoviev, the expert on international affairs on the editorial board, wrote an article summarizing its contents. This was a violation of at least the spirit, if not the letter, of the Central Committee resolution. Kaganovich's reply a few days later was that Zinoviev had to write an explanation (but had not yet done so) and at the same time said that he himself had disapproved of the Engels article.

So this was not a case of "monitoring ex-oppositionists closely" at all. Had Zinov'ev's activities been "monitored closely" his article would not have been published in the first place. Had Stalin really been a man who "held grudges" Zinov'ev would not have been appointed to the editorial board of *Bol'shevik* at all. Zinov'ev had already been expelled from the Party, sent to work in a provincial town – but then restored to a high Party position when he vowed that he now supported the Party's line.

In the specific incident under discussion Vilhel'm Knorin, another Comintern specialist, was removed as editor-in-chief. Knorin had never been associated with any Opposition. Zinoviev was removed from the editorial board because he had actually written the article in question (under a pseudonym). Stalin's letter to Kaganovich emphasized that Zinoviev was not just not the *only* person at fault but that he was not even the *main* person at fault.[49]

Lenoe has misread this incident. What this sequence of events shows, in fact, is that Stalin did *not* "hold grudges" and had gone out of his way to give Zinov'ev yet another responsible post.

Nakhaev

Lenoe states:

> The Nakhaev mutiny and numerous other incidents show that Stalin's reaction to the Kirov murder was typical for him personally and for the Bolshevik regime as a whole. The insistence that a counter-revolutionary conspiracy must be behind the assassination, the immediate resort to extrajudicial procedures, the execution of hostages, the search for a foreign connection, and the anger at the NKVD's supposed incompetence were all practically reflexive. (277)

[49] Stalin to Kaganovich, August 12, 1934. In *Stalin i Kaganovich. Perepiska. 1931-1936 gg.* Ed. Khlevniuk, O.V., et al. Moscow: ROSSPEN, 2001, p. 432.

In reality the Nakhaev mutiny shows nothing of the kind. Nakhaev tried to raise a revolt among civil defense volunteers by claiming that "Jewish Communists" were running the country. According to the sources Lenoe cites Nakhaev had quit the Party "as a protest against the expulsion of the leaders of the opposition in 1927." The authors of this note do not inform us whether the leaders whose expulsion Nakhaev was protesting were Zinov'ev and Kamenev, or Trotsky and his major supporters, or others.[50]

Given the fact that Zinov'ev, Kamenev, Trotsky and his supporters, and many other oppositionists were in fact of Jewish background, while Stalin and his Politburo were not (with the exception of Lazar' Kaganovich), it certainly must have seemed to the NKVD that something was going on that did not make sense on the surface. Sure enough, Nakhaev proved to have contact with a General Bykov, who – as far as published documents permit us to see – was in touch with Estonian intelligence.

Of course if Lenoe had evidence that something else was going on – that Nakhaev was acting on his own, that Bykov was not involved or had no connection to Estonia – he could inform his readers of that evidence. We may therefore assume that he does not.

Aside from anticommunist bias there is no particular reason to doubt Bykov's alleged ties to Estonian intelligence – or, for that matter, to doubt Nikolaev's connection with Latvian intelligence through Georgs Bissenieks, the Latvian consul. Modern scholarship has amply documented the fact that, like Germany, Japan, and Poland, the Baltics had large-scale spy operations inside the USSR, as well as the effectiveness of Soviet countermeasures and penetration of these spy networks.[51] This does not mean, of course, that all suspicions of such activity were automatically valid. But Soviet suspicions of espionage activity were realistic, not paranoid.

---

50 The list of those expelled from the Party at the 15th Party Congress in 1927 is on p. 1247 of the Transcript of the Congress. A number of the Zinovievites later involved in the Kirov murder are among them.

51 See, for example, Jeffrey Burds, "The Soviet War against 'Fifth Columnists': The Case of Chechnya, 1942-4," *Journal of Contemporary History* 42 (2007), 267-314. Despite the title Burds discusses far more than just Chechnya.

Lenoe's use of the phrase "numerous other incidents", without identifying a single one of them, is a "tell". It is a bluff, a tacit admission that he has no evidence and is fabricating what follows. No "extrajudicial procedures" were "resorted to" in the Nakhaev case. And a final point: none of the accounts Lenoe cites as his sources concerning the Nakhaev case mention "the execution of hostages." What, therefore, are we to think – except that Lenoe must have added this phrase simply to parade his anti-communist bias before his readers!

The Ezhovshchina

We now have a great deal of primary-source evidence about the so-called "Terror" – the traditional and more accurate Soviet term for this period was the "Ezhovshchina" (literally, "bad time of Ezhov") – and the reasons it took place. Rather than refer to it Lenoe attributes it to Stalin's character:

> But to return to the Terror's immediate case – Stalin ordered it. He was a vengeful and power-hungry man, and possibly a sadist in the clinical sense. ... At the same time, his resort to mass operations was a gesture of frustrated rage, or throwing up his hands...(470)
>
> Always inclined to believe the worst, ... (470)
>
> Once Stalin decided that the oppositionists were in some sense responsible, the details of individual guilt or innocence did not bother him. (471)

It is all false; none of it is supported by the evidence. Stalin ordered no "terror" but the suppression of rebel and criminal gangs which local Party leaders reported were ravaging their areas.

In this case we have a good deal of insight into Stalin's reactions to many of these events because many of the documents from that period that have been published are accompanied by marginal notations by Stalin which have also been published. But Lenoe, so eager to "psychologize" or "channel" Stalin to try to characterize his motives and thoughts, makes no reference to Stalin's notations. Perhaps this is because they show no indication whatever of "power-hunger", "vengefulness", or "rage". We have a great deal of evidence that Stalin was interested in evidence, in the details of the investigations. Yet this is what Lenoe offers as historical explanation for this complex and tragic period.

Chapter 5.
Lenoe and the Fallacy of 'Begging the Question'

The logical fallacy known as "begging the question", is well known to scholars. One source defines it as follows:

> An argument is circular if its conclusion is among its premises, if it assumes (either explicitly or not) what it is trying to prove. Such arguments are said to beg the question. A circular argument fails as a proof because it will only be judged to be sound by those who already accept its conclusion.[52]

As we will demonstrate, Lenoe commits this fallacy with astonishing frequency. This fact itself begs for an explanation. We shall suggest a hypothesis that may account for it. First, however, we will establish the truth of this claim through examination of a large number of passages where Lenoe commits this fallacy.

Lenoe states that Zvezdov was "arrested and shot on fabricated charges" (187). This is a baseless statement. This very question – the validity of the charges against the defendants in the December 1934 Kirov murder trial – is the subject of Lenoe's book. Here, early in this 800+ page book Lenoe assumes, without evidence, what he is supposedly trying to discover. As we shall see, the real state of affairs is the opposite of what Lenoe says here. There existed in 1934 and exists today a great deal of evidence attesting to the guilt of Zvezdov and the others tried, convicted and executed for conspiracy to murder Kirov. There is no evidence whatever that the charges against Zvezdov, or against any of the other defendants, were "fabricated."

---

[52] Quoted from http://www.logicalfallacies.info/presumption/begging-the-question

On page 313 Lenoe asks: "Why did Zvezdov and the other purported members of the 'Leningrad Center' confess?" He proceeds to assume that they were innocent and so must have been cajoled with "promises of clemency", threatened with torture, and so on. But it is the job of historians not to make assumptions, but to draw conclusions from evidence. Lenoe has no evidence that any of the defendants were innocent. Furthermore, Lenoe himself informs us that Zvezdov was one of those who confessed at trial to participating in the murder (360). That is, evidence exists that the charges against Zvezdov were *not* fabricated. Lenoe does not show that this evidence is faked, or is outweighed by yet other evidence. Indeed he never even attempts to do so.

When a historian wishes his readers to assume the validity of his hypothesis, a reader may be forgiven if he suspects that this must be because the historian in question knows that he does not have the evidence to prove his hypothesis. Such tactics may be understandable on the part of a defense attorney in a criminal trial who knows that his client has a very weak case – though they would evoke objections from the prosecutor. After all, defense attorneys are not after the objective truth. But tactics such as "begging the question" – "assuming that which is to be proven" – are entirely out of place in historical research.

Lenoe claims that Stalin "had by December 9 chosen a framework for the conspiracy case … the ultimate targets were Zinoviev and Kamenev." (304) This is a critical point in Lenoe's study to which we devote a special section later in the present study. In fact Lenoe cites no evidence about this or, in fact, any decision Stalin made "by December 9."

Lenoe assumes that Nikolaev's December 13 confession must be false, calling it "particularly implausible given the Russian tradition of revolutionary terrorism." But why assume that assassins always followed "tradition"? Moreover, Lenoe's statement is wrong-headed on its own terms. Lenoe argues that the "Russian tradition" was to strive "for maximum public exposure so as to propagate their views." (317) But we *know* (and Lenoe never contests this) that Nikolaev had tried to commit suicide, an act that would automatically preclude a public trial such as Lenoe claims was "traditional" Murder-suicide was never part of "the Russian tradition of revolutionary terrorism."

What's more, the "Russian tradition of revolutionary terrorism" was that of secret conspiracies like the "People's Will", not of "lone gunmen." In this sense – not at all the sense intended by Lenoe – Nikolaev's act was indeed "traditional."

Therefore the business about "the Russian tradition of revolutionary terrorism" is no argument at all. Much less is it evidence that the confession was faked. (317) Rather, it is a smokescreen, intended to take the place of evidence Lenoe does not possess. Lenoe notes that Nikolaev's early confessions were that he acted alone. But he has no evidence to support his tacit contention that only the early confessions were truthful. So he simply assumes it.

One might suspect that Lenoe "wants" Nikolaev's confession to have been faked because if it is genuine it disproves Lenoe's entire thesis. But the task of an historian is to test his hypothesis against the available evidence. When the evidence will not support his hypothesis, it is the hypothesis the historian must reject, not the evidence. Lenoe, however, does the latter.

Lenoe makes the following claim:

> Agranov continued to work Nikolaev over. On December 15 and 16 the two of them put together a story of the conspiracy's development that relied on falsifying the conversations that occurred at Nikolaev's actual meetings with Shatsky and Sokolov, and on making up meetings with Kotolynov. (321)

Since Lenoe cites no evidence of any "falsifying" or "making up" it is fair to assume that he knows of none. Evidently he assumes this "falsification" for the sake of his predetermined conclusion, to "save" it in the face of evidence that disproves it. Lenoe seems to make this clear by then saying:

> Nikolaev then had a series of almost certainly imaginary meetings with Kotolynov… (321)

What is Lenoe's evidence and argument that these meetings were "almost certainly imaginary"? He has none. In reality it is not Agranov and Nikolaev, who were "fabricating" stories – it is Lenoe who is fabricating them! Besides, the word "almost" in Lenoe's phrase "almost certainly imaginary" leaves open the possibility that the meetings might not be imaginary – that is, that they did in fact take place. But Lenoe never considers this possibility.

By this point in the book the reader can discern a pattern. When Lenoe is forced to confront evidence that contradicts his preconceived conclusion -- that Nikolaev was a "lone gunman" and all the other defendants in all the trials were "framed" – he dismisses that evidence by *assuming* it is false.

On page 336 Lenoe admits that on December 15 and 18 Iuskin "confessed" – the scare quotes are Lenoe's – that he knew from their meetings that Nikolaev planned to attack Kirov. Lenoe continues:

> It is likely that Yuskin's interrogators omitted from the protocols Yuskin's attempts to explain that his comments about killing Stalin were meant sarcastically. (321)

Why does Lenoe state that this purported omission is "likely"? He cites no evidence or even argument to support this statement. Evidently he simply assumes it because if he did not do so it would be inconvenient if not fatal to his thesis.

At the December 1934 trial Sokolov made a general confession, incriminating Zvezdov (who also confessed), Antonov, Kotolynov, and Nikolaev in the terrorist conspiracy. Lenoe says: "He followed the NKVD script closely." (361) But as we have already pointed out Lenoe fails to give any evidence whatever that such a "script" existed. Once again he seems unaware that he has to prove, not assume, that this, or any testimony that contradicts his thesis, was fabricated.

On page 460 Lenoe claims that the charges against Peterson, commander of the Kremlin garrison, were "manufactured". Lenoe's readers would never know it but a great deal of evidence against Peterson has been published. Whether it was all "manufactured" or not needs to be discussed, not assumed. As of this writing no evidence has been put forth by anyone to support a hypothesis that it was "manufactured." Other writers, notably military historian N.S. Cherushev, also *assume* that Peterson was framed but can cite no evidence that this is so.[53] Lenoe does not even refer the reader to these other historians.

---

[53] Cherushev nevertheless provides a lot of information about the arrests, charges against, and confessions of Peterson, as well as of many other military officers. A military historian, Cherushev evidently had privileged access to investigative materials unavailable

Lenoe raises the Peterson case in the midst of a discussion of the "Kremlin Affair" of 1935. Lenoe believes this case to have been fabricated as well. Once again he gives no evidence that it was. He cites Russian historian IUrii Zhukov's study of the Kremlin Affair several times. But he fails to inform his readers that Zhukov concluded that the Kremlin Affair conspiracy was not a fabrication, but was genuine.[54] Zhukov calls this conclusion "the most paradoxical" hypothesis of all. He feels compelled to spend almost five closely-printed pages outlining his evidence and reasoning. Zhukov concedes that this hypothesis would also mean that Enukidze and Peterson were guilty, and draws some of the corresponding conclusions. Zhukov, that is, does what a historian should do and what Lenoe consistently fails to do.

A few pages later Lenoe writes:

> The changes in Stalin's attitude from 1934 to 1935 had to do with his determination to deal with former oppositionists, at least those on the Left, for good… (462)

Of course Lenoe does not know what Stalin's "attitude" or "motives" were. Once again, he assumes it -- the fallacy of "psychologizing". This specific assumption is an invidious one, in that it represents only one hypothesis – that the "former" (Lenoe's description) oppositionists were innocent of the conspiracies of which they were charged. But of course the ostensible purpose of Lenoe's book is to investigate Kirov's murder and determine whether it was carried out by a "lone gunman" or, as the Soviet state contended at the time, by a clandestine terrorist conspiracy (or group of interrelated conspiracies) of oppositionists. To make the claim, as Lenoe does here, that the prosecutions in 1935 and thereafter were due not to the results of investigations but to Stalin's supposed de-

---

to anyone else. Peterson, his arrest and his confessions are discussed especially in Cherushev, *Komendanty Kremlia v labirintakh vlasti*. Moscow: Veche, 2005, 350-421; Cherushev, N.S. *Nevinovnykh ne byvaet. Chekisty protiv voennykh, 1918-1953*. Moscow: Veche, 2004, 261, 283.

[54] Lenoe 459-460 and p. 786 nn. 15-19 and note 20 (to a book by Zhukov). Zhukov, "Tainy «Kremlevskogo dela» 1935 goda i sud'ba Avelia Enukidze." ("The secrets of the "Kremlin Affair" of 1935 and the fate of Avel' Enukidze"), *Voprosy Istorii* 9 (2000), 82-113. Zhukov outlines his reasons for considering the possibility that the Kremlin Affair conspiracy really did occur at some length, pp. 108-112.

sire to rid himself of "former oppositionists" is to assume that which is to be proven, to "beg the question" of guilt or innocence entirely.

By describing the Moscow trial of August 1936 as "infamous" and claiming it was "scripted" (464) Lenoe evidently assumes he does not have to cite any evidence that the testimony given there is false. That is, Lenoe attempts to conjure away this evidence, and his duty to analyze it, with words. But the single biggest issue in the 1936 trial was the Kirov assassination. It is discussed extensively by the defendants, who outline a Zinovievite conspiracy. It is true that other scholars have also *assumed* that the trial was "scripted". But that does not make such assumptions valid. It is Lenoe's responsibility to study all the evidence in the Kirov murder case – something he neglects to do.

No one has ever proven that any of the testimony of any of the defendants at any of the three Moscow Trials of 1936, 1937 and 1938 was forced upon them[55]. Nor has anyone even cited any evidence to that effect aside from rumor and hearsay. All of the pretrial materials we now have – a small part of what still exists, still classified top secret in Russian libraries – strongly supports the hypothesis that the defendants' testimony was genuine and that it was not "scripted" or falsified by the prosecution.

In similar fashion on page 466 Lenoe dismisses all the testimony at the January 1937 Moscow Trial as "a few grotesque confessions of terrified defendants", without examining it at all, much less proving or citing any evidence that, as he claims, the confessions were "grotesque" or the witnesses "terrified".

Here is what Karl Radek, along with Iurii Piatakov one of the two most famous defendants at this trial, said in his final statement at trial:

> When I found myself in the People's Commissariat of Internal Affairs, the chief examining official realized at once why I would not talk. He said to me: "You are not a baby. Here you have fifteen people testifying against you. You cannot get out of it, and as a sensible man you cannot think of doing so. If you do not

---

[55] We advisedly do not use the words "false" or "fabrication" here because some, at least, of the defendants did make false statements – lie – to the court. But they did so because they chose to do so, to conceal conspiratorial activity that they did not wish to reveal.

> want to testify it can only be because you want to gain time and look it over more closely. Very well, study it." For two and a half months I tormented the examining official. **The question has been raised here whether we were tormented while under investigation. I must say that it was not I who was tormented, but I who tormented the examining officials and compelled them to perform a lot of useless work.** For two and a half months I compelled the examining official, by interrogating me and by confronting me with the testimony of other accused, to open up all the cards to me, so that I could see who had confessed, who had not confessed, and what each had confessed.
>
> This lasted for two and a half months. And one day the chief examining official came to me and said: "You are now the last. Why are you wasting time and temporizing? Why don't you say what you have to say?" And I answered: "Yes, tomorrow I shall begin my testimony." And the testimony I gave contains not a single correction from first to last. I unfolded the whole picture as I knew it, and the investigation may have corrected one or another personal mistake about the connections of some person with another, but I affirm that not a single thing I told the examining officials has been refuted and that nothing has been added.[56] (Emphasis added, GF)

In this passage as throughout his testimony Radek appears anything but "terrified". The same is true for the other defendants.

Lenoe, or somebody, could claim: "Maybe Radek was tortured or threatened into claiming he was not tortured or threatened?" To anyone who proposes to set forth the hypothesis that Radek, or any other defendant, was tortured, threatened, or otherwise forced to make a false confession, we must make the same demand that we make of any hypothesis: "What is your evidence that Radek was tortured, threatened, etc., to make this

---

[56] *Report of Court Proceedings in the Case of the Anti-Soviet Trotskyite Centre. Heard Before the Military Collegium of the Supreme Court of the U.S.S.R. Moscow, January 23-30, 1937....Verbatim Report.* Moscow: People's Commissariat of Justice of the U.S.S.R., 1937. (1937 Trial), p. 549. *Protsess antisovetskogo trotskistskogo tentra* (23 – 30 ianvaria 1937 goda). M.: NKIU Soiuza SSR. IUridicheskoe izdatel'stvo, s. 230.

statement?" Lenoe has no such evidence. What's more, he does not even seem to realize that evidence is necessary!

We are forced to conclude that Lenoe's words about "terrified defendants" is in reality yet another instance of a "tell", a tacit admission of defeat. By these words Lenoe is unconsciously signaling to the attentive reader that he is unable to disprove anything the defendants said and therefore must either dismiss them out of hand or concede that the evidence shows they are probably truthful – in which case, his hypothesis fails.

A page later Lenoe claims:

> The course of the murderous campaign that Stalin and Yezhov now unfolded can be summarized briefly…

But Lenoe does not do this at all. He fails even to outline, much less to study, the many and complex events of April to July 1937. A few of them are: the gradual disclosure of the Military conspiracy, the interrogations, confessions, and trial of Tukhachevsky and his seven co-defendants; the first confessions of Iagoda, Enukidze, and many others; Bukharin's first confession and those of several other of the defendants at the 1938 Moscow Trial; the June 1937 Central Committee Plenum; the requests by local Party leaders for mass repressions. A great deal has been written about these events, and we now have many primary sources for them though a large number of other primary sources are still withheld by the Russian authorities. But Lenoe does not refer to any of this scholarship or primary sources.

Failing at least a review of this research Lenoe is in no position to "summarize", "briefly" or otherwise, what ensued. Much less can he have any idea of what was actually going on and of the respective roles of Ezhov, Stalin and other important political actors. From the annotations on many documents now published[57] it appears that Stalin was reacting to events as they were reported to him, rather than controlling them. Other conclusions might be possible, but one would have to study the evidence. This Lenoe neglects to do.

---

[57] The "Lubianka" volumes published under the auspices of the Mezhdunarodniy Fond "Demokratia" record Stalin's annotations on many of the documents.

On page 471 Lenoe writes:

> In the course of the Terror, Stalin masterminded the distortion of evidence in the Kirov murder. The most persistent distortions came about in the course of Yezhov's fabrication of cases against Yagoda…

Lenoe cites no evidence in support of his claim that evidence was distorted in any of the Moscow trials. Nor does he have even a shred of evidence that Ezhov "fabricated" anything against Iagoda nor that Stalin "masterminded" such "fabrications". It is Lenoe who has "fabricated" here in asserting that these things occurred when he has not the slightest evidence that they did.

In reality we now possess a huge amount of evidence against Iagoda. This includes eight of his pretrial confessions, his testimony at trial, and his appeal to the Supreme Court published in 1992. Moreover, at his trial in March 1938 Iagoda confessed to some serious charges but stoutly and stubbornly refused to confess to others. This fact would appear to be strong evidence that his confessions were not made under compulsion. To establish otherwise would require even stronger evidence to the contrary, but Lenoe cites none.

Lenoe refers to "the imagined conspiracy" of the 1938 Trial (479) without any examination of the trial or its testimony whatsoever. A few pages later he again assumes, without any evidence or argument at all, "that the 1938 show trial version of the Kirov murder was false." (482) Lenoe never troubles himself to try to prove this. Nor does he refer to any other studies that have proven it – hardly surprising, since none exist. As we will demonstrate through an examination of the evidence the Soviet prosecution's version of the Kirov murder, as corrected by Iagoda himself in his 1938 trial testimony, is by far the most accurate account of the conspiracy to murder Kirov and, in fact, the only one consistent with the evidence.

As we have seen, on page 513 Lenoe asserts "It was not Trotsky who collaborated with foreign imperialist powers, as suggested in the indictment in the Kirov murders…" It appears that Lenoe has never studied this matter. A great deal of evidence exists that supports exactly such a hypothesis.[58] To assert the opposite would also require evidence and an argument. Lenoe shows no sign that he even knows this evidence exists!

Likewise Lenoe claims "it wasn't Trotsky who ordered Kirov's murder". But he never examines the evidence that Trotsky had in fact done so. This evidence is mainly in the Third, but also in the Second Moscow Trial. We will examine it in detail further on. Lenoe avoids all of this evidence, possibly because it thoroughly refutes his own "lone gunman" thesis.

Lenoe is quick to state:

> Given Stalin's fabrication of the case against the oppositionists… (516)

This statement assumes the very thesis that his whole book is, supposedly, an attempt to prove! If Lenoe is going to make this assumption, then there was no need to write the book at all. The truth is not simply that this "fabrication" has never been proven, but that all the evidence presently at our disposal supports the hypothesis that the confessions of the Moscow Trials' defendants were genuine, not fabricated nor the result of NKVD compulsion.[59]

On page 524 Lenoe says:

> Lobov, Pozern, and Kosaryov had been dead for twenty-five years, all shot in the Terror.

It is true that Lobov, Pozern and Kosarev were tried and executed. But it avoids – "begs" – the question again. What matters is whether or not they were guilty of the charges against them. Lenoe *assumes* they were not but without any evidence or argument. The few primary sources now available suggests that there is much evidence they were guilty, though we

---

[58] See Grover Furr, "Evidence of Leon Trotsky's Collaboration with Germany and Japan." *Cultural Logic* (2009), at http://clogic.eserver.org/2009/Furr.pdf

[59] By "genuine" we do not necessarily mean "true." We know that some of the defendants made statements that were false in order to protect other conspirators still at large.

cannot be sure of anything until the investigative materials are made public.[60]

This statement illustrates the problem of using terms such as "the Terror." The term masks an illegitimate assumption that everyone shot during this period was innocent. Applying an epithet to a very large number of historical events over more than a year's time does not free the historian from the obligation to demand and study the evidence in each case, as Lenoe appears to believe. It is similar to the practice of appealing to the "consensus" of historians – a form of the logical fallacy of "argument from authority" – rather than to evidence, to decide an historical issue.

Lenoe calls the Soviet case against Kotolynov and the other defendants a "fabrication" and an "amalgam" (529)[61] In reality he makes no attempt to prove this. As we show at length in the present study, there is a huge amount of evidence supporting Kotolynov's guilt. Nothing save his own denials support his innocence. The denials of an accused are of little weight when he is accused by many others, as is the case with Kotolynov. Bukharin himself pointed this out during the Third Moscow Trial when he said that the confession of the accused is not at all necessary for conviction and to insist that it is necessary is "medieval." What's more, Kotolynov's own denials are good evidence that he was not subjected to torture. Nor is there any evidence that those who testified against him were tortured, or threatened.

On page 544 Lenoe criticizes former Soviet NKVD man and defector Walter Krivitsky for "… the absurdity of presenting testimony from one of Stalin's kangaroo courts as established fact." Krivitsky is certainly to be blamed, for he committed the same error Lenoe has. Krivitsky accepted Moscow Trial testimony without trying to verify it, while Lenoe rejects it. The greater blame is Lenoe's, since we now have a great deal

---

[60] Khrushchev told several mutually-contradictory stories about Kosarev. But we now have more evidence against him, from former Soviet documents published within the past decade. Lobov was named by many others as a Rightist conspirator. In both cases the Russian authorities have refused to release the investigative files, as is the case in all but a few instances concerning the repressions of the 1930s. But the "rehabilitation" volumes do not cite any evidence that would support their innocence.

[61] In addition, the terms "fabrication" – something created – and "amalgam" – a mixture of two things, here of truth and falsehood – are not the same thing, though Lenoe uses them synonymously.

more evidence about the Moscow Trials than was available in Krivitsky's day. Krivitsky also falsified evidence in his own book.[62] Nor does Lenoe attempt to justify his use of the term "kangaroo court". This is another example of "assuming that should be proven."

On the same page (544) Lenoe refers to "… the dictator's fabrication of a case against the Zinovievites during the subsequent investigation." Once again, Lenoe never cites any evidence at all that the case against the Zinovievites was fabricated in any way. He simply *assumes* that it was "fabricated". On page 551 Lenoe says that Nikolaev's December 14 interrogation and December 29 trial testimony was "obviously distorted." Here the word "obvious" substitutes for evidence and reasoning, which Lenoe fails to give.

Conclusion

Lenoe commits the fallacy of "begging the question" with great frequency. Indeed, it is the single major fallacy upon which his study is based. He never comes close to proving his contention that Nikolaev was a "lone gunman". On the contrary, he tacitly gives up the attempt early in his book and thereafter relies on assertion rather than evidence.

We might consider the instances of Lenoe's question-begging to constitute a "tell", in the sense that the term is used in playing cards. Any attempt by any researcher to "beg the question", to assert what he should prove, constitutes a tacit admission of failure, a recognition that he cannot prove his case and has been reduced to hoping his readers somehow will not notice. Lenoe picked a hypothesis that, on the basis of the evidence that he cites and other evidence that he remains silent about, must be rejected as false. He should have acted as honest researchers, those who are in search of the truth, are supposed to act: When your hypothesis is contradicted by the evidence, abandon that hypothesis and con-

---

[62] For example Krivitsky states that on January 24, 1937 he was reading the transcript of the second Moscow Trial in the newspapers when he read that Karl Radek, one of the defendants, had named Tukhachevsky as "absolutely loyal" to the Party and the government. But this is impossible; Radek's statements about Tukhachevsky were not printed in the Russian transcript of the trial. They were only printed later, in the much longer English-language transcript. (*I Was Stalin's Agent*, Chapter 7; Russian edition at http://scepsis.ru/library/id_623.html)

sider others. Whatever his reason, Lenoe chose not to do this. The collapse of his hypothesis and failure of his book is the inevitable result.

wouldChapter 6.

The Leningrad and Moscow Centers.

Nikolaev and the other defendants in the December 1934 Kirov murder trial were charged with belonging to a Leningrad center of the Zinovievite underground opposition conspiracy that was in touch with a center in Moscow. Lenoe denies that these conspiratorial centers existed at all. The existence of such conspiratorial organizations would of course disprove Lenoe's hypothesis that Nikolaev was a "lone gunman".

But there's much more at stake than just the question of whether Kirov's killer Nikolaev was a "lone gunman" or whether he was part of a conspiracy. Kirov's murder was a major issue in all three Moscow Trials. The path from a Leningrad-based conspiracy, to a Leningrad center in touch with, then taking leadership from, a Moscow center led NKVD investigators to unravel a large network of interconnected opposition conspiracies which culminated in the Tukhachevsky Affair and the so-called "Great Terror" of 1937-1938.

The official position of the Soviet government since Khrushchev's day, of the Russian government today, and of all anticommunist and Trotskyist writers, is that no such conspiracies ever took place. All these trials, charges, executions, and imprisonments are said to have been faked, "scripted" by Stalin and his men, and all those charged and convicted of these conspiracies were innocent "victims of Stalinism." This is Lenoe's position too.

If Kirov really was assassinated by a conspiratorial group in Leningrad that was in touch with a similar group in Moscow led by Zinoviev and Kamenev, that fact would be fatal to the contention – for that is all it is – that all the rest of these conspiracies were fabrications. If these conspiracies were not fabricated it would follow that they actually existed. That would strongly imply that the Moscow Trial defendants, the military conspirators, and Leon Trotsky were guilty as charged. And such a result would go far to justify the actions of Stalin and the NKVD in suppressing such dangerous conspiracies.

Therefore, the question of whether Kirov was killed by a "lone gunman" or by a real conspiracy is a very important matter to ideological anticommunists. Evidence that these conspiracies actually existed poses a serious problem not only for Lenoe specifically but for the whole canonical or mainstream interpretation of Soviet history during the Stalin period.

Our hypothesis in this study is that Lenoe's book (as well as Kirilina's, Egge's, and all other books on the Kirov murder) represents an attempt not to solve the Kirov murder but to construct the best possible argument against the idea that Kirov really was killed as a result of a conspiracy. The evidence we now have contradicts, even dismantles the anti-Stalin paradigm – certainly as far as the Kirov assassination goes. Those who, like Lenoe, write from within the anticommunist or anti-Stalin paradigm of Soviet history simply cannot accept this conclusion regardless of the evidence for it. Anyone who wants to prop up the anti-Stalin paradigm is faced with the need to conjure away the evidence that it is false and invent evidence that supports it.

Lenoe introduces his attempt to disprove the existence of any such "centers" as follows:

> Stalin had by December 9 chosen a framework for the conspiracy case he was building against ex-oppositionists in Leningrad and Moscow. The ultimate targets were Zinoviev and Kamenev. According to separate reports by Olga Shatunovskaya and Party Control Committee officials, there exists a note in Stalin's archive listing members of two supposed conspiratorial groups – a "Leningrad Center" and a "Moscow Center." Control Committee officials stated in 1989 that the note is in Yagoda's handwriting, with corrections by Stalin. (Olga Shatunovskaya claimed in 1988 that the handwriting was Stalin's, and others have apparently identified it as Yezhov's.) If the Control Committee officials are correct, Stalin moved Zinoviev and Kamenev from the "Leningrad Center," where Yagoda had placed them, to the "Moscow Center." Shatunovskaya, whose testimony is sometimes unreliable, claimed in the late 1980s that there was a date on the note, December 6. It is significant that the first mention of prominent former Zinovievite Vladimir Rumiantsev in interrogations was

> also on December 6. Whatever the date of the note, by about December 10 Yezhov was outlining connections between the two 'centers" in his notebook. It seems likely that the "Leningrad Center – Moscow Center" framework, with Zinoviev and Kamenev at the head of the whole organization, was decided upon at the December 8 meeting in Stalin's office attended by Yagoda, Agranov, and Yezhov, if not a day or two earlier. (304)

We will examine carefully the following claims made by Lenoe in this paragraph:

1. "the conspiracy case he [Stalin] was building against ex-oppositionists";

2. "separate reports" by

2a. Olga Shatunovskaia, and

2b."Party Control Committee officials", testifying that

> "there exists a note in Stalin's archive listing members of two supposed conspiratorial groups – a 'Leningrad Center' and a 'Moscow Center.'"

3. "Party Control Commission officials stated in 1989 that the note is in Yagoda's handwriting";

4. "Shatunovskaya... claimed in the late 1980s that there was a date on the note, December 6."

5. "It is significant that the first mention of prominent former Zinovievite Vladimir Rumiantsev in interrogations was also on December 6."

6. "...by about December 10 Yezhov was outlining connections between the two 'centers" in his notebook."

7. "It seems likely that the "Leningrad Center – Moscow Center" framework, with Zinoviev and Kamenev at the head of the whole organization, was decided upon at the December 8 meeting in Stalin's office attended by Yagoda, Agranov, and Yezhov, if not a day or two earlier."

For the sake of clarity we will examine each statement of Lenoe's individually in the light of the evidence to us.

1. As we have argued in another part of the present study Lenoe has not proven that Stalin "was building a conspiracy case against ex-oppositionists" In fact Lenoe cites no evidence at all that Stalin was doing this. This is one of many examples in Lenoe's book of "begging the question", or "assuming that which must be proven".

2. It is clear from Lenoe's text that he has never seen this alleged "note in Stalin's archive." Lenoe appears to have taken the story of the note directly from Kirilina. (Kirilina 363-364) Quoting Shatunovskaia, Kirilina states flatly that Stalin's "final considered plan" was decided on in this note.

2a. "Separate Report" by Shatunovskaia

It appears that no such report exists – that this statement of Lenoe's is a "bluff."

A "report" is a formal document prepared for some audience – in this case, some Party or government body. But neither Lenoe nor anyone else gives any reference, even an archival one, for this supposed report, or for any document by Shatunovskaia that reproduces the text of this report or note or even discusses it or them. It is a striking omission. Therefore Lenoe refers to this report – but does not provide any reference to it and has clearly never laid eyes on it!

The note whose existence Shatunovskaia allegedly asserted has never been published. What's more, – and setting Shatunovskaia herself aside – no one who has written about the Kirov assassination claims to have ever seen it: not Lenoe, nor Kirilina, nor anyone else, including the authors of the reports and hearings published in 2004 and upon which Lenoe relies heavily. There is no reference to it in any of the documents of the commission set up by Gorbachev and Iakovlev to study Kirov's murder. Evidently there is no record of this note at all, except – allegedly – for Shatunovskaia's claim that it existed.

The only evidence that "others have apparently identified [the handwriting] as Yezhov's" are statements by Shatunovskaia. She claimed that "handwriting [*grafologicheskaia*] experts from the USSR Procurator's office" had identified the handwriting as Stalin's, and that the document was "presented to members of the Politburo" along with a "photocopy of Stalin's handwriting and the certification of the handwriting experts".

Later, Shatunovskaia continued, a "representative of the Party Control Commission claimed that the handwriting was Ezhov's, not Stalin's.[63] In her letter to Iakovlev of June 12, 1989 Shatunovskaia claimed that this was Katkov.[64] Shatunovskaia claimed that Katkov had informed her that the sample of Stalin's handwriting and the certification of the handwriting experts that had been attached to the note were now missing.

According to the published transcript one page is missing from Katkov's testimony about his meeting with Shatunovskaia. But in what remains there is no mention of this incident or of the note in question.[65]

On August 22, 1991 Katkov wrote a letter to the Central Committee in which he stated that Shatunovskaia's claims concerning the Kirov assassination were groundless. Katkov wrote:

> Shatunovskaia's communication about the substitution and disappearance of a number of "important documents" was not confirmed.

Katkov specifically stated that they failed to confirm Shatunovskaia's claims that important documents about the Kirov murder were changed or had disappeared.[66] In her letter of June 12, 1989 Shatunovskaia had listed this note as one of eight documents from the investigation of the Khrushchev era that had been tampered with.

Nowhere does Katkov even mention the supposed note, much less confirm that he had ever seen it. Therefore, of course, Katkov does not affirm that he had examined it and told Shatunovskaia the handwriting was Ezhov's, not Stalin's. Nor is it credible that Katkov could have done this without reporting it to his high-ranking superiors on this official commission. Nor would he have had any reason not to report it. The commission was intent on blaming Stalin for illegal repressions and for framing

---

[63] Shatunovskaia, O.G. *Rasskazy ob ushedshem veke.* "Prilozhenie 2. Vokrug tragedii v Smol'nom". At http://www.daabooks.net/ola/smolny.koi.html

[64] RKEB 3, 223. N.F. Katkov was a member of the commission to study the "repressions", including the Kirov assassination.

[65] RKEB 3, 217-218.

[66] RKEB 3, 597.

innocent people. This note would have been evidence to support that contention.

According to the "Reply to Iakovlev" Roy Medvedev, who included the story about the "note" without attribution in his work *Let History Judge* [67], got the story from Shatunovskaia.[68] But Medvedev does not mention her name or the December 6 date (or any other date).

2b. "Separate report" by "Party Control Committee officials"

Lenoe also speaks of a "separate report" by the Party Control Commission that discusses this note. Again, he cites no reference for this report – that is, Lenoe does not identify it. Nor can I locate it anywhere.

Shatunovskaia claimed that Katkov had seen the note, informed her that the attachments to it were now missing, and said the handwriting was not Stalin's but Ezhov's. But Katkov does not mention the note. It is possible that he did so, since one page is missing from the transcript of his remarks. But even if Katkov did see it and did report about it, neither he nor the commission members thought it important enough to mention it again. As we mentioned above, in his letter of August 22, 1991 Katkov flatly states that Shatunovskaia's statements about the Kirov assassination or claims that documents had been switched or removed could not be confirmed.

We assume that no such reports exist. Lenoe gives no reference to either of them, and we can find no trace of them. It seems clear that Lenoe himself has never seen it and cannot prove that it exists or has ever existed. Referring to it is another "bluff" – to use a polite word – on Lenoe's part.

3. Lenoe does not specify whence he learned that "Control Commission officials stated in 1989 that the note is in Yagoda's handwriting, with corrections by Stalin", as he claims. (304) This is a very vague reference to a very important document. It cannot be the archival document cited on

---

[67] Medvedev, Roil. *Let History Judge. The Origin and Consequences of Stalniism.* New York: Knopf, 1971, p. 164; Russian edition *K sudu istorii* (New York: Knopf, 1974), 318-9.

[68] RKEB 3, 501. Lenoe notes Medvedev's use of Shatunovskaia's version at p. 650.

page 775, note 38.[69] Lenoe prints excerpts from that document on pp. 654-655. He would not have omitted any reference to this note. In any case, this is not a "report" but the draft of a letter

I cannot find any reference to the note in the documents and reports by the members of the commission that re-investigated Kirov's murder in RKEB 3. Iakovlev himself, who strongly suspected that Stalin had had Kirov murdered, wrote a lengthy letter of 3900 words to the Politburo Commission setting forth his reasons. He did not mention this note. The Commission members wrote a far lengthier reply of over 23,000 words to Iakovlev's letter. They do not mention this note either. It is logical to conclude that they did not know of any such note.

If any discussion of the note by Katkov, Iakovlev, or a Party Commission could be found it would constitute evidence independent of Shatunovskaia that this note actually existed. It would be a second witness for the existence of this note. Without it, we have only – allegedly – Shatunovskaia's word that there ever was such a note. And Shatunovskaia fabricated – in plain language, lied – a great deal. Lenoe himself concludes that in 1960 Shatunovskaia invented another note out of whole cloth. (616-617)

4. Kirilina writes that Shatunovskaia asserted that the note is dated December 6. However, that date is not mentioned in the document of Shatunovskaia's that Kirilina quotes or in any other document by Shatunovskaia that Kirilina or Lenoe cites or that we can find.

The quotation in Kirilina's book on pp. 363-4 that immediately precedes Kirilina's mention of the "note" is taken directly from Shatunovskaia's letter to Iakovlev of September 5, 1988. Kirilina states (364):

> It is not so important whether Stalin himself wrote it or
> Ezhov did – and about this there are various opinions.
> What's important is something else: Shatunovskaia stated
> that there is a date – December 6 – on this note.
> Obviously, it was on this very day that the plan of

[69] "Concerning com. O.G. Shatunovskaia's letter of September 5, 1988. Draft", "O pis'me t. Shatunovskoi O.G. ot 5 sentiabria 1988g. Proekt."

> struggle against his political opponents, finally thought out in full, came to Stalin.

But Kirilina does not quote the part of the Shatunovskaia's letter where the note is mentioned. Moreover, in no published source, neither in her letter to Iakovlev nor in the account in her memoir, does Shatunovskaia mention any date on this note. Kirilina never informs her readers whence she found the information above concerning this date.

Therefore it is not any document of Shatunovskaia's but the text quoted above from Kirilina's book that is the source for the December 6 date. As far as we can determine, this is the *only* source for the date. So the "claim" Lenoe cites comes not from Shatunovskaia but from Kirilina. Of course, even if it did come from Shatunovskaia we would need confirmation of the note's existence. We can't take Shatunovskaia's, or indeed anyone's, unsupported work for an important piece of evidence.

5. Lenoe never tells us why he believes it is "significant" that Rumiantsev's first interrogation was on December 6. Perhaps we may surmise that he means something like the following:

a. If the Shatunovskaia note existed, and

b. if it really were dated December 6,

c. then it might be evidence that Stalin and/or NKVD investigators had thought of Leningrad and Moscow centers before there had been any testimony suggesting the existence of such centers.

d. And that in turn might be reason to suspect that Stalin and/or the NKVD had invented these centers and subsequently "scripted" later confessions about them by torturing, threatening, or otherwise compelling other defendants into confessing that they existed.

However, no such note is to be found, much less one with a date of December 6. This fact divests the December 6 date of Rumiantsev's first interrogation of whatever "significance" Lenoe would like to endow it with.

6. Lenoe himself states:

> ... by about December 10 Yezhov was outlining connections between the two "centers" in his notebook. (304)

We can assume that Lenoe has actually seen this document since he gives an archival identifier for this reference. We can assume he cannot date it earlier than "about December 10" or he would surely have done so. Then why does Lenoe expend so much effort on the supposed note mentioned by Shatunovskaia? I believe the following passage explains it:

> It seems likely that the "Leningrad Center – Moscow Center" framework, with Zinoviev and Kamenev at the head of the whole organization, was decided upon at the December 8 meeting in Stalin's office attended by Yagoda, Agranov, and Yezhov, if not a day or two before. (304)

Aside from an *alleged* date of December 6 on an *alleged* Shatunovskaia note the earliest date that the Leningrad and Moscow centers were mentioned by the investigators is "about December 10."

Lenoe writes:

> Stalin had by Dec 9 chosen a framework for the conspiracy case he was building against ex-oppositionists in Leningrad and Moscow. The ultimate targets were Zinoviev and Kamenev (304)

This statement is yet another example of Lenoe's "begging the question" – here, assuming that Stalin was "choosing a framework" and "building a case" in which the "ultimate targets were Zinoviev and Kamenev." Lenoe cites no evidence to support any of these assertions or the December 9 date, much less any earlier date. This is "assuming what is to be proven" with a vengeance!

On December 11 defendant Vasilii Zvezdov confirmed that he knew that a counterrevolutionary organization of Zinovievites had been revived. (309) Zvezdov identified members in Moscow, including Zinoviev and Bakaev, and stated:

> The former leaders of the Zinovievite opposition who were in Moscow and were [also] tightly connected with Leningrad hoped to drag our old Komsomol group of former Zinovievites into a battle with the party leadership.

It seems that this is why Lenoe wishes to establish a date "about December 10" or earlier for the beginning of Stalin's alleged frameup of the opositionists. Evidently Lenoe would like to convince his readers that Stalin and the NKVD had somehow forced Zvezdov to make this statement of December 11.

But this is all wrong. We know that:

> * On December 4 Nikolaev had identified Shatskii, Kotolynov and Bardin as "Trotskyites" who had influenced his decision to kill Kirov. (Kirilina 277; 281; Lenoe 281-2)
>
> * On December 5 Nikolaev had told investigators "If I'd had trouble killing Kirov myself, I'd have recruited Bardin, Shatsky, and Kotolynov, and they'd have agreed to do it." (Lenoe 288-9)
>
> * On December 6 Nikolaev confessed to a conspiracy involving at least Shatskii and Kotolynov and implicating Rumiantsev and Iuskin. (Lenoe 288)
>
> * On December 6 Shatskii had confessed that he had kept up contact with Rumiantsev. (Lenoe 291)
>
> * On December 7 Shatskii, after first denying that he knew Nikolaev, admitted that he did know him. (Lenoe 291)
>
> * On December 7 Agranov wrote to Stalin that Nikolaev's brother Piotr admitted to taking part in Kirov's murder. (Lenoe 289)
>
> * Kirilina quotes the following words from a confession of Nikolaev of about December 8 (she does not give the exact date):
>
>> The Kotolynov group was preparing a terrorist act against Kirov, and its direct implementation was entrusted to me personally. I knew from Shatskii that the same task had been given to his group as well, and that this work was being carried out by it independently of our preparation of the terrorist act.
>>
>> I first met Shatskii in 1933. Our next meeting was in the summer of 1934, at 28 Krasnye Zaria Street, where Shatskii was conducting surveillance of the apartment and establishing all Kirov's movements. He was doing this with the aim of preparing a terrorist act.
>>
>> Kotolynov said that ... getting rid of Kirov would weaken the Party leadership ... Kotolynov worked out

> the technical aspects of carrying out the act directly with me, approved this technique, specially verified how accurately I could shoot. He was my direct leader in the matter of carrying out the act. Sokolov explained how suitable this or that point in Kirov's usual route was, and in so doing made my work easier. … IUskin was informed about the preparation for the act against Kirov; he worked out with me the variant of the attempt in the Smolny. (Kirilina 281-2)

* On December 9 Nikolaev's wife Mil'da Draule had also "confessed that she shared the anti-Soviet views of her husband." (Lenoe 306)

Therefore, well *before* December 10 there was plenty of evidence of a Leningrad-based conspiracy of clandestine Zinovievites, and in fact of more than one group of such conspirators.

* On December 9 Rumiantsev had confessed to meeting with Zinoviev and Kamenev (Zinoviev and Kamenev were in Moscow).(Egge 181 & n. 115)

* On December 10 Antonov confessed that Zinoviev had organized his supporters' return to the Party and had instructed Rumiantsev to do so. (Lenoe 307)

These two confessions meant that Zinoviev was continuing to give leadership to Rumiantsev and probably others too, and that Rumiantsev was giving leadership in turn to Antonov and, probably, others.

Given all the testimony we know about, if Ezhov had been making notes about a Leningrad Center and a Moscow Center by "about December 10" that would not suggest any fabrication at all. The existence of (a) one or more Leningrad conspiracies, and (b) contact between Moscow (Zinoviev and Kamenev) and Leningrad, had been well established by December 9.

Meanwhile, Lenoe admits that he cannot prove that Ezhov's "outlining connections between the two 'centers' in his notebook" was in fact written as early as December 10. Lenoe says "about December 10." It might well have been written on subsequent days. Lenoe tacitly admits that Ezhov could not have written it before December 10. He states:

> Nikolai Yezhov returned to Leningrad with Agranov on the morning of December 9 to supervise the Kirov inquiry. His notebooks show that on December 9-10 he questioned witnesses about Leningrad NKVD negligence in guarding Kirov… (303)

Therefore there is no evidence at all to support Lenoe's statement that Stalin and NKVD chiefs invented the "Leningrad Center – Moscow Center framework." Likewise, it is logical to conclude that no such note as Shatunovskaia and Kirilina mention is available to researchers today.

This leaves a number of possibilities:

* Perhaps this note did exist at one time but has been destroyed.

* Perhaps it still exists, but the Russian government has reclassified it so that it lies among the immense number of documents from the 1930s that are still unavailable to researchers and whose very existence is still a secret.

* But probably this note never existed at all. In that case Shatunovskaia imagined it, and then perhaps came to believe it herself.

Lenoe admits that Shatunovskaia's "testimony is sometimes unreliable." (304) In fact Shatunovskaia was viewed as *very* unreliable. Lenoe himself concludes that she probably imagined another note supposedly written in 1956 concerning an alleged event in 1934 (617). He also concludes that she was probably removed from the Party Control Commission in 1962 because of the poor quality of her work (637-638). Lenoe devotes a good deal of space explaining some of the faults of Shatunovskaia's methods of investigation (607-627). As we have seen Katkov, of the Gorbachev-era commission, wrote that *none* of her claims could be confirmed.

For the purposes of our research what matters is this: neither this alleged document nor any transcript of it, or even description of it, is available to be considered for use as evidence. The very existence of this alleged note is doubtful. Lenoe cannot point to any evidence that even one person other than Shatunovskaia herself ever laid eyes on it. At best, therefore, the note falls in the category of *testis unus testis nullus* – a single source, in this case Shatunovskaia, is not enough to establish that an event occurred or, in this case, that a document once existed. Even if Lenoe could show that someone other than Shatunovskaia had seen it – and, to repeat, he does not demonstrate this – it would be of no significance unless that early date of December 6 were also on it.

But even if the note were found, and it did bear the date of December 6, it would not prove that Stalin and his men invented the Leningrad Center-Moscow Center "framework." That would still remain only one hypothesis, one possibility among others. It would not prove that the defendants who testified in detail about these two centers had been forced to do so or that their confessions had been "scripted". For the plain fact is that the Russian authorities have never permitted researchers to see all the evidence that they have on the Kirov case. Without access to all the documentary evidence we could never state with confidence that a December 6 note was the first mention of a Leningrad-based conspiratorial organization (the use of the term "center" is clearly just for convenience, the group as such would have had no name).

Lenoe wishes to argue that what he calls the "framework" of Leningrad and Moscow "centers" came not as result of deduction from the information obtained through interrogations of suspects, but rather was invented, worked out *a priori* by Stalin and his men. Ezhov's notes of "about December 10" on connections between Leningrad and Moscow will not serve the purpose. Lenoe says that Ezhov only arrived back in Leningrad on the morning of December 9 and began questioning witnesses. (303) So Ezhov's notes cannot be earlier than "about December 10". They could be from a day or two *later*.

I suggest that this is why Lenoe relies on Shatunovskaia's "note" and date. Without it there is no reason to suspect that the concept of a Leningrad Center and a Moscow Center of Zinovievite conspirators was fabricated by Stalin et al. Rather, the "framework" of the two centers is an inescapable deduction from the interrogation testimony. But Shatunovsaia's note does not exist, and Lenoe cannot show that it ever did exist, much less what it said or what, if any, date was on it; much less if such a date were on it, who wrote that date. Hence, I suggest, Lenoe's insistence on referencing this "ghost" document.

On December 12 Zvezdov outlined the memberships of both Moscow and Leningrad centers in detail, including Nikolaev in the latter (Lenoe 310-311). Before giving the text of this important interrogation Lenoe states:

> *As we have seen*, Stalin, Yagoda, and/or Yezhov were the real creators of both "centers." Zvezdov was following their script. (309; emphasis added GF)

Lenoe proceeds to speculate why Zvezdov and others would have confessed to the existence of the centers.

We can now see that this claim of Lenoe's is false, a total "bluff". "We" have not "seen" any such thing. On the contrary: Lenoe has failed to prove this claim. *Lenoe has no evidence whatsoever that Stalin et al. invented the concept of the centers or "scripted" anybody's confessions.* We recall that Lenoe writes:

> Whatever the date of the note, by about December 10 Yezhov was outlining connections between the two "centers" in his notebook.

"About December 10" could easily be a day or two later – Lenoe gives no evidence to support the December 10 date. But even by December 10 the investigators had plenty of reason to posit the existence of a Moscow Center connected to the Leningrad Centers.

7. Lenoe cites no evidence whatsoever for the following statement:

> It seems likely that the "Leningrad Center – Moscow Center" framework, with Zinoviev and Kamenev at the head of the whole organization, was decided upon at the December 8 meeting in Stalin's office attended by Yagoda, Agranov, and Yezhov, if not a day or two earlier.

The statement "it seems likely" requires some evidence and reasoning to substantiate it. Lenoe has neither. His claim that Stalin et al. "created" the concept of the two centers is a hypothesis. Like all hypotheses it must be supported by evidence or it falls by itself. There is no need to disprove statements that are not supported by any evidence, and Lenoe has no evidence to support this one.

The testimony cited above shows that it was logical and natural for NKVD investigators to form their own hypothesis of two centers of underground Zinovievite activity. This was confirmed in subsequent interrogations of Zvezdov, Tolmazov (Lenoe 314-316), Kotolynov, and others. We examine Kotolynov's interrogation of December 12 in the chapter on documents that Lenoe ignores.

Why does Lenoe insist that Stalin and his investigators invented the "framework" of the Leningrad – Moscow centers? Perhaps because, in a real sense, the whole mainstream or "anti-Stalin" paradigm of the high politics of the USSR during the 1930s depends upon the assumption that Nikolaev was not a part of a conspiracy but a "lone gunman." Lenoe is aware of this issue, as were Khrushchev and his men, as the following passage shows:

> If the official charges in the first two trials – that former Zinoviev supporters had conspired to murder Kirov – were entirely bogus, then the indictments in all of the succeeding show trials collapsed. … *But if there was some truth to the charge that Zinovievites conspired to kill Kirov, then that preserved the possibility of arguing that the latter charges were also valid, at least in part.* (591-2; emphasis added GF)

According to Lenoe this is why Khrushchev's men, undoubtedly acting under their boss's instructions, invented the notion that Nikolaev was a "lone gunman" who had acted alone and had had no connection with the Zinovievite conspiracy.

Lenoe recognizes that Khrushchev's men had to falsify matters in order to make this claim:

> Therefore Serov and Rudenko … chose to make a clear-cut argument that Nikolaev had had no relationship at all with the ex-Zinoviev supporters convicted in the trial of the "Leningrad Center".
>
> *It appears that Serov or his boss had thought through this strategy, to deny any connection at all between Nikolaev and the Zinovievites, even before the "Secret Speech."* On January 27, 1956 the KGB destroyed central records on the case file "Svoiak", the all-union surveillance operation against the Zinovievites. It seems likely that "Svoiak" contained more evidence than Serov wanted Molotov to see, either of counterrevolutionary talk among former Zinovievites and/or of Nikolaev's connections with the accused in the "Leningrad Center." Serov concealed other evidence of connections between Nikolaev and the ex-Zinovievites Kotolynov, Antonov, and Shatsky. The excerpts from Nikolaev's diaries that he released to the Molotov commission in April 1956 contained no references to these men. But we know from later releases

> of data that Nikolaev did mention all three in his diaries. Serov presumably feared that Molotov would construe such connections as evidence of criminal conspiracy.
>
> At the same time the Molotov commission was debating these issues, Rudenko, Serov, and KPK officials were already taking actions based on the assumption that the charges in the show trials were false... (Lenoe 592; emphasis added GF)

Khrushchev's men destroyed some evidence outright and concealed yet more. They did not undertake any kind of honest investigation of Kirov's murder but instead proceeded "on the assumption that the charges in the show trials were false" (Lenoe 592)

The same issue was further developed in April 1956, when the "Molotov Commission" was set to work by Khrushchev:

> Commission members asked Baranov, the KGB, and the KPK (Shvernik) to answer a series of questions related to the official 1934-1935 version of the crime. These questions boiled down to: Was Nikolaev a Zinovievite? What were his ties to Zinovievite groups? What activities in Leningrad were the Zinovievites up to? *These questions are attributable to the desire of Molotov and his allies to defend at least the 1934-1935 version of the crime as presented at the trials of the Moscow and Leningrad "Center." Nikolaev was a Zinovievite terrorist, and hence his trial, the trials of Kamenev and Zinoviev, and probably also the later show trials of 1937-1938, were justified.* (Lenoe 578; emphasis added GF)

Meanwhile Khrushchev's men were pushing the view that Nikolaev had been a "lone gunman":

> Using investigation records from the NKVD, the prosecutor's office, and the military tribunal, all of these reports explicitly denied the argument that the murder was political or that Nikolaev had connections with actual Zinovievite oppositionists. The trial of Nikolaev and the "Leningrad Center," according to these memoranda, was a fabrication created by the NKVD

> leadership in collaboration with Stalin. Nikolaev was a lone "psychopathic" killer. (579)

As Lenoe correctly points out, Khrushchev realized that the Kirov assassination was the keystone event to the subsequent Moscow Trials. In order to claim that Stalin fabricated the Moscow Trials and what flowed from them, Khrushchev's men had to claim that Nikolaev was not a part of a Zinovievite conspiracy.

We don't know whether today's Russian leaders have destroyed any evidence, as Khrushchev's men did. However, Lenoe frankly admits that today's Russian leaders keep some, perhaps much, of what they do have hidden. (14) A reasonable hypothesis would be that like Khrushchev's men in the 1950s and early 1960s today's Russian leaders must hide evidence so as to preserve some credibility for their theory that Nikolaev was a "lone gunman", that no conspiracy existed, and that all the defendants at the Kirov trials of December 1934 and January 1935, the three Moscow "Show Trials" of 1936-1938, the Tukhachevsky Affair defendants, and all others tried for conspiracy were innocent "victims of Stalin."

Lenoe follows this same construction of events. But there is no evidence to support it. It is reasonable to assume that this is the reason for his omissions and distortions, including the "Shatunovskaia note" and many other undocumented assertions, evasions, and even outright untruths that we examine elsewhere in the present study.

As we shall show, the evidence at our disposal today will not sustain the hypothesis that Nikolaev was a "lone gunman" and the Leningrad and Moscow centers were invented by Stalin and his men. On the contrary: the evidence we have points unequivocally to the opposite conclusion: that Nikolaev killed Kirov as a result of a conspiracy by a clandestine Zinovievite organization of which he was a member.

Chapter 7.

The Bloc of Rights and Trotskyites.

Shortly after the Leon Trotsky Archive at Harvard's Houghton Library was opened in January 1980 Trotskyist historian Pierre Broué discovered letters between Leon Sedov and his father Trotsky that proved the existence of a bloc between Trotskyists and other opposition groups within the USSR. Sometime in the middle of 1932 Sedov informed his father as follows:

> [The bloc] is organized. In it have entered the Zinovievites, the Sten-Lominadze group and the Trotskyists (former "[capitulators]")
>
> . The group of Safar.
> Tarkhkan. has not formally entered yet – they stand on too extreme a position; they will enter in a very short time. – The declaration of Z. and K. concerning their enormous mistake in '27 was made during negotiations with our people concerning the bloc, immediately before the exile of Z and K. –[70]

About the same time American historian Arch Getty was discovering that Trotsky had secretly sent letters to at least Radek, Sokol'nikov, Preobrazhenskii, Kollontai, and Litvinov. The first three had been Trotskyists before publicly recanting their views. Getty did not find the letters – only the certified mail receipts for them. Getty realized this meant that the Trotsky Archive had been "purged". These letters had been removed. Other materials had undoubtedly been purged as well.[71]

---

[70] Harvard, Trotsky Archive 4782 p. 1; see Broué in *Cahiers Léon Trotsky* 1980 p. 36; Broué, "Party Opposition to Stalin…", p. 100.

[71] Other materials were certainly removed – "purged" – with traces of their removal remaining. For example, excerpts from a discussion between Trotsky and Sedov concerning the slogan "remove Stalin" ("ubrat' Stalina") remain in the archive, but the full letters from which these excerpts were made are not there.

The only reason to "purge" the archives would have been to remove materials that would have seemed incriminating – that would have negatively impacted Trotsky's reputation. As an examination of the question of the letter to Radek shows, the letters that we know were removed proved, at the very least, that Trotsky lied during the 1930s by claiming he never maintained contact with oppositionists inside the USSR when, in reality, he was doing so, and by claiming that he would never agree to a secret bloc between his supporters and other oppositionist groups when in fact he had done precisely that.

Evidently Broué found the implications of this fact very disturbing. He never mentioned Getty's discoveries of Trotsky's letters to his supporters and others inside the USSR or the purging of the Trotsky archive, even though Broué cites the same Getty publications (an article and a book) in a very positive manner.[72]

Therefore it had been well established by scholars by the mid-1980s that a Trotskyite-Zinovievite bloc did in fact exist and that it was formed in 1932 and that Zinoviev and Kamenev were personally involved. Sedov also foresaw the entry into the group of Safarov, who in any case had a group of his own.

In an interview with the Dutch social-democratic newspaper *Het Volk* during the second half of January 1937, at the time of the Second Moscow Trial, Sedov stated, in a slip of the tongue, that "the Trotskyists" had been in contact with the defendants at the First Moscow Trial of August 1936.[73] Sedov specifically named Zinoviev, Kamenev and Smirnov. Concerning Radek and Piatakov Sedov went on to say that "[t]he Trotskyists have had much less contact with them than with the others. To be more exact: no contact at all." That is, Sedov tried to withdraw his "slip" about Radek and Piatakov.

But Sedov did not even try to retract the information that preceded it: that "the Trotskyists" had indeed been in contact with "the others": Smirnov, Zinoviev, and Kamenev. This interview, "slip of the tongue"

---

72 We will examine this whole question in detail in a forthcoming work.

73 "Het process te Moskou. Wie niet wil bekennen al doodgeschoten?" *Het Volk* 28 Jan. 1937 pp. 1 and 5. My sincere thanks to Sven-Eric Holmström for tracking down this article and generously providing me with a copy.

included, was published in a provincial edition of *Het Volk* on January 28, 1937. It was noticed by the Communist press, which called attention to Sedov's "slip of the tongue." (*Arbeideren*, Oslo, February 5, 1937; *Abejderbladet*, Copenhagen, February 12, 1937.) Thanks to Getty we now know that the Communist press was correct. Sedov's remark really was a "slip of the tongue." We know that Sedov was lying because Getty had found evidence of Trotsky's letter to Radek. Trotsky had indeed been in touch with Radek. Sedov's first remark, about "much less contact", was accurate.

Therefore we have good, non-Soviet evidence, confirmed by the Trotsky Archive, of the following:

> * A "bloc" of Zinovievites, Trotskyites, and others including at least the Sten-Lominadze and, perhaps, the Safarov-Tarkhanov group (with whom they were in any case in touch) and involving Zinoviev and Kamenev themselves, was indeed formed in 1932.
>
> * Trotsky had indeed been in touch with Zinoviev and Kamenev, as well as others, probably through his son and chief representative Sedov.
>
> * Trotsky was indeed in touch with at least Radek and Piatakov.
>
> * Trotsky really did send a letter to Radek, who was in Geneva at the time, in the Spring of 1932, just as Radek testified in the January 1937 Moscow Trial.
>
> * There is no reason to accept Trotskyist historian Pierre Broué's conclusion that this bloc was "ephemeral" and died out shortly after it was formed, because we know the Trotsky Archive was purged at some time, while Broué had no evidence to support his statement.

Soviet Rehabilitation Reports

The proven existence of this bloc provides additional evidence that Soviet "Rehabilitation" reports of both the Khrushchev and Gorbachev eras are dishonest and untrustworthy, politically-motivated "whitewash" or "coverup" jobs, rather than honest reviews of the cases and determinations of innocence on the basis of evidence.

The "Shvernik Report", commissioned by Khrushchev in 1962 and finished in 1964, concluded that all the accusations against the accused at the Bukharin Trial were falsified and denied the existence of a "bloc of Rights and Trotskyites" itself. (RKEB 2, 625-30)

> No "Anti-Soviet Bloc of Rights and Trotskyites" existed in reality and those convicted in this case did not engage in counterrevolutionary activity. (630)

In 1989 the Gorbachev-era "Rehabilitation Commission" of the Central Committee of the CPSU came to the same conclusion:

> It has therefore been established that after 1927 the former Trotskyites and Zinovievites did not carry out organized struggle with the Party, that they did not unite with one another either on a terrorist or on any other basis, and that the case of the "United Trotskyist-Zinovievist Center" was artificially invented by the organs of the NKVD at the direct order and with the direct participation of J.V. Stalin. (Izvestia TsK KPSS No. 8, 1989, p. 94)
>
> It has been established that the accusations against those convicted of criminal contact with L.D. Trotsky and L. Sedov are without foundation. This has also been proven by a special verification process carried out by the Procurator's Office of the USR in 1988. (Izvestia TsK KPSS 9, 1989, p. 49)
>
> As has been now established beyond doubt, the case of the so-called "Anti-Soviet Bloc of Rights and Trotskyites" was totally falsified, and the trial itself staged by J.V. Stalin and his circle. (Izvestia TsK KPSS 5, 1989, p. 81)
>
> Not a single reliable fact of the carrying-out by the former participants of the "Zinovievite" opposition after 1928 of any kind of organized activity or organized declaration that could testify to the existence of an organization or the presence of hidden underground activity. (Reabilitatsiia. Politicheskie Protsessy 30-kh- 50-kh godov. P. 166)

> In reality, neither "blocs" nor so-called "centers" existed. (RKEB 3, 342)

Aleksandr Iakovlev, Gorbachev's expert who led the anticommunist campaign from the Politburo, repeated the falsehood that no bloc had existed.

> Iagoda was artificially included among the membership of the non-existent "Right-Trotskyite" bloc. (RKEB 3, 328)

Gorbachev's commission and Iakovlev wrote long after Getty's and Broué's discoveries in the Harvard Trotsky archive had been published. In fact we know that this material became known to the Gorbachev investigators and to Iakovlev because Getty's 1986 article was published in the prestigious Party journal *Voprosy Istorii KPSS* in its May 1991 issue. Although it is possible that they did not learn of Getty's article until after 1990, when they exchanged letters on the Kirov murder, they certainly never had any evidence to support their statements that the "bloc" had never existed.[74]

Evidently, Broué's and then Getty's revelations that the bloc of Zinovievites, Trotskyites and others really did exist incited consternation within Soviet Party historical circles. The 1991 Russian publication of Getty's article is accompanied by an afterword by Boris Starkov, writing on behalf of the editors of the Party journal. Starkov's commentary clearly shows that the discoveries in the Harvard Trotsky Archive were the cause of serious concern for the official Gorbachev-era view of the Stalin years. Starkov seriously distorts what Getty wrote. He mistakenly attributes to Getty the discovery that the bloc of Trotskyites, Zinovievites, and other oppositionists did exist. He attempts to cast doubt upon it and to argue that, in any case, it could not have posed any threat to Stalin. Starkov's note contains no evidence to support his contention. Moreover, he ignores altogether Getty's own discoveries: that Trotsky had indeed been in secret contact with his supporters, such as Radek, exactly as Radek testified at the January 1937 Moscow Trial, and that the Harvard Trotsky Archive had been purged. Gorbachev's commission and

---

[74] The Shvernik Commission had also concluded that no bloc existed. See RKEB 2, p. 630.

Iakovlev simply ignore this whole issue, declaring that no such bloc existed. This is further evidence that both the Shvernik Report and the Soviet Rehabilitation Reports are falsified.[75]

The Harvard Trotsky archive yielded to Broué and Getty unmistakable evidence that the "bloc" did exist; that Trotsky was in contact with the bloc's members and his own supporters inside the USSR, and that Trotsky lied consistently about all these matters both in the *Bulletin of the Opposition* and to the Dewey Commission. No scholar today denies this. Kirilina, Lenoe, and Egge simply ignore the whole matter.

The NKVD of the 1930s termed the complexly-interlocking set of oppositional conspiracies the "klubok", or "tangle." If any of these conspiracies were acknowledged to have existed, it would be hard to deny the existence of the rest, since all the defendants implicated others in a chain that, directly or indirectly, connected them all. Admitting that the bloc of Trotskyites and Zinovievites did in fact exist would present the danger of a "slippery slope" to any historian who wanted to deny the validity of the other conspiracies. For once it is conceded that the first alleged underground opposition conspiracy really did exist, and therefore that both the Khrushchev and Gorbachev official reports, rehabilitations, and official historians were lying, it logically follows that other conspiracies, which these same sources also denied, might have existed too.

Lenoe's Error

The existence of underground organizations of Zinovievites, of Trotskyites, and of other oppositional groupings such as Safarov-Tarkhanov and Sten-Lominadze, as well as the existence of a formal "Zinovievite-Trotskyite bloc"[76] was firmly established long before Kirilina's and Lenoe's books were written. Either they were unaccountably ignorant of this fact, or they did know of it but concealed the fact from their readers.

---

[75] Parts of the "Rehabilitation" report on the Moscow Trial of August 1936 are copied verbatim, or almost so, from the Shvernik Commission of twenty-five years earlier. No one could know this in 1988, since excerpts from the text of the Shvernik Report was not published until 1993-4 and the full text until 2003. The fact of the copying does suggest that it's possible, even likely, that no new study was carried out in 1987-88.

[76] Broué conceded that Sedov and Trotsky used the term "bloc" in their correspondence with each other in 1932.

In any case, the existence of the bloc is of capital importance to any understanding of the Kirov assassination and fatal for his case that all the defendants were "framed."

Nor does Lenoe seem to be aware that their denial that the Zinovievite-Trotskyite bloc existed proves that the Shvernik Report of 1963-64, the Gorbachev-era "Rehabilitation" reports, and the "Reply to Iakovlev" document on which he relies so heavily in his book, are not honest attempts to discover the truth. On the contrary, Lenoe vouches for the honesty of the Shvernik Report:

> Although official discussion of the Kirov murder in 1963-1964 was muted, the ongoing investigation appears to have been impartial. ...there was no need to doctor conclusions. (639)

We will pass over the fact that many other parts of the Shvernik Report give evidence of dishonesty as well. This single falsehood about the bloc is obviously, blatantly incorrect – a dishonest coverup, one Lenoe either is ignorant of or deliberately remains silent about.

Lenoe reproduces the texts of letters by Zinoviev and Safarov in which they vigorously deny any oppositional activity (326-327). Zinoviev claims that he has been loyal to the Party "from the moment that I returned from Kustanaya".[77] (326) Safarov says that he "honorably and frankly broke with counter-revolutionary Trotskyism." (327)

Thanks to the Trotsky archive we know that Zinoviev and Safarov were lying. Zinoviev says he has been loyal since his return from exile, which was sometime in 1933. Safarov gives no specific time that his "break with counter-revolutionary Trotskyism" took place. We know that Safarov had been reinstated in the Party in November 1928 and served in an important position in the Comintern until his arrest in December 1934 in connection with the Kirov murder. After returning from exile Zinoviev was placed on the editorial board of *Bol'shevik*, the Party's leading political journal. They and other oppositionists were not only reinstated in Party membership but were given privileged positions – something that could never have happened without Stalin's approval and, most likely, happened at his initiative. This very lenient treatment of those who had

[77] This should be "Kustanai", the town in Kazakhstan to which Zinoviev had been exiled for a year. Apparently Lenoe does not realize "Kustanaya" is the genitive case.

strongly opposed him but who had subsequently vowed loyalty to the Party and its line shows that, far from "holding grudges" as Lenoe claims, it was Stalin who was the "moderate" in the Party leadership.

Zinoviev and Safarov could not possibly have meant, in these letters:

> "Yes, we were involved in leading secret counter-revolutionary organizations, in a bloc with Trotsky and the Trotskyites (Zinoviev) or very close to such a bloc (Safarov) – but not since 1932!"

If they had recanted since 1932 we would know about it. For one thing, it would be impossible for Khrushchev and the rest to deny the existence of the Trotskyite-Zinovievite bloc, as they would have had to expose it. We know this didn't happen thanks to Sedov and Trotsky, who record nothing of the kind. Therefore they did not recant their 1932 membership in a bloc with Trotsky, as they were obliged to do so as Party members. Furthermore, there is no way Zinoviev and Safarov would have had important posts in 1934 if they had confessed in 1932 to being in a secret anti-Soviet bloc with Trotsky.

Therefore, Zinoviev and Safarov were lying in these letters. This is an elementary deduction from what we know from the important discoveries by Getty and Broué in Trotsky Archives.

But we learn not only that Zinoviev and Safarov were lying here. By the same token we also learn that those who named them as part of the clandestine Trotskyite-Zinovievite bloc were telling the truth. A number of the defendants in the Kirov case named Zinoviev and/or Safarov. Consider the following document, omitted by Lenoe. It is a notice from the Prosecutor's office published on January 16, 1935:

> In the course of an investigation of the case of I.P. Bakaev, A.M. Gertik, A.S. Kuklin and others, brought to justice in connection with the disclosure in the city of Leningrad of an underground counterrevolutionary group that planned and carried out the murder of com. S.M. Kirov, there have been obtained facts related to underground counterrevolutionary activity by G.E. Zinoviev, E.E. Evdokimov, L.B. Kamenev, and G.F. Fedorov, whose cases have been preliminarily referred to the review of the Special Commission of the NKVD.

> In view of these facts and, in part, of confessions by I.P. Bakaev which disclose the participation of G.E. Zinoviev, E.G. Evdokimov, L.B. Kamenev, and G.F. Fedorov in the underground organization "Moscow center", and of G.I. Safarov, who has informed the investigation of a series of facts concerning the underground counterrevolutionary activity of the persons named above right up to the present time, the case concerning the accusation of G.E. Zinoviev, E.G. Evdokimov, L.B. Kamenev and G.F. Fedorov has been handed over for review to the Military Collegium of the Supreme Court of the USSR. (R-PP 156)

Lenoe tries to explain away Safarov's note in this manner:

> There is good evidence that Safarov, who had called Zinoviev "a dirty rag" in 1930, was informing on the latter as part of proving his loyalty to the party. (334)

Yet, somehow, Lenoe fails to cite any of this "good evidence." This makes us suspect that this remark is a bluff – that Lenoe does not in fact have any such evidence, "good" or otherwise. But of course Safarov was trying to "prove his loyalty to the party"– that is, he was *claiming* to be loyal. His motive is not the question. The question is, rather, whether he was telling the truth in the note of December 16, 1934 that Lenoe quotes (327), or whether he was telling the truth in the confession referred to in the note. Sedov's letter proves that Safarov was indeed telling the truth – though probably not the whole truth – in the statements referred to in the Prosecutor's note of January 16, 1935. Safarov had been discussing the entry of his and Tarkhanov's group into the Trotskyite-Zinovievite bloc in 1932, so he knew it existed.

Thanks to the Trotsky Archive we know that Safarov was lying in his letter to Stalin of December 16. He had not, as he claimed in that letter, "honorably and frankly broke[n] with counterrevolutionary Trotskyism." (327) But when he gave information about the underground Zinovievite-Trotskyite group, as outlined in the Prosecutor's note of January 16, he was telling the truth – at least with respect to Zinoviev and Kamenev.

Sedov's letter also confirms the accuracy of Tsar'kov's confession of December 12, 1934, in which Tsar'kov names Zinoviev and Kamenev as the leaders of the underground organization. Gorshenin's confession of De-

December 21, 1934 is also confirmed. He identified Zinoviev, Kamenev, Evdokimov, Bakaev, Kuklin, Fedorov and others, and said that the organization was active "up to the present."

Tolmazov confessed to belonging to the "counterrevolutionary" "Trotsky-Zinoviev bloc." (Lenoe 314-5). Moreover, Tolmazov says that during the 1920s Nikolaev "attached himself to the Trotsky-Zinoviev bloc". He also said that in 1930 Safarov "cursed Zinoviev as a 'dirty rag' in the sharpest tones." (314). This corresponds to what we know from Sedov's letter, in which he says that Safarov and Tarkhanov are "extreme" and will join the bloc in future but have not done so yet.

Kotolynov also confirmed the existence of the "Trotsky-Zinoviev bloc" and named many familiar names (Lenoe 324-5). On December 18 Kotolynov again confirmed that he was a member of the "counterrevolutionary Zinoviev-Trotskyite organization." (335)

Lenoe's ignorance, whether real or feigned, of the proven existence of the Trotskyite-Zinovievite bloc leads him far astray from the truth. He states:

> The interrogators had finally forged (in both senses of the verb) a link between the ex-Zinovievites in the USSR and Trotsky abroad. (342)

Elsewhere Lenoe writes "Zinovievites (supposedly allied with the Trotskyites)" (380) and refers to the "supposed 'Right-Trotskyite Bloc'" (482). He notes without comment Iakovlev's 1990 reference to "the nonexistent "Right-Trotskyite Bloc." (659) This, of course, is all wrong.

To sum up: it is hard to believe that, somehow, Lenoe never learned of the existence of the Trotskyite-Zinovievite bloc. Lenoe thanks Arch Getty for his help – and Getty, along with Broué, was the scholar who discovered the evidence of this bloc in the Harvard Trotsky Archive, and whose article was republished in the Soviet Party journal in 1991. If he was not ignorant of the existence of this bloc then Lenoe deliberately concealed it from his readers. The existence of the bloc; Getty's discovery that the Trotsky Archive had been purged; Broué's discoveries of various lies that Trotsky and Sedov made in publication and to the Dewey Commission hearings about their contacts with the clandestine opposition inside the USSR – all these constitute strong evidence *against*

Lenoe's hypothesis that Nikolaev was a "lone gunman" unconnected with any organized terrorist opposition group in Leningrad.

Chapter 8.

Nikolaev's First Confession.

Lenoe reproduces a text (in English translation) of Nikolaev's first interrogation dated December 1, 1934 (256-259). This document constitutes the *only* primary-source evidence for the "lone assassin" theory. It is essential to Lenoe's case. A few days after making it Nikolaev had contradicted it and thereafter consistently discussed his act as part of a conspiracy.

One would expect that Lenoe would examine this confession of Nikolaev's carefully. But he fails to do so. It is tempting to form a hypothesis to account for this failure on Lenoe's part. An analysis of the text of Nikolaev's first confession shows that we cannot accept this document, so vital for Lenoe's thesis, as genuine.

Lenoe uses, praises, and cites Kirilina's account. But he fails to inform his readers that Kirilina also reproduces a text (in Russian) of Nikolaev's first confession – and Kirilina's text is significantly different from Lenoe's. We will study these differences here.

Petukhov and Khomchik

But first we must consider a remark in a 1990 article by the Chairman of the Military Collegium of the Supreme Court of the USSR and his aide. In this article, cited by Kirilina, Lenoe, and Egge, we read the following:

> At his first interrogation on December 1 Nikolaev did not in essence give any testimony. The employees of the Leningrad UNKVD only filled out the facts on their forms. Thereafter he refused to sign the transcripts and in one case even tried to rip up the transcript.
>
> Isakov, former employee of the UNKVD who was present at these interrogations on December 1 and 2, stated in his explanations of March 15, 1961 that Nikolaev was "in some kind of state of prostration", looked like "some kind of completely alien person…

> This was not a thinking human being, but a sack of bones and muscles, without any reason… For a very long time Nikolaev completely refused to answer anything at all. In my opinion, at that time he could not think of anything … He only wept… According to his words, he had suffered enough from life troubles due to the lack of attention to him by the City Committee of the Party and personally by S.M. Kirov. Nikolaev …acted like a person in a seriously depressed condition or affect. He literally fell into hysterics every five minutes, after which a kind of stupor set in and he sat without speaking, staring at one point somewhere."[78]

We must assume that Petukhov and Khomchik had access to all the primary sources, including Nikolaev's interrogations. Here they state unequivocally that *Nikolaev did not say anything coherent at all at the first interrogation of December 1, 1934.*

Kirilina (250) also quotes the testimony of former NKVD man Fomin, which Lenoe (173) translates:

> The assistant chief of the Directorate Fedr Timofeevich Fomin afterwards described Nikolaev's behavior during the first hours after his arrest in this way: "[F]or a long time after coming to consciousness the murderer screamed, babbled, and only towards the morning began to speak and shout 'my shot rang out around the world.'"

Kirilina found Fomin's testimony in a Khrushchev-era report by Petr Pospelov, who had continued the quotation from Fomin a little further:

> I told him that he would not have anything in return for this shot except curses from the people. To the repeated questions asked by myself and by assistant chief of the Special Division Ianishevskii, "Who prompted you, Nikolaev, to carry out this shooting?" he fell into hysterics and began to shout, but did not

---

[78] N. Petukhov, V. Khomchik. "Delo o Leningradskom Tsentre" ["The Case of the Leningrad Center"]. *Vestnik Verkhovnogo Suda SSSR* 5 (1991), p. 18.

> give any answer of any kind." (Statement of com. Fomin of March 26, 1956).[79]

In an earlier article prior to writing the first edition of her book Kirilina stated that there were two medical reports on Nikolaev dated December 1, 1934, both of which attest to the fact that the suspect was incoherent.

> In Nikolaev's investigative case file there are two documents of medical observation dated December 1. One was from two hours after his arrest. It says: "Nikolaev does not answer questions; at times he moans and screams, he shows no signs of poisoning, there are signs of a general nervous excitement."[80]

Lenoe cites Isakov's testimony (173) and the article by Petukhov and Khomchik (n. 37, pp. 764-5;)., as does Kirilina (250-1). But this only compounds the problems. We'll consider them one at a time:

> * Kirilina and Lenoe both claim that Isakov was present at the December 2 interrogations of Nikolaev, citing Petukhov and Khomchik. But Petukhov and Khomchik state that Isakov was present at the interrogations of *both* December 1 *and* December 2.

Lenoe also states "Fomin's and Isakov's signatures are both on December 1 and December 2 interrogations of Nikolaev." (n. 37 p. 764). He does reproduce a December 2 interrogation signed by Fomin, Ianishevskii (named by Fomin), and Isakov (260-261). But Isakov's signature is not on either Kirilina's or Lenoe's "December 1 interrogation", while Fomin's is on Lenoe's but not on Kirilina's.

In her 1993 article cited above Kirilina stated:

> At the interrogations of December 1, 2 and 3 Nikolaev in fact did not answer one single question posed to him by the investigators. Only his personal data were written on the forms along with his statement, repeated many

---

[79] «Zapiska P.N. Pospelova ob ubiystve Kirova" (P.N. Pospelov's note about the murder of Kirov). *Svobodnaia Mysl'* 1992, No. 8, p. 68.

[80] Kirilina, A. "Sledstvennoe Delo Leonida Nikolaeva." *S.Peterburgskie Vedomosti*. December 4, 1993.

> times, "I have accomplished an act of individual terror of personal revenge." He refused to sign the transcripts.

This wording is so similar to that of Petukhov and Khomchik that Kirilina may have copied it directly from them.

So we are immediately confronted by problems with any purported confession by Nikolaev of December 1, 1934:

* Neither Kirilina nor Lenoe mention the fact that Petukhov and Khomchik deny that Nikolaev gave any coherent confession at all at his first interrogation. The statements by Isakov and Fomin too are consistent with this conclusion. They leave no doubt that Nikolaev made no confession on December 1.

* Lenoe is embarrassed by the discrepancy in the dates. He tries to resolve this problem by saying "it seems that NKVD officers were unable to conduct a real interrogation of Nikolaev until around midnight of December 1-2 or even later." (173) However, the "first interrogation" Lenoe reproduces is dated December 1. Why would the NKVD men give a false date?

* Lenoe has already conceded that there can scarcely have been a single interrogation of Nikolaev of December 1. He was forced to assume that the interrogation dated December 1 that he reproduces must be of "around midnight of December 1-2 or even later."

But if there can scarcely be a single interrogation of December 1, it follows that there surely cannot be *more* than one. So, where is the interrogation of December 1 with Isakov's signature to which Lenoe refers?

Two Different Texts of "Nikolaev's Interrogation of December 1"

We have seen that there are serious problems with accepting as genuine *any* version of a Nikolaev interrogation dated December 1. But there's more. Kirilina and Lenoe reproduce *different* texts, *both* purporting to be that of Nikolaev's interrogation of the same date, December 1.

Kirilina's text is the shorter one. For the most part it appears to be closely similar to the first part of Lenoe's text ("appears" because we only have the English translation of Lenoe's version of this confession). But there are several significant differences:

* In Kirilina's text Nikolaev refers to letters to Kirov and Stalin, while this reference is unaccountably absent from Lenoe's letter.

* Kirilina's text begins by identifying the two NKVD officers conducting the interrogation: Lobov and Medved'. No such lines exist at the beginning of Lenoe's text.

* Kirilina's text ends with Lobov's signature. Medved's signature is lacking. At the end of Lenoe's text there are five signatures: Medved', Fomin, Molochnikov, Yanishevsky, and Stromin. Lobov's name is absent entirely.

* Neither Kirilina's nor Lenoe's text bears Isakov's signature.

* Kirilina's text ends with Nikolaev's signature. But Lenoe's text informs us that Nikolaev refused to sign the transcript and tried to rip it up.

* Lenoe's text is also significantly longer than Kirilina's. It is as though Kirilina's text, minus the five words about Nikolaev's letters to Stalin and Kirov present in Kirilina's text but absent from Lenoe's, has been expanded by the addition of an extra part at the end.

Here we will examine this additional section in Lenoe's text.

* After the end of the text common to both Kirilina and Lenoe, the first sentences of Lenoe's text read as follows:

Question: Your brother Pyotr knew of this plan.

Answer: If he knew of this, he would have handed me over [to the police] instantly.

It seems highly unlikely that already on December 1, within a few hours of Kirov's murder (which took place at 4:30 p.m.) the NKVD would have been able to locate, arrest, and interrogate Nikolaev's brother about Nikolaev's written plan. Neither Kirilina nor Lenoe mention any interrogation of Piotr Nikolaev before December 3. Therefore, these lines are incompatible with any interrogation of Nikolaev of December 1 (or, as Lenoe would have it, December 1-2).

* The passage immediately following this one concerns a possible connection with Germany:

> **Question**: In your appointment book there is the address and telephone number of the German consulate in Leningrad, written in your hand. Who gave you this address and telephone number?
>
> **Answer**: The address and telephone number of the German consulate in Leningrad I copied from the 1933 telephone book.
>
> **Question**: With what purpose?
>
> **Answer**: I made that notation on purpose in order to show the party afterwards that I allegedly [sic] suffered much and in order to take the easiest route to exposure and signaling [of the wrongs done me]. I was obsessed with the idea of drawing down on myself suspicion of contacts with foreigners, and so that due to that [sic] I'd be arrested and then I would have the chance to expose all the outrages I knew about.

This alleged statement by Nikolaev appears very confused and raises a number of puzzling points.

* The interrogators had just begun to ask Nikolaev about the assassination plan they had found on his person. But after asking only one question about it they drop the matter and move on. Then the interrogators told Nikolaev that his brother Piotr knew about the plan. Nikolaev denied this, and again the interrogators just dropped the whole matter.

This is simply not the way interrogators act. They could scarcely have contented themselves with a single simple answer to questions about the assassination, let alone about the possible existence of a conspiracy.

* Nikolaev's answer about the German consulate information in his address book makes no sense at all. Visiting the German consulate *might* have drawn suspicion on him, as Nikolaev supposedly claimed he wanted to do – although we later discover that he really had visited the Latvian consulate and no one had noticed.

But it is absurd to say that copying an address into his phone book would "draw down suspicion". Who would even know it was there? Moreover, Nikolaev had clearly tried to kill himself seconds after killing Kirov, so he could not have "had the chance to expose all the outrages." However, it would indeed have had the effect of drawing the NKVD investigators onto a false scent – looking for a German connection to the assassination – if Nikolaev had in fact killed himself, as he had attempted to do. That is, it is consistent with other evidence that Nikolaev had deliberately falsified in advance some of his written materials.

> * Nikolaev was now under arrest – for murdering Kirov. Yet in none of the interrogations reproduced by Kirilina or Lenoe does he "expose all the outrages". Though he claims he committed murder to draw attention to injustices against him, he does not give any harangues about those supposed injustices, or even any details. With the attention of the whole NKVD and Party on him, here is all he says:
>
> > ...my estrangement from the party, from which I was alienated by the events at the Leningrad Institute of Party History, second my unemployment and the absence of material and most importantly moral aid from party organizations
> >
> > ....over the last eight to ten years of my life's road and work there has accumulated a backlog of unfair attitudes on the part of specific government persons towards a living human being. For a time I bore all of this as long as I was involved in directly useful civic work, but when I ended up discredited and alienated from the party, then I decided to signal all of this before the party.
> >
> > I saw and still see that attack as a political act. With this murder I wanted to get the party to pay attention to a living human being and to the heartless bureaucratic attitude towards him. (Lenoe 257-258)

All these complaints are vague and extremely general. There is not a single specific example of a supposed injustice among them. Yet Nikolaev has just testified that it was to expose specific examples of unjust treatment towards himself that he has murdered Kirov. In failing to "expose" any "outrages" Nikolaev's statements strongly suggest that he was not prepared with any list of such "outrages," and therefore that "exposing outrages" was not his motive at all.

* With all the Soviet fears of German Nazism, how likely is it that the NKVD interrogators would have stopped asking about this German connection after two short, introductory questions?

* One final point: in justifying his act of murder Nikolaev first states:

> I request that you note down that I am not an enemy of the working class and that if my recent hard experiences at the Institute had not occurred I would have borne all of the difficulties I have suffered and would not have gone so far as attempting the assassination.

But after one brief riposte by the interrogator Nikolaev both reverses and contradicts himself. He reverses himself in that he first denied being "an enemy of the working class", and then changed his mind:

> Yes, I have to admit that I really did act morally as an enemy of the working class by making my attempt on Comrade Kirov's life …

His self-contradiction about his motive is even more striking:

> …but I did so under the influence of psychological distress and the deep impression made on me by events at the Institute, which placed me in an impossible situation. (Lenoe 258)

At first he continues with his explanation of the murder as a kind of protest against "recent hard experiences at the Institute" and "difficulties", reminding us of his claim to wish to "expose all of the outrages I knew about." But then he says he acted "under the influence of psychological distress…" These latter words make the murder appear not as an act of conscious political protest, as he had insisted up to this point, but rather reduces it to the act of a psychologically disturbed person. These remarks *depoliticize* his act of murder.

Conclusions

From the preceding analysis we can draw several conclusions that are important for our evaluation of Lenoe's book and for our further inquiry into Kirov's assassination.

> * Lenoe had to be aware of these issues. But he does not point them out to his readers, much less analyze what they might mean. This glaring omission does suggest, however, that Lenoe is aware of the difficulties for his preconceived "lone gunman" thesis that the problems around this "first interrogation" create.
>
> * Thanks to Petukhov and Khomchik we can be reasonably sure that there never was any December 1 interrogation of Nikolaev. Nikolaev was incoherent. The NKVD men noted his personal details – although we apparently do not have that document – and nothing else.
>
> * But if that is the case, then both Kirilina's and Lenoe's texts are fakes, or contain falsified parts such as the date as well as more substantive falsifications.

We cannot exclude the possibility that they were created by Khrushchev's men in 1956 when, as Lenoe informs us, Khrushchev was trying to suppress any evidence that Nikolaev may have really been acting as a part of a conspiracy, and therefore trying to provide evidence that he had been a "lone gunman." If he had not been a "lone gunman", evidence would have to be created. The fake December 1 interrogations would fit that need.

But we think it more likely that these fake interrogations were created at the time, in December 1934. As we shall see later in our examination of Genrikh Iagoda's pretrial confessions Iagoda testified that he had only reluctantly agreed not to stand in the way of an attack against Kirov. Iagoda's disapproval of the assassination suggests that he might have tried to make Nikolaev's act appear like that of one individual in order to draw attention away from the conspiracy. At least Iagoda would have tried to mislead the investigation. Medved' had the direct responsibility for Kirov's security and would bear the consequences of its failure. But according to Iagoda Medved' was not initiated into the conspiracy. It would not have made any difference to Medved' whether Kirov were killed by a conspiracy or by a lone gunman.

Enukidze's Story

Thanks to a document published by Lenoe we know that Avel' Enukidze did his best to support a "lone gunman" theory virtually from the day Kirov was killed. Enukidze spread the story that Kirov was having an affair with Nikolaev's wife Mil'da Draule. Defendants in the "Kremlin Affair" of 1935 spread the same rumor. It seems likely that they got it from Enukidze. There has never been any evidence to support this rumor. Nikolaev never mentions it, or any personal animosity towards Kirov, even in his voluminous diaries. Lenoe gives good evidence on this point (691; 807 n.5)

Why would Enukidze spread this obviously false story? Lenoe thinks he did so out of "resistance" to the glorification of Stalin and to "parroting" "Stalin's" line about "class enemies." But that does not account for this specific false story, which is entirely groundless. It would be understandable, perhaps, if it originated from people who were utterly in the dark about events. But as a very high-ranking Party member and government official, Enukidze would certainly have been privy to what was going on.

Moreover, Enukidze could not possibly have known that Kirov's murder was *not* an expression of hostility to the Bolsheviks – unless, as he later confessed, he knew about the conspiracy to assassinate Kirov beforehand. *Not* to express the view that, at the very least, the assassination *might* have been the result of political opposition would be considered very suspicious, would attract unfavorable attention to him – as, in fact, it did. Why would Enukidze risk doing this – unless he had a powerful motive to do it?

Iagoda's confessions suggest an answer. Enukidze had the same motive that Iagoda had to try to deflect evidence away from any conspiracy. Enukidze and Iagoda were involved in a conspiracy of their own and therefore did not want Stalin and the NKVD to be sharply on the lookout for conspiracies. Only two 1937 interrogations of Enukidze's have been made public so far.[81] They confirm his involvement in the Rightist conspiracy. Although Enukidze does not mention the Kirov assassination in

---

[81] Lubianka 1937-1938, No. 60 pp. 144ff; Genrikh Iagoda No. 166 pp. 508-517. Between 4 and 5 pages of this latter confession have been omitted from this transcript. No reason is given for their omission (p. 517).

these two confessions he must have done so in others. Iagoda did discuss the Kirov assassination in pretrial interrogations and implicated Enukidze. NKVD interrogators would therefore certainly have interrogated Enukidze very thoroughly about the Kirov assassination too.

This alleged "December 1 interrogation" is the only one in which Nikolaev insists he killed Kirov on his own initiative alone.

> * Kirilina (216) reproduces one sentence which she states is from a December 2 interrogation of Nikolaev. Lenoe (260-1) reproduces a longer passage from a December 2 interrogation that does not contain that sentence. Nikolaev is not asked whether he acted alone or not and does not say.
>
> * We have one interrogation of Nikolaev from December 3. Kirilina (215-6 and 408-9) says she reproduces it in full. Evidently this is true, since it conforms to Lenoe's three partial quotations from it (157; 167; 249-50). Nikolaev makes no statement about whether or not he is a lone gunman.
>
> * We have one interrogation of Nikolaev of December 4. Kirilina tells us (277) that he had "new investigators". Evidently by December 4 Medved's men of the Leningrad UNKVD were under suspicion and had now been replaced by Ezhov's men. In the part transcribed by Lenoe (281-2) Nikolaev now states that his ties to Trotskyists "influenced his decision to kill Comrade Kirov", and he names Shatskii, Kotolynov, Bardin, and Sokolov. This agrees with Kirilina's brief citation (277) of this same interrogation.

This confession obviously encouraged the interrogators. Lenoe (285) says that Nikolaev was interrogated five times on December 5. Agranov's letter to Stalin of December 5, translated in Lenoe (285-287) reveals that Nikolaev had begun to implicate others among the Trotskyite-Zinovievite bloc. The Russian text has been available for a decade in Vasili Soima's *Zapreshchennyi Stalin* ("The Prohibited Stalin").

Kirilina (281) says "after December 4" – Nikolaev confessed that

> "He was a member of an underground counterrevolutionary organization", "its members stood on the platform of the Trotskyite-Zinovievite bloc", "the former Opposition had their own special accounts to

> settle with Kirov in connection with the struggle he had organized against the Leningrad oppositionists."

This document may well be the very first time anyone had disclosed to the NKVD that the bloc of Zinovievites and Trotskyites existed! (We know there was such a bloc from Sedov's and Trotsky's letters in the Harvard Trotsky Archive.) But Kirilina does not tell us how long "after December 4" Nikolaev made these statements, or why she does not seem to know. Was she able to see the actual transcript? Or is she copying from some copy of something or other that was given to her? Kirilina very often does this – withholds from her readers information vital to assess the evidence she presents. Lenoe does the same thing.

> * On December 6 for the first time Nikolaev specifically implicates Shatskii and Kotolynov as participants in the "terrorist act." (Kirilina 277) According to Lenoe (288) Nikolaev said that Kotolynov was planning to try to murder Stalin. From this point on Nikolaev and the other suspects elaborate the details of the conspiracy.

The only interrogation Kirilina or Lenoe know about in which Nikolaev explicitly claims he was a "lone gunman" and explicitly rejects the idea of a conspiracy in Kirov's murder is that of December 1. As we have shown, that interrogation is more than problematic. We do not have one text but at least two. Therefore "it" – really, "they" – cannot be genuine as they exist now. It appears as though an original confession of an early date, but not of December 1, has been seriously tampered with. Since neither can be genuine as it stands, we cannot accept either of them as evidence of anything without grave reservations.

This does not mean that Nikolaev never claimed that he was a "lone gunman". On the contrary: we can be certain that he did make this claim, since he explicitly retracts it later on. In the "Indictment" of Nikolaev and the rest, a document we will study later, we read the following statement:

> In confessions of December 13 of this year L. Nikolaev directly states:
>
> "... I was supposed to describe the murder of Kirov as an individual act in order to conceal the participation in it of the Zinovievite group." (p. 19)

This statement directly contradicts Lenoe's "lone gunman" thesis. Lenoe omits it from his lengthy excerpts from the "Indictment".

In any case we would expect Nikolaev to make an early statement of this kind. Nikolaev was caught red-handed. He could not possibly deny that he murdered Kirov. What he could deny was his participation in a conspiracy. Indeed, if he really were part of a conspiracy we would expect him to deny it. The first rule of a conspiratorial organization is not to tell the authorities about the other members so that the conspiracy may continue.

What the problematic nature of Nikolaev's "first confession" means for our inquiry is this:

* We have no reliable text of the claim Nikolaev made.

* This "first confession" has been tampered with for some reason.

Nikolaev had not planned to escape after killing Kirov. He had planned to commit suicide on the spot and almost succeeded in doing so. His ties with the Zinovievite and Trotskyite oppositionists with whom he was later to be tried and executed would, no doubt, have been discovered by the NKVD when they seized his diaries. But evidently those writings do not explicitly discuss any conspiracy. Had Nikolaev succeeded in killing himself the Leningrad Zinovievites who ultimately stood trial with him would surely have been interrogated. But there would have been no evidence to implicate them. Without something else in writing either on his person or at his home to explain the reason for his action, his diaries would have been the only thing available. In them Nikolaev does discuss his dissatisfaction in terms of his personal situation, though in a vague and general way.

According to his wife Mil'da Draule Nikolaev had researched prominent political assassins of the past like Andrei I. Zheliabov, one of the organizers of the assassination of Tsar Alexander II in 1881. (Lenoe 236; 769 n. 24). Genrikh Liushkov – not a reliable witness but one who was involved in the investigation – confirms this in a general way, although Liushkov might have simply learned about this from Draule. Zheliabov was one of probably eight members of the Narodnaia Volia who plotted the Tsar's assassination and one of five who was executed for it. Therefore, *if Nikolaev did research Zheliabov it would suggest that Nikolaev was more interested in assassins who were indeed part of an underground conspiratorial organization than in those who acted alone or from personal as opposed to political motives.*

We can conclude that Nikolaev did indeed wish to appear to the world as a "lone gunman" acting from personal motives. This would be logical whether he really acted on his own or was part of a conspiracy. A lone gunman would have no motive to name anyone else, and a conspirator would want to defend his co-conspirators. Of course NKVD investigators would have been aware of this too. Therefore, even if we did have evidence that Nikolaev claimed for a time that he was a "lone gunman" no investigator would have simply accepted this as the truth. Lenoe and Kirilina should not have done so either, if they had really been interested in an objective investigation of this murder.

Assuming for the sake of argument that Nikolaev was part of a conspiracy, what would have been the best scenario for that conspiracy? Best of all would be an assassination in which the perpetrators escaped unrecognized. That would best demonstrate the power of the conspiracy – its intelligence and reach, the depth of its support. Arguably, the next best would be a suicide assassination such as that Nikolaev planned. Therefore neither an assassination and successful suicide, nor an assassination and initial insistence by the assassin that he was acting alone, would be convincing evidence either of a "lone gunman" or of a conspiracy. NKVD investigators would have understood that too.

We can infer that Nikolaev did not implicate the oppositionists Kotolynov, Shatskii et al. before December 4, since that seems to be the first time their names are mentioned. Nikolaev mentions Kotolynov and others in his diaries. Once Nikolaev's diaries had been studied by the new NKVD team unconnected with Leningrad it was only a matter of time before Nikolaev was closely questioned about his relationships with them. Any investigator would consider it too much of a coincidence that Nikolaev should have been closely connected with several of these prominent oppositionists, and yet that this connection be completely unrelated to his assassination of the Party leader of Leningrad who had disciplined these same oppositionists and replaced their leader Zinoviev.

Lenoe (281) claims that it was Stalin who told Ezhov's investigators to "look for the killer among the Zinovievites" before December 4, when the names of the Zinovievites first appear in Nikolaev's confessions. Elsewhere in the present work we show that there is no basis for Lenoe's claim. Even if it were true, however, Stalin could simply have learned that their names were mentioned in Nikolaev's diary. Therefore it would not mean what Lenoe wants it to mean – that the NKVD interrogators, under strict instructions from Stalin through Ezhov, had somehow forced or persuaded Nikolaev to falsely accuse the oppositionists.

The Text of "Nikolaev's Confession of December 1, 1934"

Below we reproduce Lenoe's text with the insertion, in translation, of those parts of Kirilina's text that differ from Lenoe's **in boldface** (Kirilina 406-407).

Kirilina's full Russian text is at http://tinyurl.com/nikolaev-dopros

(Choose Character Encoding Cyrillic (Windows-1251) in your web browser.)

*****

Lenoe 256-259

Protocol of interrogation of Leonid Nikolaev, December 1, 1934. RGANI, f. 6,

op. 13, d. I, ll. .92-99.

[Kirilina: Interrogator: Assistant to the chief of the Special Division of the Leningrad and provincial NKVD Lobov.

Present at the interrogation: chief of the Leningrad and provincial UNKVD F.D. Medved']

Question: Today, December 1, in the corridor at Smolny you shot Central Committee secretary Comrade Kirov with a revolver. Tell us who else participated in the organization of this attack with you.

Answer: I state categorically that there were no other participants in the attack I made on Comrade Kirov. I prepared the whole thing by myself, and I told no one of my plans.

Question: Since when have you been preparing this attack?

Answer: The idea of killing Comrade Kirov actually occurred to me at the beginning of November of 1934, from that time I have been preparing for this attack.

Question: What reasons motivated you to carry out this attack?

Answer: One reason – my estrangement from the party, from which I was alienated by the events at the Leningrad Institute of Party History, second my unemployment and the absence of material and most importantly moral aid from party organizations.

My whole situation developed from the moment of my exclusion from the party /eight months ago/, which tainted me in the eyes of party organizations.

I wrote to various party instances /the Smolny Ward Committee, the party committee of the Institute of Party History, the Regional Party Committee, and the Central Committee of the Communist Party, the Leningrad Commission on Party Control, and also the Central Control Commission/, of my difficult material and moral situation many times, but **[Kirilina:... the Ward Committee, Regional Party Committee, the CC, and the letters to Kirov and Stalin did not help]** I got no real help from any of these.

Question: What specifically did you write in all of these communications?

Answer: I wrote everywhere that I had been trapped in a situation without exit and that I had reached the critical moment that pushed me to commit a political assassination.

Question: What was the main goal of the attack you made today on Comrade Kirov?

Answer: The attempt on Kirov's life had the main goal of making a political signal before the party that over the last eight to ten years of my life's road and work there has accumulated a backlog of unfair attitudes on the part of specific government persons towards a living human being. For a time I bore all of this as long as I was involved in directly useful civic work, but when I ended up discredited and alienated from the party, then I decided to signal all of this before the party.

I have fulfilled this historic mission of mine. I must show the whole party the extreme to which they forced Nikolaev for repressing self-criticism [*sic* – Nikolaev obviously means "with their repression of self-criticism"].

Question: A plan written in your hand for an assassination attempt was found on you during the personal search, tell us with whom you worked up this plan.

Answer: Who could have helped make such a plan? Nobody helped me in making it. I composed it myself personally under the influence of the events around me at the Institute of Party History. In addition I composed it under the influence of the unfair attitude towards me when I worked at the regional committee and the regional control commission.

I affirm categorically that I worked up this plan personally, nobody helped me with it and nobody knew about it.

[Kirilina:

Interrogation conducted December 1

Assistant to the chief

Special Division, NKVD for Leningrad

And province [signature]
(Lobov)

Transcribed accurately [signature]
(Nikolaev)

Kirilina's text ends here.]

Question: Your brother Pyotr knew of this plan.

Answer: If he knew of this, he would have handed me over [to the police] instantly.

Question: In your appointment book there is the address and telephone number of the German consulate in Leningrad, written in your hand. Who gave you this address and telephone number?

Answer: The address and telephone number of the German consulate in Leningrad I copied from the 1933 telephone book.

Question: With what purpose?

Answer: I made that notation on purpose in order to show the party afterwards that I allegedly [sic] suffered much and in order to take the easiest route to exposure and signaling [of the wrongs done me]. I was obsessed with the idea of drawing down on myself suspicion of contacts with foreigners, and so that due to that [sic] I'd be arrested and then I would have the chance to expose all the outrages I knew about.

Question: With what foreigners did you have ties and discuss the attack you were planning?

Answer: I never had any ties or talked with any foreigners. It would have been bad indeed if I'd given my plan to foreigners, comrades. I worked out the whole plan personally myself and I carried it out right to the end by myself.

Question: Tell us more clearly what purpose you were pursuing when you made your attack on Kirov?

Answer: I saw and still see that attack as a political act. With this murder I wanted to get the party to pay attention to a living human being and to the heartless bureaucratic attitude towards him.

I request that you note down that I am not an enemy of the working class and that if my recent hard experiences at the Institute had not occured, I would have borne all of the difficulties I have suffered and would not have gone so far as attempting the assassination.

Question: How can we make sense of your statement that you "are not an enemy of the working class" when by your actions you have joined the camp of the enemies of the working class?

Answer: Yes, I have to admit that I really did act morally as an enemy of the working class by making my attempt on Comrade Kirov's life, but I did so under the influence of psychological distress and the deep impression made on me by events at the Institute, which placed me in an impossible situation.

Transcribed correctly from my words and read back to me in its entirety.

NOTE: While confirming that the above is correctly transcribed, the interrogated prisoner Nikolaev, Leonid Vasilevich categorically refused to sign the present protocol of his testimony, and attempted to rip it up.

[…]

Interrogated by:

Chief of the Leningrad Regional Directorate of the NKVD Medved'.

Deputy Chief of the Leningrad Regional Directorate of the NKVD Fomin.

Chief of the Economic Affairs Department of the Regional Directorate of the NKVD Molochnikov

Deputy Chief of the Special Political Department of the Leningrad Military District Yanishevsky.

Deputy Chief of the Special Political Department of the Regional Directorate of the NKVD Stromin.

Chapter 9.

Stalin's Remark to "Target the Zinovievites"

The more or less "official" position on the Kirov assassination, common to the Khrushchev-era Shvernik Report, the Gorbachev-era Politburo commission, Kirilina and now Lenoe, has been that Leonid Nikolaev was a "lone gunman". According to this version everyone else was "framed" – falsely accused, in many cases somehow forced to confess, and then convicted and executed. This would include the Zinoviev supporters tried, convicted, and executed together with Nikolaev in late December 1934, and all the defendants in all three Moscow Trials who claimed to have been involved in, or to have known about, the assassination, plus all those who, like Avel' Enukidze, were accused of involvement with the assassination but were not in the public trials.

Since Khrushchev's day it has been ideologically unacceptable to conclude that Nikolaev was part of a conspiracy. For if Nikolaev's act was indeed the result of a conspiracy of underground Zinoviev supporters, then an underground conspiracy or series of conspiracies really did exist in the USSR. The whole "anti-Stalin" paradigm of Soviet politics in the 1930s would be seriously jeopardized.

Elsewhere in this study we discuss Lenoe's fear lest he be mistaken for an apologist for Stalin simply because he concluded that Stalin did not have Kirov murdered. There has never been any evidence to support that version. But that did not stop it from becoming virtually canonical both in Russia and in the West. Major scholars such as Robert Conquest and Amy Knight published whole books in which they falsely claim to have proven Stalin's guilt.

Aleksandr Iakovlev, a member of Gorbachev's Politburo and perhaps the world's leading anti-Stalinist during this time, urged the Gorbachev-era Politburo commission to investigate very seriously the possibility that

Stalin had murdered Kirov. The commission explained to Iakovlev in a very carefully crafted reply that the version he preferred simply could not be supported by the evidence. Given the fact that this commission itself did not try to discover the truth but also decided on the "lone gunman" theory, their letter to Iakovlev really means that they did not have the materials with which to "frame" Stalin for Kirov's murder. That is also why Khrushchev's Shvernik Commission decided to plump for the "lone gunman" theory: they could not satisfy Khrushchev's desire to "frame" Stalin.

With Kirilina's, and now with Lenoe's, works the "Stalin killed Kirov" hypothesis is definitively dead. Today those who adhere to the mainstream position insist that Stalin "framed" everybody except for Nikolaev. But they face a serious problem. There is no evidence at all to support the "frameup" hypothesis. Rather, we possess very strong evidence that Nikolaev was indeed part of a conspiracy, just as the prosecution in the Kirov trial of December 28-29 1934 and the three Moscow Trials, claimed. The Gorbachev-era Politburo commission, then Kirilina, and now Lenoe and Egge have striven to prove that Stalin "framed" everyone except Nikolaev. Lenoe is the latest author to do this[82] and his is the most detailed attempt in print.

The thesis of the present study is this: all the evidence now available – including, of course, all the evidence cited by Kirilina, Lenoe, and Egge, plus all the evidence available to us today and to them as well but which they did not cite – supports the hypothesis that Nikolaev was indeed a part of a conspiracy to murder Kirov. Moreover, it was Nikolaev himself who implicated the underground Zinovievite oppositionists in Kirov's murder. As we shall demonstrate, the evidence now available simply does not permit of any other conclusion.

Those who worked falsifying the history of the Stalin years for Khrushchev and Gorbachev knew this too. During Khrushchev's time a former NKVD man "remembered" that NKVD commanders had instructed him and other officers to build a case against the Zinovievite opposition. We will demonstrate that what this former NKVD man, a certain Makarov, testified in 1961, is demonstrably false. Then we will present

---

[82] Lenoe's book was published in 2010, Egge's in 2009, in Norway.

the only genuine evidence we have and prove it shows that Nikolaev himself incriminated the others who were tried and convicted with him.

The Evidence That Stalin "Framed" the Zinovievites

Lenoe cites two pieces of evidence to support his hypothesis that Stalin "framed" the Zinovievites. One of them is Genrikh Liushkov's 1939 essay in the Japanese magazine *Kaizo*. We devote a chapter later in this study to a detailed analysis of Liushkov's essay.

Here is the only other bit of evidence Lenoe cites:

> "According to Officer Makarov, Agranov, Nikolai Yezhov, and Genrikh Liushkov told interrogators at **a December 3 meeting** to press the prisoners hard for evidence implicating the Zinovievite opposition in the killing. **If this is so**, then Stalin **must have** spoken to them in the same vein **on December 2 or 3. Based in part on this evidence**, Aleksandr Yakovlev suggested in 1990 that "Stalin arrived in Leningrad with prepared, well-thought-out ideas, and immediately these began to be implemented. Stalin said from the beginning that Zinovievites had done the deed." (Lenoe 271; emphasis added, GF)

This claim by Makarov is vital for Lenoe's thesis, though even Lenoe has doubts about it, as witnessed by his phrase "if this is so". As we will show, Makarov's claim here is demonstrably false.

The source of Lenoe's statement, at note 36, page 772 to this passage on page 271, reads: "Reply to Yakovlev" 473, 482" Here are those passages, both from page 473:

> In his statement to the Party Control Commission of the CC of the CPSU of January 22, 1961 former employee of the Special Political Division of the Leningrad OGPU N.I. Makarov indicated that until January 1935 he had conducted the agent work on the underground Trotskyist, Zinovievist, and Democratic-Centralist groups and among them was the work on the "Svoiaki" file where were concentrated the materials of the

> Leningrad and Moscow agent work concerning active members of the opposition who lived in Moscow and Leningrad.
>
> On December 2, 1934 after a report to J.V. Stalin of the materials in the "Svoiaki" cases Agranov ordered him to prepare all the facts for the arrest of the former members of the Zinoviev opposition named in this file, including Rumiantsev, Kotolynov, and Bashkirov, and in the evening of that same day he was ordered to prepare facts for the arrest of Zvezdov, Antonov, and others who were not named in the "Svoiaki" file but who were in their records as Zinovievists. That same evening the arrests indicated by Agranov were carried out. (RKEB 3, 473)

Makarov may have made these statements – or he may not have. We can't verify this because we do not have his testimony. But even supposing it exists, it is false, as we shall show. Moreover, Lenoe must be aware of this too. According to Lenoe himself Kotolynov was arrested on December 5 (Lenoe 283); Rumiantsev, on December 6 (288). Antonov and Zvezdov had still not been arrested on December 7 (289-90, Agranov statement). But Makarov said they were arrested on the evening of December 2. Therefore Makarov's statement is wrong.

It is possible that Makarov, pressured by Khrushchev-era researchers to inculpate Stalin, was deliberately lying. Lenoe himself admits that Khrushchev and his aides were suborning false testimony for this purpose.

> To understand the positions that Serov and the USSR prosecutor's office took in their memoranda, it is necessary to see precisely what was at stake in the deliberations of the Molotov commission. The commission was charged with investigating the show trials of the later 1930s and determining whether the charges were valid. The Kirov murder and the trials of the "Leningrad Center" and "Moscow Center" that immediately followed were just the starting point of the inquiry, but everything that followed depended on these events. **If the official charges in the first two trials –**

> **that former Zinoviev supporters / 592 / had conspired to murder Kirov – were entirely bogus, then the indictments in all of the succeeding show trials collapsed. The latter indictments were built on the earlier ones, albeit in a confused and illogical way. But if there was some truth to the charge that Zinovievites conspired to kill Kirov, then that preserved the possibility of arguing that the later charges were also valid, at least in part.** ***Therefore Serov and Rudenko (or their subordinates who authored the memoranda) chose to make a clear-cut argument that Nikolaev had had no relationship at all with the ex-Zinoviev supporters convicted in the trial of the "Leningrad Center."***
>
> ***It appears that Serov or his boss had thought through this strategy, to deny any connection at all between Nikolaev and the Zinovievites, even before the "Secret Speech."*** On January 27, 1956 the KGB destroyed central records on the case file "Svoiak," the all-union surveillance operation against the Zinovievites. ***It seems likely that "Svoiak" contained more evidence than Serov wanted Molotov to see, either of counterrevolutionary talk among former Zinovievites and/or of Nikolaev's connections with the accused in the "Leningrad Center." Serov concealed other evidence of connections between Nikolaev and the ex-Zinovievites Kotolynov, Antonov, and Shatsky. The excerpts from Nikolaev's diaries that he released to the Molotov commission in April 1956 contained no references to these men. But we know from later releases of data that Nikolaev did mention all three in his diaries.*** (Lenoe 591-2; emphasis added, GF)

I have put in **plain boldface** above the passage in which Lenoe outlines the importance of the Kirov case for anyone wanting to understand the rest of the Moscow "show trials." Obviously, Khrushchev and his men realized that by the evidence available in the archives, these trials and the conspiracies detailed at them did not appear to have been faked. It was they themselves who would have to fake: falsify, withhold and destroy evidence, in order to build a case that these conspiracies did not take place. I have put in ***italic boldface*** the passages where Lenoe summarizes some of the falsifications that Serov, Khrushchev's man, accomplished in order to try to convince the Molotov Commission that Nikolaev was not linked to the clandestine Zinovievite conspirators.

Early in his book Lenoe explains how Khrushchev's men set out to "incriminate Stalin" (7) – in plain language, to frame him.

> The 1960-1961 investigation run by the Party Control Committee (KPK) was aimed explicitly at inculpating Stalin in the Kirov murder. (8)

Lenoe is speaking of a separate investigation from that outlined above, which took place in the period 1953-1957.

The exposure of the dishonesty of the phony Khrushchev-era investigations – we could use scare quotes and write "investigations" – is one of the most useful parts of Lenoe's book. It also fits Lenoe's purpose, which is first of all to demolish the Khrushchev-Gorbachev account that Stalin had Kirov assassinated before going on to assert his own claim that Nikolaev was a "lone gunman."

But Lenoe does not seem to realize that this also undermines the credibility of Makarov's statement (above), which was made to the Party Control Commission on January 22, 1961 – precisely the investigation Lenoe admits "was aimed explicitly at inculpating Stalin in the Kirov murder." Nor does he appear to realize that the arrest dates he himself cites prove that Makarov's statement is incorrect. At least, he fails to point out this obvious fact – obvious from the information he cites in his own book – to his readers. Lenoe does say:

> First, many of the second-, third-, or more-hand tales relating to the Kirov murder are directly contradicted by documentary evidence. (9)

But this is exactly the case with the third-hand account of Makarov (third-hand because of the supposed chain Makarov – Khrushchev-era study – "Reply to Iakovlev") of which we have only the text of the last.

The dates of December 2 and December 3 are crucial to any attempt to argue that Stalin "framed" the Zinovievites. Below is the specific passage that Lenoe cites, also from the "Reply to Iakovlev":

> On December 3 1934 at a meeting of the investigators Ezhov, Agranov and Liushkov urged them to obtain as quickly as possible confessions from those arrested that there was in Leningrad a "terrorist center" of the underground organization of Zinovievites, according to whose assignment Nikolaev had carried out the murder of S.M. Kirov. In conclusion Ezhov urged the investigators to demonstrate the greatest perseverance and in the shortest possible time to "soften up" the arrested men and to obtain from them confessions about their participation in the Zinovievist terrorist organization. (473)

But a passage on page 482 of "Reply to Yakovlev" proves that this cannot be true:

> Only on the following day, December 3, 1934, at the time of a conversation with the leaders of the UNIVD Medved' and Fomin Stalin first said: "The murder of Kirov is by the hand of an organization, but of what organization it is hard to say at this moment."

In other words on December 3 Stalin had no idea what kind of organization was responsible. The "Reply" recognizes this fact:

> We can consider it established that until December 4 there was no talk of Zinovievists, as on that day Agranov, in his report to Stalin, named Kotolynov and Shatskii Trotskyists, and not Zinovievists. (RKEB 3, 482)

Quoting the passage above from the "Reply" Lenoe (272) admits that on December 3

> "Stalin told Medved and Fomin that "Kirov's murder is the doing of some organization, but it's hard to say at the moment what organization."

But thereupon Lenoe goes on to claim:

> "He was less candid than he had been with Yezhov and Agranov, to whom he had **probably** already issued instructions to build a case against the ex-Zinovievites." (272; emphasis added, GF)

Lenoe bases this "probably" on Makarov's statement from "Reply." But, as we have already demonstrated, Makarov was wrong about the arrest date. As we have just seen, the authors of "Reply", Iurii Sedov et al. – the very work upon which Lenoe is drawing here – discount this date as well. Furthermore, as Lenoe himself admits, Makarov's testimony was part of the attempt by Khrushchev and his men to inculpate Stalin.

Lenoe himself discusses the fact that researchers have proven that false memories can be constructed by the influence of others (9-10). In addition, the passage of 16 years between the alleged event Makarov claims to "remember" (December 2-3 1934) and the date of his testimony to Khrushchev's men (January 22 1961) means that Makarov's memory of precise dates would be unreliable even if there had been no pressure to inculpate Stalin – a fact that Lenoe also recognizes (10-11).

We know that during the two following days, December 4 and 5, the NKVD investigators were still investigating possible Trotskyist involvement in the Kirov assassination. They would not have done so if Stalin had ordered them to follow up on a Zinovievite connection. Lenoe admits that in Agranov's telegram to Stalin of December 4 "There is no mention of the Zinovievites or other specific Communist opposition groups." (280)

Aside from Liushkov's 1939 article – we will return to it in detail later – Makarov's 1961 testimony is the **only** alleged evidence that Stalin in any way ordered the NKVD investigators to implicate the Zinovievites. And Makarov's 1961 testimony is false – that is, if he made it at all for, as we have already noted, we have it only at third hand.

Shortly after this Lenoe makes the following claim:

> "…interrogation protocols show a sharp turn in the investigation on December 4. On that day Agranov began pressing Nikolaev for the first time about his connection with the **Zinovievites**." (281; emphasis added, GF)

But this statement of Lenoe's is flatly false, as the evidence Lenoe cites immediately proves:

> **Question**: What influence did your connection to former oppositionists-Trotskyites have on your decision to kill Comrade Kirov?

> **Answer**: [Nikolaev] My ties with the **Trotskyites** Shatsky, Vanya Kotolynov, Nikolai Bardin, and others influenced my decision to kill Comrade Kirov. However, I knew these people not as members of any group, but as individuals… (281; emphasis added, GF)

Lenoe acknowledges that he has a problem here:

> Government investigators in 1956 and 1990 used the fact that both Nikolaev and his interrogators at first labeled Kotolynov and the other / oppositionists Trotskyites to argue that as of December 4 Stalin had not decided to target the Zinovievites. (ML 283-4)

Lenoe tries to get around this obvious contradiction thus:

> The boundary between Zinovievites and Trotskyites was not clear, either in reality or in the minds of the regime's security officers. (284)

NKVD men could not tell Zinovievites from Trotskyites? Lenoe does not even try to cite evidence to defend this absurd statement. Why does Lenoe do this, rather than following the evidence wherever it leads? Apparently Lenoe wants not to discover the truth but to argue that Nikolaev was a "lone gunman". It appears as though Lenoe may be doing what Khrushchev and his men did 60 years ago: trying to bolster a preconceived conclusion that is not supported by the evidence.

Let's review Lenoe's sleight of hand here. Lenoe states: "On that day Agranov began pressing Nikolaev for the first time about his connection with the *Zinovievites*." But what Agranov actually said was: "What influence did your connection to former oppositionists-*Trotskyites* have on your decision to kill Comrade Kirov?" On December 4 Agranov was looking for a connection not to Zinovievites but to Trotskyites. Agranov's statement *dis*proves Lenoe's contention!

"In any case, no matter what opposition groups were named, the fact of their naming would not constitute evidence that Stalin had taken the initiative to "frame", or even to implicate, either Trotskyites or Zinovievites. Rather, this evidence favors the opposite thesis – that it was Nikolaev himself, not Stalin or NKVD investigators, who first raised the issue of involvement of oppositionists in the assassination.

It might be objected that this question-and-answer could suggest that it was the NKVD interrogators, rather than Nikolaev, who had insinuated the issue of oppositionists (in this case, Trotskyists) into the investigation. But this was not the case. Lenoe admits that Nikolaev had mentioned Kotolynov, Antonov, and Shatsky in his writings:

> I remember how I. Kotolynov and I visited managerial offices collecting funds for Komsomol work. In the ward committee there was a strong team – Kotolynov, Antonov, and Shatsky on the periphery. In 1924-1926 Kotolynov joined the new opposition and at one of the Komsomol congresses traitorously declared that we are not St[alinists] but L[eninists][83], now he gnaws the granite of science. (283)

Lenoe has taken this passage too from "Reply…", p. 462:

> Nikolaev mentions Kotolynov and Antonov in his diary: "I remember how… [the paragraph quoted immediately above follows – GF]

Lenoe concedes that the NKVD would have seized these and other writings of Nikolaev's on the very day of Kirov's murder, December 1 1934:

> Leningrad NKVD officers seized this journal together with Nikolaev's "testament" and other "notes" (*zapisi*) when they raided Nikolaev's apartment on the evening of December 1, 1934, immediately after Kirov's murder. The NKVD also confiscated various other writings by Nikolaev in a raid on the apartment where his mother and sister Yekaterina lived, probably also on December 1. (193)

So from December 1 the Leningrad NKVD had Nikolaev's writings, in which he mentioned Kotolynov, Antonov, and Shatsky. And, as Lenoe admits,

---

[83] We have located Kotolynov's speech in the transcript of the Komsomol congress in question and discuss it in one of the following chapters.

> Agranov had good reason to question Nikolaev about Kotolynov and Shatsky. In the NKVD library there were informer reports on both men in a file labeled "Politikan" ("Politico"), which covered the activities of former Zinoviev supporters in Leningrad. (283)

This is also taken from the "Reply to Yakovlev", though for some reason Lenoe changes the name of the file from the plural, "politicos", to the singular[84]:

> In the archival agent materials titled "Politicos" there was a list of persons that included Kotolynov, Levin, Mandel'shtam, Miasnikov, Rumiantsev, Sositskii, Tolmazov, Khanik, Antonov, Sokolov and Zvezdov... (RKEB 3, 469)

On December 4 Agranov wrote the following note to Stalin:

> Via an agent report, based on Nikolaev's own words, it has been established that his best friends were the Trotskyites Kotolynov, Ivan Ivanovich and Shatsky, Nikolai Nikolaevich.

Although Lenoe cites an archival source for this statement in fact it too is in the "Reply to Yakovlev", which also states the following: (RKEB 3, 460)

> Together with this, in the presence of the jailhouse workers of the NKVD Nikolaev in his cell on December 4 supposedly uttered aloud in his sleep the names of Kotolynov and Shatskii. Katsafa, who had overheard this, immediately reported this to Agranov. On December 4 Agranov informed Stalin by government communication: "Through an agent it has been explained from the words of Leonid Nikolaev that his best friends were the Trotskyists Kotolynov and Shatskii." Subsequently in a talk on February 3, 1935 at a meeting of the operatives of the NKVD of the USSR,

[84] Lenoe does the same thing with the file he calls "Svoiak", "brother-in-law." In the Russian original it was called "Svoiaki", in the plural.

> Agranov said that once they had received these facts "we seized upon this slip of the tongue and developed the investigation in this direction."

The Khrushchev-era report of 1956, which Lenoe cites approvingly, claims:

> Katsafa... could have received from them [NKVD officials] the task of persuading Nikolaev to confess to being a participant in the Zinovievite opposition, and [sic] they also gave him [Katsafa] the names of Kotolynov and Shatsky. (Lenoe 285)

This is not evidence but pure speculation. Nothing could more clearly show the desperation of the Khrushchev-era researchers! They were obviously so frustrated by their inability to find any evidence to support either the story that Stalin had ordered Kirov's assassination or that Nikolaev was a "lone gunman" that they were forced into distortions like this one.

Katsafa's testimony was as inconvenient for Khrushchev's men as it is to Lenoe's preconceived notions. Lenoe calls Agranov's recounting of Katsafa's story a "schoolboy lie" (284) but never gives any evidence or reason for calling it a "lie". This is the equivalent of "wishing it away", as Khrushchev's men had done. Once again, this is a "tell", a tacit but obvious admission by Lenoe that his hypothesis runs counter to all the evidence.

Lenoe is forced to rely heavily on the interpretation of the April 1956 KGB report from which he cites this statement.

> Katsafa claimed that several days after his arrest Nikolaev gave revealing testimony of his participation in the Zinovievite organization. Katsafa at the time supposedly heard Nikolaev pronounce in his sleep the phrase, "If they arrest Kotolynov, there's no need to worry, he is a strong man, but if they arrest Shatsky, he's a punk [*meliuzga*], he'll give everything away." Katsafa then supposedly wrote this phrase down in his notebook and immediately reported it to Agranov and Mironov, after which he received an order to prepare a detailed official report. (Lenoe 284-285)

As we have seen, by Lenoe's own admission the 1956 investigation was set up for the purpose of fabricating a case against Stalin. But Lenoe needs to have a reason not only to cast doubt upon Katsafa's story but to suggest that the NKVD had instructed Katsafa to get Nikolaev to inculpate the Zinovievites.

The April 1956 report continues:

> Katsafa's claim is dubious, as Radin, whom we [also] questioned, who was together with Katsafa in the cell with Nikolaev, does not confirm it, but says that Nikolaev [...] often spoke deliriously in his sleep, mentioned some last names, but never pronounced complete phrases.
>
> For this reason **it is to be supposed that** Katsafa, who was the person [the guard] closest to the leaders of the USSR NKVD /a relative of Leplevsky [I.M. Leplevsky, a prominent security official in Ukraine and Belarus in 1933-1935]/ **could have received** from them the task of persuading Nikolaev to confess to being a participant in the Zinovievite opposition, and [sic] they also gave him [Katsafa] the names of Kotolynov and Shatsky. (Quoted by Lenoe 285; emphasis added, GF)

This is just more desperate speculation by Serov, who was trying to provide Khrushchev with the phony evidence his boss needed to begin "rehabilitating" the Moscow Trials defendants. Kirilina, upon whose account Lenoe often relies and whose work he praises highly, does not suggest that this account was fabricated and gives the date: "the night of December 4". Given the date of Agranov's report to Stalin, this would have been December 3-4. (Kirilina 277)

Kirilina gives as her source for Katsafa's story the article by IU. Sedov in *Trud* of December 4, 1990. But in reality this time the quotation from Katsafa is not in that article but in the 1963 "Zapiska" of the Shvernik Commission. There it reads as follows:

> From the materials of the case and the verification it is clear that one of the reasons for the arrest of the so-called co-participants of Nikolaev was the report of the NKVD worker Katsafa, who was guarding Nikolaev in

> his prison cell. In this report, written on December 4, 1934, he reported to Agranov that Nikolaev in his sleep had supposedly uttered the following words:
>
> "If they arrest Kotolynov there's no need to worry, he is a strong-willed person, but if they arrest Shatskii – he is a punk, he will give up everything." (Archive of the KGB attached to the Soviet of Ministers of the USSR delo [case] No. OV-5, vol. 1, p. 39)
>
> Despite the obvious clumsiness and meaninglessness of these words and of the report itself Agranov immediately reported to Stalin by telegraph that by "agent work" it had been established that Nikolaev's "best friends" were the former Trotskyist Kotolynov and the former anarchist Shatskii, "from whom he had learned much" (Archive of the KGB, archival investigative file No. 100807, vol. 15, pp. 221-222).
>
> Soon Kotolynov and Shatskii, who really were former Zinovievists, were arrested, and confessions were obtained from Nikolaev that his ties to these persons influenced his decision to carry out the murder of Kirov.[85]

But all the effort expended by Khrushchev's men and by Lenoe in attempting to discredit Katsafa's statement was pointless. For, as Lenoe has already admitted, the NKVD men had more than enough reason to question Nikolaev closely about his ties with proven opposition figures. No investigator would have ignored or chalked up to mere coincidence the fact that prominent oppositionists, with good reasons to harbor hatred of Kirov, should have been so close to Nikolaev as to appear in his diaries.

According to Sedov et al., "Reply to Iakovlev" (RKEB 3, 460) it was Nikolaev himself who began talking about Kotolynov and Shatskii:

---

[85] "Zapiska Komissii Prezidiuma TsK KPSS v Prezidium TsK KPSS of Rezul'tatakh Raboty po Rassledovaniiu Prichin Repressiy I Obstoiatel'stv Politicheskikh Protsessov 30-kh Godov." In RKEB 2, 541-670. (Zapiska). Here at 546-547.

> On December 4, 1934 Nikolaev explained during interrogation that he knew Kotolynov, Shatskii and Bardin "individually", and not as members of any grouping, and that these persons, in his words, had not taken part in the crime he had committed. In an interrogation of December 5 Nikolaev again stated: "I did not draw Kotolynov into this, since I wanted to be the sole perpetrator of the terrorist act against Kirov according to my own convictions."
>
> At a second interrogation, also on December 5, Nikolaev confessed that "if for some reasons or other I was delayed in carrying out the murder of Kirov then I would have set about creating a group to carry it out and would have drawn in, first of all, Bardin, Kotolynov, and Shatskii."

Lenoe translates the relevant parts of Nikolaev's confessions of these dates on pp. 281 and 287.

Nikolaev's statements here would have immediately aroused the suspicions of any investigator. First Nikolaev implies that Kotolynov would have agreed to be "recruited" to the murder scheme if Nikolaev had asked him, then he states openly that Bardin, Kotolynov, and Shatskii would have agreed to do it.

Nevertheless, Agranov's December 5 telegram to Stalin (Lenoe's document #45, 285-287) is further evidence that the NKVD was still not looking for Zinovievites but for Trotskyites. That means that as of December 5 Stalin had not directed investigation toward Zinovievites.

Agranov wrote:

> 1. According to Leonid Nikolaev's testimony the Trotskyists Shatskii, Bardin and Kotolynov were of a terrorist frame of mind.
>
> Nikolaev confessed: "Nikolai Bardin is unquestionably of a terrorist frame of mind; he had the same frame of mind as I did, and I even consider that Bardin's frame of mind was more strongly disposed than was my own."
>
> Further, in answer to the question whether Kotolynov had been drawn into the preparation of the terrorist act

> against com. Kirov Nikolaev confessed: "I did not draw Kotolynov into this, since I wanted to be the sole perpetrator of the terrorist act against Kirov according to my own convictions. Secondly, I thought Kotolynov would not have agreed to the murder of Kirov but would have wanted to aim higher, that is, to carry out a terrorist act against com. Stalin, to which I would not have agreed."

Lenoe cites this document from archives. It would have been helpful of Lenoe to inform his readers of the fact that it has long been available in print and on the Internet in Russian.[86]

There is no talk of Zinovievites. Agranov calls Shatskii, Bardin and Kotolynov "Trotskyites". Agranov et al. certainly knew the difference between Zinovievites and Trotskyites, despite Lenoe's lame attempt to confuse the two (284; see above)

But more than that: in order to "save" his hypothesis that it was the NKVD investigators, under Stalin's instructions, who inculpated the Zinovievites as terrorists, Lenoe has to account for Nikolaev's statement here. If Lenoe wished to argue that this statement of Nikolaev's was false, then he would have to argue that the investigators either (a) had somehow forced Nikolaev to make this statement; (2) had somehow persuaded him to falsely accuse them; or (3) had fabricated the statement outright and Nikolaev never made it at all.

But Lenoe does not claim any such explanation. It's easy to see why – he has no evidence. But this means that *here Lenoe tacitly concedes it was Nikolaev and no one else who first accused the Zinovievites of terrorist aims.*

Lenoe continues to try to rescue his theory that Stalin, via the NKVD, fabricated the involvement of the Zinovievites:

> On December 5…[b]y encouraging him to monologue about the "moods" of his old Komsomol acquaintances, Agranov and Dmitriev seem to have nudged Nikolaev

---

[86] See http://delostalina.ru/?p=1633 Once again it is in Vasilii Soima's book *Zapreshchennyi Stalin*.

> towards incriminating them directly in Kirov's murder. (287)

It appears that Lenoe would like very much to imply that the interrogators somehow forced Nikolaev to incriminate these men. But he has no evidence at all, so he has to make do with mere assertion. Here Lenoe also misconstrues normal investigative procedure. Any interrogator would have done as Agranov and Dmitriev did – follow the investigator's adage to "keep the suspect talking". Particularly since Nikolaev had just claimed the Zinovievites had terrorist intentions themselves.

Lenoe continues:

> For example, they had him describe again his meeting with Shatsky in August. In Nikolaev's quite plausible account Shatsky expressed anger at Stalin's Seventeenth Party Congress speech calling for the firing of former oppositionists… (287)

But *Stalin never called for any such thing at the 17th Party Congress* – a fact that the interrogators could easily check since the transcript of the Congress had already been published, and in addition Stalin's speeches had been printed separately. Therefore, if Nikolaev really said this – Lenoe does not quote the text and it has not been published elsewhere – then he was now telling flagrant and therefore more desperate lies. This in turn would have been a signal to the investigators that Nikolaev had exhausted any cover story he might have worked out in advance and was now nearing the end of his endurance. For in addition to being false this story would not have helped Nikolaev even if it had been true.

Why does Lenoe not point this out? We can't say, but even if this story of Shatskii's motive were true it would not provide any evidence for Lenoe's contention that the NKVD men somehow compelled Nikolaev to inculpate the Zinovievites.

Lenoe continues:

> Agranov and Dmitriev also prompted Nikolaev about the supposed terrorist moods of Kotolynov and Bardin until he said that "If I'd had trouble killing Kirov myself, I'd have recruited Bardin, Shatsky, and Kotolynov, and they'd have agreed to do it." (287-288)

Again Lenoe cites an archival document here, and once again it is in Sedov et al., "Reply to Yakovlev". We have already quoted it above; here it is again.

> At a second interrogation, also on December 5, Nikolaev confessed that "if for some reasons or other I was delayed in carrying out the murder of Kirov then I would have set about creating a group to carry it out and would have drawn in, first of all, Bardin, Kotolynov, and Shatskii." (RKEB 3, 460)

Sedov et al. don't claim that the NKVD men "prompted" Nikolaev's statement. But in a way they must have done so. They would have been fools not to just keep Nikolaev talking about his terrorist intentions. Nikolaev was running out of plausible lies. Sooner or later he would begin to contradict himself, let something of the truth slip.

When Lenoe comes to discuss the first occasion when Nikolaev directly implicated Shatsky, Kotolynov, Rumiantsev, and IUskin in Kirov's assassination he puts quotation marks around the word "confession:"

> Eventually Nikolaev "confessed" that he had recruited Shatsky to watch Kirov's apartment for him, and strongly implied that Kotolynov had masterminded a conspiracy to murder Kirov. Moreover, he said that Kotolynov was planning to go to Moscow to assassinate Stalin. Nikolaev also implicated Vladimir Rumiantsev, the former Zinovievite who had returned to a prominent position on the Vyborg Ward executive committee, and Ignat Grigorevich Yuskin, a longtime acquaintance. (288)

This "argument by scare quotes" is a characteristic of Lenoe's presentation that we discuss in more detail elsewhere in this essay. It appears that Lenoe employs it when he wants his readers to doubt or discount the veracity of some statement but he cannot give any reason why they should do so. The reason in this case appears obvious: the statement contradicts Lenoe's preconceived conclusion that Nikolaev was a "lone gunman", so presumably Lenoe would like to discredit it or otherwise conjure it away. But Lenoe has no grounds to do that, so the scare quotes are his only recourse.

Therefore the scare quotes are also a "tell". Like a poker player trying unsuccessfully to bluff Lenoe's unjustified quotation marks "telegraph" his anxiety to the attentive reader: "I have nothing in my hand." If Nikolaev's confession is genuine, Lenoe's whole thesis – that Nikolaev was a "lone gunman", that all the defendants were "framed" and murdered – falls apart. But Lenoe has no evidence whatsoever to suggest that Nikolaev's confession is anything but genuine! Hence, the "bluff."

Lenoe has also read a number of these December 6 interrogation-confessions of Nikolaev's (n.16, pp. 773-4). According to this note there are *seven* confessions totaling 41 pages in length (Lenoe concedes that this may be a single long confession with alternating interrogators). These would appear to be very important texts!

But Lenoe does not quote anything from these documents. Why not? If he were an objective researcher Lenoe would be obligated to inform his readers why he is omitting all these confessions. He is especially obliged to do so since these seven confessions come at a crucial time in the investigation, when Nikolaev was beginning to directly implicate others, to change his story from "lone gunman" to conspirator.

Lenoe correctly notes that the better treatment Nikolaev was given when he proved cooperative was normal investigator practice.

> How were these and later confessions extracted from Nikolaev? Like police interrogators all over the world, NKVD officers alternated soft treatment with coercion, threats, promises, and bargaining. (288)

It is interesting that Lenoe takes it for granted Nikolaev was not tortured. But it is less than forthright of Lenoe to refer to "coercion" and "threats", since he has no more evidence of them than he does of torture.

Lenoe tries hard to find some form of "coercion" or "threats". For example, he states:

> Nikolaev was almost certainly promised that his family would not be harmed if he cooperated with the investigation."

He has no evidence whatsoever for this statement so he tries to invent some. At note 18 (p. 774) to this passage Lenoe writes:

> Kirilina, *Neizvestnyi Kirov*, 251, provides the evidence that Nikolaev hoped to save his family. Unfortunately she does not provide a citation for her quotes.

But this statement is not accurate. Here is what Kirilina writes at that page:

> Nikolaev undoubtedly loved his wife very much. At his interrogations he repeatedly said that "my wife did not know anything", "did not guess anything", asked for "mercy towards her."

Lenoe has distorted what Kirilina wrote. According to Kirilina Nikolaev was not at all asking to "save his family". He was simply trying to deny any guilt on the part of his wife. We can better understand why when we see the evidence that Mil'da Draule was a full participant in the conspiracy to murder Kirov.

Lenoe writes that "Kirilina...provides the evidence". But this is false. Kirilina does not even provide a source for these short phrases in quotation marks. And they would mean nothing if she had provided sources for them, for they are not evidence that the investigators used his family either as bait or as a threat.

However, thanks to Lenoe we know:

* that Nikolaev's brother Piotr confessed to participating in the murder of Kirov along with his brother; (Lenoe 289)

* that on or about December 9 Mil'da Draule "confessed that she shared the anti-Soviet views of her husband" (306).

Thanks to Kirilina we know that on December 11 Draule confessed that she had been hiding the fact that her husband held oppositional views.

> Nikolaev blamed the CC of the AUCP(b) for its militaristic policy, for spending huge sums on national defense, building military factories, and by doing so raising an artificial furor about an invasion threatening the USSR. This hubbub, in his words, was calculated to distract the attention of the workers from the hardships caused by the erroneous policy of the CC... The character of his sentiments and exasperation against the

> Party apparatus took an especially sharp character after his expulsion from the Party. (Kirilina 258)

Although Kirilina is one of his main sources Lenoe omits any mention of this. Why? He does mention the following facts concerning Draule:

> * that on January 10, 1935 "Milda Draule signed testimony asserting that Nikolaev had visited [Latvian consul in Leningrad] Bissenieks to discuss 'the question of detaching various national regions from the USSR"; (Lenoe 387)
>
> * that at her trial on March 11, 1935 Mil'da Draule confessed that she had been seeking a pass to the Party meeting of December 1 in order to "help" her husband. (Kirilina 374-5; Lenoe 387-388). When asked "Help him in what?" she answered, somewhat vaguely, "It would have been obvious there, according to the circumstances."
>
> > To the question what aim she was pursuing by obtaining a pass to the December 1 meeting of the Party active at which com. Kirov was to have made a report Mil'da Draule replied that "she wanted to help Leonid Nikolaev". In what? "It would have been obvious there, according to the circumstances." In this way we have established that the accused wanted to help Nikolaev to carry out the terrorist act.

There must be other interrogations of Draule, plus her trial transcript, in which she states that she really was trying to get a pass to the Party meeting to which her husband was also trying to get a pass. These materials would no doubt help complete the picture of Draule's involvement in the murder. We can be sure that if these materials exculpated Draule in any way they would have been made public, as Gorbachev's men were trying hard to find any and all evidence that Nikolaev was a "lone gunman."

The matter of the time of Draule's first interrogation has always been somewhat of a mystery. But Draule's confession of March 11, 1935, cited above, implies that Draule must have been at Smolny at or near the time of the assassination. And this in turn could explain IUrii Zhukov's claim that Draule's first interrogation began at 4:45 p.m., only a quarter of an hour after the assassination. As Lenoe notes, this too implied that Draule was arrested near Smolny. It might still be the case that Draule was not arrested until 6:45 p.m., as Lenoe suggests (176). But it would be a considerable coincidence if Draule had been seeking a pass to the meeting, and therefore had been at Smolny, but had then left and was arrested at her home.

Since Draule's presence in or near Smolny at the time of the assassination would naturally be incriminating, this may explain why Draule's interrogations and the transcript of her trial have not been made public to researchers. But whatever the case, the fact that she had been seeking a pass is itself deeply suspicious, given that her husband had been doing the same thing on the same day and with the intention of killing Kirov. Judge Ul'rikh interpreted this as a confession that Draule was an accessory to Kirov's murder and was prepared, if necessary, to act as an accomplice. It's difficult to interpret her words any other way. And, unlike us today, Ul'rikh had before him the transcripts of her interrogations and had heard her testimony at trial.

Neither Lenoe nor Kirilina present any evidence that any of Piotr's, or Mil'da Draule's, or for that matter, Nikolaev's own testimony, was obtained through compulsion. All the evidence we have points towards Nikolaev's brother's and wife's guilt in helping him.

Therefore there is no evidence at all that Stalin ordered or suggested the NKVD men to inculpate any oppositionists, whether Trotskyites or Zinovievites. This is strong evidence in itself that these men were guilty. When taken together with the other evidence, including the fact that a number of them confessed, while others implicated those who did not confess, any objective student is forced to conclude that the case against the Zinovievites was very strong.

Chapter 10.

Iurii Sedov, "Reliable Researcher"

Early in his book Lenoe states:

> The archives of the Federal Security Service… are effectively closed, although a number of KGB documents on the murder have been released and *reliable researchers (such as Yu.I. Sedov)* have seen and reported on relevant files. (14; emphasis added, GF)

Late in the book Lenoe quotes from an article by Sedov in *Trud* of December 4, 1990 (668-9 and n. 103, p. 807). This article proves that, far from being "reliable", Sedov is a liar.

"Svoiaki"

In this article Sedov wrote:

> We brought to light several archives [where the authorities] … do not like the eyes of outsiders, and which to this day are still closed… These are the agent surveillance documents on persons counted as Zinovievites and other well-known oppositionists. We are talking about, for example, … the operational file "Svoiaki" on which Stalin was briefed on December 2, 1934… (Lenoe 668)

Lenoe has to know that Sedov is not being truthful here, for earlier in his book Lenoe noted:

> On January 27, 1956 the KGB destroyed central records on the case file "Svoiaki", the all-union surveillance operation against the Zinovievites. It seems likely that "Svoiaki"contained more evidence than Serov wanted Molotov to see … (592)

Here, in the text, Lenoe prevaricates: "destroyed central records on the case file 'Svoiak'" might suggest that some of the "Svoiaki" file might have been preserved. But the relevant part of Lenoe's footnote, which references a June 14, 1990 report by Sedov and other official Soviet researchers, simply reads

> (469 destruction of "Svoiaki");
>
> - n. 49, p. 799.

About the original text of this report we are left in no doubt: "Svoiaki"did not exist when Sedov et al. did their work:

> Unfortunately, the file "Svoiaki" itself has not been preserved; it was destroyed on January 27, 1956. (RKEB 3, 469)

On the same page the report does state that some of the materials from this file were included in the files on some specific defendants:

> In the Directorate of the KGB of the USSR for Leningrad province materials from this case file are only partially present, discovered in the files on V.I. Zvezdov, V.S. Levin, and N.P. Miasnikov (all convicted in the case of the "Leningrad center") and in the agent file "Undergrounders."
>
> ...Here there are documents for the year 1928 under the heading "Zinovievites", in one of which it is stated that at a meeting of "Left Zinovievites" at Gertik's Rumiantsev was present, and in another it is stated that Kotolynov was maintaining contact with Trotskyists for the mutual exchange of information and of literature.
>
> In this same file there is a series of documents headed "Svoiaki", in which is given a short list of the contents of statements of 1928-1930 of an informational character concerning the political affiliations of the persons under investigation and their meetings with each other, and also a list with the lists of first, middle, and last names of those covered in the case file, to the total of 26 persons, among whom of those brought to criminal justice in the case of the murder of S.M. Kirov Rumiantsev, Mandel'shtam, Kotolynov, and Levin are named.

In his 1990 article in *Trud* Sedov plainly states that "the operational file [delo] Svoiak" was one of the archives he and other Soviet investigators "brought to light" (подняли – a better translation would be "took up"). The USSR was still in existence when Sedov wrote this article in *Trud* in 1990.

The July 14, 1990 report he co-authored and in which he revealed that the "Svoiaki" *delo* (case file) had been destroyed in 1956 was not published until 2004. Therefore, no one reading Sedov's article in 1990 could know that Sedov was not telling the truth about the "Svoiaki" file.

Nor is this the only falsehood in Sedov's 1990 *Trud* article. Sedov wrote:

> Under such circumstances, when all 13 of the defendants unanimously denied their guilt, and in which there is no other evidence aside from the oral, contradictory, and abstract confessions of Nikolaev, the direct perpetrator of the crime, the court had no legal basis to sentence these persons to death.

As we now know, this statement is false. Of course, Sedov and the other Gorbachev-era investigators knew this in 1990, when Sedov published this article. They had access to the investigative materials and the trial transcript. But no one else at that time had any way of knowing that Sedov was lying. It is hard to understand how Lenoe could have missed this, as he must have done when he called Sedov a "reliable researcher."

According to Alla Kirilina four of the defendants, in addition to Nikolaev, confessed both during the preliminary investigation and at trial. These were Antonov, Iuskin, Zvezdov, and Sokolov.

> …of the 14 persons brought to trial in the case of the "Leningrad center" only three (not including Nikolaev) – Zvezdov, Sokolov, and Antonov – confessed their participation in the murder of Kirov at interrogation during the preliminary investigation. (Kirilina 283)
>
> At the investigation and from the beginning at the trial Antonov, IUskin, Zvezdov and Sokolov admitted their guilt in participating in the terrorist group and in the preparation for the murder of Kirov and gave similar confessions against other defendants. (301)

According to Lenoe things were a bit more uncertain than Kirilina's account allows.

> Late in the course of the investigation (December 17 and after), Antonov, Zvezdov, and Sokolov all claimed that they had heard in general that the organization of ex-Zinovievites was planning terrorist activities against the Soviet leadership (Antonov and Zvezdov said that Kotolynov had told them). This was as far as any of the ex-Zinovievites the NKVD placed in the "Leningrad Center" went in confessing terrorist activities. The indictments' assertions that Antonov and Zvezdov had "confessed themselves guilty in full" were deceptive. (Lenoe 353)

But Lenoe cannot possibly know that the indictments were "deceptive." He would only be able to say this honestly if he had access to all the investigative materials, including all the interrogations of Antonov, Zvezdov, and Sokolov. For all anyone knows, they may well have "confessed themselves guilty in full" in materials to which Lenoe did not have access. But Lenoe states himself that he did not have access to everything. Therefore he cannot know whether the indictments were "deceptive" or not.

> Agranov's report to Yagoda [during the trial of December 28-9, 1934], transmitted at 7:30 p.m. on December 28, noted that Antonov pled guilty, confirming all of his depositions, that Zvezdov did the same, and that Yuskin confessed that they knew of Nikolaev's plans to murder Kirov, but did not take them seriously. Sokolov testified to being a member of a counterrevolutionary organization, and to knowing about preparations for an unspecified terrorist act.
>
> Agranov was once again glossing over or ignoring inconvenient testimony. Antonov had in fact denied specific knowledge of preparations for any terrorist attack, and declared that "Terrorist acts are against my principles." Under questioning by Ulrikh he confessed that he still bore responsibility for the murder because he had done nothing to stop it. Antonov also said that he had only met Nikolaev once since 1923, and that was in 1932. This of course would put into serious question

> whether the two could have worked together on any plot at all in 1934. Zvezdov denied knowledge of any terrorist plot against the Soviet leaders, declaring that he had hoped that they could be removed from their posts through political action. He claimed not to have met Nikolaev since the spring of 1934.
>
> Careful reading of Yuskin's testimony in one archival transcript reveals that although he pled guilty to all charges, he admitted no wrongdoing under examination. … In spite of aggressive questioning from Ulrikh, Yuskin insisted that he had had no idea Nikolaev was planning a murder. …
>
> Sokolov, who had been the first witness to link Nikolaev to a "counterrevolutionary" group of former Zinovievites in Leningrad (December 6), was the most cooperative of this group of defendants. He followed the NKVD script closely, incriminating Zvezdov, Antonov, Kotolynov, and Nikolaev in a terrorist conspiracy, but without giving specifics. (Lenoe 360-361)

Evidently Lenoe has had access to "one archival transcript" of the trial. But he fails to give us any analysis of the evidence presented at the trial as recorded in this transcript. Instead Lenoe only reports a few instances where the accused themselves tried to minimize their own guilt. Lenoe should have cited and discussed other testimony and evidence against each of the accused as well.

For example, Lenoe informs us that a number of the defendants accused Rumiantsev, another of the defendants. Kotolynov named him as one of the leaders of the "Leningrad Zinovievites." (362) Yet in his own testimony Rumiantsev denied any political relations with any of the Zinovievites after 1929, whereupon several others denounced him. (364) Obviously Rumiantsev's, or any defendant's, own denials of guilt would not be taken at face value by any court in any country at any time. Lenoe gives us some idea of the testimony of other defendants against Rumiantsev. But he fails to do the same thing in the case of the other defendants whose testimony he summarizes.

We can't account for the apparent discrepancies between Kirilina's and Lenoe's accounts of the defendants' testimony. Since Lenoe has stated that he relied heavily on Kirilina's account and respects it, he should have addressed this important issue directly. Instead he fails to inform his readers of it at all. Again, Lenoe's reference to "one archival transcript" suggests that there are, or may be, others. But Lenoe does not discuss this important document in any way, so we have no information with which to evaluate it. This omission is a serious error for any professional historian to make.

Lenoe presents excerpts from the "draft indictments", though not of the actual indictment. In another chapter we have compared Lenoe's text (Document #72, 345-52) with the published indictment. There we discuss some of the important parts of the indictment that Lenoe deleted. In it we can see that the fourteen defendants did not make similar confessions. In the cases of Antonov, Zvezdov, and Sokolov, the three named (above) by both Kirilina and Lenoe,

- Antonov "confessed himself guilty in full";

- Zvezdov "confessed himself guilty in full";

- Sokolov "confessed that he was guilty of belonging to an underground counterrevolutionary group, but denied his direct participation in Nikolaev's preparations for the murder of Comrade Kirov." (Lenoe 351-2)

This corresponds exactly to the text of the printed indictment (Indictment 22). Naturally, the indictment summarizes what the defendants confessed *before* trial, not what was stated *at* the trial.

We will examine the question of guilt or innocence in another place. It is enough for the present to note that Lenoe agrees that some of the defendants did plead guilty to some crimes.

Therefore, IUrii Sedov was lying when he wrote in the *Trud* article that "all thirteen defendants denied with one voice their guilt". Furthermore, Lenoe was well aware that Sedov was lying. How, then, could Lenoe describe Sedov as a "reliable researcher"? Two serious lies in one short article – about the "Svoiaki" file, and also about the defendants' "unanimously denying their guilt" – prove that Sedov is anything but the "reliable researcher" that Lenoe called him. Why would Lenoe make such a statement when the very evidence he himself cites refutes that statement?

One hypothesis might be that this is one of Lenoe's many "tells." Lenoe embraces the preconceived conclusion promoted by the Khrushchev-era

Soviet leadership, the Gorbachev-era Soviet leadership, the Russian leadership since 1991, and anticommunist researchers such as Kirilina, that Nikolaev acted alone and that the rest of the defendants were innocent, "framed" by the NKVD and, ultimately, by Stalin. Sedov promotes this view strongly. But he evidently cannot do so without having recourse to falsifications.

The same is true of Lenoe. We shall see many examples of this. There is, in fact, virtually no evidence that Nikolaev acted alone, and a huge amount of evidence that he was part of a conspiracy. At times it appears that Lenoe's main task throughout his book is not to try to uncover the truth about Kirov's murder but to try to cover up the evidence that Kirov was murdered by the Zinovievite conspiracy.

Before leaving Sedov we note one more lie – more accurately, a deception – of his. In his *Trud* article Sedov wrote:

> The OGPU agents worked "tirelessly", reporting in writing to their unsleeping chiefs about every meeting, party, trips to other cities of the so-called … oppositionists. Those whom the snoops were hunting did not realize that they were being thoroughly covered. The old OGPU-NKVD reports give off a bad, a very bad odor.

Let's set aside the phrase "so-called oppositionists" – although this too is a deception, a dishonest turn of phrase, since none of those in question ever denied being involved in oppositional activities and we have plenty of evidence that they still were active oppositionists – evidence that was, however, not available to Sedov's readers in 1990.

The truth is that the NKVD investigation of these oppositionists made perfect sense. We now know that Zinoviev, Kamenev, some leading Trotskyists, Safarov, and others too had formed a "bloc of Rights and Trotskyites" in 1932, because Trotsky and Leon Sedov discuss this fact in private letters preserved in the Harvard Trotsky archive. We know that Trotsky and Sedov, through Soviet-based Trotskyists, were in touch with Zinoviev and Kamenev. From this same unimpeachable source we know now – though Trotsky publicly denied it at the time – that Trotsky had written Radek in 1932 exactly as Radek testified at the January 1937 Moscow Trial, and had written to Preobrazhenskii, Sokol'nikov and other oppositionists as well.

Furthermore, we know that the promises of many oppositionists that they were loyal again to the Party line were false. Finally – for now – we know that some of Bukharin's followers had met in 1932 to discuss, among other things, the assassination of Stalin, and that Bukharin himself was already plotting with his followers to assassinate Stalin in 1927 or early 1928. And there is much more. We will discuss this topic more fully in the section of this study titled "dvurushnichestvo", or "two-facedness."

Given all this, NKVD surveillance of these "former" oppositionists was appropriate and, as it turned out, necessary. According to Iagoda's own testimony, this surveillance could have prevented Kirov's assassination – if Iagoda himself had not intervened to stop it.

We know this – and IUrii Sedov had to have known it in 1990 as well, since he and his fellow researchers had access to everything in the Soviet archives, as well as to the Trotsky archives in the USA. Sedov knew it, but fraudulently hid it from his readers in 1990. In 2010 Lenoe did the same thing.

Chapter 11.

Documents Lenoe Ignores.

Lenoe ignores a great deal of the available evidence concerning the Kirov assassination. In terms of quantity, most of this is comprised by the testimonial evidence related to the three public Moscow Trials. This Moscow Trial evidence is so extensive that we will reserve examination of it for later chapters.

As he describes in his Introduction, Lenoe did manage to obtain privileged access to much archival material. But despite this unparalleled, though far from complete, access to unpublished materials concerning the Kirov assassination Lenoe fails to discuss some of the evidence that has long been publicly available. Here we'll examine the evidence Lenoe passes over very briefly or ignores altogether.

I am aware of ten such documents:

- Kotolynov interrogation of December 12, 1934 (Lubianka 1922-1936)
- Tsar'kov interrogation of December 13, 1934; (Volkogonov Archive ((VA))
- Kotolynov interrogation of December 19, 1934; (VA)
- Gorshenin interrogation of December 21, 1934; (VA)
- Mil'da Draule interrogation of December 11, 1934; (Kirilina 258)
- Rumiantsev interrogation of December 22, 1934; (K 364)
- Tarasov interrogation of December 22, 1934; (K 364)
- Evdokimov interrogation of December 24, 1934; (K 365)
- Gorshenin interrogation of December 24, 1934; (K 365)

In addition, Lenoe omits altogether some parts of the Indictment of the Kirov defendants of December 24-25. (Lenoe 345-352) I will discuss those parts here as well.

Kotolynov Interrogation of December 12, 1934

On page 316 Lenoe briefly summarizes this testimony by Kotolynov:

> Kotolynov confessed that after the defeat of the opposition in 1927 the Zinovievites continued to maintain "an autonomous organization," and that their rejoining the party in 1928 was a "deliberate maneuver." He admitted that the ex-Zinovievites bore "political and moral responsibility for the murder of Kirov" because they had "nourished Nikolaev in an atmosphere of hostility to the Communist Party leadership.

The note to this passage is to an archival document that, naturally, none of his readers can see. For some reason Lenoe conceals from his readers the fact that this testimony has long since been published. (Lubianka 1922-1936, 577-8). Lenoe also omits some of the most important matters it contains.

In this confession Kotolynov does the following:

* He confesses to "dvurushnichestvo" – "two-facedness", or duplicity.

* Kotolynov directly incriminates Zinoviev and Kamenev by naming them as the leaders of the secret Zinovievite organization.

* He names members of both the Leningrad and Moscow organizations of Zinovievites.

Perhaps most striking is this:

* Kotolynov confirms that Nikolaev was a member of the secret anti-Party Leningrad group of Zinovievites.

"Dvurushnichestvo"

Kotolynov goes into some detail in confessing that the Zinovievites' statements that they now supported the Party line, the requirement for rejoining the Party, were deliberately false.

> **Answer**: After the complete defeat of the Zinovievite-Trotskyite bloc by the Party the Zinovievites continued to exist as an independent organization.
>
> All of us Zinovievites continued to maintain organizational contact and regarded all of ZINOVIEV'S declarations about his rejection of his antiparty views and of struggle with the party as a tactical maneuver.
>
> ZINOVIEV'S written directive of June 30, 1928 is a direct confirmation of this tactic. I have already confessed about it and how it gave instructions about deceiving the Party. Together with other members of the organization I personally concealed from the Party this letter of ZINOVIEV'S and thereafter carried out its instructions.
>
> In particular, at the moment we returned to the Party in August 1928 I, RUMIANTSEV, and I. TARASOV, when we were conducting negotiations with com. IAROSLAVSKII, in fact were being directed by KAMENEV who, after our informing him about our negotiations with com. IAROSLAVSKII, edited the final text of our statement of admittance into the Party.

Lenoe omits the fact that here Kotolynov directly accuses both Zinoviev and Kamenev of giving leadership to those who lied to the Party when they rejoined it. When NKVD investigator Liushkov asked him: "Who is the leadership of this counter-revolutionary organization?" – present tense – Kotolynov's answer is significant:

> **Question**: Who is the leadership of this counter-revolutionary organization?
>
> **Answer**: ZINOVIEV, KAMENEV, and EVDOKIMOV, BAKAEV, KHARITONOV, and GERTIK, who are in contact with the former.

Here Kotolynov directly implicates Zinoviev and Kamenev in leading the underground Zinovievite organization. This passage establishes the existence of a Moscow Center of clandestine Zinovievite anti-Party activists led by Zinoviev and Kamenev. Lenoe conceals Kotolynov's accusation of them here. Perhaps he does so because Kotolynov's admission is very inconvenient for Lenoe's unsubstantiated theory that no "Moscow Center" really existed and that Zinoviev and Kamenev were "framed" by Stalin (as, indeed, Lenoe insists everybody other than Nikolaev was).

Zinoviev and Kamenev Were Lying

During December 1934 and January 1935 Zinoviev and Kamenev were both testifying that they no longer led such an organization. In an interrogation of December 22, 1934 that Lenoe partially reprints Zinoviev made the following statements:

> The moods I have described remained with me until 1932. Naturally, in such a mood I cursed the party leadership and Comrade Stalin personally. But from the time I returned from Kustanaya[87] I have had no such unhealthy feelings. I did not meet with anyone, I did not have any antiparty conversations, I know of no organization nor do I know about any center. (330)

Kamenev made a similar statement in the one interrogation we have of his from December 17, 1934 from the Volkogonov archive:

> I deny not only leadership of any c-r anti-Party organization, but also membership in it, and also that I was informed about the existence of such an organization. From the moment of my departure to Minusinsk in November 1932 I did not have any contact with any of the former participants of the Zinovievite-Trotskyite bloc and did not see any of them.

(Lenoe also fails to mention this document or its contents.)

Elsewhere in his book Lenoe tries to claim that it was Stalin and the NKVD who invented the idea that there were Moscow and Leningrad "centers" of the Zinovievite conspiracy. We examine those arguments of Lenoe's in another chapter. But in discussing this December 12 confession by Kotolynov Lenoe omits the fact that Kotolynov not only agrees

---

[87] The name of Zinoviev's place of exile was Kustanai, in Kazakhstan (now Kostanai). Lenoe has mistaken the genitive case for the nominative case of the noun.

that there were Leningrad and Moscow groups but also names some of their members.

Kotolynov also confirmed that the Leningraders had contact with Moscow through Rumiantsev.

> **Question**: Who among the members of the Leningrad counter-revolutionary organization are known to you?
>
> **Answer**: V. RUMIANTSEV, S. MANDEL'SHTAM, A. TOLMAZOV, F. FADEEV, IA. TSEITLIN. In the industrial institute: ANTONOV, ZVEZDOV, M. NADEL'. I was in contact with all of them. I was also in contact with the Trotskyite SUROV, who it seems has been exiled for counter-revolutionary activity. Besides which I was in contact with NATANSON until his exile and with BOGOMOL'NIY.
>
> I know LEVIN as an active Zinovievist and I assume that around him are the participants in the group of "the 23", specifically MIASNIKOV and ZELIKSON.
>
> **Question**: Who else besides you maintained contact with the Moscow center of the counter-revolutionary organization?
>
> **Answer**: RUMIANTSEV also maintained contact with Moscow. He was always kept informed and informed me about the latest political news. Specifically, at one of our meetings RUMIANTSEV told me about the removal of ZINOVIEV from the editorial staff of the journal "Bol'shevik". RUMIANTSEV expressed regret about ZINOVIEV and dissatisfaction with the Party leadership's relations with him.

A few pages earlier (310-311) Lenoe prints part of a December 12, 1934 interrogation of Vasilii Zvedzov. Asked to list the members of the Leningrad Center – evidently he did not say "group" – Zvedzov named all the persons Kotolynov names here except for Mandel'shtam, plus a few more. One of those Zvezdov identified as a member of the Leningrad group but whom Kotolynov did not explicitly name was Nikolaev. Kotolynov's and Zvezdov's confessions corroborate each other.

The fact that Kotolynov did not name Nikolaev as a member of the Leningrad group is not surprising. Nikolaev had just murdered Kirov, so who would have wanted to volunteer that he had contact with Nikolaev? We possess other testimony, including the evidence of Nikolaev's diary and Nikolaev's statement in his cell on December 4 (whether literally made in his sleep or while talking to himself during the night), that Nikolaev and Kotolynov were close.

We might expect, therefore, that Kotolynov would deny an association with Nikolaev whether he had one or not. But Kotolynov did *not* deny it. On the contrary: he *affirmed* it, though in an indirect manner.

> **Question**: What can you confess concerning the terrorist act against com. KIROV by the member of your counter-revolutionary group L. NIKOLAEV?
>
> **Answer**: Our organization bears political and moral responsibility for the murder of com. KIROV by NIKOLAEV. Under its influence NIKOLAEV was nourished in an atmosphere of hostility towards the leadership of the AUCP(b).

Kotolynov's statement is in fact an admission that Nikolaev was indeed a member of the Leningrad organization. For one thing, Kotolynov did not object when Liushkov referred to Nikolaev as "member of your organization." Moreover, Nikolaev could not possibly have been "nourished" by "our organization" "in an atmosphere of hostility" towards the Party leadership to the extent that it bore "political and moral responsibility" for the murder unless he had maintained regular contact with the organization over a period of time.

That means that Kotolynov here admits that Nikolaev had indeed been a member of the organization. After all, this was not an organization with "membership cards" or "general meetings" with all members in attendance. It was a conspiratorial communist organization. Probably members met in small groups of 2, 3 or 4 at a time. Such a "cell structure" is the usual manner of meeting for conspiratorial organization. Its members were those who met and whom everyone else considered to be members. There can be no "candidate members" or "one-time guest visitors" for an illegal conspiratorial group of oppositionists! Clearly Nikolaev was a member.

Furthermore, the fact that Kotolynov did not name Nikolaev as a member of the Leningrad center, while Zvezdov did, is evidence that neither Zvezdov's nor Kotolynov's confessions were the result of "means of physical pressure" and were not fabricated. If Zvezdov's (and, as we shall see, Tsar'kov's) naming of Nikolaev had been the result of torture, then torture could also have been applied to Kotolynov so as to make their confessions agree.

Therefore, this extract of Kotolynov's December 12 interrogation-confession, short as it is, contains important and damning evidence. Lenoe's failure to fully discuss it and its implications suggests that Lenoe may have suppressed it because Kotolynov's testimony in it goes counter to Lenoe's contention that Nikolaev was a "lone gunman." Whatever his reasons Lenoe did conceal its contents from his readers.

Tsar'kov Interrogation of December 13, 1934

This interrogation-confession is of primary importance. Neither Kirilina nor Lenoe mentions it at all. For all we know, Kirilina may have never seen it. But Lenoe does not have this excuse. The document is in the Volkogonov Archive and has been available to the public since 2000 either through Inter-Library Loan on microfilm from the Library of Congress or at the LOC itself. Lenoe spent years researching and writing his book. He should have checked the Volkogonov Archive as a matter of course.

Tsar'kov's confession is important for the following reasons:

> * He confirms that an oppositional underground Zinovievite group did exist in Leningrad.
>
> * He confirms that Rumiantsev was the leader of the Leningrad group.
>
> * He names Kotolynov as among the four persons who "were our direct leaders, who headed up our struggle against the Party".
>
> * Tsar'kov explicitly states that the group "regarded Kirov with especial enmity, since it was he who personally defeated our leaders in the open struggle in front of the broad masses."
>
> * He confirms that Zinoviev and Kamenev were the "leaders of the Zinovievite organization".

* Tsar'kov admits that the Zinovievites had two plans for overcoming the Party leadership and bringing their own leaders back to power. One was an invasion by imperialist countries, which they initially believed to be inevitable. He explicitly implicated Zinoviev and Kamenev in these plans.

* He confirms that the Zinovievites advocated the "removal of Stalin from the Party leadership" by assassination and explicitly links the Kirov assassination to this.

* Tsar'kov not only confirms that Nikolaev was a member of the Leningrad Zinovievite underground group but that he was "closest to Kotolynov."

We will discuss these last three points in more detail.

Plan To Get Rid of Stalin And His Leadership

Here is the relevant part of the text of Tsar'kov's confession:

> The directives which were issued significantly later by the center set forth the view that the possibility of the return of the leaders of the Zinovievite organization – ZINOVIEV, KAMENEV, and others, to the Party leadership could only be realized under one of two conditions:
>
> 1/ An invasion of the USSR by imperialist countries. The ensuing war – inevitable, as we believed – must of necessity lead to the return of our leaders to the Party leadership. In this case our policy coincided with the hopes and aspirations of all counter-revolutionary and fascist forces within the country and abroad.
>
> 2/ The removal of STALIN ("ustranenie Stalina") from leadership of the Party.
>
> Our first hope was not justified: no war took place. Therefore, in our arsenal in our struggle against the Party, of our effective arguments only one remained: To remove STALIN. On this basis there appeared and grew among us young members the very most extreme sentiments. NIKOLAEV'S shooting of KIROV, as a

> result, is a direct and immediate enactment of the sentiments that exist in our organization.

"Ustranenie Stalina" – The Removal of Stalin

Tsar'kov's confession is important not only for the Kirov murder investigation, but for understanding the oppositions of the 1930s generally. The term "removal of Stalin" – *ustranenie Stalina* – was said to come directly from Trotsky, who used it in an article in his *Bulletin of the Opposition*. Elsewhere in this book we show that Bukharin also used it early on, perhaps before Trotsky did, and that his young supporters understood it to mean "by any means necessary" including murder.

In the January 1937 Moscow Trial Karl Radek said that he never had any doubt that it meant "assassination", though Trotsky had not used the word "assassination". Here Tsar'kov, several years before the January 1937 trial, says the same thing – assassination. Therefore, Tsar'kov has confessed that the "young" members of the group were bent on putting their leaders, Zinoviev and Kamenev, back into power through the assassination of Stalin and other party leaders, explicitly naming Nikolaev's murder of Kirov as an expression of this sentiment.

It's important to note what Tsar'kov does *not* say. He does not claim that anyone, including Nikolaev, was "ordered" or assigned to kill anyone. Rather, he claims that the younger member's "very most extreme sentiments" – this must mean an inclination towards assassination – were the result of two things: (a) the strong hatred towards the Stalin party leadership; (b) the lack of any alternative but the "removal of Stalin" to achieve this goal.

Nikolaev As Member of the Leningrad Zinovievite Organization

Tsar'kov's preceding statement firmly situated Nikolaev's murder within the overall aims of the underground Zinovievite group, and so it was natural that NKVD interrogator Kogan asked him for more details about Nikolaev.

> **Question**: What do you know about the murderer of com. KIROV – NIKOLAEV, Leonid?

> **Answer**: I know NIKOLAEV through our joint work in the Vyborg region [of Leningrad]. He is a Zinovievite. He was closest to KOTOLYNOV. I do not precisely remember whether he took part in our legal struggle with the Party during the first years of the appearance of the Trotskyite-Zinovievite bloc, or whether he signed the platform of the bloc (all signatures to the platform went through myself and MURAV'EV, Mikh.), or whether he belonged to the category of persons who remained in an illegal position and did not stand forth openly as members of the organization. Our counter-revolutionary organization bears political responsibility for the terrorist act of NIKOLAEV, member of the organization, in whose ranks he was nourished.

Importance of Tsar'kov's Confession

Tsar'kov confirms that Nikolaev was a member of the underground Zinovievite group. He does so in a forthright manner, by identifying him as a member. We recall that Kotolynov tacitly admitted that Nikolaev was a member without explicitly stating that he was one. Although Tsar'kov does not say that Nikolaev was assigned or ordered by the group to assassinate Kirov, he does say that murderous intentions were held by the younger members of the Leningrad organization..

This is confirmed by a passage from the face-to-face confrontation between Ignatii Iuskin and Nikolaev on December 19 and partially reprinted by Lenoe.

> **Question to Yuskin**: Did you suggest to Nikolaev that he organize a terrorist attack on Comrade Stalin and did you agree to be a participant in preparation of that act?
>
> **Answer**: Yes, in conversation with Nikolaev I told him that to kill Kirov [sic] it was necessary to kill Stalin.
>
> **Question to Nikolaev**: Do you confirm Yuskin's testimony?
>
> **Answer**: Yes I confirm it. I want to add that in this conversation Yuskin also talked with me about a trip to Moscow to make preparations for a terrorist act on Stalin. (337)

This evidence goes against Lenoe's hypothesis that Nikolaev acted alone. Rather than honestly acknowledging that this evidence goes counter to his hypothesis Lenoe states:

> It is likely that Yuskin's interrogators omitted from the protocols Yuskin's attempts to explain that his comments about killing Stalin were meant sarcastically. (336)

Lenoe has no evidence at all to support this "likely" interpretation. On the contrary: judging from Tsar'kov's confession it is quite possible that Iuskin urged Nikolaev to assassinate Stalin instead of Kirov and offered to help him in that act rather than in the Kirov assassination. That is, it is likely that Tsar'kov was an accessory before the fact in the case of Kirov's assassination but may well not have played any role in planning or carrying out this specific murder.

According to Lenoe's summary of the indictment, no fewer than five members of the Leningrad Zinovievite group "attested to 'terrorist moods' among the former oppositionists", thus confirming what Tsar'kov said. In addition, Lenoe says that "Yuskin testified that he knew Nikolaev was planning to attack Kirov beforehand" (354), confirming our interpretation of the passage above.

On the same page Lenoe states:

> Kotolynov now suspected that the investigators had lied when they told him that Nikolaev had belonged to the Zinovievite opposition. (354)

This statement refers to something Kotolynov evidently said during the trial and which Lenoe briefly summarizes (362). It would have been more accurate for Lenoe to say that Kotolynov *claimed* he suspected the investigators had lied to him. In reality there is plenty of evidence that Nikolaev really was a member of the Zinovievite group; moreover, Kotolynov had, indirectly but unmistakably, identified him as a member as well. Tsar'kov's testimony that Nikolaev was indeed a member refutes Lenoe's statement here.

Kotolynov continued to deny that he knew anything about Nikolaev's membership or intentions. But denials of guilt are to be expected both from the guilty as well as the innocent. For example, Kotolynov testified that Rumiantsev was one of the leaders of the Leningrad organization

(362), in which he agrees with Zvezdov and others. Yet Rumiantsev himself stoutly denied even being a member, much less a leader! (357) Clearly one of the two was lying, and it must have been Rumiantsev. Similarly, Kotolynov was lying when he denied knowing about Nikolaev's membership in the Zinovievite group. With all the testimony we have that Nikolaev was close to Kotolynov, including Tsar'kov's, there is no reason to believe Kotolynov's denials.

Gorshenin Interrogation of December 21, 1934

There is also at least one interrogation of Ivan Gorshenin in the Volkogonov Archive. Neither Kirilina nor Lenoe refers to it.[88]

The points of interest for our purposes are the following:

> * Gorshenin blames Zinoviev and Kamenev personally, and the Moscow Zinovievite center – he does use the word "center" – for Nikolaev's crime.
>
> * Gorshenin testified that the Moscow center held meetings at which all the members of the center were present. Gorshenin himself claims to have been a member of this center.
>
> * He stated that he himself was "especially" close to Zinoviev, with whom he has had a number of discussions not only in 1932 and before, but since Hitler's taking power (January 1933) and "the revolution in Spain". The reference to Spain probably refers to the events of 1932, but those to Hitler's taking power certainly refer to a later year, 1933 at the earliest. Gorshenin also states that he met with Zinoviev after the latter's dismissal from his position on the editorial board of the Party journal *Bol'shevik* in August 1934, less than four months before Kirov's murder.[89]

---

[88] Because the photocopy is poor I have been unable to decipher a few words, especially on the first page.

[89] Zinoviev was dismissed from the editorial board of *Bol'shevik* by a Politburo decision of August 16, 1934 initiated by Stalin. Khlevniuk, O.V. et al., *Stalin i Kaganovich. Perepiska. 1931-1936 gg.* (Moscow: ROSSPEN, 2001), n. 2 p. 433.

Gorshenin explicitly states that the Moscow center continued to spread hostility against the Party leadership "up to the present day", December 1934.

> **Question**: What do you know about the political policies of the Moscow center and about its attitude towards the leadership of the VKP(b)?
>
> **Answer**: The Moscow political center of the counter-revolutionary organization of Zinovievites has remained up to the present with its position of critical attitude towards the decisions of the Central Committee of the VKP(b) and its hostile attitude towards the Party leadership. I know about this from what individual members of the centers have said and, mainly, from its leader–ZINOV'EV G.E., with whom I met in his apartment on Kalominskii pereulok.

Zinoviev testified that he had no disagreements with the Party's line after 1932. Therefore, Gorshenin's testimony is strong evidence that Zinoviev had been lying. The NKVD interrogator was probably referring to this very confession of Gorshenin's in the following exchange during the December 22, 1934 interrogation of Zinoviev:

> **Question**: The depositions of Gorshenin establish that at the end of 1933 [at the time of] the Fascist coup in Germany and Hitler's coming to power, you personally explained to him the incorrect line of the Comintern and the Central Committee of the Communist Party, which facilitated Hitler's coming to power.
>
> **Answer [Zinoviev]**: I cannot confirm that in any way. (Lenoe 333)

Zinoviev, like Kamenev, continued to change his story. In January 1935, at the time of his trial, he admitted that he was not telling the truth here. Arrested again in July and August 1936, in pretrial confessions both Zinoviev and Kamenev went much further still and admitted direct involvement in the Kirov assassination. We examine those statements elsewhere in this study.

Gorshenin testified that Zinoviev and Kamenev represented the overall leadership of a clandestine oppositional group that continued to meet and conspire against the Party leadership's line right up to December 1934.

> In your admissions of 19 December of this year you stated that the political and moral responsibility for the terrorist act against com. KIROV, carried out by NIKOLAEV Leonid, falls upon the Moscow center of Zinovievites and, in the main, personally upon ZINOVIEV and KAMENEV. Tell us what you know about ________ of this center, about its activities and its personnel.
>
> Concerning the Moscow Zinovievite center I know that, despite the fact that after the 15th Party Congress it was formally dissolved and liquidated, in reality, judging by the meetings and _________ it has in fact continued to exist until today.
>
> In the personnel of the center, in my _______, until the present time, are the following persons: ZINOVIEV, Grigorii Evseevich, KAMENEV, Lev Borisovich, EVDOKIMOV, Grigorii Eremeevich, KUKLIN, Aleksandr Sergeevich, BAKAEV, Ivan Petrovich, and SHAROV, Iakov Vasil'evich. In comparison with the old Moscow Zinovievite _______ center that existed in the period before the XV Congress consisting ____________ only in that in it also participated _________ _________, __________ Mikhail, and FEDOROV Grigorii.
>
> _________ in the personnel ________ of the center in the recent period also ____________ I assume that GERTIK, Artem Moiseevich also ____ _________ as a member of it.

Kotolynov Interrogation of December 19, 1934

Kirilina reprints the text of this interrogation (411-412) but Lenoe never mentions it. The significant points in this short document are these:

* Kotolynov admits to being one of the leaders of the "Leningrad group":

> In this connection I admit that I have been in an organization and have been one of the leaders of the Leningrad group.

* He agrees that the mood created by this organization "objectively was bound to lead [*ob"ektivno dolzhny byli privesti*] to terror against the leaders of the Party and government" and that he shared responsibility for this.

> I admit that our organization bears the political and moral responsibility for the shooting by NIKOLAEV. We have created a mood that objectively had to lead to terror against the leaders of the Party and government. As an active member of this organization I too personally bear responsibility for this.

* He repeated that Kamenev had edited the statement he had written asking for readmission to the Party in 1928 and admitted it amounted to "dvurushnichestvo" or duplicity and that Kamenev helped him in this.

> My declaration concerning my readmission to the Party, given in 1928, was first edited by KAMENEV, to whom I went for advice. This declaration was two-faced (*dvurushnicheskim*) and the declaration was in essence a deceiving of the Party. KAMENEV, in editing this declaration, aided me in this deception.

* Kotolynov stated that "after that" his duplicity against the Party continued, since he did not break with the opposition.

> After that this deception of the Party on my part continued, since I did not break with the opposition.

* He admits he knew that Zinoviev and Kamenev continued to lead their organization from Moscow and that he had read a letter from Zinoviev to Rumiantsev.

> That ZINOVIEV and KAMENEV and their followers lead our organization from Moscow I could have guessed and supposed, since they continued their contact with us. For example, I read the letter of ZINOVIEV to RUMIANTSEV.

This document repeats what Kotolynov confessed earlier, especially in his interrogation of December 12. He claims he had not met with Nikolaev since 1932 or 1933. Specifically:

> * By accepting blame, both on his own part and on the part of the organization, for Nikolaev's murder of Kirov Kotolynov tacitly agrees that Nikolaev was a member of the Leningrad group, since it was that group that spread the mood of hostility against Party leaders.
>
> * He states that someone was bound to commit such violence, while never even claiming that he himself tried to do anything to prevent such a result.
>
> * Kotolynov agrees with Gorshenin and others that Zinoviev and Kamenev continued to lead the underground Zinovievite group, and thereby impugns their claims that they had abandoned all oppositional activity and contacts after 1932.

Mil'da Draule Interrogation of December 11, 1934

Kirilina quotes two passages from this interrogation-confession. Lenoe does not mention it.

> At the interrogation of December 11, 1934 M. Draule testified: "Nikolaev blamed the CC AUCP(b) for its militarist policy, spending immense resources on national defense, on building military factories, and for this reason it raised an artificial hubbub about the preparation of an invasion of the USSR … This hubbub, in his words, was calculated to distract the attention of the working people of the USSR from the hardships caused by the incorrect policy of the CC." Draule also asserted that "his mood and hostility against the Party apparatus took an especially sharp character after his expulsion from the Party." (K 258)

* Draule stated that Nikolaev accused the Party of spending great resources on military preparedness, which he said were meant to distract the attention of Soviet workers from the hardships caused by the Party's incorrect policies.

* Draule said that Nikolaev's mood and hostility were especially sharp against the Party apparatus after his expulsion from the Party.

This statement strongly implicates Draule herself. Kirilina states that she, Kirilina, had interviewed R.O. Popov, who had been in charge of the Special Political office of the Leningrad NKVD in 1934 and who claimed that he had personally interrogated Draule and written the transcript himself. On December 2 Draule had stated that:

> She considered him (her husband – A. Kirilina) a secretive person and never heard political conversation from him. (Kirilina 252)

Evidently quoting from the same source, Kirilina summed up Draule's confessions of December 1 through 3 this way:

> In general, the confessions of Mil'da Draule of December 1 and 3 come down to the following: "He (i.e. Nikolaev – A. Kirilina) was dissatisfied about his expulsion from the Party, but his sentiments did not take an anti-Soviet character. It was more a case of an affront at the insensitive, as he put it, relationship towards him. During the more recent past Nikolaev was of a depressed condition, was more silent, rarely spoke to me. His mood was also influenced by our unsatisfactory material situation and the lack of his ability to help his family."
>
> Describing Nikolaev as a person Mil'da Draule noted that he was "a nervous, quick-tempered", "however these traits did not assume any especially sharp forms." (Kirilina 252)

According to a report to Stalin by Agranov on December 9, as summarized by Lenoe, Mil'da Draule had "confessed that she shared the anti-Soviet views of her husband". (306) This means Draule admitted that she had been lying earlier when she stated that Nikolaev's attitude had not been "anti-Soviet." By December 9 Draule was not only admitting that her husband's did indeed harbor anti-Soviet views, but also conceded that she herself shared them.

Draule's statement of December 11 amounts to a further admission that she had been lying. She knew Nikolaev's anti-Soviet views in some detail.

It is apparent that Lenoe has deliberately avoided discussion of these gradually escalating admissions by Draule. After the one clause Lenoe devotes to Agranov's December 9 statement about her (306, above) Lenoe next mentions Draule in connection with a January 10, 1935 statement:

> On January 10, 1935 Milda Draule signed testimony asserting that Nikolaev had visited Bissenieks to discuss "the question of detaching various national regions from the USSR." (387)

Lenoe also reveals that Draule stated on March 8, 1935 that she knew Nikolaev had visited the Latvian consulate in Leningrad in October 1934 and knew about consul Bissenieks' 5000-ruble "loan" to Nikolaev. (387) Lenoe clearly does not believe Draule told the truth in these statements. But he gives no evidence or any reason for doubting them. Absent evidence, neither Lenoe's nor anybody else's "doubts" are of any relevance. Later in his book Lenoe states that Bissenieks has been "rehabilitated" by the Soviets. But that is not evidence that he or Draule were innocent. Anticommunist researchers have conceded that Soviet-era and post-Soviet "rehabilitations" are made for political reasons only. Those we have been able to examine seldom contain any evidence of the innocence of the persons "rehabilitated."[90]

On p. 387-8 Lenoe reproduces a statement by Ul'rikh, the judge in Draule's case, to the effect that Draule admitted being an accessory to Nikolaev's murder of Kirov. Given the fact that Draule first lied about Nikolaev's attitude, then revealed more about it, and at length admitted that she shared his anti-Soviet views, further progressive admissions by Draule should not be surprising. They certainly do not constitute evidence that her confessions were "scripted" or are otherwise faked.

Rumiantsev, Tarasov, Evdokimov, Gorshenin Interrogations, December 22 - 25, 1934

Kirilina quotes briefly from these four interrogations. For some reason Lenoe does not mention them. We'll examine Kirilina's quotations here.

---

[90] A number of "rehabilitation" reports are studied in detail in Grover Furr, *Khrushchev Lied*...(Kettering, OH: Erythrós Press & Media LLC, 2011).

N.N. Tarasov, December 22, 1934:

> On December 22, 1934 N.N. Tarasov stated at interrogation: "The country finds itself in a difficult situation. The Party leadership sees no exit from this situation. Stalin is leading the country to getting involved in a war, proceeding from the position that it is better to perish in war with the bourgeoisie than as a result of the failure of an internal policy that is the result of bad leadership … Stalin is leading the proletarian revolution to its doom. (Kirilina 364)

V.V. Rumiantsev, December 22, 1934:

> In a statement that supported Tarasov V.V. Rumiantsev, interrogated the same day, confessed as follows: "…as concerns the conversation about resorting to war, which would lead to the doom of the proletarian revolution, I deny that… In the event a war breaks out the current leadership of the AUCP(b) will not be able to deal with the problems that will arise, and the return of Kamenev and Zinoviev to the leadership of the country will be unavoidable. (Kirilina 364)

These two short paragraphs confirm that the Zinovievite group in Leningrad had a political position or "line" on the Party leadership: that they were relying on war with one or more capitalist countries to bring Zinoviev and Kamenev to power. This confirms the first part of Tsar'kov's confession of December 13, 1934, which we have discussed above.

Did Rumiantsev or Tarasov continue and confirm the second part of Tsar'kov's confession: that, once it had become clear that no war was going to take place, the Zinovievites planned to "remove Stalin" by the only remaining means – violence? Kirilina does not tell us. She too is wedded to the preconceived idea that Nikolaev was a "lone gunman". But any investigator, seeing that these two men confirmed the first part of the Zinovievites' plan as outlined by Tsar'kov, would certainly have examined them closely about the second part – assassination.

G.E. Evdokimov, December 24, 1934:

> At interrogation on December 24 G.E. Evdokimov stated: "In November 1934 he (Zinoviev – A. Kirilina)

> criticized the work of creating a united front (in France – A. Kirilina), and blamed the French Communist Party and also the Comintern leadership because in France they were going for a united front." (Kirilina 365)

I.S. Gorshenin, December 25, 1934

> I.S. Gorshenin went even further in his criticism of the foreign policy of the USSR. On December 25 he confirmed at interrogation: "com. Stalin is consciously not activating the activity of the Comintern and is transferring the center of all attention to the official diplomacy of the Commissariat of Foreign Affairs and, in essence, is sacrificing the interests of the world proletarian revolution to the idea of building socialism in one country." (Kirilina 365, quoting Zhukov)

Both of these statements reflect the viewpoint, common to both the Trotskyists and the Zinovievists, that the Comintern could have stimulated revolutions in advanced industrial countries if the Soviet leadership had chosen to do so. We know from the Trotsky archives that it was in part on this basis that the Zinovievites joined with the Trotskyites in a bloc in 1932.

Evdokimov's statement affirms that Zinoviev was lying when he said that after 1932 he neither met nor engaged in political discussions with the "former" oppositionists. Both Zinoviev and Kamenev later admitted that they had been lying when making that claim. The confessions of Kotolynov, Gorshenin, and Evdokimov are good evidence that Zinoviev and Kamenev were not "forced" by some nefarious means to admit to oppositional activity they never did but, on the contrary, were lying when they denied such activity when they were interrogated in December 1934.

Prosecutor's Indictment of December 25, 1934

On pages 345-352 Lenoe translates most of the text of the indictment of the defendants composed by Prosecutor Andrei Ia. Vyshinskii. However, there are some ellipses – places where the text has been omitted. Lenoe notes them by inserting [...]. He doesn't tell the reader what he has omitted.

Lenoe also fails to tell the reader that the complete text of the indictment has been published, much less where. Lenoe quotes it from an archival copy, obviously inaccessible to readers. In short, Lenoe makes it very difficult to find the complete text of the indictment and discover what he has omitted.

However, the indictments were published at the time. I have taken the text of the indictment from the pamphlet *Obvinitel'nye materialy po dely pod-pol'noi kontrrevoliutsionnoi gruppy zinov'evtsev* (Moscow: Partizdat TsK VKP(b), January 1935; hereafter OM). A comparison with the translated text published by Lenoe shows that the texts are identical, except that the country name "Latvia" and the name of the Latvian consul Bissenieks are omitted in the published Russian text, these omissions being marked with the *troetochie* or three dots that indicate an ellipsis.

We will first give the full text and translation of the sections of the indictment omitted in Lenoe's text. Then we'll examine them. Materials in square brackets [ ] are part of Lenoe's text inserted to make sense of the omitted parts.

Omission #1: Lenoe 347; OM 10-11.

["Nikolaev, L.V. himself, in his testimony of December 13, attested that he belonged to the group of former oppositionists consisting of Kotolynov, Shatsky, Yuskin and others, which carried out counterrevolutionary work"],

> ... and added:
>
> "... The participants in the group stood on the platform of the Trotskyist-Zinovievist bloc. They considered it essential to replace the existing Party leadership with all possible means..."
>
> (vol. 1, l.d. 266).
>
> As the investigation has established, the whole work of the underground counterrevolutionary terrorist group was carried out under conditions of strict conspiracy. Concerning the strictly conspiratorial character of the relations within this group literally all the members of

> this group summoned as accused in the present case. In particular the accused Khanik has confessed:
>
> "... For conspiratorial reasons only the members of the center had information about the organizational structure of the organization. However, according to Rumiantsev I knew that our organization had a number of links in places where youth are concentrated..."
>
> (vol. 2, l.d. 35)
>
> On the conspiratorial nature of the underground counterrevolutionary group Miasnikov, one of the leaders of the Leningrad group, speaks in his confessions. It was at his direction that a full archive of the Trotskyist-Zinovievist opposition was seized at one of the apartments of the participants of this group.

Omission #2: Lenoe 349; OM 15-16.

["The other group, according to the words of Nikolaev himself, acted under the leadership of Shatsky, N.N."]

> The Kotolynov group, – Nikolaev stated further – was preparing a terrorist act against Kirov, and the immediate accomplishment of it was assigned personally to me.
>
> I knew from Shatskii that the same task had been given to his group too, and that this work was being carried out by it independently of our preparation for a terrorist act. I know from Kotolynov that his group was preparing a terrorist act against Stalin, utilizing those contacts that it had in Moscow. As I stated in my interrogation of December 6 1935 Shatskii and evidently his group were also preparing a terrorist act against Stalin. So each of the groups had a special assignment concerning terror and were pursuing them independently of each other, though their immediate aims often coincided. This is obvious from the way the preparation for the murder of Kirov went; it was being prepared by myself, mainly in the area of the Smolny, and by Shatskii, mainly in the area of Kirov's apartment..."

(vol. 1, l.d. 273-273)

Speaking about Shatskii's role in this affair Nikolaev confessed:

" ... I first met Shatskii in 1933. Our next meeting was in the summer of 1934, at 28 Krasnykh Zor' Street, where Shatskii was carrying out surveillance on the apartment and establishing all of Kirov's movements. He was doing this in connection with the preparation of a terrorist act....

During October 1934 I met Shatskii again near Kirov's apartment where he was continuing his surveillance. Since Shatskii was surveilling Kirov's apartment I shifted my attention to the Smolny and intended to kill Kirov at this spot..."

(vol. 1, l.d. 50-51)

Concerning the circumstances that immediately preceded the defendant Nikolaev's making his final decision about carrying out the terrorist act against com. S.M. Kirov, they may be described in the following manner.

Omission #3: Lenoe 349; OM 17.

Detailing the contents of this conversation L.V. Nikolaev confessed that it was precisely then that he and Kotolynov worked out the possible variants of the assassination attempt and it was decided that:

"...Which one of the variants of the attack that were under discussion should be taken would have to depend on the circumstances...."

(vol. 2, l.d. 82).

At that time, according to L.V. Nikolaev's confessions, Kotolynov said that – "... the removal of Kirov will weaken the existing leadership of the AUCP(b), that the former opposition has its own accounts to settle with Kirov in connection with the struggle he had organized against the Leningrad oppositionists..."

(vol. 2, l.d. 81).

Afterwards...

Omission #4: Lenoe 350, top; OM 18, top.

> [Nikolaev confessed that;]
>
> Sokolov explained Kirov's route before the October 1934 celebrations.

Omission #5: Lenoe 350, second ellipsis from top; OM 18, center of page:

> The investigation has established that L. Nikolaev, as a result of decision taken by the counterrevolutionary underground terrorist group to murder com. S.M. Kirov, during a long period of time together with his accomplices prepared very carefully for the accomplishment of this revolting crime.

Omission #6: Lenoe 350, third ellipsis, center of page; OM 19.

> ["The accused Nikolaev L. himself admitted the falsehood and artificiality of such a version of events, explaining that he created this version with the previous agreement of members of the terrorist group, who decided to present {the} murder of Comrade Kirov as an individual act, and in this fashion to hide the real motives of this crime."]
>
> In his confessions of December 13 of this year NIKOLAEV L. directly states this:
>
> "… I was supposed to portray the murder of Kirov as an individual act in order to conceal the participation of the Zinovievist group in it.".
>
> (vol. 1, l.d. 266)

Omission #7: Lenoe 350, bottom of page; OM 20.

> In one of his confessions the accused Nikolaev directly states: "I informed him (Kotolynov) that I had decided not to accept employment during the period when I was preparing the act, in order to have enough free time to

> carry out the murder of Kirov. Kotolynov approved my decision."
>
> (vol. 2, l.d. 85).
>
> Mil'da Draule, the wife of the accused L. Nikolaev, confirms the same thing. She testifies:
>
> "...From the end of March 1934 until his (i.e. L. Nikolaev's) arrest he did not work anywhere. The explanation for this is not that Nikolaev could not find work, but that he had a determined aversion to being occupied by any kind of work. Having devoted himself wholeheartedly to preparing the terrorist act, I assume that he did not want to tie himself down with work anywhere...".
>
> (vol. 3, l.d. 201).

The final omission (Lenoe 352; OM 22-24) is a list of the 14 defendants with short biographies. It will not be reproduced here.

Discussion of Passages Omitted By Lenoe

Some of the passages above add considerably to our evidence in the Kirov assassination matter. Lenoe does not explain why he has omitted them.

Omission #1: Nikolaev confirms the existence of a Trotskyite-Zinovievite bloc. The very existence of such a bloc was denied during Khrushchev's time and again during Gorbachev's. But we know that it existed because we have the letters in which Sedov and Trotsky exchanged information about it. So Nikolaev's statement confirms other evidence that Khrushchev's and Gorbachev's men were lying. Yet Khrushchev-era and Gorbachev-era "research" – really, coverups – constitute Lenoe's main evidence that Nikolaev was a "lone gunman"!

Khanik's statement about "links ... in places where youth were concentrated" confirms Zvezdov's confession (Lenoe 310-11) in which he lists the members of the various "links" of the conspiracy, including Nikolaev in the "Leningrad center."

Omission #2 confirms the existence of parallel conspiracies and gives another explanation for Shatskii's role. According to this passage Shatskii was not mainly helping Nikolaev at all, but instead was involved in a parallel plot to kill Kirov at or near his home. This gives the lie to Genrikh Liushkov's statement at one of his press conferences arranged for propaganda purposes by the Japanese. Lenoe takes Liushkov's statement and articles at face value. We discuss Liushkov, and Lenoe's treatment of him, in a separate chapter.

In **Omission #3** Nikolaev directly accuses Kotolynov of helping him to plan different scenarios for the assassination of Kirov. He also testified that Kotolynov gave a motive: revenge for Kirov's actions against the opposition in Leningrad.

Omission #4 gives Nikolaev's claim that Sokolov was directly involved in planning the Kirov assassination. We already knew that Sokolov was one of those who confessed to being a knowing accomplice in Kirov's assassination – a confession that discomfits both Kirilina and Lenoe.

Omission #7 is very significant. Lenoe's (and Kirilina's) case that Nikolaev was a disgruntled loner relies heavily on his supposed inability to find work, and on his sense of victimization at the hands of Leningrad authorities. Here Nikolaev confessed that he had refused work in order to concentrate on the assassination. Moreover, his wife Mil'da Draule confirms that Nikolaev could have obtained work but chose not to.

Draule's statement is not easily compatible with any assumption that she was innocent, either. She says "I assume", by which she gives the impression that she did not know Nikolaev was preparing for the murder. But she also states that she knew he did not want to get any job. This directly contradicts her claim in her first confessions that Nikolaev was unable to work because (a) he was waiting for the resolution of his appeal to the Party; and (b) he could not work in production because of his health. This constitutes important additional evidence that Draule was an accessory to her husband's crime. She assumed that his decision not to seek work was related to his planning the assassination. Moreover, this puts his act in a quite different category: not one of individual revenge because of perceived injustice towards him, but of political opposition.

Evidently many investigative materials in the Kirov case have been withheld even from Kirilina, head of the Kirov museum for many years, and from Lenoe as well. From what we have, however, it seems clear that what has been withheld must strongly incriminate Nikolaev's wife and the other 13 men tried and executed with him. After all, the official Russian government position is that all but Nikolaev were "framed". Had there been anything at all that pointed towards their innocence it would surely have been released. Yet there is no evidence to support that conclusion.

Kirilina and Lenoe try to support this official position. They too would hardly have missed the opportunity to cite any evidence that supported it. Yet they have nothing.

None of the documents and passages omitted by Lenoe contains any evidence that would strengthen his contention that Nikolaev was a "lone gunman." All of those that contain information of evidentiary value run counter to this contention of Lenoe's and strengthen the other evidence we possess that Kirov was murdered as a result of a Zinovievite conspiracy. In light of these facts it seems likely that Lenoe omitted some of them deliberately because an examination of them weakens, rather than strengthens, his preconceived conclusion. It is also possible that he did not bother to check the Volkogonov Archive for material relevant to the Kirov assassination, though it had been publicly available for a decade by the time his book was published in late 2010.

Chapter 12.
Evidence Lenoe Ignores: Kirov Murder to 1936 Trial

Kirilina and Lenoe examine most of the available evidence from the December 1934 investigation, indictment and trial of Nikolaev and his codefendants, albeit with some important exceptions. We have carefully reviewed and studied both the evidence Kirilina and Lenoe did examine and that which they ignored, and have critically dissected Kirilina's and Lenoe's treatments of it.

We reached the following conclusions:

> * On the evidence now available to researchers there is simply no room for doubt that all of Nikolaev's co-conspirators were guilty of conspiracy to murder Kirov. The evidence of their guilt is overwhelming.
>
> * In fact, there is virtually no evidence that suggests any other conclusion. We devote an entire chapter to each of the two exceptions: Nikolaev's alleged first confession, and Liushkov's 1939 article in *Kaizo*. Upon close inspection we find that neither document is really evidence.
>
> * Lenoe and Kirilina fail in their attempt to refute the validity of the evidence against Nikolaev's co-conspirators.
>
> * Like the Khrushchev- and Gorbachev-era official commissions before them and upon whose work they draw heavily, both Kirilina and Lenoe proceed from the preconceived idea that the Kirov codefendants must have been innocent.
>
> * Neither Lenoe nor Kirilina investigated the Kirov murder objectively. Rather, they have tortured the evidence in order to arrive at the respectable but preconceived conclusion that Stalin "framed" everybody but Nikolaev. As we have shown, the evidence will not sustain that hypothesis.

Kirilina's book stops at the December 1934 trial. Lenoe claims to have studied all the relevant evidence, including that which became available after the trial.

But this is not so. Lenoe did not study all the relevant evidence.

> * Between the end of 1934 (the Kirov trial) and the end of the third Moscow Trial in March 1938 a large amount of new evidence came to light. The Kirov murder figured prominently in the so-called "Kremlin Affair" of 1935 and in all three of the Moscow Trials.
>
> * In addition, some of the pre-trial investigative materials never before available have been published since the end of the USSR in 1991, including a significant body of material dealing directly with the Kirov assassination and the Moscow Trials.

Lenoe fails to study *any* of this evidence. Instead, he either dismisses it unexamined with disparaging remarks about it, or ignores it , in effect concealing its existence entirely from his readers.

In this chapter we will:

> * assemble and study all of the evidence that came to light after the December 1934 trial but before the 1936 Moscow trial, which we will examine in a separate chapter;
>
> * outline and expose how Lenoe omits, dismisses, and/or distorts this evidence. One must assume Lenoe is compelled to resort to these devices in service to his preconceived idea that the defendants were "framed".

The evidence available to us from the Nikolaev investigation and trial of December 1934 by itself is more than sufficient to justify the conviction of all the December 1934 defendants. Naturally the Prosecution had all the pre-trial investigative material available to it, including much that was not available to Kirilina or Lenoe and is still secret today. However, we can be reasonably certain that none of the evidence that remains classified and unavailable today supports the "lone gunman" hypothesis, for if it did, it would have been published by the Russian authorities to support their official position that Nikolaev acted alone. (Khrushchev-era researchers could not find any such evidence either.) The additional evidence uncovered during the period 1935-1938 both confirms Nikolaev's role as a part of a conspiracy in Kirov's murder and exposes the wider network of conspiracies of which the Kirov assassination was one part.

1935

Lenoe was not permitted to read the transcript of the January 15-16 trial of Zinoviev, Kamenev, and others of their supporters. He states: "Zinoviev apparently continued to deny that any organized 'center' existed." (378) But this statement cannot be true. Moreover, Lenoe ought to have been aware that it cannot be true.

Lenoe does not mention that on January 13, 1935, just *before* the trial took place, Zinoviev wrote a statement more than 3000 words in length in which he confessed that there was indeed a "center". This statement was first published in the official journal *Izvestiia TsK KPSS* No. 7, 1989, and republished in the collection *Reabilitatsii ι – politicheskie protsessy 30-50-kh godov* in 1991.

In it Zinoviev stated the following:

> I stated during the investigation that since 1929 we in Moscow have had no center of former "Zinovievites." And I have often thought about this: What kind of a "center" is this – it is simply Zinoviev, plus Kamenev, plus Evdokimov, plus two or three more persons. And they practically never see each other any more and no longer carry out any systematic antiparty fractional work.
>
> But, in fact, this was a center.
>
> The remaining cadres of former "Zinovievites" regarded it as such. They either did not know how to really dissolve their group into the Party or did not want to do so (especially the remaining "Leningradists").
>
> All the other antiparty groups and grouplets also regarded it as such. … All the antiparty elements once again set forth our candidacies [in discussions about the Party leadership – GF] [91]

Surely Lenoe knows about this document because he cites both the journal in which it was originally published and the 1991 book in which it and

---

[91] *Reabilitatsiia. Politicheskie Protsessy 30-kh – 50-kh godov* (Moscow, 1991), 160-161. (R-PP)

other similar documents were collected.[92] But he never mentions this statement by Zinoviev.

The statement is significant for a number of reasons. In it Zinoviev in effect admits he was lying in his earlier statement of December 22, 1934, large parts of which Lenoe reproduces on pp. 328-333 of his book.

Zinoviev admits that a "center" existed. While claiming that the center did not "carry out any systematic anti-Party factional work" Zinoviev still admits that it was viewed as a "center" by "former Zinovievites" and other anti-Party groups, that it fostered "hostility" towards the Party leadership; that it was a "center of struggle against the Party." Most telling, he also admitted that, like all Party members, he was obliged to inform the Party of anti-Party activity by his "former" supporters but did not do so.

Zinoviev's statement is hard to believe in places even for a person who, like most readers of Lenoe's book, is not independently familiar with the evidence in the Kirov case and that from the Harvard Trotsky Archive. For example he states that he was unaware that a "Leningrad organization of 'Zinovievites'" even existed and admits that this was, at the very least, extremely naïve on his part since he met with at least one of its members, Levin, in 1932 and was aware that Levin considered him an "authoritative person", someone whose views would be spread among others in Leningrad.

Zinoviev Continued To Lie

That Zinoviev was continuing to lie in this statement we can affirm with certainty. For one thing, as we have seen Gorshenin testified that he had heard anti-Party statements from Zinoviev "up to the present day", something that Zinoviev had already denied in his December 16 letter to Stalin and his December 22, 1934 interrogation. (Lenoe 330)

There is other important evidence that Zinoviev was lying here. He concealed the existence of the bloc with the Trotskyites formed in 1932 about which we know from the Sedov-Trotsky correspondence in the Harvard Trotsky archive. Clearly the prosecutors did not yet know about

---

92 Zinoviev's statement was first published in *Izvestiia Tsentrral'nogo Komiteta KPSS* 7 (1989), 74-80 (IzvTsK KPSS) and was reprinted in R-PP 159-164.

the Trotskyite-Zinovievite bloc or its existence would have surfaced at the January 1935 trial. Just as clearly, Zinoviev did not want them to know about this bloc. He could have told them, made a complete confession as he claimed he was doing. But he did not tell them. As we shall see in another chapter, Zinoviev could not tell them everything without putting his own head, and those of many of his fellow conspirators, in a noose.

Both the statement on the January 15-16, 1935 trial (Indictment 42) and Agranov's statement of February 3, 1935 (Lenoe 378; Kirilina 366) make it clear that in the first months of 1935 the prosecution could not prove that the Moscow Center encouraged or knew about the Kirov assassination. These important admissions are further evidence that no one was tortured or otherwise threatened to confess. However, they take on another dimension when we put them together with Genrikh Iagoda's pretrial admissions of 1937, which we will examine later.

Renewed Investigation of the Kirov Assassination

The Russian government still keeps all but a small number of the investigative materials from the 1930s top secret. We don't know precisely the stages by which the investigation proceeded or how the investigation into another antigovernment conspiracy, the "Kremlin Affair" of 1935, led to the reopening of the Kirov murder investigation – as it seems to have done. One of the "Kremlin Affair" defendants was B.N. Rozenfel'd, Kamenev's nephew (his father, N.B. Rozenfel'd, was Kamenev's brother). From the testimony that we now have it seems clear that the investigators concluded that Kamenev had not told the truth at the time of the January 1935 trial. We will examine Rozenfel'd's testimony along with that of others in the chapter "Enukidze and the Lone Gunman Story". Along with other evidence in the "Kremlin Affair" that bear directly on the Kirov murder.

IUrii Zhukov's article published in *Voprosy Istorii* in 2000 is the only detailed study of the materials of this affair. Zhukov concluded that this conspiracy probably did exist in fact.

Ezhov reported to the June 1935 Central Committee Plenum that the investigation of Enukidze and a subsequent interrogation of Kamenev showed that Zinoviev and Kamenev had organized the murder of Kirov and had planned other murders. (Getty & Naumov 165) Getty points out that Stalin and other Politburo members did not follow up on this accusation. Evidently they were not ready to believe it on the basis of the evidence that was then available. This is yet more evidence, if more were needed, that Stalin was not out to "frame" anyone.

On January 5, 1936 Valentin Ol'berg was arrested.

> On January 5, 1936, in Gorky, without any evidence of criminal activity, V.P. Ol'berg, who had just arrived from Germany in order to live permanently in the USSR, was arrested. A month after his arrest he had confessed that he arrived in the USSR from abroad supposedly with a special assignment from L.D. Trotsky to carry out counterrevolutionary work and to organize a terrorist act against J.V. Stalin.[93]

According to Arch Getty, who has had access to some archival materials:

> His [Ol'berg's] wife testified that Olberg had received money and false passports from Trotsky's son Sedov and other Trotskyists in Paris and Prague. (Yezhov, 190)

We know that Ol'berg's wife was telling the truth insofar as that he had indeed been in touch with Trotsky, for letters of his to Trotsky are in the Harvard Trotsky archive. He had also attracted suspicion by travelling on a Honduran passport, obviously obtained illegally. Evidently Ol'berg began to implicate others, including Trotsky.

Ia. A. Mirovitskii's Confession

On January 2, 1936 during the investigation of another Zinovievite conspiratorial group in Leningrad Iagoda and Vyshinskii sent to Stalin a report revealing that one of these defendants, Mirovitskii, claimed he had been recruited by Kotolynov for the purposes of assassinating Party leaders. (Lubianka 1922-1936, No. 559) Mirovitskii said that Kotolynov had recruited him to the clandestine Leningrad Zinovievite group in October 1933.

> KOTOLYNOV told me that our views concerning collectivization and other measures of the current Party

---

[93] *Izv. TsK KPSS* 8 (1989), 82; R-PP 176.

> leadership are shared by many Party members who, like he himself, KOTOLYNOV, are members of the underground Zinovievite group that exists in Leningrad and which sets as its task the removal of the existing Party leadership and putting at the head of the leadership ZINOVIEV, KAMENEV, EVDOKIMOV, and others. KOTOLYNOV proposed that I join this organization and I gave him my assent.
>
> ...
>
> The last time I met with KOTOLYNOV was in October of 1934 when he gave me the assignment of selecting especially reliable people and preparing them for active terrorist activity.
>
> When he gave me this assignment Kotolynov stated that the time was coming when we would have to take up arms and shoot at the Party leadership from above, since by democratic methods the current incompetent leadership could not be forced to depart from the leadership of political life. (Lubianka 1922-1936, 718)

Mirovitskii named three persons whom he had recruited. Others arrested at this time also confessed that they considered themselves to be acting for Zinoviev, Kamenev, and Trotsky. This corroborates what we know from the Trotsky Archive materials: that Zinoviev and Kamenev, together with others, really were in a "bloc" with Trotsky from 1932 on.

M.N. Iakovlev's Confession

On June 1, 1936 Iagoda sent to Stalin the transcript of an interrogation of a certain M.N. Iakovlev, who had been interrogated on May 27, 1936 as a member of a Trotskyite-Zinovievite organization in Leningrad. Iakovlev, who had been arrested in 1935 and sentenced to five years imprisonment as a member of a counter-revolutionary Zinovievite group, stated the following:

> * In June 1934 Kamenev, who had traveled to Leningrad, informed him that the center had decided to prepare and carry out the assassination of Kirov in Leningrad and a further assassination in Moscow.

* Iakovlev was supposed to prepare to assassinate Kirov and not to mention Zinoviev's or Kamenev's name when talking with other participants in the group.

* Kamenev told him that Bakaev, who was subsequently one of the Zinovievite defendants at the January 1935 trial, had organized the Rumiantsev-Kotolynov group to prepare Kirov's assassination also.

> IAKOVLEV and MATORIN confessed that from KAMENEV'S and BAKAEV'S words they knew that the Trotskyists and Zinovievists had united on the basis of terrorist struggle against the leadership of the AUCP(b) and that there exists a unified center made up of ZINOVIEV, KAMENEV, BAKAEV, SMIRNOV, TER-VAGANIAN, and MRACHKOVSKII. (758)

We can independently verify that this center existed. Sedov's letter to Trotsky in the Harvard Trotsky Archive reveals that Trotsky was in touch with Smirnov:

> several
> days before his arrest IN said to our informer:
> X has begun to name names, I await arrest any day. [94]

Smirnov (= "I.N." for Ivan Nikitich, Smirnov's name and patronymic[95]), an old-time Trotsky supporter, would logically have been the contact for Ter-Vaganian and Mrachkovsky as well. Basic conspiratorial principles dictate that one person makes contact for the group.

By the same letter, confirmed by Sedov's January 1937 "slip of the tongue", we know that the Trotskyists were in a bloc with Zinoviev and Kamenev.

> [The bloc] is organized. In it have entered the
> Zinovievites,
> the Sten-Lominadze group and the Trotskyists
> (former "[capitulators]". The group of Safar.
> Tarkhkan. has not formally entered yet – they

---

[94] Sedov to Trotsky 1932; Trotsky Archive 4782.

[95] This identification was made by Pierre Broué, the world's leading Trotskyist historian, who discovered the document in 1980.

> stand on too extreme a position; they will enter
> in a very short time. – The declaration of Z. and K.
> concerning their
> enormous mistake in '27 was made during
> negotiations with our people concerning the bloc,
> immediately before
> the exile of Z and K. –

No one denies that Bakaev was a Zinovievite. The Sedov letter constitutes corroborating evidence that Iakovlev and Matorin were telling the truth about the makeup of the Trotskyite-Zinovievite bloc.

But how about the crucial claim that the bloc was formed "on the basis of a terrorist struggle"? The real question is: What constitutes "confirmation" or "disconfirmation" of this claim? As we shall see, ALL the evidence we have – and there is a great deal of it – confirms that this bloc was formed for "terrorist" purposes, including assassination. At the same time we have no evidence to disconfirm this hypothesis.

Here are some passages from Iakovlev's confession:

> **Answer**: … I started on the road of direct terrorist struggle against the leaders of the Party and government in the middle of 1934.
>
> **Question**: Under what circumstances do you start on this road?
>
> **Answer**: In June 1934 L.B. KAMENEV travelled to Leningrad. I was in contact with KAMENEV through our mutual counterrevolutionary activity in the Zinovievist organization and went to tell him about the situation in the Leningrad organization and to receive directives from KAMENEV about further work. After hearing me out and discussing with me the situation in the Leningrad organization KAMENEV gave me the decision of the center concerning the organization of struggle against the leaders of the AUCP(b) and the government by means of terror.
>
> He asked me what I thought about this, received my positive response, and set forth his direct proposal that it

was essential to prepare a terrorist act against Kirov while at the same time telling me that in Moscow an attempt on Stalin's life was under preparation by the organization.

Question: Confess what specifically KAMENEV told you about the decisions of the center of the organization about the preparation of terrorist acts against the leaders of the AUCP(b) and government.

Answer: KAMENEV told me that in the current conditions terror was the sole possible method of struggle against Stalin. KAMENEV said that every other way would inevitably lead to our final destruction. The only chance for success lay in terror. Therefore, while we have forces, we must use this last means. (Lubianka 1922-1936, 759-760)

[…]

Question: Did KAMENEV tell you in June 1934 that other groups also were preparing a terrorist act against com. KIROV, in particular, the terrorist group that carried out the murder of S.M. KIROV on December 1, 1934?

Answer: Yes, KAMENEV spoke to me about this.

When we were discussing the question about the preparation of a terrorist act against KIROV, KAMENEV asked me whether I was in contact with the RUMIANTSEV-KOTOLYNOV group. I answered him in the negative. KAMENEV then said that instructions about preparing and carrying out the murder of KIROV were also given to the RUMIANTSEV-KOTOLYNOV group and recommended that I avoid contact with this group on conspiratorial grounds.

Question: Did KAMENEV tell you who among the members of the center had organized the terrorist RUMIANTSEV-KOTOLYNOV group?

Answer: KAMENEV told me that the RUMIANTSEV-KOTOLYNOV group was organized by BAKAEV on

> the instructions of the center. Besides that, from MATORIN, the former secretary of Zinoviev's and active member of the organization I know that he, MATORIN, had a personal meeting in the summer of 1934 in Leningrad with BAKAEV, who gave him, MATORIN, the task of organizing a terrorist group for the murder of KIROV, and also said to MATORIN that he had assigned the RUMIANTSEV-KOTOLYNOV group to make preparations in a parallel manner for a terrorist act against KIROV. (761)

Getty describes some ensuing parts of the investigation as follows:

> By 23 July, Kamenev was admitting membership in a counterrevolutionary center that planned terror, but he denied being one of the organizers; he implicated Zinoviev as being closer to the matter. Three days later Zinoviev was confronted by one of his followers, Karev, who directly accused him. Zinoviev asked that the interrogation be stopped because he wanted to make a statement that, in the event, amounted to a full confession of organizing assassination and terror.[43] (Yezhov, 191)

The Secret Letter of the Central Committee of July 29 1936

The footnote 43 to this passage is to an interrogation of Kamenev of July 23-24 and of Zinoviev of July 26, 1936, both in an archive. Neither of these has been published. But we do have some other pretrial materials.

On July 29, 1936 the Central Committee sent a "closed letter" to all party leadership bodies above the very local levels. It was evidently drafted by Ezhov and revised by Stalin, whose handwritten editions remain in the original.[96] It appears to be the first attempt to outline the breadth and depth of the network of conspiracies as it was then understood by the

[96] A facsimile of a page of this report with Stalin's handwritten editions is reproduced in *Izvestiia TsK KPSS* 8 (1989), p. 102.

Party and NKVD leadership. It also set the stage for the first Moscow Trial three weeks later.

The "closed letter" cites selected quotations from interrogations of Zinoviev, of July 23-25; of Kamenev, of July 23, July 24, and July 23-24; of Mrachkovskii of July 4 and July 19-20; of Karev, of June 5; of Matorin, of June 30; of Bakaev, of July 17-19; of Pickel', of July 22; of Dreitser, of July 23; of V. Ol'berg, of February 15 and May 9; of Berman-IUrin, of July 21; of Natan Lur'e, of July 21; of I.S. Esterman, of July 2; of Mukhin, of December 11, 1935; of Moisei Lur'e, of July 21; of Konstant, of July 21; of A.A. Lavrent'ev of November 9, 1935; of Reingol'd, of July 9 and July 17. The full texts of these interrogations probably still exist in the archives but as of 2012 are still being kept top-secret, unavailable to researchers.

The whole letter concerns the discovery by the NKVD of a large-scale Trotskyite-Zinovievite conspiracy that planned the Kirov assassination and much else. The letter provides a context for the Kirov assassination, which was only one part of the alleged aims of the conspiracy. We cite below only those quotations from the confessions that mention the Kirov assassination directly:

Kamenev:

> ...we, that is the Zinovievist center of the counterrevolutionary organization, the membership of which I have named above, and the Trotskyist counterrevolutionary organization in the persons of Smirnov, Mrachkovskii and Ter-Vaganian, agreed in 1932 about the union of both, i.e. the Zinovievist and Trotskyist counterrevolutionary organizations for cooperative preparation of terrorist acts against the leaders of the CC and first of all against Stalin and Kirov. (Kamenev, July 23 1936; Izv. TsK KPSS 8 (1989), 101; R-PP 198)
>
> [...]
>
> "Yes, I am forced to admit that even before the meeting in Il'inskoe Zinoviev informed me about the planned decisions of the center of the Trotskyist-Zinovievist bloc concerning the preparation of terrorist acts against Stalin

> and Kirov. At that time he told me that the representatives of the Trotskyists in the center of the bloc – Smirnov, Mrachkovskii, and Ter-Vaganian – categorically insist upon this decision, that they have a direct instruction from Trotsky on this and that they demand a practical transition to this undertaking towards the realization of the aims which form the basis of the bloc… I agreed to this decision since I shared it completely.
>
> - Kamenev. Transcript of interrogation of July 23-24, 1936.; Izv. TsK KPSS 8 (1989) 104; R-PP 199)

Zinoviev:

> I was indeed a member of the united Trotskyist-Zinovievist center organized in 1932.
>
> The Trotskyist-Zinovievist center considered as its chief task the murder of leaders of the VKP(b) and, first and foremost, the murder of Stalin and Kirov. The center was connected with Trotsky through its members I.N. Smirnov and Mrachkovsky. Direct instructions from Trotsky for the preparation of Stalin's murder were received by Smirnov.
>
> - Getty & Naumov, 251-252; Izv. TsK KPSS 8 (1989) 101; R-PP 198.
>
> I also confess that Bakaev and Karev, members of the organization, were entrusted by me, in the name of the united center, with the organization of terrorist acts against Stalin in Moscow and Kirov in Leningrad. These instructions by me were given in Il'inskoe in the fall of 1932.
>
> - Zinoviev. Transcript of interrogation of July 23-25, 1936; translation by Getty & Naumov, 232 (they omit the words "in Il'inskoe"); (Izv. TsK KPSS 8 (1989) 104; R-PP 199)

Karev:

> Zinoviev stated that at the basis of the admission by the Zinovievist center of terror as the basic means of struggle with the existing Party leadership contact had been established with the leaders of the Trotskyist organization in the USSR, Ivan Nikitich Smirnov and Mrachkovskii, and that a decision of the unified Trotskyist-Zinovievist center exists concerning the organization of terrorist acts against Stalin in Moscow and Kirov in Leningrad. Zinoviev said that the preparation of terrorist acts against Stalin and Kirov was assigned to Bakaev, who was supposed to use for these ends his contacts with the Zinovievist groups in Leningrad and Moscow.
>
> Zinoviev also proposed to me in turn to select people close to me from the organization which I led in the Academy of Sciences in Leningrad who would be capable of carrying out a terrorist act against Kirov.
>
> ...at my conversation with Bakaev I found out that for the organization of the terrorist act against Kirov he intended to use the Zinovievist groups of Rumiantsev and Kotolynov that existed in Leningrad and that were in contact with himself, Bakaev.
>
> - Karev, N.A. Transcript of interrogation of June 5 1936. (Izv. TsK KPSS 8 (1989), 104; R-PP 200)

Motorin:

> Zinoviev instructed me that the preparation for a terrorist act should be accelerated as much as possible and that by the winter Kirov must be killed. He chided me for insufficient decisiveness and energy and told me that on the question of terrorist methods of struggle it was necessary to reject all our prejudices."
>
> - Motorin, N.M. Transcript of interrogation of June 10, 1936. (Izv. TsK KPSS 9 (1989) 105; R-PP 200).

This whole document concerns the discovery of a broad conspiracy, only part of which was concerned with the assassination of Kirov. As such all of it is in fact relevant evidence, since the Kirov assassination was but a part of this larger conspiracy.

Pretrial Confessions of Zinoviev and Kamenev

The texts of only two pretrial interrogations of Zinoviev are available to researchers. The first is dated July 28, 1936. It begins with an explicit reference to the confrontation with Karev to which Getty refers. Although it may not be the very first confession of Zinoviev's after he broke off his face-to-face confrontation with Karev, it does fit Getty's description of "a full confession of organizing assassination and terror."

Zinoviev said the following about the Kirov assassination specifically:

> **Question**: What concretely was done by the united center to carry out the terrorist plans?
>
> **Answer**: At that time, in 1932, the center took a decision to organize terrorist acts against Stalin in Moscow and Kirov in Leningrad.
>
> [...]
>
> **Question**: You confess that GERTIK was in touch with the participants of the organization in Leningrad. We wish to turn once more to the question of GERTIK's ties to KOTOLYNOV. We know for certain that GERTIK in 193? [year not legible – GF] returned from Leningrad to Moscow and spoke about the terrorist character of his ties to KOTOLYNOV. You must have known about this?
>
> **Answer**: Yes, I admit that in 1934, I can't remember the month but in the middle of the year, EVDOKIMOV told me about one of GERTIK'S trips to Leningrad, during which GERTIK got into contact with KOTOLYNOV. In addition, as a result of this meeting KOTOLYNOV told GERTIK that he was taking a direct role in the preparation of the murder of KIROV.

Zinoviev goes on to link Kamenev with M.N. Iakovlev, whose only published confession we have discussed above.

> **Question**: With which of the participants of the organization did KAMENEV maintain contact in Leningrad?
>
> **Answer**: In 1934 KAMENEV told me that in Leningrad he met with IAKOVLEV Moisei, a member of the organization, to whom he confirmed the decisions of the united Trotskyite-Zinovievite center to organize the murder of Kirov.
>
> **Question**: Was IAKOVLEV carrying out the work of preparation for the murder of com. Kirov together with the RUMIANTSEV-KOTOLYNOV group or independently?
>
> **Answer**: IAKOVLEV was preparing the murder of Kirov in parallel with the RUMIANTSEV-KOTOLYOV group.
>
> [...]
>
> I must add that a plan was developed for hiding the traces of the crimes that were under preparation by the united Trotskyite-Zinovievite center. **The forcible removal of the leaders of the Party and government had to be very carefully disguised as** White Guardist acts or **acts of "personal vengeance."** (Emphasis added, GF)

Zinoviev's statement about "disguising" the murder as an "act of personal vengeance" is of capital importance, in that it constitutes strong evidence against Kirilina's and Lenoe's hypothesis that Nikolaev was a "lone gunman."

Elsewhere in this study we examine a passage from a confession by Nikolaev, reproduced in the text of the December 1934 Indictment, that he had tried to disguise the assassination as an individual act. Avel' Enukidze and those with whom he was in contact in the Kremlin were spreading precisely this rumor – that Nikolaev had acted from personal motives. Enukidze's remarks are also consistent with Iagoda's pretrial confessions. We will examine them later.

We also have the text of a shorter confession of Zinoviev's of sometime in August, 1936. The month and year are clearly readable, but not the date. Zinoviev's statements in this confession are numbered in the text. The second and third points concern the Kirov assassination. It reads as follows:

> 2. After KAREV'S arrest since 1933 the matter of organizing of terrorist acts in Leningrad was transferred to the Zinovievite M. IAKOVLEV, about which this had been preliminary agreed with KAREV.
>
> In 1934 it was assigned by the united center to KAMENEV to meet in Leningrad with IAKOVLEV. KAMENEV fulfilled this in the summer of 1934 and at that time I told KAMENEV that it was necessary to give the control and general leadership of this action to BAKAEV.
>
> 3. KAMENEV informed me in November 1934 that he had met with BAKAEV who had just returned from Leningrad and who informed him that he (BAKAEV) had met in Leningrad with LEVIN, RUMIANTSEV, KATALYNOV, and I think MANDEL'SHTAM. At this meeting was decided the question about where and when to murder Kirov. **Nikolaev, the murderer of Kirov, with whom BAKAEV spoke, was at that meeting.** [Emphasis added, GF]
>
> BAKAEV familiarized himself in detail with the state of the preparation of the terrorist act against Kirov and finally sanctioned the attempt in the name of the united Trotskyite-Zinovievite center.

Here Zinoviev again reveals that the Moscow Center, which he headed, had directed the assassination of Kirov. He also reveals that Nikolaev had been present at the meeting, evidently in the fall of 1934, between Bakaev, representing the Moscow Center, and the main leadership of the Leningrad Center.

Zinoviev's revelation that Nikolaev was also present at the meeting is strong evidence of Nikolaev's direct participation in the Leningrad group of Zinovievites and, of course, it is evidence too of the central role in the Kirov murder of both the Moscow and Leningrad centers. It contradicts Lenoe's hypothesis of Nikolaev as a "lone gunman."

We have only one pretrial confession by Kamenev, of August 10, 1936. Concerning the Kirov assassination Kamenev confessed as follows:

> **Question**: What precisely did SOKOL'NIKOV know about the bloc that existed between Trotskyists and Zinovievists?
>
> **Answer**: He knew that this bloc was being organized on the basis of terror and that the practical task of the bloc was the organization of assassination attempts against STALIN and KIROV.
>
> [...]
>
> **Question**: That means SOKOL'NIKOV not only knew from you, that terrorist attempts on coms. STALIN and KIROV were being prepared by the center of the Trotskyist-Zinovievist bloc, but that he personally participated in the decision to create the leading terrorist group.
>
> Do you confirm this?
>
> **Answer**: Yes, I confirm it.

Kamenev's accusation of Sokol'nikov set off an investigation that was to lead to the second Moscow Trial of January 1937.

In the early 1980s Arch Getty discovered evidence in the Harvard Trotsky Archive that in 1932 Trotsky had sent a letter to Sokol'nikov, no doubt urging him to return to clandestine opposition. There may – almost certainly were – more letters of this kind, for Getty also discovered that the Trotsky Archive had been purged, no doubt of incriminating material.

Chapter 13.

Evidence Lenoe Ignores – The First Moscow Trial

In this chapter we examine the Kirov testimony in the First Moscow Trial of August 1936. There is a great deal of it. Lenoe simply omits discussion of it entirely.

Lenoe evidently takes the position that the testimony in this and in the other two Moscow Trials was fabricated by the NKVD in some way. But he fails to give any evidence that this is so, nor does he make any kind of argument to justify these very considerable omissions. In effect Lenoe simply chose to ignore this and a great deal of other evidence. This may be because this evidence contradicts his preconceived conclusion that Nikolaev was a "lone gunman."

In reality, no one has ever come close to proving that any of the Moscow Trials were faked. However, in the highly politicized and biased field of Soviet history the position that the Moscow Trials were all fabrications and all the defendants "framed" is not merely the "mainstream" position – it is the only position that is tolerated. Anyone who suggests that the Moscow Trials may not have been fabrications faces ridicule or worse. So there is a great deal of professional pressure to regard the trials as fabrications and little incentive to do any serious research on them.

Any objective investigation must always confront the question of verification. Therefore in this chapter we will discuss two questions. First: What is the Kirov testimony in the first Moscow Trial? Second: To what extent can we confirm or disconfirm the testimony in the first Moscow Trial?

The first public Moscow Trial of August 19-24 1936 was preceded by a great deal of investigation. Only a very small amount of the documentation this investigation produced – confessions, statements, and some physical evidence as well – has ever been made public. Most of it by far is still top-secret in Russia today. Neither Kirilina nor Lenoe had access to anything like the full extent of it. Nor, of course, do we.

But in the materials we do have there is a great deal of testimony about the Kirov assassination. All of it corroborates the hypothesis that the defendants in the December 1934 trial of Nikolaev and others were guilty, and that the trial was not in any sense a "frameup." However, it goes beyond the December 1934 trial, in that some of the defendants in the January 1935 Kamenev-Zinoviev trial later confessed to direct planning of Kirov's murder.

Like Lenoe, or like any researcher or investigator, we are faced with the task of evaluating all this evidence according to objective criteria. We have already seen that Lenoe ignores material from between the December 1934 trial and the August 1936 trial, and also ignores the pretrial materials of the 1936 Trial. Likewise he ignores the testimony at the 1936 Trial itself. In his brief two-page summary of this trial Lenoe does not examine any of the testimony. He simply assumes that there was no merit to the charges and that Stalin was out to destroy the "former" oppositionists.

> Whatever the specific trigger, if any, for reopening the Kirov investigation, Stalin's decision was obviously part of his ongoing drive to crush former party oppositionists. (464)
>
> The show trial of Zinoviev and Kamenev made it clear that Stalin's agenda was total destruction of the former Left opposition. (465)

In reality there is nothing "obvious" or "clear" about these conclusions. There is no evidence whatsoever that Stalin had a "goal" of "crushing" or "destroying" former oppositionists. On the contrary: there is good evidence that prior to the Kirov murder Stalin was trying to conciliate former oppositionists – or people whom he believed were former oppositionists, whose opposition he believed was in the past, as they promised it was.

The omission of any study of the 1936 trial is yet another of many examples of Lenoe's committing the logical fallacy of "Begging the Question" by "assuming that which should be proven." Lenoe does not prove or even argue, but instead assumes, that the August 1936 trial is a fabrication. Lenoe dismisses the pretrial and trial testimony without bothering to examine it. The word "obviously" serves as Lenoe's excuse for the lack of any evidence to support his statement. It is another of Lenoe's "tells", a sign that what he has to say is a "bluff", that he has no evidence to back it up.

This makes no sense if Lenoe's goal is to re-examine the Kirov murder and find out what really happened. It makes sense only if Lenoe has a preconceived conclusion that he wants to promote at any cost – that Nikolaev was a "lone gunman" and that all other defendants were framed, forced or induced somehow to give false testimony. One who commits the fallacy of "assuming that which should be proven" demonstrates that he is not interested in finding out the truth. And he certainly will not stumble across it by accident, as it were, by refusing *a priori* to seriously examine the evidence that does not support his hypothesis.

In the present study we assume, as any investigator or researcher should, that the result of our inquiry is not a foregone conclusion. Therefore we must study all the evidence – not just that which Lenoe examines, but also the very considerable amount of evidence that Lenoe leaves unexamined.

Questions of Methodology

How can these materials be assessed as to their truthfulness? What, in fact, can we reasonably expect to learn from them? This problem confronts Egge, Lenoe and Kirilina as well, though they do not directly address it. They have some interrogations, trial transcripts, and investigative materials, so we too have whatever of these materials they have chosen to disclose to us. In addition, we have all the evidence that, for whatever reasons, they omit.

Although a full examination of the Moscow Trials is beyond the scope of this study, we do wish to emphasize the following point: There is no evidence that any of the defendants in these trials was framed, falsely convicted, innocent. Not one shred of evidence has ever been produced that the defendants in the three Moscow Trials were anything but guilty of those charges to which they confessed. No one has ever produced any evidence that the defendants were forced to testify in some manner dictated by the prosecution or NKVD. None of the "rehabilitation" documents and reports produced during Khrushchev's and especially during Gorbachev's era contains any evidence that the defendants were innocent. All the conclusions of all these rehabilitation reports are assertions only.

As we shall see, there is good evidence that some of the defendants at least did not tell "the whole truth" and that both Iagoda and other defendants, as well as Ezhov, distorted and concealed some matters at the trials. But none of this deception tends to exculpate any of the trial defendants either. It simply adds another dimension to their guilt, and to the picture of the conspiracies that we already have. From what we know, the defendants' testimony reflects what they wanted to say.

A central problem in evaluating the Moscow Trials testimony is the question of independent corroboration of statements made at the trial through evidence that could not have been arranged, planted, or otherwise created by the prosecution. Of course the lack of independent corroboration would not mean that the trial testimony and confessions were faked by the prosecution. In the case of a skillful conspiracy there might be no independent evidence at all. It would just mean that we would have no way of comparing this testimony with independent evidence. Even if we had no independent corroboration, we could evaluate the internal consistency of the statements made by different defendants at different times.

Fortunately some evidence external to the Moscow Trials and even to the USSR itself does exist. All of this external evidence tends to corroborate the confessions of the accused.

The Bloc: Its Formation and Composition

The major prosecution claim that frames the 1936 Trial is that a bloc was formed in 1932 between Trotskyites and Zinovievites, with other forces also joining. This bloc really did exist, as is confirmed in Sedov's letter to Trotsky of sometime in mid-1932 (Trotsky Archive 4782). Sedov names Zinovievites, "the Sten-Lominadze group", "the group of Safar[ov]-Tarkhan[ov]"; and "I.N. [Smirnov]", as well as Zinoviev and Kamenev ("Z. and K.").

All of these groups were named by prosecution and defendants in the August 1936 Trial. Sedov identified I.N. Smirnov as the leader of the Trotskyite group and this is confirmed in the trial transcript. Sedov's letter and the trial transcript confirm that the bloc was formed by 1932.

Active planning for murder of Kirov

According to testimony at the 1936 Trial active planning for Kirov's assassination began in the summer of 1934 and Leningrad conspirators were contacted in the autumn of 1934. This appears to coincide with certain indications in Nikolaev's diary upon which Lenoe has remarked. Concerning Nikolaev's "farewell letters" to family members, dated August 1934, Lenoe comments:

> Moreover, some "farewell" letters that he wrote to family members in August, but may not have delivered, suggest that he was considering suicide, or possibly the assassination of party officials. (216)

For Nikolaev the murder and suicide went together. We recall that he tried to kill himself seconds after shooting Kirov.

According to trial testimony specific organizational plans for Kirov's assassination began in the autumn of 1934.

> In order to prepare the murder, Bakayev went to Leningrad in the autumn of 1934 and there established contact with the active members of our organization: Kotolynov, Levin, Rumyantsev, Mandelstamm and Myasnikov, who formed the so-called Leningrad terrorist centre.The Leningrad centre had an active group of terrorists, directly engaged in preparations for the murder of Kirov. (Vol. XXXVI, p. 6.)[97]
>
> This was also fully confirmed during the investigation by the accused Evdokimov, who stated the following:
>
> "I learned from Bakayev that in the autumn of 1934, he, Bakayev, together with one Trotskyite terrorist, whose name I do not know, went to Leningrad to establish contact with the Leningrad terrorist centre and to organize the assassination of Kirov.
>
> "While in Leningrad, Bakayev and the above-mentioned Trotskyite terrorist met Nikolayev and arranged with him

[97] *Report of Court Proceedings. The Case of the Trotskyite-Zinovievite Terrorist Centre.* Moscow: People's Commissariat of Justice of the U.S.S.R., 1936, 30-31. (Report 1936)

> that he would assassinate Kirov." (Vol. XXXVI, pp. 7, 8.) (Report 1936, 33-34)
>
> At the end of Mrachkovsky's examination Vyshinsky asks Bakayev in what part of 1934 he went to Leningrad.
>
> Bakayev: In the autumn.
>
> Vyshinsky: For what purpose?
>
> Bakayev: To ascertain the preparedness of the organization to assassinate Kirov.
>
> Vyshinsky (to Kamenev): Did you give the instructions to make preparations for assassination of Kirov?
>
> Kamenev: Yes, in the autumn.
>
> Vyshinsky: In the autumn you and Evdokimov instructed Bakayev to go to Leningrad to check up on the progress which was being made by the Leningrad Trotskyite-Zinovievite group in its preparations to assassinate Kirov? Is that right, do you confirm that?
>
> Kamenev: Yes that is true. I confirm that.
>
> (Report 1936, 46)
>
> Continuing, Evdokimov says that for this purpose Bakayev, in the autumn of 1934, went to Leningrad to check up on the progress of preparations for the terroristic act against Sergei Mironovich Kirov by the Leningrad terrorists. These terrorist groups began to shadow Sergei Mironovich Kirov and waited for an opportune moment to commit their terroristic act.
>
> (Report 1936, 48)

The time period – autumn 1934 – corresponds with Nikolaev's lengthy diary entries of October 1934 in which he writes of "dying for my political convictions" (Lenoe 228) and his letter of "explanation before the Party and the Fatherland." (229-234). Nikolaev also wrote a letter to Kirov on October 30, 1934 (237-8). Within the next few days he "tried to outline concrete plans for assassinating Kirov" (238; 239-241).

Marxism and Terrorism

The question of reconciling the use of terror with Marxism which, as is well known, rejects the use of terror, arose at the trial.

> Vyshinsky: How did Zinoviev and Kamenev reconcile terroristic activities with Marxism?
>
> Reingold: In 1932, Zinoviev, at Kamenev's apartment, in the presence of a number of members of the united Trotskyite-Zinovievite centre argued in favor of resorting to terror as follows: although terror is incompatible with Marxism, at the present moment these considerations must be abandoned. There are no other methods available of fighting the leaders of the Party and the Government at the present time. Stalin combines in himself all the strength and firmness of the present Party leadership. Therefore Stalin must be put out of the way in the first place. Kamenev enlarged on this theory and said that the former methods of fighting, namely, attempts to win the masses, combinations with the leaders of the Rightists, and banking on economic difficulties, have failed. That is why the only method of struggle available is terroristic acts against Stalin and his closest comrades-in-arms, Kirov, Voroshilov, Kaganovich, Orjonikidze, Postyshev, Kossior and the others.
>
> (Report 1936, 55)

Trotsky and Terror

Trotsky proclaimed repeatedly in print and at the Dewey Commission hearings that he was unalterably opposed to "terror" – in English, to the use of violence and assassination against political opponents. In the words of Trotsky's advocate Goldman:

> The accusation of individual terror, as will be shown on the basis of Trotsky's numerous articles, beginning in 1902, is in direct contradiction with the whole bent of his thought, with his political education, with the lessons

> of his revolutionary experience, and finally, with the entire tradition of Russian Marxism.[98]

Trotsky spoke many times in opposition to terror. Almost the whole of the seventh session of the Dewey Commission hearings was devoted to this point. For example:

> On the 28th of December, 1934, four weeks after the Kirov assassination, Trotsky wrote in the Bulletin of the Opposition: … If Marxists have categorically condemned individual terrorism ….even when the shots were directed against the agents of the Tsarist government and of capitalist exploitation, then all the more relentlessly will they condemn and reject the criminal adventurism of terrorist acts directed against the bureaucratic representatives of the first workers' state in history.
>
> (Case of Leon Trotsky, 259-260)

Sedov devoted chapter 10 of his *Livre rouge* [99] ("Red Book") to demonstrating how vigorously Trotsky opposed terror.

> *Entrer maintenant dans la voie de la terreur individuelle, renoncer au marxisme, signifierait pour Trotsky non seulement renoncer à lui-même, mais aussi réduire à néant le fruit de quarante années d'activité révolutionnaire. Cela signifierait se suicider politiquement. (70)*
>
> To now take the path of individual terror, to renounce Marxism, would signify for Trotsky not only renouncing himself, but also reducing to nothing the fruits of forty years of revolutionary activity. That would signify political suicide.
>
> *Lors du coup de revolver de Nikolaïev, les communistes internationalistes ont déjà condamné la terreur individuelle de la*

[98] *The Case of Leon Trotsky. Report of hearings on the charges made against him in the Moscow trials. By the Preliminary Commission of Inquiry: John Dewey, chairman [and others].* New York: Harper & Brothers, 1937. 1st Session, p. 11. (Case of Leon Trotsky)

[99] L. Sedov. *Livre rouge sur le procès de Moscou.* Paris: Éditions Populaires, 1936.

> *façon la plus impitoyable, la plus résolue. Ils maintiennent aujourd'ui ce point de vue plus fermement que jamais. Si Staline, par sa politique, son régime et l'extermination de l'opposition, peut créer un état d'esprit terroriste, le devoir rélutionnaire dicte impérieusement aux bolchéviks-léninistes de répéter encore une fois de toute leur énergie: la voie de la terreur individuelle n'est pas notre voie, elle ne peut être que la voie qui mène à la perte de la révolution. (72)*
>
> At the time of Nikolaev's revolver shot we, the communist-internationalists, had already condemned individual terror in the most pitiless and most decisive fashion. Today we maintain this point of view more firmly than ever. If Stalin, by his policy, his regime and the extermination of the Opposition, can create a terrorist state of mind, then revolutionary duty imperiously demands that the Bolshevik-Leninists repeat once again with all their energy: the path or individual terror is not our path, it can only be the path to the destruction of the revolution.

In interviews with his biographer Feferman former Trotsky secretary Jan van Heijenoort insisted that in his own opinion Stalin should have been assassinated but that Trotsky would never consider it.

> When he later described the enormous amount of work the Trotskyites had to do to prepare for the hearings, van Heijenoort wrote the odd sentence: "Needless to say, in all this work, there was nothing falsified, nothing hidden." Why needless to say? Why wouldn't Trotsky, the ex-commissar of war, have plotted a return? Why wouldn't there have been many plots against Stalin by those who, early on, were keenly and painfully aware of his diabolical cruelty and singlemindedness?
>
> Fifty years after the Moscow trials, van Heijenoort's response to such questions was excited and emphatic:

> Yes, that's exactly my opinion. … But Trotsky always said 'We are against personal terrorism'. I say that is bunk. Of course Stalin should have been eliminated.[100]

But we know that, like Kamenev, Sedov did in fact believe that "terror" was an appropriate tactic for Marxists. Mark Zborowski was an NKVD agent who managed to gain Sedov's confidence. Zborowski wrote reports to his handlers while acting as one of Sedov's closest collaborators. In a report dated February 8, 1937 Zborowski wrote that on January 22, 1937, the eve of the Piatakov-Radek trial, Sedov suddenly began speaking to him of "terror":

> February 8, 1937
>
> On January 22 L. Sedov in our conversation at his apartment about the question of the second Moscow trial and the role in it of some of the accused (Radek, Piatakov and others) stated: "Now there is no reason to hesitate. Stalin must be killed."
>
> For me this statement was so unexpected that I did not manage to react to it in any way. L. Sedov immediately redirected the conversation onto other questions.
>
> On January 23 L. Sedov, in my presence and also that of L. Estrina, uttered a sentence with the same content as that of the 22nd. In answer to this statement of his L. Estrina said "Keep your mouth shut." They did not return to this question again.[101]

---

[100] Anita Burdman Feferman. *Politics, logic, and love : the life of Jean Van Heijenoort*. Wellesley, Mass.: A K Peters, Ltd., 1993, 140.

[101] Zborowski archive, F.31660 d. 9067 Papka No. 28. In Volkogonov Archive, Library of Congress. Online at
http://msuweb.montclair.edu/~furrg/research/zbor_sedov_stalin0238.pdf

Some of these same documents are confirmed by John Costello and Oleg Tsarev, *Deadly Illusions* (New York: Crown, 1993). Tsarev, a former KGB man, had privileged access to KGB files for a time in the early 1990s.

Mark Zborowski

In a report with a handwritten date on it of February 11, 1938 but which is possibly from the previous year, 1937, Zborowski reported again:

> Since 1936 "Sonny" had not talked with me about terror. Only about two or three weeks ago, after a meeting of the group, "Sonny" again began to speak on this subject. At first he only tried to "theoretically" prove that terrorism does not contradict Marxism. "Marxism" – in Sonny's words – rejects terrorism only insofar as the conditions of the class struggle are not suitable for terrorism, but there are situations in which terrorism is essential. The next time "Sonny" began to speak about terrorism when I arrived at his apartment to work. While reading newspapers "Sonny" said that since the whole regime of the USSR is held up by Stalin, it would be enough to kill Stalin for everything to fall apart. He had stated this thought earlier too, but until this time he had never formulated it this sharply. This last time he repeatedly returned to it, and underscored the necessity to kill com. Stalin with special care.
>
> In connection with this conversation "Sonny" asked me whether I feared death generally and whether I would be capable of carrying out a terrorist act. To my answer that it all depends on the circumstances and whether it was called for, Sonny said that I do not at all correctly understand what a "real" terrorist is and began to explain to me what kind of persons people suitable for carrying out terrorist acts are.
>
> Moving to the tactics of terror he stopped on the question of cadres, considering that this is the basic point. A terrorist – in Sonny's words – just always be ready for death, death must be for the terrorist a daily reality, and he illustrated this thesis with the example of the psychiology of the Narodovoltsy. Here he tossed out

> the remark that I, in his opinion, am too soft a person for this kind of affair.[102]

Sedov was surely reflecting his father's view here. Sedov himself had no political organization or goals independent of those of his father whose primary and, on very sensitive issues, sole political confidant he was.

In his testimony at trial Smirnov had claimed that first Sedov, in his meeting with him in 1931, and later Trotsky, through Gaven, had endorsed violence ("terrorism") as the only way to take power. In his *Livre rouge* Sedov conceded that he had met with Smirnov in Berlin in July 1931 (96). Soviet agent Zborowski's reports that Sedov recommended assassination and specifically Stalin's assassination, is consistent with what Radek and others testified that Trotsky had advocated in letters and communications to them.

It is to be expected that Trotsky and Sedov would publicly deny the use of "terror" (assassination). Thanks to Pierre Broué's research in the Harvard Trotsky archive we know they lied to preserve their conspiracy when they thought it useful to do so.

The Rights and Terror

Despite his denials, therefore, the evidence now available supports the hypothesis that Radek was telling the truth when he testified at the January 1937 Moscow Trial that Trotsky, along with other oppositionists, did advocate that Stalin be assassinated. This is to be expected in light of what we now know about the plans of the Rightists, with whom Trotsky's supporters had, with Trotsky's blessing, formed a bloc.

We can be certain that Bukharin, one of the main leaders of the Rights, was indeed advocating that Stalin be assassinated. In his memoirs published in Switzerland in 1971 Jules Humbert-Droz, a Swiss communist in the Comintern and close ally of Bukharin's, revealed that Bukharin told him the Rights were planning to kill Stalin as early as 1928.

---

102 Costello, John, and Oleg Tsarev. *Deadly Illusions*. NY: Crown, 1993, 283; 469 n.44. Tsarev & Kostello, *Rokovye Illiuzii*, 322-3, and n. 44 p.531 (Russian original). The other texts of Zborowski's reports are in facsimile in the Volkogonov Archiv, LOC. This archive also contains facsimiles of the reports published by Costello and Tsarev, thus verifying that they are the same ones.

Humbert-Droz met and talked with Bukharin for the last time in early 1929. The Swiss communist was about to leave for a conference of Latin American communist parties. In his memoirs, published in Switzerland in 1971, Humbert-Droz recalled this incident as follows:

> Before leaving I went to see Bukharin for one last time not knowing whether I would see him again upon my return. We had a long and frank conversation. He brought me up to date with the contacts made by his group with the Zinoviev-Kamenev fraction in order to coordinate the struggle against the power of Stalin. I did not hide from him that I did not approve of this liaison of the oppositions. "The struggle against Stalin is not a political programme. We had combatted with reason the programme of the Trotskyites on the essential questions, the danger of the kulaks in Russia, the struggle against the united front with the social-democrats, the Chinese problems, the very short-sighted revolutionary perspective, etc. On the morrow of a common victory against Stalin, the political problems will divide us. This bloc is a bloc without principles which will crumble away before achieving any results."
>
> **Bukharin also told me that they had decided to utilise individual terror in order to rid themselves of Stalin.** On this point as well I expressed my reservation: the introduction of individual terror into the political struggles born from the Russian Revolution would strongly risk turning against those who employed it. It had never been a revolutionary weapon. "My opinion is that we ought to continue the ideological and political struggle against Stalin. His line will lead in the near future to a catastrophe which will open the eyes of the communists and result in a changing of orientation. Fascism menaces Germany and our party of phrasemongers will be incapable of resisting it. Before the debacle of the Communist Party of Germany and the extension of fascism to Poland and to France, the International must change politics. That moment will then be our hour. It is necessary then to remain

disciplined, to apply the sectarian decisions after having fought and opposed the leftist errors and measures, but to continue to struggle on the strictly political terrain."

Bukharin doubtlessly had understood that I would not bind myself blindly to his fraction whose sole programme was to make Stalin disappear. / 380 / **This was our last meeting.** It was clear that he did not have confidence in the tactic that I proposed. He also certainly knew better than I what crimes Stalin was capable of. In short, **those who, after Lenin's death and on the basis of his testament, could have destroyed Stalin politically, sought instead to eliminate him physically,** when he held firmly in his hand the Party and the police apparatus of the state. (Emphasis added, GF.)[103]

---

[103] *Mémoirs de Jules Humbert-Droz. De Lénine à Staline. Dix ans au service de l'internationale communiste 1921-1931.* Neufchâtel: A la Baconnière, 1971, pp. 379-380. The original French text is as follows:

Avant de partir, j'allai voir une dernière fois Boukharine, ne sachant si je le reverrais á mon retour. Nous eûmes une longue et franche conversation. Il me mit au courant des contacts pris par son groupe avec la fraction Zinoviev-Kamenev pour coordonner la lutte contre le pouvoir de Staline. Je ne lui cachai pas que je n'approuvrais pas cette liaison des oppositions: «La lutte contre Staline n'est pas un programme politique. Nous avons combattu avec raison le programme des troskystes sur des problèmes essentiels, le danger des koulaks en Russie, la lutte contre le front unique avec les social-démocrates, les problèmes chinois, la perspective révolutionnaire très courte, etc. Au lendemain d'une victoire commune contre Staline, ces problèmes politiques nous diviseront. Ce bloc est un bloc sans principles, qui s'effritera même avant d'aboutir.»

Boukharine me dit aussi qu'ils avaient décidé d'utiliser la terreur individuelle pour se débarrasser de Staline. Sur ce point aussi je fis d'expresses réserves: l'introduction de la terreur individuelle dans les luttes politiques nées de la Révolution russe risquait fort de se tourner contre ceux qui l'emploieraient. Elle n'a jamais été une arme révolutionnaire. «Mon opinion est que nous devons continuer la lutte idéologique et politique contre Staline. Sa ligne conduira, dans un avenir proche, à une catastrophe qui ouvrira les yeux des communistes et aboutira à un changement d'orientation. Le fascisme ménace l'Allemagne et notre parti de phraseurs sera incapable de lui resister. Devant la débâcle du Parti communiste allemande et l'extension du fascisme à la Pologne, à la France, l'Internationale devra changer de politque. Ce moment-là sera notre heure. Il faut donc rester disciplinés, appliquer les décisions sectaires après les avoir combatues et s'opposer

Humbert-Droz, who published this account in 1971 wrote without any pressure from the NKVD. He wrote, and lived most of his life, in his native Switzerland. Moreover, he was Bukharin's friend and political ally. At the time of writing he hated Stalin, as is clear from his remark about "crimes Stalin was capable of". Thus he had no motive that we know of to lie or to exaggerate what he knew. Furthermore, Humbert-Droz claims he heard of the plans to murder Stalin from Bukharin's own lips.

This corroborates the confessions of many other Rightists, some of which have been published. It also corroborates Bukharin's recently-published first confession and his testimony at his 1938 trial.[104]

Thanks to Sedov's letter to his father and Trotsky's reply we know that Trotsky did enter a bloc with the Zinovievites and others. If Trotsky had held any kind of principled objection to assassinating Stalin he would not have entered into a bloc with persons whose goal that was.

He would also have not advocated "removing the leadership", a phrase which could not have reasonably been understood any other way than by assassination. No forms of activity except illegal ones were available to the defeated oppositions. Moreover, this same phrase is used by the oppositionists in the USSR to mean "assassination". We know the Rights had been planning to assassinate Stalin. Trotsky seems to have arrived at the same conclusion.

---

aux fautes et aux measures gauchistes, mais continuer la lutte sur le terrain strictement politique.»

Boukharine a sans doute compris que je ne me liais pas aveglément à sa fraction, dont le seul programme était de fair disparaître Staline. / 380 / Ce fut notre dernière entrevue. Manifestement il n'ávait pas confiance dans la tactique que je proposais. Il savait aussi bien sûr, mieux que moi, de quelles crimes Staline était capable. Bref, ceux qui, après la mort de Lénine, sur la base de son testament, auraient pu liquider politiquement Staline, cherchaient à l'élimer physiquement, alors qu'il tenait fermement en main le parti et l'appareil policier de l'Etat.

104 Grover Furr and Vladimir L. Bobrov, "Nikolai Bukharin's First Statement of Confession in the Lubianka". *Cultural Logic* 2007. At http://clogic.eserver.org/2007/Furr_Bobrov.pdf This article was first published in the St. Petersburg historical journal *Klio* 1 (36), 2005, 38-52. I have put the Russian version online at http://tinyurl.com/furr-bukharin

Yurii Gaven

In 1990 Pierre Broué announced that he had discovered that Trotsky and Sedov lied concerning their ties to some Party members inside the USSR. One of these figures was an Old Bolshevik of Latvian background, IUrii Petrovich Gavenis or, in its Russian form, Gaven. At the 1936 Moscow Trial Gaven was named by I.N. Smirnov, one of the chief defendants and a longtime Trotskyist, as the person who had met with Trotsky in 1932 and received terrorist instructions from him – that is, instructions to assassinate Stalin and, perhaps, others.

Vyshinskii, quoting Smirnov:

> I admit that the attitude which regarded terrorism as the only way of changing the situation in the Soviet Union was known to me from a conversation with Sedov in Berlin in 1931 as his own personal position. I admit that this line on terrorism was confirmed by L. Trotsky in 1932 in his personal instructions conveyed to me through Y. Gaven.
>
> (Report 1936, 17)

> Vyshinsky: Another question to Smirnov. Do you corroborate the testimony of Mrachkovsky that in 1932 you received a reply from Trotsky through Gaven?
>
> Smirnov: I received a reply from Trotsky through Gaven.
>
> Vyshinsky: And in addition, did you receive verbal information on the conversation with Trotsky?
>
> Smirnov: Yes, also verbal conversation.
>
> Vyshinsky: You, Smirnov, confirm before the Supreme Court that in 1932 you received from Gaven the direction from Trotsky to commit acts of terrorism?
>
> Smirnov: Yes.
>
> Vyshinsky: Against whom?
>
> Smirnov: Against the leaders.

> Vyshinsky: Against which?
>
> Smirnov: Stalin and others.
>
> (Report 1936, 42)

Smirnov stated that he had also had contact with Sedov but that Gaven had conveyed to him a letter from Trotsky himself.

> Vyshinsky: Was the letter you received through Gaven sent by Sedov or by Trotsky?
>
> Smirnov: Gaven brought a letter from Trotsky.
>
> (Report 1936, 83-84)
>
> [...]
>
> Vyshinsky: What then do you admit?
>
> Smirnov: I admit that I belonged to the underground Trotskyite organization, joined the bloc, joined the centre of this bloc, met Sedov in Berlin in 1931, listened to his opinion on terrorism and passed this opinion on to Moscow. I admit that I received Trotsky's instructions on terrorism from Gaven and, although not in agreement with them, I communicated them to the Zinovievites through Ter-Vaganyan.
>
> Vyshinsky: And, while not in agreement, you remained a member of the bloc and worked in the bloc?
>
> Smirnov: I did not resign officially from the bloc, but actually I did no work.
>
> (Report 1936, 85)

Smirnov's behavior seems inconsistent with a "forced" or faked confession. Smirnov continued to stubbornly insist that he was not a member of the bloc even though he passed on the instructions about terrorism to the Zinovievites, a point Vyshinsky energetically contested.

Smirnov returned to this topic in his last plea.

> This was the mistake I made, which later grew into a crime. It induced me to resume contact with Trotsky, it induced me to seek connections with the Zinovievite group, it brought me into a bloc with the group of

> Zinovievites, into receiving instructions on terrorism from Trotsky through Gaven in November 1932, it brought me to terrorism. I communicated Trotsky's instructions on terrorism to the bloc to which I belonged as a member of the centre. The bloc accepted these instructions and began to act.
>
> (Report 1936, 171)

Both Sedov and Trotsky publicly denied any meetings with Gaven.

Sedov, *Livre rouge*:

> *Gaven, par exemple, dont nous parlerons plus amplement, bien qu'il ait été mentionné à diverses reprises comme ayant transmis les instructions terroristes de Trotsky à Smirnov, est absent du procès. (49)*
>
> Gaven, for example, whom we will later discuss more fully, is mentioned several times as a courier of terrorist instructions from Trotsky to Smirnov, – and is absent from the trial.
>
> *Celui qui est mentionné comme ayant transmis les instructions de Trotsky sur la terreur, ce n'est pas Goltzman, mais I. Gaven, qui aurait personnellement reçu de Trotsky des instructions terroristes et les aurait transmises à I.N. Smirnov. C'est de Gaven, comme de l'unique personne qui ait transmis des instructions terroristes de Trotsky au Centre unifié que parle l'acte d'accusation…* (99-100)
>
> The one named at the trial who figures as the transmitter of Trotsky's instructions about terrorism is not Holtzman, but Y. Gaven, who supposedly personally received terrorist instructions from Trotsky, and passed them on to I.N. Smirnov. The charges speak of Gaven as the only person who had passed on terrorist instructions from Trotsky to the "Unified Center,"…
>
> […]
>
> *Faut-il répéter que Trotsky n'a pas transmis par l'intermédiare de I. Gaven, pas plus que par l'intermédiaire de quelqu'un d'autre, des instructions terroristes et ne s'est pas rencontré à l'étranger avec Gaven, pas plus qu'il ne s'est recontré avec aucun des accusés?* (100)

> Is it necessary to say that Trotsky did not transmit through I. Gaven, any more than through anyone else, any kind of terrorist instructions and did not meet with Gaven abroad, any more than he met with a single one of the defendants?

Trotsky, at the Dewey Commission hearings:

> GOLDMAN: Did you ever hear of a man by the name of Gaven?
>
> TROTSKY: Yes.
>
> GOLDMAN: Who is he?
>
> TROTSKY: He is a Latvian Bolshevik. He, if I remember, gave all his sympathies at a certain time to the Opposition. As Holtzman, for example. In 1926 or 1927, he was connected for a time with Smilga, a member of the Central Committee. But he disappeared from my eyes absolutely after 1926.
>
> GOLDMAN: In the testimony of Mrachkovsky, and also Smirnov, there is a reference that you sent communications through Gaven to Smirnov about the necessity of killing Stalin.
>
> TROTSKY: I don't know anything about it. No, it is an absolute falsehood. He is not among the defendants.
>
> GOLDMAN: No, he is not. He is a witness.
>
> TROTSKY: Not even a witness.
>
> GOLDMAN: That's right.
>
> TROTSKY: He disappeared.
>
> GOLDMAN: It is simply mentioned by Mrachkovsky, by the defendant Mrachkovsky.
>
> (*Case of Leon Trotsky*, 6th session, 225-226)

But in 1990 Broué revealed that Trotsky and Sedov had lied. Gaven did meet with Sedov at least.

> In 1936 Trotskii and Sedov denied having any contact with him [Gaven]. In fact, they had. Allowed to go to

> Germany in order to receive medical care, Gavenis wrote to Trotskii and got an interview with Lev Sedov, who wrote an account of it. Gavenis gave information about the bloc, supplementing Holzman's. He also gave information about his own "O"-group (probably Osinskii) and seems to have agreed to bring back to the Soviet Union a message to the Trotskiite group itself – in spite of his worry about the latter having been infiltrated by the OGPU.[105]

Broué does not identify the letter or letters either in the Sedov Papers at the Hoover Institution or in the Trotsky Archive at Harvard in which Trotsky and his son discuss Gaven. According to Vadim Rogovin, one of those letters may be Trotsky Archive 4858.[106] Broué suggests that other letters are at Hoover but gives no further details. In Broué's 1988 biography *Trotsky* we read only this:

> *Gaven, l'ancien « émissaire » de Trotsky, est fusillé sur une civière.*[107]

The detail of being shot "on a litter" is taken from Roi Medvedev, *Let History Judge,* a unreliable book full of Khrushchev-era falsifications. In the same chapter Broué also accepts Medvedev's account that Stalin had Sergo Ordzhonikidze assassinated, a story for which there is no evidence at all and which has long been abandoned even by anticommunists who insist that Sergo committed suicide – also a falsehood, as Vladimir Bobrov has demonstrated.[108]

---

105 Pierre Broué. "Party Opposition to Stalin (1930-1932) and the First Moscow Trial." In John W. Strong, ed. *Essays on Revolutionary Culture and Stalinism.* Columbus, OH: Slavica Publishers, 1990, pp. 98-111, p. 99. (Broué POS)

106 Rogovin, *Byla li Al'ternativa?*, Chapter 9; in Russian at http://web.mit.edu/people/fjk/Rogovin/volume4/ix.html

107 Chapter 56; at http://www.marxists.org/francais/broue/works/1988/00/PB_tky_56.htm

108 Vladimir L. Bobrov, "Taina smerti Ordzhonikidze", at http://vif2ne.ru/nvz/forum/archive/238/238967.htm ; fully footnoted Russian version at http://msuweb.montclair.edu/~furrg/research/bobrov-ordzhon08.html ; English translation at http://tinyurl.com/furr-bobrov

Broué writes:

> The correspondence between Trotskii and Sedov demonstrates that father and son were astounded at the beginning of the trial when they saw that Smirnov and Holzman, already guilty in Stalin's eyes, did not content themselves with confessing the truth but accused themselves of fantastic crimes. (Broué POS 99)

It would be important to see the text of such letters. If they are as Broué describes, they might constitute evidence that Smirnov's and Gol'tsman's testimony was false. But Broué neither quotes the text nor cites the specific letters in which this exchange supposedly took place. Therefore we can't verify Broué's claim that Trotsky and Sedov were "astounded" or that they discussed between themselves which of the accusations made by Smirnov and Gol'tsman were true and which were not.

Vadim Rogovin may have been informed of the contents of the Trotsky Archive by Broué; I have not found any evidence that he had access to the Trotsky Archives himself. We know that these men, the two most prominent Trotsky scholars in the world at the time, were in communication with each other.[109] Yet Rogovin cites only a letter in which Sedov discusses what he and Trotsky should admit and what they should conceal. This does not constitute evidence that they thought Smirnov's and Gol'tsman's testimony false.

Therefore we have evidence that Trotsky and Sedov lied about Gaven. Gaven had indeed met with Sedov and, in Broué's words, "seems to have agreed to bring back to the Soviet Union a message to the Trotskyite group itself". Smirnov confessed that this letter, which he dates to November 1932, contained terrorist instructions. Broué and Rogovin deny this but give no evidence for this denial.

Neither Broué nor Rogovin have any coherent explanation for Trotsky's and Sedov's lying here. Broué attempts to explain it thus:

> Sedov at first wondered whether he should tell the truth, publicly, but finally decided to deny everything, except

---

[109] I know this from the person who drove Broué when he was doing research in the Nicolaevsky Archive at the Hoover Institution during the 1980s.

> proven contacts, which seemed to him the only way of hindering the annihilation of the defendants. (Broué POS 99)

Rogovin opines:

> Facts such as these argue that Trotsky and Sedov decided to deny everything that was not already thoroughly known to Stalin's inquisitors. (op.cit.)

Such statements do not explain why Trotsky did not simply publish the letter he did give to Gaven, with the names of individuals deleted. Gaven and many others were already known to the NKVD, so this would not have further endangered them. Publishing the letter would have been a major challenge to Stalin and the NKVD, and be strong documentary evidence that Smirnov, Gol'tsman, and others were lying when they said that Trotsky was urging "terror" – assassination.

But if the letter Sedov passed to Gaven really did advocate "terror", as Smirnov and Vyshinsky claimed, then of course Trotsky and Sedov could not publish it. Therefore their failure to admit to the discussion with and message to Gaven, and their failure to publish the message they gave Gaven, at the very least leaves open the possibility that Trotsky had indeed advocated "terror" in this letter. As we shall see in our examination of the Kirov evidence in the second Moscow Trial of January 1937, exactly the same situation arose a few months later with respect to the letter to Radek.

In the early 1980s Getty revealed that the Trotsky Archive at Harvard had been "purged" of incriminating materials. No further evidence of Trotsky-Sedov contacts with Gaven or the other clandestine oppositionists inside the USSR during the 1930s can be expected from that source. This suggests that Trotsky's letter to the bloc sent by Gaven was incriminating in some way and so was among the materials purged from the archive. It is possible that such materials may be held in former Soviet archives still top-secret in Russia.

The "Hotel Bristol" Question

In 2010 Swedish researcher Sven-Eric Holmström proved that Trotsky laid down a smokescreen of lies and fabrication before the Dewey Commission. In his careful study of Gol'tsman's testimony at the 1936 Moscow Trial, the testimony by Trotsky and his witnesses at the Dewey Commission hearings, photographs of the Grand Hotel Copenhagen and Bristol Konditori (café), and the communist press of the time, Holmström has shown that the communist press was correct. Gol'tsman was telling the truth about the "Hotel Bristol". It was Trotsky and his witness, Esther Field, who were lying.[110]

As Holmström points out, Trotsky took a serious risk in lying about the Hotel Bristol matter. The Danish Communist Party did check up on his story and published their findings in their newspaper. Had anyone in the mainstream press followed up on this story the fact that Trotsky had lied would have become broadly known. This in turn might have discredited the Dewey Commission's investigation. In fact the Commission itself could have easily taken the trouble to verify the "Hotel Bristol" issue. That it failed to do so is additional evidence that the commission was heavily biased in Trotsky's favor.

If Gol'tsman really had been lying in his testimony about meeting Trotsky, Trotsky could have simply denied meeting Gol'tsman anywhere in Copenhagen in November 1932, though it is a matter of record that Trotsky was indeed present in Copenhagen at the time. Gol'tsman had no other proof of the meeting. The fact that Trotsky took the risk of lying about it for the purpose of raising what amounted to a "red herring" concerning the name of the hotel in question suggests that he may have had something to hide that was worth the risk of being caught in a lie in order to conceal.[111]

Conclusion

There is no direct confirmation from sources outside the Soviet Union of the charge that the Trotskyite-Zinovievite bloc conspired in the murder of Kirov. But such confirmation is hardly to be expected. In the interests

---

[110] Holmström, Sven-Eric. " New Evidence Concerning the 'Hotel Bristol' Question in the First Moscow Trial of 1936." *Cultural Logic*, 2008. At http://clogic.eserver.org/2008/Holmstrom.pdf (Published 2010)

[111] Holmström suspects that Gol'tsman did meet with Trotsky but that he did not meet with Sedov, as he claimed at the 1936 Moscow Trial, but with someone else whose identity he wanted to conceal. Holmström's study of the question of IUrii Piatakov's claim that he visited Trotsky in Norway in December 1935 is well advanced.

of secrecy the details of such a conspiracy would be confined to a small number of persons. Experienced conspirators like Trotsky and his son would not have told anyone who did not "need to know".

We do have confirmation of a number of details in the Moscow Trial from the best possible source outside Soviet control – Trotsky and his son. Trotsky and Sedov publicly denied these allegations – evidence that they believed this information would add to the credibility of the chief criminal allegations made in the Trial, as in fact they do. Corroboration of those allegations we can check does not, of course, prove that all allegations and accusations made at the Trial were equally correct. But it does add to the credibility of those charges that cannot be directly corroborated.

We also know that Trotsky's and Sedov's public statements cannot be taken at face value. To the extent that we have corroborated allegations made at the Trial that Trotsky and Sedov publicly denied, we can be assured that they would probably also deny other, even more incriminating accusations, especially if they were in fact true.

Chapter 14.

Evidence Lenoe Ignores – The Second and Third Moscow Trials

The second Moscow Trial is formally known as "the case of the Anti-Soviet Trotskyite Centre" and informally as the Piatakov-Radek trial after the two most famous defendants. It took place between January 23 and January 30, 1937. Lenoe dismisses the evidence given at this trial even more briefly than that of the first trial.

> The second major show trial of the Terror opened on January 23, 1937. Stalin and Yezhov supervised. The state constructed a giant conspiratorial edifice on the basis of private grumbling about Stalin and a few grotesque confessions of terrified defendants. (466)

This is another example of Lenoe's recourse to the fallacy of "begging the question", assuming that which must be proven.[112] Lenoe has no evidence that the defendants' confessions are false or that the state, not the defendants, "constructed" the conspiracy. The reason is simple: no such evidence exists.

As for Lenoe's claim that the defendants were any more "terrified" than defendants in any capital trial anywhere, I suggest that no objective person who studies the transcript could come away with that opinion. On the contrary: the principal defendants gave the impression of calmness and lucidity. A well-known example is the following passage from Karl Radek's closing statement:

> When I found myself in the People's Commissariat of Internal Affairs, the chief examining official realized at

---

[112] One famous definition: "*Petitio principia* is, therefore, committed when a proposition which requires proof is assumed without proof." James Welton. *A Manual of Logic. Volume II.* (London: W.B. Clive, 1896), p. 279. "Petitio principia" is translated as "begging the question"

> once why I would not talk. He said to me: "You are not a baby. Here you have fifteen people testifying against you. You cannot get out of it, and as a sensible man you cannot think of doing so. If you do not want to testify it can only be because you want to gain time and look it over more closely. Very well, study it." For two and a half months I tormented the examining official. **The question has been raised here whether we were tormented while under investigation. I must say that it was not I who was tormented, but I who tormented the examining officials and compelled them to perform a lot of useless work.** For two and a half months I compelled the examining official, by interrogating me and by confronting me with the testimony of other accused, to open up all the cards to me, so that I could see who had confessed, who had not confessed, and what each had confessed.
>
> This lasted for two and a half months. And one day the chief examining official came to me and said: "You are now the last. Why are you wasting time and temporizing? Why don't you say what you have to say?" And I answered: "Yes, tomorrow I shall begin my testimony." And the testimony I gave contains not a single correction from first to last. I unfolded the whole picture as I knew it, and the investigation may have corrected one or another personal mistake about the connections of some person with another, but I affirm that not a single thing I told the examining officials has been refuted and that nothing has been added.[113] (Emphasis added, GF)

This passage is famous. But other defendants were almost as cool under Vyshinsky's questioning.

Such passages expose Lenoe's purpose in describing the defendants as "terrified". Lenoe appears to be unwilling to deal with the testimony

---

113 *Report of Court Proceedings in the Case of the Anti-Soviet Trotskyite Centre. Heard Before the Military Collegium of the Supreme Court of the U.S.S.R. Moscow, January 23-30, 1937....Verbatim Report.* Moscow: People's Commissariat of Justice of the U.S.S.R., 1937, 549. (1937 Trial)

about the Kirov assassination. Perhaps this is because, like so much other evidence, it is incompatible with his preconceived conclusion that Nikolaev was a "lone gunman" and everybody else was "framed." Whatever his motives, Lenoe uses language in an attempt to justify ignoring the testimony. Declaring the testimony "grotesque" and the defendants "terrified" is also a "tell", a tacit admission that he has no evidence to refute the trial testimony and so is reduced to the "bluff" of denial.

Was the Trial Testimony Falsified?

Lenoe "begs the question" in that he assumes that the trial testimony was falsified in some way he does not specify. In this he follows the example of ideologically anticommunist researchers. It is easy to find historians of Soviet history who make this assumption. But it is impossible to find one who proves it, or indeed has any evidence for it at all. There has never been any evidence that the testimony at the Moscow Trials was falsified, the defendants forced to mouth confessions composed or dictated by others.

But though there is no evidence that the testimony in this trial was falsified, there is a lot of evidence of the contrary: that it was genuine. Here are a few examples of corroboration between testimony at the January 1937 trial and other established facts:

> * Radek and others testify that they disagreed with the assassination of individuals (1937 Trial 71; 101-2). This corresponds to what Iagoda testified independently, as we will see in the chapter devoted to him.
>
> * Radek's claim that he had received a letter from Trotsky in the spring of 1932 is confirmed by a certified mail receipt found by Getty in the Harvard Trotsky archive. (92)
>
> * Radek testified that Bukharin had told him he (Bukharin) had "taken the path of terrorism." (99) We know from the memoirs of Jules Humbert-Droz, published in Switzerland in 1971, that Bukharin had decided to assassinate Stalin long before this.
>
> * Sokol'nikov testified that the "united centre" of Zinovievites and Trotskyites had decided on planning terrorist acts against Stalin and Kirov "as early as the autumn of 1932." (147) This corresponds with the testimony of Valentin Astrov, one of Bukharin's followers,

one of whose confessions has been published. Astrov had the chance to recant this after the fall of the USSR but explicitly refused to do so. Astrov also insisted that the NKVD investigators had treated him with respect and used no compulsion against him.

* Muralov stated that Ivan Smirnov had told him about his meeting abroad with Sedov. (217) In his *Livre rouge* Sedov admitted that he had met with Smirnov, though he claimed the meeting was entirely innocent.

* Muralov stated that Shestov had brought a letter from Sedov in 1932 with a secret message written with antipirin, or invisible ink. (218) We know that Sedov used antipirin to write secret messages since at least one such letter of Sedov's survives in the Harvard Trotsky archive. In it he recommends that his father Trotsky write him back with antipirin as well.

* Radek stated that it was he who had recommended to Trotsky that Vitovt Putna, a military commander loyal to Trotsky, be the person to negotiate with the Germans and Japanese on Trotsky's behalf. This corresponds with Putna's later confessions as recorded by Marshal Budienniy.[114]

Most of this evidence might be explained as faked – if there were any evidence that the confessions, and the alleged plots, had been scripted by the NKVD. But there is no evidence of any such conspiracy to fabricate the trials, while we do have evidence that they were not scripted.

In light of these facts it is impermissible for any competent and objective researcher to simply dismiss without any consideration the very significant evidence given in the trial transcript concerning Kirov's assassination.

The Kirov Assassination

Radek had the most to say about the Kirov assassination plans. The following text is from the English version of the trial transcript, which is

114 Furr, Grover, and Vladimir L. Bobrov. "Marshal S.M. Budiennyi on the Tukhachevsky Trial. Impressions of an Eye-Witness" (in Russian). *Klio* No. 2 (2012), pp. 8-24. At http://msuweb.montclair.edu/~furrg/research/budennyi_klio12.pdf Reprinted in *M.N. Tukhachevskii. Kak My Predali Stalina.* Moscow: Algoritm, 2012, 174-230.

more than twice as long as the Russian version and so contains far more detail.

> Vyshinsky In what year was this?
>
> Radek: This was in 1930-31. And here there were those transgressions which would have justified my being brought to trial even if I had not belonged to the bloc. There was the fact that, knowing from these talks of their vacillations – which already exceeded the bounds of vacillations – I did not consider it possible to inform the leadership of the Party of it. For example, if you were to ask me about my responsibility for the murder of Sergei Mironovich Kirov, I must say that this responsibility began not from the moment I joined the leadership of the bloc, but from that moment in 1930 when a man with whom I had close relations – Safarov – came to me looking black in the face and tried to convince me that the country was on the verge of ruin, and I did not report this – and what were the consequences? Safarov was connected with Kotolynov. If I had told the Party about Safarov's frame of mind, the Party would have got at the group of the former leaders of the Leningrad Young Communist League who later became the leaders of the assassination of Kirov. And so I declare that my responsibility dates not only from the time I joined the bloc, but that the roots of this crime lie in the Trotskyite views with which I returned and which I had not thoroughly abandoned, and in the relations I had retained with the Trotskyite-Zinovievite cadres. (83-4)

This specific passage is not in the Russian transcript, where Safarov is not mentioned at all.

Both the Russian and English texts contain the following passages by Radek:

> Vyshinsky: Did you know from Mrachkovsky about the preparations for terrorist acts against the leaders of the Party and the government?

> ...
>
> Radek: The conversation about Kirov was connected with the fact that in April 1933 Mrachkovsky asked me whether I could mention any Trotskyite in Leningrad who would undertake the organization of a terrorist group there.
>
> Vyshinsky: Against whom?
>
> Radek: Against Kirov, of course.
>
> Vyshinsky: He requested your assistance?
>
> Radek: Naming a person is assistance, that is clear.
>
> Vyshinsky: And then?
>
> Radek: I named such a person.
>
> Vyshinsky: You named?
>
> Radek: Yes.
>
> Vyshinsky: Who was it?
>
> Radek: Prigozhin.
>
> Vyshinsky: Prigozhin? Who could find a murderer?
>
> Radek: Yes.
>
> Vyshinsky: This was in April 1933?
>
> Radek: Yes.
>
> Vyshinsky: And when was Kirov killed?
>
> Radek: Kirov was killed in December 1934. (Report 90)[115]

We know from the Trotsky Archive that Sedov informed Trotsky in 1932 that Safarov would shortly join the newly-minted bloc of Zinovievites, Trotskyites, and some others. Radek testified that Safarov told him in 1930 that "the country was on the verge of ruin" and, by implication, that

---

115 The account in the Russian transcript is slightly abbreviated.

Stalin must be stopped. Further, Safarov "was connected with Kotolynov", thus implying that the Zinovievite underground group existed as early as that date.

Radek testified that the decision to turn to terror came from the Spring 1932 letter from Trotsky and this meant terrorist acts should be planned against "Stalin and his immediate colleagues", including Kirov.

> Vyshinsky: Did you know anything about the preparations for the assassination of Sergei Mironovich Kirov?
>
> Radek: When we discussed the projected terrorist struggle, the question arose against whom it should be directed in the first place.
>
> Vyshinsky: This was in 1932?
>
> Radek: When the question arose against whom terrorism should be directed, it concerned terrorism directed against the leading core of the Central Committee of the C.P.S.U. and the Soviet government. And although not a single name was mentioned during this conversation, I know very well who are the leaders and did not have the slightest doubt that the acts were to be directed against Stalin and his immediate colleagues, against Kirov, Molotov, Voroshilov and Kaganovich.
>
> Vyshinsky: Were those your deductions or did he say this?
>
> Radek: There was no necessity to say it because I knew very well who lead the Party and the Soviet government. (89)
>
> ...
>
> Vyshinsky: And so it may be considered established that you learned about terrorism from Mrachkovsky?
>
> Radek: Yes.

> Vyshinsky: This was before you received the letter from Trotsky?
>
> Radek: This was after I received the letter from Trotsky. The letter from Trotsky was received in February or March 1932.
>
> Vyshinsky: That is, in February 1932 you received a letter from Trotsky in which he already spoke of the necessity of getting rid of .... .
>
> Radek: Removing.
>
> Vyshinsky: . . of the necessity of removing; consequently you understood that terrorism was meant?
>
> Radek: Of course. (93)

In April 1933 Mrachkovsky asked Radek if he could find someone in Leningrad to assassinate Kirov. Radek mentioned someone who might be able to organize a terrorist group there – Prigozhin.

Then Mrachkovsky told him that the Trotskyists had no one in Leningrad but that the Zinovievites did and were planning to assassinate Kirov. Mrachkovsky named Bakayev as overall leader of the Zinovievite terrorist groups.

> Vyshinsky: Consequently, many months before this villainous crime, you, Radek, knew that the Trotskyites were preparing to murder Kirov?
>
> Radek: I can say even more. I knew that it was being prepared in general, and by the Zinovievites because since it had been decided to strike at the leaders – Kirov was one of the most prominent leaders, and the Zinovievites had their main centre in Petrograd – it was clear that their terrorist organization intended to strike at Kirov. Moreover, Mrachkovsky told me then that we had nothing in Leningrad; the Zinovievites were preparing there and of course we ought to have our own group. That much in this connection he told me; but he did not tell me when and what would be. He only told me that the Zinovievites in Leningrad / 91 / were preparing for an assassination. He told me that, and I

> very clearly, without any ambiguity, knew that this concerned Kirov.
>
> Vyshinsky: When you say here that Mrachkovsky informed you of the role of Bakayev, what do you mean by that?
>
> Radek: He did not tell me that Bakayev personally directed the assassination of Kirov, but he named him as the leader of all the terrorist groups of the Zinovievites. I did not know whether Bakayev would commit this assassination or entrust it to somebody else, but it was clear to me that the preparations for the assassination could not proceed without Bakayev. (90-1; not in the Russian transcript)

Sokol'nikov, another leader with Radek and Piatakov of the "reserve center" of Trotskyites, also claimed he knew of terrorist planning in 1932 and of Bakayev's role. Sokol'nikov said that Kamenev had told him in the autumn of 1934 about an impending assassination attempt against Kirov. He also confessed that he knew as early as 1932 that the Leningrad center included Kotolynov, Mandelshtam, Levin "and others".

> The President: Did you know of the preparations in 1934 for the assassination of Comrade Kirov? Did you know who were the members of the terrorist centre which prepared and carried out the assassination of Comrade Kirov?
>
> Sokolnikov: I knew in the beginning of the autumn, or the end of the summer of 1934, I cannot say definitely, that an attempt on the life of Kirov was being prepared in Leningrad. As to who was to carry it out, that I did not know. I was not informed about the details of this affair. But in 1932 I heard who the members of the Leningrad centre were.
>
> The President: Thus, you confirm your testimony that you knew of the existence in Leningrad of the terrorist centre, and in particular, that the members of this centre were Levin, Kotolynov, Mandelstamm and others. You confirm this?

Sokolnikov: Yes, I confirm it, I knew that in 1932.

The President: Did you know that the preparations for the terrorist act against Comrade Kirov were carried out under Bakayev's personal direction?

Sokolnikov: I was not told about that directly, but I knew that the direction of the preparation of a terrorist act was entrusted to Bakayev.

The President: To what extent were you connected with Reingold and his activities?

Sokolnikov: Reingold directed the terrorist groups in Moscow. I used to meet him, but he gave me no information about his work. About the functions that he was carrying out I learned from Kamenev.

The President: Reingold had more direct connections with you than with Kamenev?

Sokolnikov: But he gave me no information about his activities.

The President: Reingold frequently visited you and discussed things with you more than he did with Kamenev. How is it that you did not know about his activities?

Sokolnikov: I met him, but he gave me no infomation about his terrorist activities, and I cannot testify to the details of his work.

The President: If you did not know the details of Reingold's terrorist activities, how is it you knew such a detail as the fact that in November 1934 Bakayev went to Leningrad personally to prepare the murder of Comrade Kirov?

Sokolnikov: I had no connection whatever with the preparations for the murder of Kirov except that, as a member of the organization, I bear responsibility for all the actions and all the crimes committed by the organization. The reason why I knew about Bakayev is that Kamenev mentioned him to me. I had known

> Bakayev for a long time, and evidently Kamenev, in conversation with me, mentioned him. (165-166)

This corresponds with Kamenev's confessions both before and at the 1936 trial. We have discussed them in a previous chapter. It also confirms the confessions of Valentin Astrov, a former follower of Bukharin's. Astrov confirmed these confessions in articles published in the post-Soviet period.[116]

Muralov confirmed that I.N. Smirnov had told him in 1931 of his visit with Sedov and of "Trotsky's new line about resorting to terrorism against the leadership of the Communist Party and the government."

> Vyshinsky: Tell us about the part you played in the West-Siberian underground Trotskyite centre.
>
> [...]
>
> Muralov: In the beginning of 1931. While I was on an official business trip in Moscow I met Ivan Nikitich Smirnov. He told me that he had been abroad and had seen Sedov. He told me about Trotsky's new line about resorting to terrorism against the leadership of the Communist Party and the government.
>
> Smirnov advised us to re-establish the Siberian centre to consist of persons known to me and him, those who returned to the Party in 1929. These names were mentioned – Sumetsky and Boguslavsky. The first task of this centre was to gather Trotsky-ite forces and to organize serious terrorist acts. On my arrival in Novosibirsk I arranged to meet Sumetsky and Boguslavsky and told them what Ivan Nikitich Smirnov had proposed, which I accepted as proper. They also agreed with me and we three began to function as the Trotskyite counter-revolutionary centre in Siberia. I was the leader; Sumetsky was to gather the cadres chiefly among the young people in the universities. I instructed the Trotskyite Khodoroze to organize a terrorist group. He formed it in 1932. The designated object of the terrorist act was

[116] We discuss Astrov elsewhere in the present work, and at greater length in our essay "Verdikt – Vinoven" ("Verdict – Guilty"), Chapter One of Grover Furr and Vladimir Bobrov, 1937. *Pravosudie Stalina. Obzhalovaniiu ne podlezhit!* Moscow: Eksmo, 2010.

> the secretary of the Territory Committee of the C.P.S.U., Eiche. In the same year, 1932, Shestov arrived in Novosibirsk and brought a letter from Sedov.
>
> This letter contained a lot of fiction and was written in the ordinary way, but what was not fiction was written with antipirin and when made visible was found to be Trotsky's directive to proceed to terrorist activities. The letter confirmed what Smirnov had said. (216-217)

This confirms what Broué was told by Lilia Dallin: that Sedov was the only person who knew all of Trotsky's plans. It is also consistent with Mark Zborowski's reports to Moscow that Sedov had confided to him that Stalin should be assassinated, despite the fact that both Sedov and Trotsky publicly denounced assassination as contrary to Marxism. We also have at least one letter in the Harvard Trotsky Archive by Sedov written with antipirin, a kind of invisible ink made visible when heated with an iron.

Like Radek and Piatakov – and, as we shall see, like Iagoda – Muralov was opposed to "working by Socialist-Revolutionary, guerrilla methods" of individual assassination, but nevertheless participated in plans for assassination.

> Vyshinsky: Tell the Court please, did you meet Pyatakov after the murder of Sergei Mironovich Kirov?
>
> Muralov: I did.
>
> Vyshinsky: In Moscow?
>
> Muralov: In Moscow.
>
> Vyshinsky: And did you discuss the murder of Sergei Mironovich Kirov?
>
> Muralov: We did, we discussed the impression this act had left on everybody, and noted that after all, the directive was being carried out; one man had already been removed.
>
> Vyshinsky: One had been removed!
>
> And did not Pyatakov say that now it was the turn of the others?

Muralov: He did not say that now it was the turn of the others; on the contrary, he said that it was necessary to do this in an organized way. Generally speaking, we did not say that it must be each in turn, or all at once; at all events we said that we must be well prepared, and reproaching me in this respect, he said that we must not act in this blunt soldier-like fashion, but cautiously, in an organized way, and so forth.

Vyshinsky: Cautiously, in an organized way, but act?

Muralov: Yes.

Vyshinsky: At the preliminary investigation, when you were examined at the office of the Procurator of the U.S.S.R., you testified as follows. Permit me to read Vol. XXV, p. 109:

"In 1934, after the murder of Sergei Mironovich Kirov, I met Pyatakov in Moscow and in conversation with me he said: 'One of those listed in the plan has been wiped off, now it is the turn of the rest; but we must not be impetuous.'"

Is that right?

Muralov: I confirm it, that is what I said.

(224-225)

[...]

Vyshinsky: But was it not said that terrorism in general produces no result if only one is killed and the others remain, and therefore it is necessary to act at one stroke?

Muralov: Both I and Pyatakov felt that it was no use working by Socialist-Revolutionary, guerrilla methods. We must organize it so as to cause panic at one stroke. We regarded causing panic and consternation in the leading ranks of the Party as one of the means by which we would come into power. (226)

The Second Moscow Trial: Conclusion

The testimony at the second Moscow Trial concerning the Kirov assassination situates that act in the context of a much broader conspiracy composed of a number of independent underground groups in touch with one another through a co-ordinating center. It also exculpates the Trotskyite conspiracy from direct participation in the Kirov assassination.

The conventional explanation of the anti-Trotskyite campaign of the 1930s is that it was a fabrication that demonstrated how Stalin saw Trotsky as his main rival and wanted to demonize him for that reason. However, if that had been the case, why would the NKVD "script" confessions that showed the Trotskyites were not directly involved in Kirov's murder? Of course they knew such an attempt was being planned by the Zinovievites. In a legal sense this made them responsible as well. But there is clearly a moral and a legal difference between being informed that an assassination is being planned and actively assisting in its accomplishment. Trotsky is portrayed as demanding assassinations, but his men did not carry them out.

It is also hard to square with the fact that two of the leading Trotskyite defendants, Radek and Sokol'nikov (along with two minor defendants), were given only prison sentences on the grounds that they did not participate either in the assassination of Kirov or in the sabotage to which the rest of the defendants confessed. Why would this have happened if Trotsky had been the main target of the trial?

The fact that some parts of Radek's confessions can be verified and that we have no evidence of any "scripting" of the confessions by Stalin or at his direction ought to compel any honest investigator to treat these confessions as genuine unless and until evidence of such "scripting" or other evidence of falsification were to come to light. Absent such evidence, the confessions at this trial reveal that the conspiracy to assassinate leading Party members goes back to the formation of the bloc in 1932, and plans to murder Kirov to at least April 1933. Nikolaev's act appears as the culminating stage of a much broader conspiracy.

Evidence Lenoe Ignored: The Third Moscow Trial

Genrikh Iagoda was the only one of the defendants in the March 1938 trial who had a close connection with the actual murder of Kirov. The testimony of other defendants gives more information concerning the conspiracy of the Rights, but it does not reveal anything more about the assassination plot or execution itself.

We will also examine the other testimony related to the Kirov assassination because it gives convincing evidence that the testimony of the defendants was not "scripted" or "fabricated" in the least, but genuine. Defendants Ivanov, Rykov, and Bukharin insist that they had no prior knowledge about the conspiracy to assassinate Kirov despite their prominent roles in the conspiracy of the Rights and the relationship of the Rights to the Trotskyite and Zinovievite conspiracies. Sharply differentiated confessions in which a defendant admits to some capital crimes while staunchly denying his guilt in others, is strong evidence that the defendant was not acting under torture or threats. This is especially striking in the case of Bukharin.

Bukharin claimed that he had no prior knowledge of the Kirov assassination plot despite his admitted membership in the bloc of Rights and Trotskyites.

> VYSHINSKY: Did the bloc stand for the organization of terrorist acts, the assassination of leaders of the Party and the Soviet government?
>
> BUKHARIN: It did, and I think that the organization of this must be dated back roughly to 1932, the autumn.
>
> VYSHINSKY: And what was your relation to the assassination of Sergei Mironovich Kirov? Was this assassination also committed with the knowledge and on the instructions of the "bloc of Rights and Trotskyites"?
>
> BUKHARIN: That I did not know.
>
> VYSHINSKY: I ask you, was this assassination committed with the knowledge and on the instructions of the "bloc of Rights and Trotskyites"?
>
> BUKHARIN: And I repeat that I do not know, Citizen Procurator.
>
> VYSHINSKY: You did not know about this specifically in relation to the assassination of S. M. Kirov?
>
> BUKHARIN: Not specifically, but...

VYSHINSKY: Permit me to question the accused Rykov.

THE PRESIDENT: You may.

VYSHINSKY: Accused Rykov, what do you know about the assassination of Sergei Mironovich Kirov?

RYKOV: I know nothing about the participation of the Rights or the Right part of the bloc in the assassination of Kirov.

VYSHINSKY: In general, were you aware of preparations for terrorist acts, for the assassination of members of the Party and the government?

RYKOV: As one of the leaders of the Right part of this bloc, I took part in the organization of a number of terrorist groups and in preparations for terrorist acts. As I have said in my testimony, I do not know of a single decision of the Right centre, through which I was related with the "bloc of Rights and Trotskyites" about the actual commission of assassinations... .

VYSHINSKY: About the actual commission. So. Do you know that one of the aims of the "bloc of Rights and Trotskyites" was to organize and commit terrorist acts against leaders of the Party and the government?

RYKOV: I said more than that, I said that I personally organized terrorist groups. But you are asking me whether I knew of such aims through some third person.

VYSHINSKY: I am asking whether the "bloc of Rights and Trotskyites" had any relation to the assassination of Comrade Kirov.

RYKOV: I have no information regarding the relation of the Right part to this assassination, and therefore I am convinced to this day that the assassination of Kirov was carried out by the Trotskyites without the knowledge of

> the Rights. Of course, I might not have known about it.[117]

Bukharin's and Rykov's stubborn refusal to admit any knowledge of the role of the bloc in the assassination of Kirov is strong evidence that his testimony was not forced or fabricated. As we shall see, Vyshinsky had to address the court with the claim that he had successfully proven their complicity despite their denials.

In their concluding statements both Bukharin and Rykov again insist that they were ignorant about the assassination:

> Rykov: ...The assassination of Kirov has formed the subject of two trials. Both the direct perpetrators and the organizers and leaders of this assassination have appeared in Court. I do not recall that my name was mentioned then. (1938 Trial, 738)

> Bukharin: ... I categorically deny my complicity in the assassination of Kirov, Menzhinsky, Kuibyshev, Gorky and Maxim Peshkov. (771)

Of course, it might be the case that Rykov and Bukharin were lying here and really had known about the Kirov murder in advance. It is possible they thought that the question of complicity in these murders might have been a decisive one in determining whether they and others would face the death penalty or merely receive prison terms, as Radek and Sokol'nikov had at the January 1937 Moscow Trial. Both Radek and Sokol'nikov knew of Kirov's assassination but did not play any role in it, and had been spared execution.

Vyshinsky, the prosecutor, argued that it was highly unlikely that such leaders of the Rights as Rykov and Bukharin could have been ignorant about the Kirov murder no matter what they said at trial. Genrikh Iagoda testified that they had to know of the Kirov murder plot.

---

[117] *Report of Court Proceedings in the Case of the Anti-Soviet "Bloc of Rights and Trotskyites" Heard Before the Military Collegium of the Supreme Court of the U.S.S.R. Moscow, March 2-13, 1938... Verbatim Report.* Moscow: People's Commissariat of Justice of the U.S.S.R., 1938, 373-374. (1938 Trial)

VYSHINSKY: Very well; please be seated. Permit me to question the accused Yagoda. Accused Yagoda, do you know that Yenukidze, of whom the accused Rykov just spoke, represented the Right part of the bloc and that he had direct relation to the organization of the assassination of Sergei Mironovich Kirov?

YAGODA: Both Rykov and Bukharin are telling lies – Rykov and Yenukidze were present at the meeting of the centre where the question of assassinating S. M. Kirov was discussed.

VYSHINSKY: Did the Rights have any relation to this?

YAGODA: Direct relation, because it was a bloc of Rights and Trotskyites.

VYSHINSKY: Did the accused Rykov and Bukharin in particular have any relation to the assassination?

YAGODA: Direct relation.

VYSHINSKY: Did you, as a member of the "bloc of Rights and Trotskyites" have any relation to this assassination?

YAGODA: I did.

VYSHINSKY: Are Bukharin and Rykov telling the truth when they say that they knew nothing about it?

YAGODA: That cannot be so, because when Yenukidze told me, that they, that is, the "bloc of Rights and Trotskyites" had decided at a joint meeting to commit a terrorist act against Kirov, I categorically objected... .

VYSHINSKY: Why?

YAGODA: I declared that I would never permit any terrorist acts. I regarded it as absolutely unnecessary.

VYSHINSKY: And dangerous for the organization?

YAGODA: Of course.

VYSHINSKY: Nevertheless? :

> YAGODA: Nevertheless Yenukidze confirmed …
>
> VYSHINSKY: What?
>
> YAGODA: That at this meeting they …
>
> VYSHINSKY: Who were they?
>
> YAGODA: Rykov and Yenukidze at first categorically objected… .
>
> VYSHINSKY: To what?
>
> YAGODA: To the commission of a terrorist act. But under the pressure of the remaining part of the "bloc of Rights and Trotskyites"…
>
> VYSHINSKY: Principally the Trotskyites?
>
> YAGODA: Yes, under the pressure of the remaining part of the "bloc of Rights and Trotskyites" they gave their consent. So Yenukidze told me. (375-376)

Iagoda insisted that both Rykov and Bukharin were lying in denying that they had prior knowledge of the plot to kill Kirov. Yet when pressed by Vyshinskii Iagoda admitted that he did not know this at first hand but had heard it from Enukidze. This is evidence that this testimony was genuine. Vyshinskii was eager to prove that Bukharin and Rykov had prior knowledge of Kirov's murder. But none of his star witnesses would oblige him by admitting this.

In his summation to the court Vyshinskii claimed that this prior knowledge was "proven." But it is clear from the transcript that it was not in fact proven. There is no direct testimony to that effect; this is only Vyshinskii's deduction.

> Yenukidze and Yagoda were members of the centre and closest associates of Bukharin and Rykov. How can we believe that Yenukidze and Yagoda who had a share in the assassination of Sergei Mironovich Kirov, who were closest associates of Rykov and Bukharin, and who were the centre of the whole system of terrorist acts against leaders of the Party and the government -- how can we believe that Rykov and Bukharin did not know what was known to Yenukidze, the immediate friend, accomplice

> and coadjutor of Bukharin and Rykov, and what was known to Yagoda, the closest friend, accomplice and coadjutor of Bukharin and Rykov?
>
> These are the circumstances which completely prove the participation of Rykov and Bukharin in the organization of the assassination of Sergei Mironovich Kirov.
>
> - Report 679-680

Had Iagoda been subject to torture or threats he could have claimed direct knowledge of Bukharin's and Rykov's prior knowledge, thus substantiating Vyshinskii's case. Had Rykov and Bukharin been subject to torture or threats they could have done likewise. The fact that they insisted upon their innocence in this regard while admitting to other very serious crimes argues that they were guilty of at least what they confessed to. Bukharin devoted his own final statement to the court to a detailed denial of a number of the charges against him, charges of which the prosecution spent a great deal of time and effort trying to prove him guilty. We will discuss the issue of "torture" in a separate section of the present study. Bukharin's biography Stephen Cohen, perhaps the greatest authority on Bukharin in the world, has stated his conviction that Bukharin was not tortured.[118]

Bulanov's Testimony

Bulanov's testimony appears to corroborate Iagoda's in one respect while contradicting it on another important matter. Bulanov testified that Iagoda informed him in 1936 that he and Zaporozhets had had prior knowledge of the Kirov murder plot. This far Bulanov's testimony agrees with that of Iagoda.

But then Bulanov testified that Iagoda had arranged the murder of Borisov, Kirov's bodyguard, supposedly because Borisov had been ordered not to prevent the assassination attempt.

> Yagoda further told me that Borisov, an employee of the Leningrad Administration of the People s Commissariat

---

118 Cohen, Stephen. "Bukharin na Lubianke." *Svobodnaia Mysl'* 21, No. 3 (2003), 58-63, at 60-61.

> of Internal Affairs, had a share in the assassination of Kirov. When members of the government came to Leningrad and summoned this Borisov to the Smolny to interrogate him as a witness in connection with the assassination of Kirov, Zaporozhetz, being alarmed by this and fearing that Borisov would betray those who stood behind Nikolayev, decided to kill Borisov. On Yagoda's instructions, Zaporozhetz so arranged it that an accident occurred to the automobile which took Borisov to the Smolny. Borisov was killed in the accident, and in this way they got rid of a dangerous witness. (1938 Trial 558-559)

This is from the published trial transcript. But in 1995 Russian researcher IUrii Murin revealed that the original transcript of Bulanov's remarks says something quite different here:

> In the original transcript:
>
> "Bulanov .. I can't tell you exactly – the story was rather confused, but I seem to remember also that commissar Borisov, who was the sole participant in the murder [sic – GF] , who was supposed to give to the members of the government, who themselves had travelled there and were conducting the investigation, was supposed to give confessions, which he could have given, that Iagoda had also been there, then this commissar Borisov could not appear at the interrogation and was killed through an automobile accident. When he told me that he had been informed of the murder, then I understood that unusual concern of Iagoda's which he showed when Medved', Zaporopzhets and the other employees had been arrested and given over for trial as ordered."[119]

In the original transcript Bulanov admitted that his memory of the details was imprecise – "I seem to remember." Bulanov did remember Borisov's death. It seemed suspicious to him, as it did to others at the time. But in

[119] IUrii Murin. "Ubiystvo v Smol'nom" [Murder in the Smolny]. *Rodina* 10 (1995), p. 66.

the original transcript Bulanov could not be certain that Iagoda had told him this. In fact he does not even directly attribute this story to Iagoda.

Lenoe states that this is an example of how "almost totally incoherent" Vyshinskii's case was. (480) But Lenoe is mistaken. Iagoda claimed he did not order Borisov to be killed, and Bulanov was unable to contradict him. Iagoda's testimony was not shaken on this point. Lenoe's false conclusion is based upon his claim that Iagoda "retracted" his testimony about Kirov's murder. That Iagoda never did so we have demonstrated in a separate section of this study.

This passage is evidence that yet another defendant testified honestly. Bulanov could have been forced to directly inculpate Iagoda in Borisov's death. But Bulanov was not forced. Instead he admitted his recollection was unclear.

Genrikh Iagoda was the only defendant in the March 1938 trial who had a close connection with the actual murder of Kirov. The testimony of other defendants gives more information concerning the conspiracy of the Rights, but it does not reveal anything more about the assassination plot or its execution.

Here we will examine the other testimony related to the Kirov assassination because it gives convincing evidence that the testimony of the defendants was not "scripted" or "fabricated" in the least, but genuine. (By "genuine" we mean that the defendants said what they chose to say; we don't claim that they always told the truth.) Defendants Ivanov, Rykov, and Bukharin insist that they had no prior knowledge of the conspiracy to assassinate Kirov despite their prominent roles in the conspiracy of the Rights and the relationship of the Rights to the Trotskyite and Zinovievite conspiracies.

Bukharin's and Rykov's stubborn refusal to admit any knowledge of the role of the bloc in the assassination of Kirov is strong evidence that their testimony was not compelled or "scripted". As we shall see, Vyshinsky believed that they were lying. As we saw above, when he addressed the court Vyshinskii claimed that he had successfully proven their complicity. But in their concluding statements both Bukharin and Rykov once again insisted that they were ignorant about the assassination. (1938 Trial 737-8; 771)

There are no logical or rational grounds – much less evidentiary grounds – for doubting that the defendants at this trial testified what they wanted to testify. Had Iagoda been subject to torture or threats he could have claimed direct knowledge of Bukharin's and Rykov's prior knowledge, thus substantiating Vyshinskii's case. Likewise, had Bukharin or Rykov been tortured or threatened, or their families threatened, they would hardly have strenuously denied their guilt when the prosecution was eager to inculpate them.

Chapter 15.
Iagoda's Confession

Lenoe claims that Genrikh Iagoda, NKVD commissar from 1934 to 1936 and later defendant at the March 1938 Moscow Trial, "recanted" a confession concerning Kirov's assassination. Lenoe quotes from a report by Khrushchev-era NKVD chief Ivan Serov of August 31, 1956:

> In his final words to the court Yagoda declared:
>
> Not only is it false to say that I was an organizer but even to say that I was an accomplice in the murder of Kirov. I am guilty of a very serious dereliction of duty, that is true. I will answer for that in full measure, but I was not an accomplice. 'An accomplice' – you know as well as I do, comrade procurator, what that means. None of the materials of this trial or the preliminary investigation show that I was an accomplice in this villainous murder.
>
> Yagoda in essence recanted his earlier testimony with regard to the participation of the Rightists in the murder of Kirov… (Lenoe 598)[120]

Lenoe accepts Serov's interpretation of this passage, writing:

---

120 For some reason Lenoe does not use the official Soviet translation of this passage, from the trial transcript published in Moscow in 1938. As a convenience to the reader who may wish to check this for herself, this passage is on p. 786 of the trial transcript, and is as follows:

"It is not only untrue to say that I was an organizer but it is untrue to say that I was an accomplice in the murder of Kirov. I committed an extremely grave violation of duty – that is right. I answer for it in an equal measure, but I was not an accomplice. Citizen Procurator, you know what complicity is just as well as I do. The entire material of the Court proceedings and the preliminary investigation has failed to prove that I was an accomplice in this vile murder."

> As we have seen, Yagoda recanted his confession at the trial's end. (666)

Lenoe's statement is false. In this section we shall show that Iagoda did not at all "recant his confession" concerning Kirov's assassination and his role in it. On the contrary: Iagoda confirmed all the essential aspects of his confession concerning his role in the Kirov assassination. The only thing he did "recant" was that he was legally an accomplice (*souchastnik*) – a technical legal matter concerning the definition of which he and Soviet prosecutor Andrei Vyshinskii disagreed.

We will first prove that this is the case. Then we will conclude this section with a discussion of how it is that Lenoe could have misunderstood what Iagoda said. Briefly: Iagoda's confessions disprove Lenoe's thesis that Nikolaev acted alone, that there was no conspiracy to kill Kirov. Lenoe evidently misread Iagoda's testimony accordingly. Lenoe's misreading was possibly facilitated by the fact that Serov had also misread it back in the 1950s. But, as Lenoe himself notes, Serov was deliberately falsifying matters as a part of Khrushchev's attempt to malign Stalin. Lenoe ought to have been more cautious in accepting Serov's interpretation.

Iagoda's Testimony

In his introductory remarks at the March 1938 Moscow trial Soviet Prosecutor Andrei Vyshinskii introduced the matter of Iagoda's involvement with Kirov's murder this way:

> The investigation has established that the vile assassination of S. M. KIROV committed by the Leningrad Trotskyite-Zinovievite terrorist centre on December 1, 1934, was also committed in pursuance of a decision of the "bloc of Rights and Trotskyites," members of which are being charged in the present case.
>
> The investigation has established that one of the participants in this vile murder was the accused YAGODA, who testified as follows:
>
> "That preparations for the assassination of S. M. KIROV were being made in accordance with a decision of the conspiratorial centre, I had previously learnt from

> YENUKIDZE. YENUKIDZE told me not to hinder the organization of this terrorist act, and I agreed. With this purpose I summoned ZAPOROZHETZ from Leningrad and instructed him not to hinder the terrorist act that was being prepared against S. M. KIROV." (Vol. II, p. 209.)
>
> (1938 Trial 22)

This is the essence of the charge against Iagoda concerning Kirov's murder.

We shall show that, in Iagoda's view, this meant he was not an accomplice in Kirov's murder, while Vyshinskii insisted that he was indeed an accomplice. All that Iagoda and Vyshinskii disagreed about was the legal definition of "accomplice."

We now have the entire text of the specific pretrial interrogation of Iagoda from which Vyshinskii quotes here. It is in a collection of documents related to Iagoda that includes the texts of seven of Iagoda's pretrial interrogation-confessions. The paragraph above is taken word for word from the pretrial interrogation-confession of Iagoda that is dated January 10, 1938.[121] Elsewhere we have examined the *bona fides* of these confessions, demonstrated that they are genuine, and shown that even anticommunist authors have accepted them.[122]

The fact that we have the texts of all these pretrial interrogations is important for several reasons.

> * They prove that Vyshinskii honestly quoted from the pre-trial investigation materials. That is, these pretrial interrogations are evidence that the trial was conducted honestly, insofar as the prosecution quoted accurately from real pretrial evidence.

---

121 *Genrikh Iagoda. Narkom vnutrennikh del SSSR, General'niy komisar gosudarstvennoi bezopasnosti. Sbornik dokumentov*. Kazan', 1997. (Genrikh Iagoda), p. 235. The Russian-language quotation in this 1997 volume is the same, word for word, as that in the Russian-language trial transcript.

122 Grover Furr, "Evidence of Leon Trotsky's Collaboration with Germany and Japan." *Cultural Logic* (2009), at http://clogic.eserver.org/2009/Furr.pdf, p. 140 and notes 91 and 92. Hereafter cited as "Furr, Evidence".

> * The pretrial interrogation-confessions contain no indication that Iagoda was forced to testify falsely because of threats or "torture." Iagoda denies guilt in the earliest of these pretrial confessions. In subsequent confessions Iagoda gradually discloses more and more details as he confesses to more crimes.

This conforms to a pattern common in the investigation of criminal defendants: an initial wholesale denial of guilt, followed by gradually escalating confessions to more and more crimes as the suspect becomes convinced that the investigators have enough evidence from other sources to convict him despite his denials and decides that his best course is to cooperate.

> * Lenoe knows about these pretrial confessions by Iagoda, as we shall prove. But he never cites them, even in his footnotes. Perhaps this is because these pretrial confessions disprove his preconceived idea that Nikolaev was a "lone gunman." Rather, they corroborate the hypothesis that Kirov was indeed assassinated by a Right-Trotskyite conspiracy, thereby also corroborating Moscow Trial testimony generally.

Lenoe claims that his goal in his book is to solve Kirov's murder ("Introduction"). But what Lenoe's book really does is to set forth a "best possible case" for the hypothesis that Nikolaev was a "lone gunman" and that Stalin "framed" the defendants in the December 28-29 1934 trial and in the three public Moscow Trials of August 1936, January 1937, and March 1938.

Here from the official transcript of the March 1938 Moscow Trial is Iagoda's trial testimony about the Kirov assassination and his role in it (we have already quoted the first part of it in the previous chapter):

> VYSHINSKY: Are Bukharin and Rykov telling the truth when they say that they knew nothing about it?
>
> YAGODA: That cannot be so, because when Yenukidze told me, that they, that is, the "bloc of Rights and Trotskyites" had decided at a joint meeting to commit a terrorist act against Kirov,
>
> I categorically objected. ...
>
> VYSHINSKY: Why?

YAGODA: I declared that I would never permit any terrorist acts. I regarded it as absolutely unnecessary.

VYSHINSKY: And dangerous for the organization?

YAGODA: Of course.

VYSHINSKY: Nevertheless? :

YAGODA: Nevertheless Yenukidze confirmed …

VYSHINSKY: What?

YAGODA: That at this meeting they - …

VYSHINSKY: Who were they?

YAGODA: Rykov and Yenukidze at first categorically objected…

VYSHINSKY: To what?

YAGODA: To the commission of a terrorist act. But under the pressure of the remaining part of the "bloc of Rights and Trotskyites"...

VYSHINSKY: Principally the Trotskyites?

YAGODA: Yes, under the pressure of the remaining part of the "bloc of Rights and Trotskyites" they gave their consent. So Yenukidze told me.

VYSHINSKY: After this, did you personally take any measures to effect the assassination of Sergei Mironovich Kirov?

YAGODA: I personally?

VYSHINSKY: Yes, as a member of the bloc.

YAGODA: I gave instructions…

VYSHINSKY: To whom?

YAGODA: To Zaporozhetz in Leningrad. **That is not quite how it was.**

VYSHINSKY: We shall speak about that later. What I want now is to elucidate the part played by Rykov and Bukharin in this villainous act.

YAGODA: I gave instructions to Zaporozhetz. When Nikolayev was detained...

VYSHINSKY: The first time?

YAGODA: Yes. Zaporozhetz came to Moscow and reported to me that a man had been detained...

VYSHINSKY: In whose briefcase...

YAGODA: There was a revolver and a diary. And he released him.

VYSHINSKY: And you approved of this?

YAGODA: I just took note of the fact.

VYSHINSKY: And then you gave instructions not to place obstacles in the way of the murder of Sergei Mironovich Kirov?

YAGODA: Yes, I did. **It was not like that.**

VYSHINSKY: In a somewhat different form?

YAGODA: It was not like that, but it is not important.

VYSHINSKY: Did you give instructions?

YAGODA: I have confirmed that.

VYSHINSKY: You have. Be seated.

(1938 Trial 375-376)

The passage above constitutes Iagoda's confession of guilt in Kirov's murder. Iagoda said that he had vigorously opposed any "terrorist acts" but had been outvoted in a meeting of the bloc of Rights and Trotskyites. He admitted to having prior knowledge that an attempt on Kirov's life would be made.

But in answering Vyshinsky's questions some matters are left unclarified here:

> * What did Iagoda mean by his answer: "To Zaporozhetz in Leningrad. That is not quite how it was"?
>
> * What did he mean by denying he had "approved of" releasing Nikolaev but rather admitting "I just took note of the fact"?
>
> * When Vyshinsky asked whether he, Iagoda, "gave instructions not to place obstacles in the way of the murder of Sergei Mironovich Kirov", what did Iagoda mean by saying: "It was not like that… It was not like that, but it is not important"?

Lenoe does not ask these questions, much less answer them. But they can be answered. At the end of this chapter we will return to them and answer them.

Later in the trial Vyshinskii returned to Iagoda, peppering him with a long list of more than twenty rapid-fire questions. On the whole, Iagoda appears to have handled this series of questions rather well. He answered "Yes" to most of them, but was careful to give differentiated replies, while also refusing to assent to some of them. As an example we cite the following exchange:

> VYSHINSKY: Did you know of their espionage activity and did you shield this espionage activity?
>
> YAGODA: Yes.
>
> (1938 Trial 576)

Vyshinskii then draws an apparently logical conclusions from Iagoda's admission:

> VYSHINSKY: I consider that since you shielded this espionage activity, you helped them, assisted them.
>
> YAGODA: No, I do not admit being guilty of that. Had I been a spy, I assure you that dozens of states would have been compelled to disband their intelligence services.
>
> […]

> VYSHINSKY: So they passed on materials to foreign intelligence services with your knowledge?
>
> YAGODA: No.
>
> VYSHINSKY; Were you informed that they passed on materials to foreign intelligence services?
>
> YAGODA: Undoubtedly.
>
> VYSHINSKY: Since you were informed of it, then it was with your knowledge?
>
> YAGODA: With my connivance.
>
> (577)

In this passage Iagoda agrees that he had "shielded" espionage activity, yet denies that he "helped…assisted" this activity. He agrees that he was "informed"' that spies were "passing materials to foreign intelligence services" – yet insists that, though this occurred with his "connivance", it did not occur with his "knowledge." The word *pokrovitel'stvo,* which is translated here as "connivance", might be more accurately translated as "protection."[123]

After a few more rapid-fire questions Vyshinskii raises the issue of the Kirov murder:

> VYSHINSKY: And do you admit being guilty of organizing and effecting terrorist acts: first the murder of Comrade Kirov on the orders and instructions of the bloc?

Iagoda replied:

> YAGODA: I admit being guilty of complicity in the murder.
>
> (1938 Trial 577)

As we shall see, this – the legal matter of "complicity", *souchastie,* is the *only* confession Iagoda really did "recant" later in the trial.

---

[123] See the Russian text at http://www.hrono.ru/dokum/1938buharin/vec8-5-38-1.php

Later in the trial Vyshinskii addresses the question of the legal definition of complicity:

> First of all, the question of complicity. The Court investigation has shown that not all the accused participated to an equal extent in the crimes which were reviewed at this trial.
>
> Hence the question: To what extent and in what degree can and should each of the accused be held answerable for the charges preferred against them in the indictment?
>
> The second question: To what extent and in what degree have the charges preferred against the accused been proved?
>
> (693-694)

Vyshinskii argues that Iagoda, Bukharin, and other members of the bloc of Rights and Trotskyites are "accomplices" in every one of the crimes undertaken by any of the bloc's members.

> Each of the accused must be held answerable for the sum total of the crimes as a member of a conspiratorial organization whose criminal objects and aims, and whose criminal methods of carrying out these aims, were known to, approved of and accepted by each of the accused. ... There is an opinion current among criminologists that in order to establish complicity it is necessary to establish common agreement and an intent on the part of each of the criminals, of the accomplices, for each of the crimes. This viewpoint is wrong. We cannot accept it and we have never applied or accepted it.
>
> [...]
>
> To establish complicity, we must establish that there is a common line uniting the accomplices in a given crime, that there is a common criminal design. To establish complicity, it is necessary to establish the existence of a united will directed toward a single object common to all the participants in the crime. If, say, a gang of robbers will act in such a way that one part of its members will

> set fire to houses, violate women, murder and so on, in one place, while another part of the gang will do the same in another place, then even if neither the one nor the other knew of the crimes committed separately by any section of the common gang, they will be held answerable to the full for the sum total of the crimes, if only it is proved that they had agreed to participate in this gang for the purpose of committing the various crimes.
>
> (694-695)

Iagoda insistently disagreed with Vyshinsky's definition of "complicity" (*souchastie*). In his final statement to the court he made the following statement – the same one quoted, as we have seen, by Serov in his report of August 31, 1956. This passage is also quoted by Lenoe on page 598 of his book and referred to again on page 666.

> Not only is it false to say that I was an organizer but even to say that I was an accomplice in the murder of Kirov. I am guilty of a very serious dereliction of duty, that is true. I will answer for that in full measure, but I was not an accomplice. 'An accomplice' – you know as well as I do, comrade procurator, what that means. None of the materials of this trial or the preliminary investigation show that I was an accomplice in this villainous murder. (Lenoe's translation; slightly different at 1938 Trial 786)

Lenoe, following Khrushchev's man Serov, writes "Iagoda recanted his confession at the trial's end." In reality, as the passages above make clear Iagoda never retracted the confession he made which we have quoted above from pages 375-6 of the trial transcript. The sole statement Iagoda did retract was the one he made on page 577 and quoted above: "I admit being guilty of complicity in the murder."

Iagoda did not accept Vyshinskii's view that his agreement with the overall aim of the bloc of Rights and Trotskyites made him an "accomplice" to Kirov's murder. Iagoda evidently believed – to use Vyshinsky's language – "that in order to establish complicity it is necessary to establish common agreement and an intent on the part of each of the criminals, of the accomplices, for each of the crimes." Since Iagoda opposed Kirov's murder, did not actively aid it, but nevertheless agreed not to stand in its way, we may say that, in English usage, Iagoda considered himself not an accomplice – one who actually *participates* in the commission of a crime – but an accessory – one who *assists* in the commission of a crime.[124]

*****

Now we can return to Iagoda's enigmatic words that we put in boldface in his confession above, in which he leaves somewhat vague the precise nature of what he did and did not do: "That is not quite how it was"; "It was not like that"; "It was not like that, but it is not important." In clarifying what Iagoda meant by these phrases we can confirm that in Iagoda's confession at trial he did claim a role in Kirov's murder which he never retracted or, as Lenoe writes, "recanted".

In his pretrial interrogation-confession of April 26, 1937 published in 1997 we read the following:

> Question… Above you admitted that if it had not been for your and Molchanov's traitorous role in the OGPU-NKVD the centers of the organization of Rights, Trotskyites and Zinovievites, or more accurately, the centers of the bloc of these organizations could have been liquidated in time?
>
> Answer: Yes, that is undoubtedly the case.
>
> Question: That means that the murder of com. Kirov could have been prevented?
>
> Answer: Unquestionably.

---

124 The *Oxford English Dictionary*: "Complicity. 1. The being an accomplice; partnership in an evil action.." "Accessory. B. adj. 1. Of persons: Acceding or adhering to; assisting as a subordinate. In Law: Participating or sharing in a crime, though not the chief actor; participant, privy." *Black's Law Dictionary* (1910 edition): "Accessory. Contributing to or aiding in the commission of a crime. One who, without being present at the commission of a felonious offense, becomes guilty of such an offense, not as a chief actor, but as a participator, as by command, advise, instigation, or concealment; either before or after the fact of commission." (13) "An accessory after the fact is a person who, knowing a felony to have been committed by another, receives, relieves, comforts or assists the felon, in order to enable him to escape from punishment." (14)

> Question: And you did not do this?
>
> Answer: No.
>
> Question: **That means you are an accomplice to this vile murder?**
>
> **Answer: No, I cannot admit to that.**
>
> Question: You had materials about the active terrorist centers?
>
> Answer: I had.
>
> Question: Kirov was killed by them?
>
> Answer: By them.
>
> Question: You concealed the activity of these terrorist organizations?
>
> Answer: I did.
>
> Question: How can you dare to deny your complicity in the vile murder of com. Kirov?
>
> Answer: **I am not an accomplice in this murder, but undoubtedly must be responsible for the fact that I did not prevent the murder of com. Kirov.**
>
> (Genrikh Iagoda 121-122; emphasis added, GF)

To the interrogator's continued astonishment at Iagoda's denial of complicity in Kirov's murder Iagoda answered:

> Answer: You must understand that such disparate acts as the murder of com. Kirov would not enter my personal plans as People's Commissar of Internal Affairs.
>
> I well understood that such acts could lead if not to my complete downfall as a participant in the organization of Rights, then in any case to my complete responsibility as Commissar and responsible for the security of the members of the government. So nothing could come of this for me personally but loss. And at just this same period my own personal plans had gone rather far and did not fully coincide with the plans of the bloc.

> (Genrikh Iagoda 122-123)

Later in the same interrogation-confession Iagoda explained how his fears were realized:

> The murder of Kirov, **about the concrete preparation for which I did not know**, elicited in me a natural alertness in the CC. I was put under the supervision of Ezhov, who pressed me and demanded the complete defeat of the organization of Trotskyites, Zinovievites and Rights. (Genrikh Iagoda 130; emphasis added, GF)

These passages in his pretrial confessions explain through amplification what Iagoda stated at trial.

Lenoe knew about the *Genrikh Iagoda* volume. But he does not quote from it nor mention its existence to his readers. These confessions disprove Lenoe's contention that Iagoda "retracted his confession". They also provide additional evidence confirming the existence of a Right-Trotskyite-Zinovievite conspiracy to assassinate Kirov.

The existence of this conspiracy also dismantles – refutes – the main thesis of Lenoe's book. No one who examines these passages carefully and objectively would assent to Lenoe's contention that Nikolaev was a "lone gunman" and everyone else – those tried, convicted, and executed along with Nikolaev on December 28-29, 1934, and the defendants at the three public Moscow Trials of 1936-8 – was innocent, "framed" by Stalin.

In a later pretrial interrogation-confession of May 19, 1937 Iagoda gave more details about the events leading up to the decision to murder Kirov. For the readers' convenience I have boldfaced certain sections of the text.

> Answer: The second meeting of the center of the conspiracy took place during the summer of 1934. Not long before this meeting I was at Enukidze's. He said that during the next few days a meeting of the center of the conspiracy would take place, at which the Trotskyites and Zinovievites will demand that their plan for terrorist acts against members of the Politburo of the AUCP(b) be confirmed.
>
> **In the most determined fashion I told Enukidze that I would not permit the carrying-out of disparate**

terrorist acts against members of the CC, that I will not permit them to pay with my head in order to satisfy Trotsky's appetite. I demanded of Enukidze that he bring this declaration of mine to the knowledge of Rykov, Bukharin, and Tomskii. My categorical tone must have had its effect on Enukidze and he promised me that at the meeting the Rights would oppose disparate terrorist acts.

Enukidze and I agreed that he would inform me about the center's decision immediately after the meeting.

A few days later Enukidze called me and I went again to see him, and he informed me that the meeting had already taken place, that Kamenev and Piatakov had presented a big plan for the commission of terrorist acts, in the first place against Stalin and Voroshilov, and then against Kirov in Leningrad.

Enukidze said that the Rights had succeeded, with great difficulty, in postponing the terrorist acts against Stalin and Voroshilov and, yielding to the Trotskyite-Zinovievite parts of the center, had sanctioned a terrorist act against Kirov in Leningrad.

Enukidze told me that Kamenev and Piatakov had presented to the meeting a demand for carrying out a terrorist act against Stalin and Voroshilov, which was received from Trotsky. They declared that their terrorist organizations were energetically preparing for these acts and that they scarcely had the power to stop them. But, remembering their agreement with me, Rykov, Tomskii and Enukidze actively protested and then, in the way of compromise, Kamenev submitted a proposal to immediately sanction a terrorist act against Kirov in Leningrad. He declared that it was essential to give an outlet to the mounting energy of the terrorist groups, which could rot on the vine without action. Kamenev also argued that if the center did not approve even a single terrorist act, then partisan actions of individual terrorist groups would become essential. **And**

> **it was sanctioned. In the name of the center of the conspiracy Enukidze proposed that I not try to prevent this terrorist act, and I promised to do that.**
>
> (Genrikh Iagoda 179-181)

The text in boldface further elucidates Iagoda's insistence that he was not an "accomplice". He took no active part in the assassination of Kirov, but did take steps to assure it was not prevented.

He elaborated this point a bit more in the succeeding passage. Here Iagoda explained precisely what kind of instructions he gave to Zaporozhets.

> Question: At interrogation you constantly insist that you were opposed to terrorist acts against members of the CC because you were responsible for the security of members of the government. How then did you permit the terrorist act against com. Kirov?
>
> Answer: Kirov was in Leningrad, and a terrorist act against him would have to be committed there. I supposed that if they were successful in killing Kirov it was Medved' who would have to answer for it. And I was not opposed to ridding myself of Medved'. He was hostile towards me. Everybody knew about my bad relations with Medved' and also that I was preparing to remove him, and that, I thought, would serve as yet another argument in favor of my innocence and Medved's guilt for the poor security around Kirov.
>
> Question: Therefore, you mean, you accepted the proposal of the conspiratorial center that Enukidze gave you: "Do not try to prevent this terrorist act against Kirov in Leningrad"?
>
> Answer: Yes.
>
> Question: And you promised to do this?
>
> Answer: Yes. I was forced to do this.
>
> **Question: What did you do, concretely?**

Answer: I summoned Zaporozhets (the assistant chief of the Political Division) from Leningrad, informed him of the possibility of an attempt on Kirov's life, and proposed to him that he not hinder it.

Question: You proposed this to Zaporozhets? Why him? What relation did he have to the conspiracy?

Answer: I forgot, when I was naming my confederates, to name Zaporozhets among their number. I had recruited him to the conspiracy at the end of 1933, during one of his trips from Leningrad to Moscow.

Before this I learned that Zaporozhets was recruited by German intelligence while abroad. He himself told me about this before he was appointed to Leningrad in 1931. He said that despite the fact that many years had passed since his recruitment no one had contacted him and he had done no work for them.

Question: Under what circumstances was Zaporozhets recruited by German intelligence?

Answer: It's possible that he told me about this, but I don't recall it now.

Question: And under what circumstances did you recruit him to the conspiracy?

Answer: Zaporozhets has always been a person of the Right. He was a Ukrainian SR for many years. I used all this plus his contact with German intelligence and recruited him rather easily.

I should say that already in 1931, when I sent Zaporozhets to Leningrad, I told him that he was going there as my man, since Medved' in Leningrad was not, and that Zaporozhets was to replace Medved' and take his place.

Question: So what did you tell Zaporozhets in connection with the decision of the conspiratorial

center concerning the terrorist act against com. Kirov?

Answer: I have already said that I summoned him from Leningrad, told him about an imminent attempt on Kirov's life and proposed to him, in case facts about preparation of the terrorist act should enter agents' materials, not to act upon these materials and to inform me. I did not entrust the details to him.

Zaporozhets fulfilled my directives.

Queston: But we know that Nikolaev, Kirov's murderer, was detained by the Operational Division in Leningrad some time before his carrying out the terrorist act against com. Kirov. With him was a weapon and documents that exposed him as a terrorist and, despite this, he was released.

Answer: Zaporozhets informed me about this some time after Nikolaev had been freed.

Question: What did he tell you?

Answer: Zaporozhets was in Moscow, dropped in on me, and told me that a certain Nikolaev, who was surveilling Kirov's automobile, had been detained by officers of the Operod in Leningrad. He was brought to the Political Division and after he had been searched in Gubin's presence materials were found on him that gave evidence of terrorist intentions. Gubin reported this to him and Zaporozhets released Nikolaev.

(Genrikh Iagoda 181-183; emphasis added GF)

In the text above Iagoda explains that Zaporozhets had reported to him about Nikolaev some time after Nikolaev had been apprehended, detained, searched, and then released. In short, Iagoda learned about this after the fact. He did not specifically give Zaporozhets any "instructions" about Nikolaev, or about any specific person or act. This is why he denied "personally taking any measures to effect the assassination of" Kirov

– as Vyshinsky put it – and why he answered, as we have seen, "That is not quite how it was."

Vyshinsky kept trying to get Iagoda to confess that he had in some way actively participated in Kirov's murder. But Iagoda insisted on precision in his confessions. In the passage below from Iagoda's pretrial interrogation of May 19, 1937 the NKVD interrogator tries to do the same thing by charging that Iagoda had given orders to weaken Kirov's personal security. Iagoda flatly denies this charge.

> Question: Your role in the murder of com. Kirov is not limited to the fact that you did not take measures to prevent the terrorist act against him and that you freed the murderer who had been detained by the officers of the Leningrad Operod. **You took steps to weaken as much as possible com. Kirov's physical security, and thereby facilitated the murderer's access to him.**
>
> **Answer: I do not admit this. I gave no instructions about weakening the physical security of com. Kirov. Perhaps Zaporozhets did this on his own initiative, but he did not tell me about it.**
>
> **Question: You not only made arrangements about weakening Kirov's security but after the accomplishment of the terrorist act you took measures to get rid of a witness. We are speaking about the murder of Borisov, an officer of the Operod who was guarding Kirov.**
>
> **Answer: I also cannot admit to this. I myself did not give any instructions about getting rid of Borisov. At this time Zaporozhets was not in Leningrad at all. If this was indeed a case of murder, and not an unfortunate accident, then Gubin is responsible for it, but I do not know about that.**
>
> Question: You are not telling the truth. You will be exposed in your lie by the confessions of Zaporozhets and Gubin. **We propose that you tell the truth right now about the circumstances under which Kirov was murdered.**

> **Answer: I am not hiding anything. I am speaking sincerely and truthfully. I have nothing to add to my confessions about this matter.**
>
> I can admit that after Kirov's murder I personally tried, or rather intended, to "squelch" this matter and limit it to arrests only in Leningrad. But the strengthened supervision by the CC and the participation of Ezhov in the investigation hindered this. As you know, Zinoviev, Kamenev, Bakaev and others were arrested in Moscow.
>
> The attempt to protect Zaporozhets from being brought to answer in the case of the Leningrad Chekists was also unsuccessful. Ezhov became involved, and Zaporozheets was arrested.
>
> (Genrikh Iagoda 184, emphasis added GF)

In the passage above Iagoda admits to taking definite steps with regard to Kirov's murder but only *after* it had taken place. He also confesses to trying to sabotage or sidetrack the investigation into Kirov's murder. Again, this crime was committed *after* the fact.

A week later, on May 26, 1937, Iagoda continued his discussion of the Kirov murder and his role in it.

> Question: Let us continue the interrupted interrogation.
>
> You have confessed that after the murder of com. Kirov you intended to "squelch" the investigation into this case.
>
> Circumstances beyond your control hindered this plan. **But we are interested to learn how you intended to avert, or as you say, "squelch" the investigation?**
>
> **Answer: I had no ready plan of action. Already during the investigation, when it had been determined and was clear that the murder of Kirov had been at the hands of the Trotskyite-Zinovievite organization, I greatly regretted that I had not remained in Leningrad myself to lead the investigation of the case. It's clear that if I had remained in Leningrad, the murder of Kirov would**

> **have been depicted in some way, but the real culprits, the Trotskyites and Zinovievites, would never have been caught.**
>
> (Genrikh Iagoda 185; emphasis added GF)

Iagoda testifies above that he would have much preferred to be in Leningrad when Kirov was murdered so he could have turned the investigation in a false direction. This is evidence that he did not know anything specific about it in advance.

In the passage that follows Iagoda admits that he could not prevent the Zinovievite-Trotskyite group – Nikolaev, Kotolynov, and those others convicted of Kirov's murder – from being discovered. He was more successful in preventing the discovery of the Leningrad NKVD men ("Chekists") who were also accomplices and they were not exposed.

> Of course all this is very conditional and suppositional, for it was not I who led the investigation but, as you know, Ezhov stayed in Leningrad and the real situation came to light, more or less.
>
> **But I was compensated in Moscow in that I redirected the investigation in the case of the former Leningrad Chekists and put it on a false trail.**
>
> Question: How did you do this. What precisely was concealed in the case of the former Leningrad Chekists?
>
> Answer: First, at the beginning **I did not arrest Zaporozhets, who participated in the conspiracy. Zaporozhets' name is not on the list of the Leningrad Chekists, those fired from the NKVD and brought to trial (the list was published in the newspaper).**
>
> **He was arrested much later, at the direction of the CC.**
>
> **Second, before the beginning of the investigation into the case I called Prokof'ev and Molchanov to me and proposed that they lead the investigation personally. I assigned them two tasks:**

> **1. That nothing that might compromise the central apparatus of the NKVD or its employees (most of all, me personally) should be in the investigative materials.**
>
> **2. To reduce the case to simple carelessness and by doing so to protect Zaporozhets and Gubin, who had known about the preparations for the murder of Kirov.**
>
> **My instructions were carried out in full.**
>
> I must state here that Mironov took part in this affair. He was not acting on my direct orders but on his own initiative, he was actively protecting me in all the interrogations in which he took part.
>
> (Genrikh Iagoda 185-186; emphasis added GF)

Iagoda explains how he attempted to blame Medved' for failing to protect Kirov.

> If you look at the materials of the investigation of Medved' you'll undoubtedly notice that almost all the interrogation transcripts are composed in such a way that I, Iagoda, supposedly repeatedly warned him about the necessity of strengthening Kirov's physical security, but Medved' failed to do it. The outcome was that it appeared as though I was not guilty of anything, but Medved' and his apparatus were guilty.
>
> As far as I recall Medved' was interrogated by Mironov and Prokof'ev or Mironov and Molchanov.
>
> (Genrikh Iagoda 186)

At the same time Iagoda testifies that he successfully covered up the fact that, when Nikolaev was arrested, a gun and other incriminating materials were indeed discovered on him.

Lenoe notes that in his interrogation of December 8, 1934 Nikolaev admitted having a gun in his possession when he was detained by the Leningrad NKVD on October 15, 1934. (401) Nikolaev said that he did have a gun with him but asserted that he had not been searched.

But Lenoe first suggests, then states, that Nikolaev did not really have a gun in his possession, despite the fact that Nikolaev had stated clearly that he did have one. If Nikolaev really did have a gun with him as he had claimed, and if Nikolaev was searched, as the Leningrad NKVD men, including Gubin, stated he was, then it would be obvious that there was a conspiracy involving people in the Leningrad NKVD. That would mean Nikolaev was not a "lone gunman" – a conclusion fatal to the thesis of Lenoe's book. So Lenoe had a strong motive to conclude that Nikolaev did not have a gun with him when he was detained despite all the testimony, including from Nikolaev himself, that he was carrying a gun (and incriminating papers as well).

Likewise Lenoe had a strong motive not to examine this pretrial testimony of Iagoda's or to inform his readers about its existence.

> There was one other circumstance in this investigation that could have caused unpleasantness if it had flared up.
>
> Question: What circumstance?
>
> Answer: In 1933-1934 the SPO of the UNKVD of Leningrad oblast' uncovered and liquidated a rather serious Trotskyite-Zinovievite organization. In the investigative materials that were sent from Leningrad to Molchanov and me there were facts about the existence of this center in Moscow.
>
> Neither I nor Molchanov did anything about these materials – we hid them.
>
> The danger lay in the fact that the accused in the case of the Leningrad Chekists could have raised this question in their interrogations, while they were justifying their actions.
>
> Molchanov and I spoke about this and agreed that these facts would not appear in the investigation. And that was done.
>
> **There was also another danger. It was that someone among the arrested Leningrad Operod officers (Gubin and others) could have blurted out during interrogation that Nikolaev, Kirov's killer, was**

> **searched when he was first detained (before the murder) and that on him were found materials that attested to his terrorist intentions, and a weapon. But Molchanov was correct when he assured me that none of them would say this, if only out of a sense of self-protection.**
>
> Question: That means Molchanov knew that Nikolaev, the murderer of com. Kirov, was freed in the Leningrad Operod after it had been established that he was a terrorist?
>
> Answer: Yes, he knew. **I told Molchanov and Prokof'ev about all the circumstances related to the Kirov murder after his arrival from Leningrad during the first days of December 1934.**
>
> **What did you tell them?**
>
> **Answer: I told them that Kirov had been killed by a decision of the center of the Trotskyite-Zinovievite bloc, that I was warned in advance about this, that I had proposed to Zaporozhets not to hinder it and told them about Zaporozhets having freed Nikolaev when he had been detained in Leningrad.**
>
> **I was forced to warn Molchanov and Prokof'ev about all this because they were leading the investigation of the case of the former Leningrad Chekists and had to know all the circumstances of the case so as not to permit these facts to enter into the interrogations.**
>
> (Genrikh Iagoda 187-188; emphasis added GF)

In these pretrial interrogation-confessions Iagoda gives more detail about the conspiracy, one part of which was the murder of Kirov. He describes how he and others of the Rights never liked the idea of individual assassination.

> Question: You confessed above that at the time of the investigation into the "Klubok" case you did not meet with Enukidze in order to preserve the conspiracy. The

> investigation into "Klubok", as you know, began in 1935. Did you and Enukidze meet before that?
>
> Answer: I met with Enukidze after the Kirov murder, soon after the arrests of Zinoviev, Kamenev, and the others in Moscow. Our conversation took place, as usual, in Enukidze's office. He was asking me how matters stood in Leningrad, whether there was any danger of a total failure and expressed his outrage about the partisan actions of the Trotskyites and Zinovievites that expressed themselves in the murder of Kirov.
>
> Question: What partisan activities are you talking about? The murder of com. Kirov had been sanctioned by the general center of the conspiracy, hadn't it?
>
> Answer: That's true. But I have already said at the previous interrogation that the Rights were forced to go along with sanctioning the terrorist act against Kirov only by compromise.
>
> In general we opposed individual terrorist acts that were not coordinated with the general plan for the conspiracy and the seizure of power.
>
> This is what Enukidze had in mind when he spoke about partisan actions.
>
> (Genrikh Iagoda 192-193)

Iagoda also mentions the accession of Sokol'nikov to the conspiratorial center after Kamenev's arrest.

> At that time Enukidze told me that in the place of the arrested Kamenev the Trotskyite-Zinovievite bloc had promoted Sokol'nikov into the general center of the conspiracy.
>
> Enukidze told me that in the conspiracy's new orientation Sokol'nikov's role had first-class importance.
>
> (Genrikh Iagoda 192-193)

Iagoda echoes Radek's conclusion that the assassination of Kirov was counterproductive for the conspiracy. He claims that this lack of support among the Soviet population is what turned them towards Germany.

> Second, the Kirov murder caused great alertness by the Party and the whole country to the Trotskyite and Zinovievite cadres, and we could not count upon any kind of support within the country.
>
> "Watchfulness, about which people shout on every street corner, will cost the heads of our people", Enukidze told me.
>
> These were the considerations that lay at the basis of the orientation of the conspiracy beginning with 1935, towards Germany. And it was precisely in connection with them that the role of Sokol'nikov, who was then the assistant Commissar for Foreign Affairs, in the general conspiratorial center had special meaning, because contact with official circles in Germany could be established through him.
>
> **Question: You say that contact with the Germans "could be" established through Sokol'nikov. But wasn't this possibility realized?**
>
> **Answer: I cannot say. At that time during my talk with Enukidze we only spoke of possibilities. Whether they were realized after that, I don't know.**
>
> (Genrikh Iagoda 194; emphasis added GF)

Elsewhere we have analyzed a statement in an unpublished confession by Sokol'nikov that a Japanese official had approached him and informed him that the Japanese were in contact with Trotsky.[125]

Iagoda returned to the question of Kirov's murder briefly on December 28, 1937. Here he explained how he objected to individual terrorism, and why he at length relented to the demands of the Zinovievites and Trotskyites yet kept a certain distance from the assassination.

---

[125] Furr, Evidence 66-68.

Question: That means we can confirm that V.R. Menzhinskii and M.A. Peshkov were killed by your direct order, and that in both cases you acted out of base person reasons?

Answer: Yes, that is true. I admit my guilt in this.

I would like to tell about the circumstances that forced me to commit this even more monstrous crime, the organization of the killing of such persons as V.V. Kuibyshev and A.M. Gor'kii.

Question: Tell us.

Answer: At one of these interrogations I told how the unified center of the Right-Trotskyite organization carried out its decision about the murder of S.M. Kirov. I told also about how I did not take part in this decision. Moreover, when Enukidze informed me about it, I protested. And it is clear to you, of course, why I did so. I feared direct terrorist acts because I was responsible for the security of members of the government.

In the transcripts of my previous interrogations it is written that I was forced to warn Zaporozhets (in Leningrad) not to hinder the terrorist act against S.M. Kirov.

You know all this already from my confessions, but I did not tell everything then. What did I remain silent about? **I did not tell how, when Enukidze told me in the summer of 1934 about the decision to organize a terrorist act against S.M. Kirov, I proposed to him my own variant of killing Kirov by means of "death from disease."**

I also told him then that this method had already been verified by me in practice (M.A. Peshkov and V.R. Menzhinskii), and that it was also safe for me, as assistant Chairman of the OGPU, responsible for security.

> **Enukidze rejected my proposal in relation to S.M. Kirov. He explained that the Zinovievites and Trotskyites were organizing a terrorist act against Kirov and that our job was simply not to hinder them, nothing more.**
>
> "Death from disease" will not have the necessary resonance in the country. We must test how the country will react to the shooting of Kirov," – Enukidze told me.
>
> But at the same time Enukidze also seized upon my proposed method. He made me inform him in detail about how, technically, and who concretely would carry it out. I told him.
>
> A little while later Enukidze again asked me to drop in on him. He told me that he had informed the center about my method, and that it had been decided to implement it without delay.
>
> (Genrikh Iagoda 210-211; emphasis added GF)

The passage above concerning the medical murders of Gorky's son (Peshkov) and of Iagoda's former boss Menzhinskii confirm Iagoda's sensational testimony at the March 1938 trial. This testimony is widely, if not quite universally, dismissed today as a fabrication. However, the *Genrikh Iagoda* volume contains pretrial testimony from a number of figures besides Iagoda that bears witness to such a conspiracy. Moreover, there's nothing fantastic about it. The NKVD and its successors had a history of assassination by poison made to appear natural.

Iagoda's final pretrial remarks concerning Kirov's murder are in his interrogation of January 10, 1938. This includes the passage quoted by Vyshinsky above:

> In the NKVD I established a counterrevolutionary group of a number of individual officers of the NKVD whom I drew into counterrevolutionary activity. Earlier I have confessed in detail about this counterrevolutionary group and its membership. I also confirm the facts given by me in my earlier confession about my part in the murder of S.M. Kirov.

> I knew before Enukidze that the murder of S.M. Kirov was being prepared by decision of the conspiratorial center. Enukidze proposed that I not hinder the organization of this terrorist act and I agreed to this. **With this goal Zaporozhets was summoned by me from Leningrad, and I instructed him not to hinder the terrorist act against S.M. Kirov that was in preparation.**
>
> **After the freeing of Nikolaev, the murderer of S.M. Kirov, when Nikolaev was detained the first time, Zaporozhets informed me about this.**
>
> (Genrikh Iagoda 236-237; emphasis added GF)

Iagoda repeated this same version of events later during the trial:

> Yenukidze insisted that I was not to place any obstacles in the way; the terrorist act, he said, would be carried out by the Trotskyite-Zinovievite group. **Owing to this, I was compelled to instruct Zaporozhetz, who occupied the post of Assistant Chief of the Regional Administration of the People's Commissariat of Internal Affairs, not to place any obstacles in the way of the terrorist act against Kirov. Some time later Zaporozhetz informed me that the organs of the People's Commissariat of Internal Affairs had detained Nikolayev, in whose possession a revolver and a chart of the route Kirov usually took had been found. Nikolayev was released.**
>
> (1938 Trial 572-573; emphasis added GF)

Lenoe Concealed These Confessions

It appears that Lenoe may have deliberately concealed these confessions from his readers. In note 22 on page 786 of his book Lenoe writes (in part):

> See Mikhail Il'inskii, *Narkom Yagoda: Dvadtsat'let v maske* [Moscow: "Iauza", "ESKMO," 2005], 157, based on transcripts of Yagoda's interrogations in 1937.

Lenoe is familiar with the Il'inskii book. But the source for the quotations from Iagoda's pretrial confessions quoted extensively in Il'inskii's book is this same 1997 volume: *Genrikh Iagoda.* Since Lenoe read and cites Il'inskii Lenoe had to at least be aware that this latter work exists.

In the "Editor's afterword" to Il'inskii's book we read:

> Of importance are the documentary publications, especially the collection "General'nyi komissar gosudarstvennoi bezopasnosti Genrikh Iagoda", prepared by A.L. Litvin and V.K Vinogradov … (Il'inskii, 763).

This is more or less the way the book in question is listed in Il'inskii's bibliography as well:

> "General'nyi komissar gosudarstvennoi bezopasnosti Genrikh Iagoda. Sbornik dokumentov. Kazan', 1997. (Il'inskii 761).

The accurate bibliographical reference is slightly different:

> Genrikh Iagoda. Narkom vnytrennikh del SSR. General'nyi komissar gosudarstvennoi bezopasnosti. Sbornik dokumentov. Kazan', 1997. – 542 pp. ISBN 5-900975-16-9

A.L. Litvin[126] is named as the "scientific editor" (*nauchnyi redactor*) and V.K. Vinogradov is one of six men, including Litvin again, named as "compilers" (*sostaviteli*).

Il'inskii quotes directly from many of the confessions and other documents published in this book without, however, specifically identifying their source. And it would have been hard, perhaps, to locate this volume from the incorrect title given by Il'inskii if one did not know the actual title. But surely Lenoe knows the real title, for this book has been in circulation among American scholars for some years. For example, it is cited accurately in Jansen and Petrov's 2002 book on Ezhov, which Lenoe cites.

---

126 Alter L'vovich Litvin is a well-known Russian scholar, very anticommunist and anti-Stalin.

Therefore Lenoe ought to have known of this volume and these documents. But he never refers to them at all in his book. Moreover, Lenoe chose to ignore even those passages from Iagoda's pretrial interrogations that his source Il'inskii quotes.

Iagoda's testimony refutes Lenoe's hypothesis. The texts of Iagoda's pretrial interrogation-confessions are strong evidence that a conspiracy did indeed exist. They also help corroborate the hypothesis that the Moscow Trials were not fabricated by Stalin or anybody else. This evidence demolishes Lenoe's "lone gunman" hypothesis.

What Iagoda's Pre-Trial Confessions Reveal

We have reproduced here all the parts of Iagoda's published pretrial interrogation-confessions in which the murder of Kirov is discussed. None of this very important material has ever been made available in English before. They strongly corroborate Iagoda's testimony at trial. They also corroborate the testimony of the other defendants. These documents disprove Lenoe's allegations. They constitute strong evidence against the fraudulent claim that Iagoda (and, by extension, other defendants at the March 1938 Trial) was tortured, threatened, or otherwise induced to testify falsely to a conspiracy in order to hide a "frameup" of innocent people instigated by Stalin and/or others.

During his interrogation-confession of April 26, 1937 Iagoda insists that his actions, though criminal, did not constitute "complicity":

> Question: How can you dare to deny your complicity in the vile murder of com. Kirov?
>
> Answer: I am not an accomplice in this murder, but undoubtedly I must be responsible for the fact that I did not prevent the murder of com. Kirov.
>
> (Genrikh Iagoda 122)

This testimony is entirely consistent with Iagoda's position at the March 1938 trial. Iagoda went into considerable detail about his contribution to the success of Kirov's murder. He insisted repeatedly that he helped facilitate Kirov's assassination. He admits that he had general, though not specific, prior knowledge of it. This was what he confessed to.

Therefore, despite what Lenoe (and before him Serov) asserts *Iagoda never retracted this confession.* Iagoda denied only that he was an "accomplice". He did so emphatically and consistently. His testimony explains his qualifications at pages 375-6 of the trial transcript that we have quoted above.

> * First, Vyshinskii asked Iagoda whether he "personally took any measure to effect the assassination of ...Kirov." Iagoda naturally answered "That is not quite how it was."

As we can see from his pretrial testimony Iagoda stated that he had only given orders to Zaporozhets that no obstacle be placed in the way of such an attempt. He never "took any measure to effect the assassination" itself.

> * In the second passage Vyshinskii refers to Nikolaev's release and then asks whether "then" – that is, subsequently to Nikolaev's release – Iagoda "gave instructions not to place obstacles in the way..." Again Iagoda replies: "It was not like that... but it is not important."

This is fully consistent with Iagoda's pretrial testimony. There he stated that he *first* gave orders not to hinder any attempt against Kirov. He never gave such orders "then" – that is, *after* Nikolaev's detention and release. In fact Iagoda confessed that he was informed of Nikolaev's detention and release only *after* it had occurred.

Iagoda's confession is strongly differentiated. He insisted on confessing only to those crimes he believed he had actually committed, and refused to confess to others. Both in the pretrial interrogations and at trial he stubbornly refused to agree that he was an accomplice. In this he was like Bukharin, who also confessed to many serious, capital crimes, but nevertheless spent much of his time on the stand and most of his final speech to the court strenuously denying certain of the accusations made by the prosecution.

Such behavior, both in pretrial interrogations and at trial, appears to be incompatible with torture or other compulsion, or with "terrified defendants." Yet Lenoe makes such allegations time and again:

> * "a few grotesque confessions of terrified defendants." (Lenoe 467)
>
> * "evidence that was extracted under torture in the process of fabricating a case against arrested NKVD chief Yagoda." (573)

> * "[Klimov] made extensive use of 1937-1938 depositions from Gubin, Zaporozhets, other Leningrad NKVD officers, Yagoda, and Yagoda's former deputy Bulanov, extracted under torture and used to incriminate Yagoda at the March 1938 trial." (622)

Lenoe employs the verbiage of "torture" when he wishes to dismiss without consideration some testimony that fails to fit into his preconceived schema. We'll analyze his use of "torture as smokescreen" later.

Vyshinskii's discussion of the legal definition of "complicity" which we reproduced above from the trial transcript proves that Iagoda never "recanted his confession", as Lenoe claimed. Iagoda only "retracted" one sentence – his admission of "complicity". Lenoe had to know this, of course, and therefore has concealed this from his readers.

Chapter 16.

Bukharin and Kotolynov

On page 135 of Lenoe's study we read:

> Vyborg Ward party secretary Pyotr Smorodin (together with Nikolai Bukharin) sponsored a request by the physicist and secret police collaborator D.L. Talmud that OGPU chief Filip Medved assign the former Leningrad Komsomol official Ivan Kotolynov, now an ex-Zinovievite, to work in his lab.

Lenoe does not return to the question of Bukharin's recommendation of Kotolynov. The entry on Bukharin in the index of Lenoe's book (818) has a number of subheadings, but this reference is simply lumped in with other miscellaneous references to him.

Lenoe gives one footnote to this paragraph, though the note does not mention Bukharin:

> 75. On Talmud's request that Kotolynov be posted to his lab, see "Ubiistvo v Smol'nom," *Rodina*, no.10 (1995): 62-66.

The reader would never guess from Lenoe's footnote that this article is devoted entirely to an exploration of the connection between Bukharin and the Kirov murder. The author, Iurii Murin, has specialized in studying Bukharin and the March 1938 Trial.

A firm anticommunist, Murin rejects any suggestion that Bukharin was guilty even of those crimes to which he confessed. But Murin has usefully gathered some primary source evidence of Bukharin's involvement with the Kirov murder. Lenoe fails even to mention, much less examine, any of this evidence. Here we will consider only the question of Bukharin's recommendation of Kotolynov, reserving discussion of the other evidence linking Bukharin to the Kirov assassination for our chapters on the January 1937 and March 1938 Moscow Trials.

Bukharin's explanation of his recommendation of Kotolynov is contained in his letter to Stalin of April 15, 1937. This was published separately, also by Murin, in 2000.[127] We have been able to compare it with a photocopy of the archival copy of Bukharins' letter that Murin used.[128] This is a long letter written personally to Stalin by Bukharin from the prison where he and Rykov had been confined after their arrest on February 27, 1937 at the conclusion of the discussion of the evidence against them at the February-March 1937 Central Committee Plenum. On page 19 of the typescript of this letter (Murin 1995, 64; 2000, 53-54) Bukharin writes:

> In the concluding remarks of N.I. Ezhov at the plenum, as evidence that I also supposedly maintained contact with my "friends" whom I have condemned, there figured two of my letters:
>
> 1) to E. Iaroslavski concerning Vladimir Slepkov, and 2) to Medved' concerning Katalynov.
>
> The last letter can be explained in this way (in general, I never had any contact with Katalynov): D. L. Talmud, a physicist and GPU employee, whom I had helped in constructing a laboratory of special assignment under GPU direction, came to me. He asked me to write Medved' to give him [Talmud] Katalynov, about whom he, Talmud, knew from Smorodin. Then, at Talmud's request, having no idea who Katalynov was (he told me his name was Vania Katalynov) I wrote to Medved' and as Talmud said that there were some kind of oppositional sins against K[atalynov], I wrote in this same letter to Medved' about this and instructed him that it was necessary to verify K[atalynov] specially along these lines (all this can be read in the original of the

---

[127] Murin, Iurii. "'No ia to znaiu, chto ia prav.' Pis'mo N.I. Bukharina I.V. Stalinu iz vnutrennei tiur'my NKVD." *Istochnik*, No. 3 (2000), 46-58.

[128] The archival identifiers given by Murin are handwritten on the first page of this copy. But they are written incorrectly. The precise archival identifiers are given at the end of the letter in larger handwriting, and show that Murin misread starting page 129 as "12⁻"

> letter, and also verified by Talmud). So, what kind of contact is this. What kind of correspondence with friends is this letter of mine to a chief of the GPU at the request of an employee of the GPU?

Bukharin refers to two letters that Ezhov produced at the February-March 1937 Plenum. Lenoe never discusses them or anything about the context in which Bukharin's recommendation of Kotolynov came to light. We examine it here as it bears directly on the question of evidence against Bukharin.

In the course of his detailed indictment of Bukharin before the Central Committee Plenum in February 1937 Ezhov cited evidence that Bukharin, along with Rykov, had continued to be involved in a hostile oppositional fraction against the Stalin leadership while claiming to have long ago abandoned any opposition. That is, Ezhov accused Bukharin of "dvurushnichestvo" or "two-facedness", a subject that we explore in another chapter of the present work.

Immediately before discussing the two letters mentioned above Ezhov cites some evidence that we can now verify. Ezhov said:

> Three main charges were presented. First, that Bukharin and Rykov, after they had given statements about their full submission to the Party and their renunciation of their right opportunist views, deceived the Party, two-facedly disguised themselves, while renouncing their right opportunist views they retained their fraction, the members of whom went underground, continued to stand on their old political platform, did not cease their struggle against the Party, and submitted only to their own internal fractional discipline. For the leadership of this fraction a center, which continued to exist until recently, had already been established in 1928. Bukharin and Rykov were very active participants and members of this center.
>
> (*Voprosy Istorii* No. 2, 1993, 26)

In 1929 Bukharin personally told the Swiss Communist Jules Humbert-Droz, a member of the Executive Committee of the Comintern and one of Bukharin's few supporters on that body, that he and his people intended to kill Stalin:

> Boukharine m'a dit aussi qu'ils avaient décidé d'utiliser la terreur individuelle pour se débarrasser de Staline. (Humbert-Droz 379-380)
>
> Bukharin also told me that they had decided to use individual terror to get rid of Stalin.

As we have written elsewhere there is no reason to doubt this evidence:

> Humbert-Droz wrote without any pressure from the NKVD. He was Bukharin's friend and hated Stalin. He had no reason to lie or to exaggerate what he knew. And these are not "rumors," since Humbert-Droz wrote that he heard of the plans to murder Stalin from Bukharin's own lips.[129]

In his famous and influential book on Bukharin Stephen F. Cohen quoted from Humbert-Droz's memoirs. But Cohen failed to inform his readers about the Swiss communist's revelation that Bukharin and his faction were conspiring to murder Stalin not in 1932, as later testimony also confirms, but as early as 1929 or even perhaps a few months earlier, in 1928.[130]

By the time Ezhov spoke to the February-March 1937 Plenum there had been a great deal of testimony that Bukharin had continued his oppositional activity, including supporting other, especially younger, Party members in his fraction hostile to Stalin. At the time of this writing five face-to-face confrontations between Bukharin and his supporters have been published: those with Astrov, Kulikov, Piatakov, Radek, and Sosnovski. We have carefully studied all these accounts elsewhere.[131]

---

[129] Grover Furr, Vladimir L. Bobrov, "Nikolai Bukharin's First Statement of Confession in the Lubianka." *Cultural Logic* 2007 17, n.34.

[130] *Bukharin and the Bolshevik Revolution. A Political biography 1888-1938.* New York: Oxford University Press, 1980 (1971), 294, 300, 309. Humbert-Droz's memoir is cited at 453 n.170.

[131] "Verdikt: Vinoven!". Ch. 1 of Furr and Bobrov, *1937. Pravosudie Stalina.* (Moscow: EKSMO 2010), 13-63. We hope to publish an English version soon.

We have no evidence or any other reason to believe any compulsion was applied to these men. But we can have confidence in the case of one of them. Born in 1898, Valentin Astrov survived till after the end of the USSR. In 1989 and again in 1993 when anticommunist and anti-Stalin articles were welcomed in the Russian press, Astrov continued to insist in print that he had not been manhandled, threatened, tortured, or even treated with any disrespect. For example, he stressed that his NKVD investigators never even called him "ty" ("thou", a term of disrespect unless used to a close friend, relative, or lover). Astrov retracted only one statement he had made in the 1930s: that he had heard Bukharin personally call for "terror" against Stalin. He refused to retract anything else. No one would have contradicted Astrov if he had said that his confessions were due to torture or threats. In fact he would have gained the sympathy of many.

Astrov's account, plus that of Humbert-Droz, constitutes strong evidence that Bukharin continued his clandestine oppositional activities after having publicly sworn off them.[132]

Letter To Radek, 1932

After passing very briefly over the second accusation against Bukharin and Rykov (that they continued to support the re-establishment of capitalist relations in the countryside) Ezhov continued:

> And, third, we have accused Bukharin and Rykov of having had direct recourse to a bloc with Trotskyites, Zinovievites, "Leftists", SR's, Mensheviks, and with all the other fractional groupings that had long since been smashed, in order to attain their end of overthrowing the Leninist-Stalinist leadership. In a bloc with all the enemies of the Soviet Union they adopted the method of . terror, organzing an armed insurrection, and to sabotage. (*Voprosy Istorii* No. 2, 1993, 26)

---

132 It is likely that Astrov lied when he stated that he did not really hear Bukharin call for "terror" against Stalin. During the 1940s Astrov had boasted of his role in helping to unmask the Rights. And we know from Humbert-Droz that Bukharin was plotting Stalin's assassination as early as 1928.

Thanks to the opening of the Harvard Trotsky archive in 1980 we now know that a "bloc" of this nature was indeed formed with Trotsky's approval. In January 1986 American historian Arch Getty revealed that the Trotsky archive at Harvard closed to the public until 1980 (and so long known as the "Closed Archive") had been "purged". Someone had removed materials from it at some point before it was opened.

In Getty's words:

> At the time of the Moscow show trials, Trotsky denied that he had any communications with the defendants since his exile in 1929. Yet it is now clear that in 1932 he sent secret personal letters to former leading oppositionists Karl Radek, G. Sokol'nikov, E. Preobrazhensky, and others. While the contents of these letters are unknown, it seems reasonable to believe that they involved an attempt to persuade the addressees to return to opposition.[18] (Getty, Trotsky in Exile 27-8)

Getty's note to this passage reads as follows:

> [18] Trotsky Papers, 15821. Unlike virtually all Trotsky's other letters (including even the most sensitive) no copies of these remain in the Trotsky Papers. It seems likely that they have been removed from the Papers at some time. Only the certified mail receipts remain. (Getty, Trotsky in Exile 34)

In his 1985 book Getty was less hesitant in concluding that the archive had been purged. He also revealed some new information about dates and destinations for some of the missing letters.

> Although Trotsky later denied that he had any communications with former followers in the USSR since his exile in 1929,[19] **it is clear that he did**. In the first three months of 1932 he sent secret letters to former oppositionists Radek, Sokolnikov, Preobrazhenskii, and others.[20] Although the contents of these letters are unknown, it seems reasonable to believe that they involved an attempt to persuade the addressees to return to opposition. (Getty Origins 119; emphasis added, GF)

The two footnotes:

> (Origins n. 19 p. 245) The Dewey Commission, *The Case of Leon Trotsky,* New York, 1937, 91, 264, 273. See also *Bulletin of the Opposition* No. 52-3, Oct. 1936, 38-41."
>
> (Origins n. 20 p. 245) Trotsky Papers II, 15821. The letters are dated from April 1932 to December 1932. Those to Sokolnikov and Preobrazhenskii were sent to London, **that to Radek in Geneva**. Other letters were sent to Kollontai and Litvinov. **Copies of these letters have been removed** from Trotsky's papers, but whoever removed them failed to retrieve the certified-mail receipts signed by Trotsky's secretaries. (Emphasis added GF)

Getty concluded the footnote of his 1986 article with these words:

> At his 1937 trial, Karl Radek testified that he had received a letter from Trotsky containing 'terrorist instructions', but we do not know whether this was the letter in question. (34)

But we can in fact be certain that this was indeed the letter in question. In his testimony at the January 1937 trial Radek mentioned a number of letters from Trotsky, beginning with one that he received in February 1932. A little later Radek said:

> Preliminarily, that preparations were being made, I learned from the letter Trotsky wrote to me in February-March 1932.
>
> (1937 Trial 85)

We have obtained copies of the certified mail receipts of Trotsky's letters from the Houghton Library, Harvard University. The receipt of the letter to Radek is dated March 3, 1932. Radek stated:

> Radek: This was after I received the letter from Trotsky. The letter from Trotsky was received in February or March 1932. (92)

This is strong evidence that the letter of which Radek is speaking was the same one as the letter purged from Trotsky's archive.

Radek described the contents of this letter of Trotsky's as follows:

> Radek: Trotsky wrote that the information he possessed led him to conclude that I had become convinced that he was right, and that without the realization of the Trotskyite demands the policy would find itself at an impasse. Trotsky further wrote that since he knew me to be an active person he was convinced that I would return to the struggle.
>
> Vyshinsky: And did Trotsky summon you to the struggle?
>
> Radek: At the end of the letter Trotsky wrote approximately as follows: "You must bear in mind the experience of the preceding period and realize that for you there can be no returning to the past, that the struggle has entered a new phase and that the new feature in this phase is that either we shall be destroyed together with the Soviet Union, or we must raise the question of removing the leadership." The word terrorism was not used, but when I read the words "removing the leadership," it became clear to me what Trotsky had in mind. … Trotsky informed me that not only the Trotskyites but also the Zinovievites had decided to return to the struggle and that negotiations for union were under way.
>
> (1937 Trial 86-87)

Sedov's letter to Trotsky partially reprinted in French translation by Broué confirms Radek's words about the Zinovievites.

> [The bloc] has been organized. In it have entered the Zinovievites, the Sten-Lominadze group and the Trotskyists
>
> (former "[capitulators]".

Radek testified that he had confirmed that Trotsky intended "terrorism" in a talk with Sergei Mrachkovsky that took place at the end of October or beginning of November 1932.

> Vyshinsky: What did Mrachkovsky reply?

> Radek: He replied quite definitely that the struggle had entered the terrorist phase and that in order to carry out these tactics they had now united with the Zinovievites anld would set about the preparatory work.
>
> Vyshinsky: What preparatory work?
>
> Radek: It was clear that since terrorism was the new position, the preparatory work must consist in assembling and forming terrorist cadres.
>
> [...]
>
> Vyshinsky: Did you know from Mrachkovsky about the preparations for terrorist acts against the leaders of the Party and the government ?
>
> [...]
>
> Radek: The conversation about Kirov was connected with the fact that in April 1933 Mrachkovsky asked me whether I could mention any Trotskyite in Leningrad who would undertake the organization of a terrorist group there.
>
> Vyshinsky: Against whom?
>
> Radek: Against Kirov, of course.
>
> (1937 Trial 89-90)

As a result, Radek testified, a plot to assassinate Sergei Kirov, Party leader in Leningrad, was hatched in April 1933, and Kirov was actually killed in December 1934.

"Remove The Leadership"

Radek claimed that in February or March 1932 – we know now that it was on March 3, 1932 – he had received a letter from Trotsky while he, Radek, was in Geneva. That letter was a directive to "remove the leadership" ("ustranit' rukovodstvo") – which Radek understood to mean through "terror".

Getty surmised that this letter "involved an attempt to persuade the addressee[s] to return to opposition." Radek confirmed that Trotsky's letter did contain such an appeal but that it closed by saying "we must raise the question of removing the leadership" ("nado postavit' vopros ob ustranenii rukovodstva"). The terms *ustranit'* ("to remove") and *ustranenie* ("removal") are used many times by the defendants in the first Moscow Trial. All claimed that they understood it in the way Radek did – as meaning assassination. It was natural that they did so, for there was no other means of "removing the leadership" aside from winning a majority of the Central Committee – something they had been unable to do during the 1920s when they could campaign openly within the Party in the USSR.

According to Valentin Astrov Bukharin used exactly the same words in speaking to his clandestine faction:

> I return to my exposition of BUKHARIN'S speech at the January 1930 meeting.
>
> BUKHARIN said that it was not possible to determine how long the period of uprisings would be, it might last for a number of years. It was possible that during the process of the struggle for power it would be necessary to conclude temporary blocs with the SRs or the Mensheviks. BUKHARIN focused on STALIN'S very important role and said that as the main force in this leadership it would be necessary at any cost to remove STALIN ("STALINA… ustranit'")
>
> (Lubianka 1937-1938, 27)

Trotsky later wrote publicly that by "ustranit'" he did not mean "kill." According to Astrov, the meaning of the admittedly ambivalent word received clarification at the same conspiratorial meeting of January 1930:

> BUKHARIN further referred to the approaching military intervention and said that the USSR in its present condition and with the policy of the Stalin leadership would be unable to defeat the imperialists. In the case of intervention the Rights should make use of the wartime situation, preserve their underground organization for the continuation of the struggle to overthrow the Stalin leadership.
>
> The participants in the meeting who spoke after BUKHARIN expressed solidarity with him. In his

> speech KUZ'MIN spoke out for the tactic of a "palace coup", with the arrests of STALIN and of other members of the Soviet government.
>
> KUZ'MIN'S speech ended with his loud declaration, which he made in the heat of extraordinary hostility: "Give me a revolver and I will shoot Stalin." He was asked not to shout about this, since people under the window might be listening. SLEPKOV said that "hatred of Stalin is a sacred hatred", but that it should not be expressed so loudly.
>
> A few days later, in MARETSKII'S apartment in my and KUZ'MIN'S presence BUKHARIN said to KUZ'MIN that such legitimate wishes, generally speaking such as "I will kill Stalin" must not be expressed where many people are present, since the GPU might find out about it.
>
> (Lubianka 1937-1938, 27)

Later in the same statement Astrov recounted the story of how Bukharin had told him in the summer of 1931 that Stalin must be killed, since there was no other way to "take the Party leadership into our hands."

> I remember my conversation with BUKHARIN that took place in the summer of 1931 or 1932, during which BUKHARIN this time in a direct manner stated the necessity of killing STALIN. Developing this thought further BUKHARIN emphasized that once STALIN was gone no one could consolidate the Party, and that would give us the possibility to take the leadership in our hands. (29)

The only thing that Astrov later denied was that he had heard Bukharin expressly utter the word "kill".

The Bloc

As we have seen, in 1932 Trotsky and Sedov wrote of a bloc between the Trotskyites, the Zinovievites, and the Sten-Lominadze group, and that in January 1937 Radek also spoke of a bloc formed in 1932 between the Trotskyites and Zinovievites. Astrov testified that Bukharin had announced to his clandestine faction, also in 1932, the need to form a bloc with the Trotskyites.

> In the Fall of 1924 BUKHARIN, with SLEPKOV present, told me that we must "make up" with TROTSKY at any cost, so as to later form a bloc with him against the Stalin leaders and change the Leninist line of the Party in his, BUKHARIN'S, direction.
>
> [...]
>
> In particular SLEPKOV made a similar reference in his speech at the illegal conference of Bukharinites at the end of August 1932, in explaining the necessity of a bloc of Rights with the Trotskyites.
>
> [...]
>
> In the Spring of 1932 SLEPKOV in his apartment directly expressed to me the necessity of killing STALIN ("either we, or STALIN, we cannot both continue to live") and informed me that the center of Rights had moved to the tactic of terror.
>
> Parallel to this the practical formulation of our former idea about a bloc with the other counterrevolutionary and White Guardist organizations was proceeding. At the beginning of 1932 SLEPKOV in his apartment at a meeting of the active members of the organization explained the necessity of concluding a bloc with the Trotskyites. He said that "the Trotskyites had accepted the economic platform of the Rights and the Rights, the inner-Party platform of the Trotskyites. The tactic of terror united us. Disagreements between us and the Trotskyites are not essential.
>
> [...]
>
> SLEPKOV informed the meeting that his point of view concerning the necessity of concluding a bloc with the Trotskyites had been confirmed with BUKHARIN, that is, with the center of the Rights, and the meeting adopted this viewpoint. A few days later at SLEPKOV'S

> apartment with MARETSKII present BUKHARIN confirmed the necessity of such a bloc. …
>
> At the first session of the conference SLEPKOV informed those present that STEN had recently come to him and had proposed to conclude a bloc with them in the name of the group of "Leftists."
>
> (Lubianka 1937-1938 32;23; 32; 35)

Astrov described how the Bukharinist group discussed the need for blocs with the "leftist" Sten-Lominadze group, with S-Rs, and with Mensheviks. As we've seen Sedov informed Trotsky of the formation of a bloc between the Trotskyites, Zinovievites, and the Sten-Lominadze group.

Sedov and Trotsky cannot possibly have been lying in their letters to one another. Astrov cannot have been lying either. He could have written anything at all in 1993, when his last published article on this matter appeared. If he had claimed he had been tortured, beaten, threatened, no one would have been able or willing to refute him. Indeed, such testimony would have been welcomed by those who are already committed to the proposition that all the testimony of the accused is false. Instead Astrov refused to do any of this.

The Two Bukharin Letters

We recall that in the April 15, 1937 letter to Stalin Bukharin referred to two letters brought forth by Ezhov:

> In the concluding remarks of N.I. Ezhov at the plenum, as evidence that I also supposedly maintained contact with my "friends" whom I have condemned, there figured two of my letters:
>
> 1) to E. Iaroslavskii concerning Vladimir Slepkov, and 2) to Medved' concerning Katalynov.

At the Plenum on February 26, 1937 Ezhov described the letter about Vladimir Slepkov as follows:

> Moving on – a second argument: I, he says, you see, have long since distanced myself from all these people, have called them counterrevolutionaries, have not defended them, and therefore they are naturally angry at

me and are slandering me. Here I will show Bukharin several documents, about how he has distanced himself. He really did distance himself from Slepkov, that is, more accurately, he distanced himself from all the Slepkov brothers, distanced himself a long time ago, after their arrest, and in particular distanced himself from this Slepkov, when he was expelled from the Party and arrested. Here I mean Vladimir Slepkov. And nonetheless a little time later he secretly phoned Emel'ian Iaroslavskii and, having first asked him, sent him a letter. I tell you about this because he was arrested, expelled from the party, and after that you write Emel'ian. (Bukharin: True, but he had no relationship to this group.) But that's not true, you know very well that he had a direct relationship. (Bukharin: No, no.)

Wait, listen to the documents, be patient. He [Bukharin] writes a letter about Slepkov, the youngest of the brothers. "I can only say that I know very well that Vladimir Slepkov has never taken part in any trouble or fractional activities. It is possible that he had some doubts at one time, but he has kept himself politically at a distance from Aleksandr." And he asks that he be readmitted to the Party. (Stalin. To whom is Bukharin writing this?) He is writing this to Iaroslavskii. In fact he knows very well that Vladimir Slepkov, just like Vasilii, took part in that famous meeting in Pokrovskoe-Streshnevo, where there were 17 people, where Kuz'min first stated that if everything depends on Stalin, then let's remove him ["uberiom", from "ubrat'" – GF]. All of them talk about this and talk about it openly just like Vasilii and Vladimir Slepkov, who have been in this organization from the moment of its existence, that is, from the moment when their brothers recruited them. This Vladimir Slepkov took part in almost all the meetings. (Bukharin. But he was living in Leningrad.) Yes, he was living in Leningrad, quite true. This same Slepkov is arrested in 1933 and then is released and is expelled from the Party, and in 1934 Nikolai Ivanovich

> Bukharin intercedes for this person and then says that "they are slandering me because I distanced myself from them". That's how his two-faced behavior is evidence, even in these small details." (*Voprosy Istorii* No. 2, 1993, 27-28)

In his April 15, 1937 letter to Stalin from prison Bukharin tried to explain this accusation as follows:

> 2) The letter about Vlad. Slepkov. (Vlad. Slepkov must not be confused with Vasilii Slepkov). I received by mail an almost insane letter from Vlad. Slepkov (he was in a psychiatric hospital). I had never seen him and did not know that this "Volodia" was one of the Slepkov group. And I then wrote a letter to the CCC, to E. Iaroslaavskii. Not to Slepkov, but to a member of the Party troika of the CCC. And this is a sin? And this is my "contact" with the Slepkovites whom I have condemned? (Murin 2000 54; Volkogonov Paprs 20)

However, in his January 1937 statement Valentin Astrov specifically implicated Vladimir Slepkov as well as his brothers.

> In 1928-1930 our filial groups were created and conducted underground work, with the following membership:
>
> 1. Samara – SLEPKOV, LEVIN, AREF'EV, AREF'EVA, KROTOV, VOROB'EVA, Galina SHALAKHOVA, ZHIROV.
>
> 2. Saratov – PETROVSKII, ZAITSEV, SLEPKOV, SHALAKHOVA, ZAITSEVA, LEVINA, ALEKSANDROV, LAPKIN, IVANOV and others.
>
> 3. Kazan – Vas. SLEPKOV (I don't remember the rest of the members of the group).
>
> 4. Ivanovo – I (ASTROV), BASHENKOV, BOL'SHAKOV, BOGDANOV, ABOLIN.
>
> 5. Leningrad – MARETSKII, AIKHENVAL'D, **Vl. SLEPKOV**, KANIN and others
>
> (Lubianka 1937-1938, 28; emphasis added GF)

Astrov also discussed the conference in Pokrovsko-Streshnevo (near Moscow) to which Ezhov referred, saying that "V. Slepkov" was present, but we can't tell whether this was Vasilii or Vladimir. Ezhov may have been confusing two separate meetings. After outlining the meeting at Pokrovsko-Streshnevo in the winter of 1930-1 Astrov spoke as follows:

> At another meeting in this same apartment of MARETSKII'S that same winter of 1930-31 TSETLIN, in BUKHARIN'S presence, talked about the relationship of the Rights to Trotskyism as follows: we just once and for all admit, said TSETLIN, that in inner-Party questions we were incorrect in 1923-1928 and the Trotskyites were completely correct. They saw earlier than we did where the "Stalin regime" was leading us. This is where KUZ'MIN interrupted TSETLIN, crying out "kill STALIN".
>
> (Lubianka 1937-1938, 31)

Astrov refused to recant his testimony on this point, so there is no reason to doubt that Vladimir Slepkov was in fact involved in the underground opposition group.

As leader of this group it is hardly possible that Bukharin would not have known about Vladimir Slepkov's participation, even if he were less active than his brothers – and we do not know that. Vladimir Slepkov's participation would fully explain Bukharin's letter on his behalf to Iaroslavskii, since it was the plan of the underground opposition groups to penetrate the party. Therefore it would expose Bukharin as a "double-dealer" just as Ezhov charged.

Bukharin's Letter To Medved' About Kotolynov[133]

Bukharin does not dispute Ezhov's summary of and quotations from the letter, which is as follows:

> The second document – is also such a friendship, rather suspicious: there was a famous little man, the terrorist Katalynov, the organizer of the murder of com. Kirov, the person who directed Nikolaev. So here, you see, also in 1934 Bukharin writes ... (Voice from the room: To whom?). To Medved' in Leningrad. He writes: "Dear comrade Medved', you lack one worker – and then he asks – it would be good to unload some administrative matters, you have in Leningrad a young man, Vania Katalynov", in a word, he sends him a detailed character reference from the words of others, tells him that Smorodinov can recommend him. Then he writes: "I leave to one side that he was expelled from the party, and only know that I have heard about him as a very talented Party volunteer." (Bukharin. One very prominent, very staunch Chekist...) Yes, but that's neither here nor there. (Bukharin. A Chekist, a scientific worker, asked me to give [a reference to] this Katalynov. I wrote Medved' and asked him to verify this person.) A strange acquaintance with terrorists. (Bukharin. I can summon the witnesses on whose request I did this.) (*Voprosy Istorii* No. 2 1993, 27)

Concerning Bukharin's letter to Iaroslavskii Ezhov pointed out that Bukharin wrote a recommendation that Vladimir Slepkov, expelled from the Party, be admitted, all the while knowing that he was a member of an underground oppositional faction. Astrov had testified that Bukharin actively led this clandestine opposition group in which Vladimir Slepkov was a member of the Leningrad branch.

Bukharin did not deny writing this letter or Ezhov's characterization of its contents. But Bukharin claimed he did not know of Vladimir Slep-

---

133 This is only part of the context in which we should consider Bukharin's letter recommending Kotolynov. For by February 26, 1937, the date of Ezhov's report, the second Moscow Trial of January 23-30 1937 had concluded. Of course the testimony against Bukharin at that trial also forms a part of the context in which Ezhov gave his report about Bukharin's two letters. In another part of this present study we examine how the Kirov assassination figured in the January 1937 trial.

kov's oppositional activity, thus directly contradicting Astrov's testimony. Bukharin's only response to the testimony of Astrov and of others – apparently many others – of his followers who testified against him was that they "had it in for him" since he had attacked and criticized them.

In his letter to Stalin Bukharin did not even try to explain why he would recommend reinstatement in the Party for a person in a psychiatric hospital who had written him one "insane letter" and who had been expelled from the Party not long before. Stalin could hardly have failed to notice this omission.

Moreover, Bukharin wrote not to Slepkov's original Party body, to the next highest body, or to any of the Leningrad Party leadership. He did not even write to Kirov, whom Bukharin professed to admire. Instead Bukharin went right to the top, to Emil'ian Iaroslavskii, member of the Central Control Commission (or, depending upon the date of the letter, the Commission of Party Control). Iaroslavskii was not only a person who could directly urge that someone be readmitted to Party membership. It was also unlikely that he would have known about Vladimir Slepkov. The leading party bodies in Leningrad, and of course Kirov himself, would have known about Slepkov and his oppositional past. Thus it appears that Bukharin was trying to get Slepkov readmitted to the Party by going over the heads of the Leningrad Party organization.

It would have made no sense for any ordinary Party member to recommend a person like Vladimir Slepkov. But it would indeed make sense if Bukharin knew that Slepkov was a co-conspirator. The whole point of the "double-dealing" tactic was to "bore from within", to retain as many, and as powerful, positions in the Party as possible. It is hard to explain Bukharin's action in any other way. At the very least it would have excited suspicion.

It is in this context that we need to view Bukharin's letter recommending Kotolynov to Medved'. While insisting that he did not know him personally Bukharin wrote a letter recommending Kotolynov to a position as an administrator in the Leningrad NKVD, despite the fact that Kotolynov had been expelled from the Party for oppositional activity. Here too Bukharin was going over the head of the Leningrad Party leadership, including Kirov. Any investigator would wonder why he would do that. Bukharin's explanation that he had done this because Talmud had asked him to do so would not have excused Bukharin's action either. Party members were supposed to recommend persons whom they knew and in whom they had confidence.

We possess evidence that Bukharin had long known about Kotolynov and his oppositional sympathies. At the 7th Congress of the Komsomol in March 1926 Kotolynov spoke up against the supporters of Stalin:

> ...comrades, we must take a look at the psychology of a few Party workers who are carrying out these transfers. They show this kind of psychology: Whom do you support? Are you a Stalinist or not? If you are not a Stalinist – press him, crush him, drive him far away so we don't hear even a squeak from him. In our organization this has nothing in common with a Leninist upbringing, and it must be clearly explained that our organization is not Stalinist, but Leninist.[134]

Kotolynov's speech is recorded on pages 104-108 of the transcript; at the fifth session. Bukharin was present and spoke during the ninth session; his speech is on pages 230-258.

At the 15th Party Congress Kotolynov, as well as Bakaev, Gertik, Evdokimov, Kamenev, Kuklin, Levin, and Rumiantsev, all of whom reappear in the Kirov case, were expelled from the Party as "activists in the Trotskyite opposition". Kotolynov's name, spelled "Katalynov"[135] just as Bukharin spelled it in his letter to Stalin, is in the list of expellees on pages 1247 and 1318 of the transcript of the Congress. The letter signed by many expellees agreeing with the Party's line, renouncing oppositional activity, and requesting reinstatement in the Party, is in the Appendix on pages 1334-1335. It is countersigned by Kamenev, who states that he has verified the signatures of all the co-signers, and dated December 3, 1927.

Bukharin spoke several times during this Congress. He would probably have voted in favor of the expulsions. We know from Bukharin's friend Humbert-Droz that at this very time Bukharin was already fractionalizing against Stalin and probably already discussing plans to kill him. Kotolynov was a prominent Leningrad Zinovievite and one of those reinstated

---

134 *VII s"ezd vsesoiuznogj leninskogo kommunisticheskogo soiuza molodezhi. 11 – 22 marta 1926 goda. Stenograficheskii otchet.* (Moscow-Leningrad: Molodaia gvardiia, 1926), p. 108.

135 In most parts of Russia an unstressed "o" is pronounced as though it were a short "a", so "Kotolynov" would be pronounced "Katalynov", with stress on the third syllable.

along with Kamenev. It seems more than unlikely that Bukharin would not have known who Kotolynov was.[136] Rather, it appears likely that Bukharin knew that Kotolynov was an active underground Oppositionist, a Zinovievite allied with his own Rightists and with clandestine Trotskyites in the bloc that was planning to assassinate Kirov, Stalin, and others.

Conclusion

Ezhov said that the two letters of Bukharin's constituted "a strange acquaintance with terrorists" – strange, that is, if Bukharin were innocent of any clandestine oppositional activity, as he claimed to be. But given all of the evidence available by February 26, 1937 of Bukharin's involvement with an underground Rightist conspiracy, it must have appeared unlikely to the investigators that his recommendation of Kotolynov, whom he admitted he did not know, was simply a very strange coincidence. Investigators, like historians, are professionally suspicious of coincidences.

Evidence given at the January 1937 and March 1938 Moscow Trials indicated that Bukharin agreed with the tactic of terror. In the March 1938 Trial Iagoda and Vyshinsky expressed disbelief that Bukharin could have been ignorant of the fact that a plan was afoot to murder Kirov. But Bukharin's letter in favor of Kotolynov was apparently never raised again, either in the trials – whose transcripts we have – or in those few pre-trial investigative materials that have been released to researchers.

So either Bukharin did not know that Kotolynov was in a secret Zinovievite group that was preparing an assassination attempt upon Kirov, or the prosecution was not able to prove that he did and so did not raise this matter at the March 1938 Moscow trial. That would not mean his recommendation of Kotolynov was necessarily innocent. We do not have whatever investigation materials are available on Talmud, on whose behalf Bukharin claimed he wrote the letter in question. Talmud's name does not appear in the most extensive list of "victims of Stalinism", the

---

[136] My thanks to my colleague Vladimir L. Bobrov of Moscow, who informed me of the references to Kotolynov in the 7th Komsomol and 15th Party Congresses (personal email October 31, 2011).

list maintained by the Memorial Society. The biographical information available about him is extremely sketchy and cites no repression.[137]

---

137 http://www.ipme.nw.ru/mirrors/PRAN/www/info/44/4429.htm A Stalin prize laureate, Talmud signed the unpublished letter to *Pravda* in early 1953 critical of the Jewish Anti-Fascist Committee and the Joint Distribution Committee. A slightly longer biography of Talmud at the semi-official Aleksandr Iakovlev site mentions no collaboration with the NKVD; see http://www.alexanderyakovlev.org/almanah/inside/almanah-doc/person/1004070 The text of the unpublished letter is available in many places, including at http://www.alexanderyakovlev.org/almanah/inside/almanah-doc/55578

Chapter 17

Liushkov's Essay

NKVD general Genrikh Samoilovich Liushkov defected to the Japanese on June 13, 1938 by crossing the border into Japanese-occupied Manchuria. He gave some press conferences and wrote articles attacking Stalin and the Soviet party and government. In at least one press conference, a report of which was published in *Asahi Shimbun* on July 2, 1938 and in *Yomiuri Shinbun* the following day, and in a long article in the Japanese journal *Kaizo* of March 1939 Liushkov discussed the Kirov assassination. As an NKVD investigator Liushkov had been directly involved in the Kirov assassination investigation and the later interrogations of Zinoviev and Kamenev prior to their August 1936 Trial.

On pp. 680-1 (Document #126) Lenoe prints an English translation of Liushkov's press statement of July 3, 1938. This brief document has long been available in Russian translation.[138] On pp. 681-686 (Document #127) Lenoe publishes a translation of that part of the *Kaizo* article in which Liushkov discusses the Kirov assassination at much greater length. As far as we can determine this article has never been published in full in English or Russian translation. We have arranged for a complete translation into English of Liushkov's *Kaizo* article and will refer to it here.

Lenoe states that Liushkov's account is of primary importance for our knowledge of the Kirov assassination:

> Liushkov's evidence, which has been ignored or downplayed by Western writers on the Kirov killing, is in fact the most important in the case. (687)

In this chapter I study Liushkov's account in detail. This detailed study concludes that Lenoe is mistaken about the value of Liushkov's article in understanding the Kirov assassination. I will demonstrate that Liushkov

---

[138] See the entry in the Russian language Wikipedia at http://ru.wikipedia.org/wiki/Люшков,_Генрих_Самойлович and at the biographical site at http://www.hrono.ru/biograf/bio_l/ljushkov_gs.php

deliberately falsified his writings in order to make anti-Soviet, and specifically anti-Stalin, propaganda for the Japanese.

My study shows that, ironically, Lenoe is correct – though not at all for the reasons he states. Liushkov is in fact "the most important evidence" – but not of the Kirov assassination. Rather, it turns out that Liushkov is the most direct non-Soviet testimony that the conspiracies during 1936-1938 in the USSR, and specifically the 1938 Moscow Trial and the military conspiracies known to history as the "Tukhachevsky Affair" of 1937, later discussed by defendants in the 1938 Moscow Trial, really did exist.

Lenoe notes correctly that all the alleged conspiracies, from the Kirov Affair in 1934 to the Bloc of Rights and Trotskyites in 1938, were linked to each other by overlapping leadership and inter-communication. This is why the NKVD referred to them all as the *klubok*, or "tangle." As we have seen in our study of the March 1938 Moscow Trial, the defendants there testify to their connection with the Zinovievites who murdered Kirov. Therefore Liushkov provides evidence not that Nikolaev was a "lone gunman", but of precisely the opposite – that the conspiracies as outlined in the December 1934 Kirov trial and the other Moscow Trials were genuine.

Our study of Liushkov's account is in three parts. First we will examine what Liushkov wrote on the Kirov assassination in the 1939 *Kaizo* article as translated by Lenoe and reprinted in his book. After that we will study the rest of Liushkov's *Kaizo* article – the part not translated by Lenoe. Then we will compare what Liushkov wrote for publication with what we know he told the Japanese privately. At the end we will return to Lenoe's view of what Liushkov wrote.

Liushkov's account of the Kirov affair in *Kaizo*, March 1939

Liushkov wrote when no details about the Kirov assassination were available other than what had been published in Soviet newspapers. None of the other evidence – interrogation transcripts, for example – was available. The evidence we have today permits us to immediately discern some of Liushkov's falsifications simply by reading his 1938 and 1939 accounts.

For example, in the July 1938 interview Liushkov wrote:

> Nikolaev definitely did not belong to the Zinoviev group.[139]

In his *Kaizo* article some months later he had altered this claim:

> ...[W]hen he was a member of the Komsomol, he [Nikolaev] had sympathies for the Zinovievite faction. (683)

Lenoe has printed parts of a confession of December 12, 1934 in which Zvezdov specifically identified Nikolaev as a member of the Leningrad Center, along with Rumiantsev, Kotolynov, Tsarkov, Severov, Tseitlin, Surov, and Tolmazov (310 Doc. 55; Lenoe has declined to make the Russian original public):

> Question [to Zvezdov]: Lay out for us the membership of the Center and the other branches of the Leningrad organization [of underground Zinovievites – GF].
>
> Answer: The membership is as follows:
>
> 1. The Leningrad Center.
>
> a. Rumiantsev, Vladimir – leader of the organization.
>
> b. Kotolynov, Ivan.
>
> [...]
>
> h. Nikolaev, Leonid. (310)

Moreover, in a confession of December 13, 1934 in the Volkogonov Archive Tsar'kov confirms that Nikolaev was a Zinovievite:

> Question: What do you know about the murderer of com. KIROV – NIKOLAEV, Leonid?
>
> Answer: I know NIKOLAEV through our joint work in the Vyborg region [of Leningrad]. He is a Zinovievite. He was closest to KOTOLYNOV. I do not precisely

---

139 « □□□□□,□□□□□□ □□□□□□□□□□ ». http://hrono.ru/biograf/bio_l/ljushkov_gs.php ; Lenoe, p. 681.

> remember whether he took part in our legal struggle with the Party during the first years of the appearance of the Trotskyite-Zinovievite bloc, or whether he signed the platform of the bloc (all signatures to the platform went through myself and MURAV'EV, Mikh.), or whether he belonged to the category of persons who remained in an illegal position and did not stand forth openly as members of the organization. Our counter-revolutionary organization bears political responsibility for the terrorist act of L. NIKOLAEV, member of the organization, in whose ranks he was nourished.

Tsar'kov's confession contains details that we can now confirm from other evidence, including the fact that a Trotskyite-Zinovievite bloc did indeed exist, as we know from Trotsky's own correspondence.

As we have seen, Kotolynov agreed that his Zinovievist group bore responsibility for Nikolaev's murder of Kirov since it had nourished in him hostility towards the Party. As we have argued above, this could not have happened unless Nikolaev were a member of the Zinovievist group. Finally, Nikolaev himself admitted close contact with Kotolynov and the Zinovievist group.

Liushkov's other remarks concerning the Kirov assassination are of little interest to our inquiry. He insists that Borisov was not killed by Iagoda's order but by accident. This corresponds both to the conclusion the NKVD reached in December 1934 and to the position of the Russian government, Kirilina, and Lenoe today. Iagoda freely confessed to other heinous crimes, but he always insisted that he had nothing to do with Borisov's death. We examine this testimony elsewhere in this present study.

About Kamenev and Zinoviev Liushkov has little to say except to simply declare their confessions false:

> … [A]t the August 1936 show trial, Zinoviev and Kamenev were the leaders of the conspiratorial organization and Bakaev was presented as the direct organizer [of the killing]. Here I myself can serve as a witness. I was the person who conducted the interrogation of the aforementioned three men and I can confirm that their confessions were completely false.

> Yagoda transmitted Stalin's orders to me and these orders were embodied in the text of Zinoviev, Kamenev, and Bakaev's confessions. (Lenoe 685)

This does not come close to answering the questions that arise just from the evidence that we now have. Why did Zinoviev and Kamenev testify as they did in the public trial? Even more important: why did they, and all the other defendants whose confessions we now have, confess in the way they did *before* the multiple trials of December 1934 (the Kirov murder trial), January 1935 (the Zinoviev-Kamenev "Moscow Center" trial), and the Moscow Trial of August 1936? Liushkov did not have to account for these confessions – they were unknown to the public.[140]

We have good evidence today that Liushkov was lying here. Arch Getty was apparently the first scholar to see recently-opened Ezhov materials. Concerning Zinoviev's and Kamenev's pretrial behavior he writes as follows:

> By 23 July [1936], Kamenev was admitting membership in a counterrevolutionary center that planned terror, but he denied being one of the organizers; he implicated Zinoviev as being closer to the matter. Three days later Zinoviev was confronted by one of his followers, Karev, who directly accused him. Zinoviev asked that the interrogation be stopped because he wanted to make a statement that, in the event, amounted to a full confession of organizing assassination and terror. Shortly thereafter, he submitted to his interrogators a 540-page manuscript he had written in prison. In "A Deserved Sentence" he wrote:

[140] Liushkov was not being quite frank here. We know today that he did not conduct all the interrogations of Zinoviev and Kamenev. He was only one of the NKVD investigators who cosigned Zinoviev's interrogation-confession of July 28, 1936. Liushkov was the only NKVD man to cosign Zinoviev's confession of an unknown date in August, 1936. But Liushkov was not one of the three NKVD men who cosigned Kamenev's confession of August 10, 1936.

> There is no question about it.... It is a fact. Whoever plays with the idea of "opposition" to the socialist state plays with the idea of counterrevolutionary terror. ... Before each who finds himself in my position this question stands in sharp relief. If tomorrow war comes – it stands yet a million times sharper and bigger. And for myself this question in prison for a long time is irreversibly decided. Rise from the dead! Be born again as a Bolshevik! Finish your human days conscious of your guilt before the party! Do everything to erase this guilt. (Getty, Yezhov 191)[141]

Liushkov mentions nothing about this huge manuscript by Zinov'ev. Of course! It would have been absurd for him to state that "Moscow" dictated all this material, none of which was even cited at the 1936 Moscow Trial, to NKVD officials so that Zinov'ev might "sign" it. Nor did Liushkov have to account for Zinov'ev's repeated confessions of guilt while in prison in 1935, for these too were unknown to the public at the time.

Nor does Liushkov's claim of falsification account for Zinoviev's and Kamenev's appeals to the Soviet Supreme Court following their death sentences. These secret documents were only made public in 1992. In them both Kamenev and, at greater length, Zinoviev, repeat their confessions of guilt and throw themselves upon the mercy of the court.

However, we have still stronger evidence that Liushkov was lying and that Lenoe knew it and covered it up.

Liushkov's Other Claims in his *Kaizo* Article

In order to accurately assess Liushkov's assertions about the Kirov murder we need to look at them in two additional contexts. First, we need to study that part of Liushkov's *Kaizo* article that Lenoe does not make available to his readers. Then we need to compare what Liushkov says in

---

141 We have obtained a copy of this 540-page document. It was clearly written when Zinoviev was still refusing to confess to being involved in assassination plots. It could not have done him any good at this point.

his published articles with what he told the Japanese privately. Lenoe fails to do either.

Kirilina uses Liushkov's *Kaizo* article in a dishonest manner. She simply states that Liushkov's article "categorically refutes Iagoda's participation in Kirov's assassination." (Kirilina 353) In reality it does nothing of the kind. What Liushkov does is refute Bulanov's account at the March 1938 trial. But Iagoda also rejected Bulanov's account. As we show in another part of this review, Iagoda never claimed that he was free of guilt in Kirov's assassination.

But how would Kirilina's readers know what Liushkov wrote in *Kaizo*? We can be reasonably certain that Kirilina had not read this article herself, or she would have more to say about it. Any genuine scholar would inform her readers where they could obtain a translation of the article to check for themselves, or at least tell them how they themselves had done so. So Kirilina is "bluffing" here: she is claiming she has read Liushkov's article while she never has. This is consistent with other evidence that Kirilina's book is less than honest. Like Lenoe, Kirilina did not "begin with a clean slate" – try to determine who killed Kirov and how on the basis of the evidence now available. Instead she wrote a work of political propaganda to "prove", i.e. to convince her readers, of the preconceived position that Nikolaev was a "lone gunman" – a position that happens to be that of the Gorbachev and of the subsequent Russian regimes.

Lenoe says nothing about the rest of the *Kaizo* article, as though it does not bear on the Kirov assassination. But it does – because an examination of the rest of the article proves that Liushkov was lying. We can specify a number of individual falsehoods by Liushkov. For example, he wrote:

> … Stalin exploited the deaths of the influential figures to show that the terrorist acts were not made-up but real stories and that the conspiracies were not fantasies. Briefly, he established political resources thanks to their deaths. It may be questioned why he did not exploit the death of Ordzhonikidze. This main reason was that Ordzhonikidze complained about the wholesale arrests just before his death. … Ordzhonikidze aggressively debated with Stalin because he had bitter experiences during that period. (*Kaizo* 107)

Khrushchev and his men spread a similar story about Ordzhonikidze's supposed opposition to arrests. But we know now that there is no evidence whatsoever to support this claim. Getty has shown that Ordzhonikidze agreed with the arrests in his Commissariat of Heavy Industry, particularly that of Piatakov. He reprints a speech the commissar gave in early February 1937, only days before his death, that demonstrates this conclusively.[142] This passage about Ordzhonikidze is enough in itself to establish that Liushkov was either inventing a story or, perhaps, repeating a rumor among opposition sympathizers. In any case, Liushkov would have had no way of knowing about discussions within the Politburo.

In the part of his essay not published by Lenoe Liushkov claims to have attended the February-March 1937 Central Committee Plenum.

> Stalin addressed this issue in the February-March Plenum of the Central Committee of the All-Union Communist Party. I also attended these assemblies.

There Stalin criticized the recently-deceased Ordzhonikidze for not telling the Politburo about some oppositional communications he had received. This must also be the source for Liushkov's claim that "after a certain period of time, he ordered through Yezhov, to whom he had entrusted the investigation, that the Zinoviev group be targeted", as Ezhov made such a statement during that Plenum (Lenoe 683)

What Liushkov Told the Japanese

The heart of the rest of the *Kaizo* article is Liushkov's assertion that *all* the conspiracies of the 1930s were fabrications.

> Of course, these do not cover all the dubious fabrications I know. Yet, is it still necessary to show more facts about the fabricated charges and trials? I do not think so. However, I want to mention one more thing. With simple logic, this could demolish the scenario of the conspiracy fabricated by Stalin. According to him, there was consistent conspiracy while each incident was revealed individually. As conspiracy members were

---

[142] Getty & Naumov 292-294. Also online at: http://www.red-channel.de/books/ordzhonikidze.htm

> arrested almost all commissars, commanders of military districts, senior commanders, clericals of committees of the party and the chairmen of the executive committees in each state, directors of NKVD, diplomats, and businesspeople. It could be judged by seeing the situations in the supreme organ of the party how intense those arrests were. Arrested were 49 out of 71 members of the central committee of the party (more than 2/3), 54 out of 68 alternate members of the same committee (more than 3/4), 16 out of 22 members of the central control office (more than 3/4), 3 out of 7 bureaucrats of the control office of the party (approx. 1/2), and finally 5 out of 16 Politburo members and alternate members (approx. 1/3). (Page 119) I affirm that these figures are accurate. If a part of them had engaged in the conspiracy against Stalin, who could have prevented them from carrying that out? They took enough power and had the practical forces, the army and the GPU. Suppose that they had contacted foreign staff headquarters and just waited for their interference against the Soviet Union? However, since badly failing at the cases in Leningrad and the Kremlin, at the public trial in August 1936, and so on, the conspiracy group could have immediately carried out their plan as their only solution. Also, although the dismissal of Yagoda, which could have kept the conspiracy from completely failing, was the last alarm, the fact that they still did not take any actions is to be considered. Nobody but a psychotic would act like a rabbit waiting to be killed, just passively observing. **This also demonstrates that no conspiracy did or could exist.** (*Kaizo* 118-119; emphasis added GF)

The statement I have put in boldface contradicts what Liushkov privately told the Japanese.

The late Alvin D. Coox spent many years studying Japanese-Soviet relations. In 1968 he published a preliminary survey of what he could discover about Liushkov's defection from the Japanese side. Thirty years later in 1998 he published two long articles with many more details. Coox managed to locate Liushkov papers long believed lost. He also studied the surviving report on Liushkov made by Soviet spy Richard Sorge. Most important, he was able to conduct extensive interviews with some of the Japanese military men who were in charge of Liushkov, worked with him, and spent much time with him. What follows here is a summary of those parts of Coox's study that are most relevant to our present purposes.[143]

For our purposes Coox's most important discovery is this: Liushkov confirmed to the Japanese that real conspiracies did indeed exist in the USSR. Before being sent to the Far East Liushkov had a private meeting with Stalin during which Stalin made it clear that he believed that a military plot did exist. According to Liushkov Stalin informed him:

> War with Japan is inevitable; the Far East is undoubtedly a theater of war. It is necessary to clean up the army and its rear in the most determined manner from hostile spy and pro-Japanese elements. The plot of Tukhachevsky, Gamarnik, and others, and also the arrest of Sangurski, Aronshtam, and Kashcheev show that all is not well with the army, that there are plotters with the leaders of the NKVD in the Far East. Deribas, Zapadni, and Barminski are Japanese spies, and Japan has a large base for spying and insurrection work by means of Koreans and Chinese. (Coox 1, 151)

Sent to the Far East to deal with these conspiracies Liushkov reported to the Japanese that they did indeed exist. By mentioning Gamarnik, who committed suicide when NKVD men went to arrest him, Liushkov indirectly confirmed the genuineness of the charges against Tukhachevskii and the other seven high-ranking officers tried and executed together with him, as Gamarnik was one of them.

> According to Lyushkov, the interrogations of Deribas, Zapadni, and Barminski established that in the NKVD and the border guard forces, a plot centering on Gamarnik had been fomented.

---

143 Coox, Alvin D. "The Lesser of Two Hells: NKVD General G.S. Lyushkov's Defection to Japan, 1938-1945." *Journal of Slavic Military Studies* 11, 3 (1998) 145-186 (Part One) (Coox 1); 11, 4 (1998) 72-110 (Part Two). We will refer to these articles in the text as Coox 1 and Coox 2 respectively.

Liushkov also confirmed the connection of the Rights, convicted in the March 1938 Moscow Trial, with the military conspirators. For example, Liushkov told the Japanese:

> For a long time Deribas had been in contact with Rykov and was the latter's 'hidden conspirator.'

Liushkov mentioned Rykov elsewhere as well (see below). He also revealed that the charges against Lavrent'ev (Kartvelishvili), arrested in July 1937 but not tried and executed until August 1938, were true. Khrushchev's man Aleksei V. Snegov later charged Beria with framing and then killing Lavrent'ev; Liushkov's testimony here proves that Snegov was wrong.

Liushkov also confirmed at least the intention of these Party and military conspirators to conspire with the Japanese.

> In concert with Lavrenty Lavrentiev (former First Secretary of the Regional Committee of the Party until January 1937), with Grigory Krutov (shot in April 1938), and with the army plotters Sangurski, Aronshtam, and others, Deribas supposedly intended to conduct a putsch in the Far East and to reach agreement with the Japanese for help and for combined operations against the Soviet Union. In the NKVD the plotters had recruited Transtok, Chief of the 2nd Section, and many others. Lyushkov gave the names of about 20 officials, mostly NKVD types, and of ten border guards, all of whom he asserted were involved in the plots. (Coox 1, 156)

Coox emphasizes that Liushkov outlined this information to the Japanese in a manner that convinced them that he believed they were genuine:

> About this murderous period as a whole, Lyushkov said little to the Japanese, but his enumeration of the suspects was straightforward, without any admission of NKVD-fabricated evidence, such as he said had occurred at Leningrad in the era of the Kirov assassination. (Coox 1, 156).

It is important to note that Coox's account of what Liushkov had to say about the Kirov murder is taken exclusively from an interview in *Asahi*

Shimbun of July 2, 1938. (Coox 1, 149) Though we have not been able to obtain that specific newspaper, we assume the Liushkov interview reported in it must be the same interview printed in *Yomiuri Shimbun* on July 3, 1938, which is a report of the same news conference. We will discuss the importance of this fact in some detail below.

Briefly, however, it is this: Liushkov said one thing in public, but contradicted his public statements in private. For example, in the *Yomiuri Shimbun* article Liushkov said:

> At the trial that took place in August 1936 the accusations that the Trotskyites through Ol'berg 1) had contact with the German Gestapo, the accusations of espionage against Zinoviev and Kamenev, the accusations that Zinoviev and Kamenev were connected with the so-called "Right center" through Tomskii, 2) **Rykov** and Bukharin – are complete fabrications. Zinoviev, Kamenev, Tomskii, Rykov, Bukharin and many others were executed as enemies of Stalin who acted to oppose his destructive policies.
>
> Stalin used the convenient possibility which the Kirov case presented to him in order to rid himself of these people by fabricating broad anti-Stalin conspiracies, espionage trials, and terrorist organizations.[144] [Emphasis added, GF]

But in private conversations to Japanese officers and others with whom he interacted Liushkov incriminated Rykov along with Marshal Bliukher and others:

> [One] group of traitors belonging to the staff of the Far Eastern Army, people near to Blyukher himself, such as [Yan] Pokus, Gulin, Vasenov, Kropachev and others, tried to get round Blyukher and to draw him into

[144] Only the second of these two paragraphs is translated by Lenoe, 681; I have taken the other from the text at the Russian-language Wikipedia page, which is the same as that in the biographical encyclopedia at Hrono.ru. See http://ru.wikipedia.org/wiki/Люшков,_Генрих_Самойлович and http://hrono.ru/biograf/bio_l/ljushkov_gs.php

> politically dangerous conversations. Blyukher showed them the secret confessions of arrested plotters [without] the authority to do so. After his arrest Gulin told me that after the recall of Pokus to Moscow, Blyukher, when drinking with them, cursed the NKVD and the arrests recently carried out, and also Voroshilov, [Lazar] Kaganovich and others. **Blyukher told Gulin that before the removal of Rykov he was in connection with him and had often written that the 'right wing' wished to see him at the head of the armed forces of the country.** (Coox 1, 158; emphasis added, GF)

Publicly Liushkov was saying that all the conspiracies were fabrications by Stalin. But at the same time he was privately informing the Japanese that serious conspiracies did in fact exist. Moreover, what Liushkov told the Japanese is consistent with the charges at the January 1937 and March 1938 Moscow Trials (the guilt of Rykov) and with the charges against the military conspirators, both the Tukhachevsky Affair figures (Gamarnik) and those against military and Party officials in the Far East.

This is important for our purposes because Liushkov spoke about the Kirov assassination in published articles only. Coox did not know of any such remarks made privately to the Japanese. Since Liushkov lied in his published materials – writings that were first and foremost anti-Soviet propaganda – and since it was only in those published materials that Liushkov discussed the Kirov assassination, then it follows that, at a minimum, we can't put any store at all in what Liushkov wrote about the Kirov affair.

What's more, Liushkov wrote in his public article in *Kaizo* that "no conspiracy did or could exist" while at the same time he confirmed to the Japanese that a number of serious conspiracies had indeed existed. That is, we know that the existence of conspiracies is one of the things that Liushkov deliberately lied about in his public statements.

At a news conference on July 13 1938 called by the Japanese to give the press a chance to ask Liushkov questions, Liushkov said the following, as summarized by Coox:

> ...though Lyushkov doubted that there was any basis for it, Gamarnik had been charged with conspiring with

> elements in the Soviet Far East. In particular, Stalin fabricated allegations that the party secretaries in Siberia – Y.M. Vareikis, Karlenev, and L.Y. Lavrentiev – plotted with Gamarnik and other important individuals to wreck military preparations in the Far East. (Coox 1, 175)

Here Liushkov directly contradicted what he was saying privately to the Japanese, to whom he affirmed the existence of a conspiracy or conspiracies involving Gamarnik, Lavrent'ev, and others (see quotations from Coox 1, 156 above and Coox 2, 85 below). Head of the Political Directorate of the Red Army Ian Gamarnik was questioned by NKVD men in connection with the arrests of Marshal Tukhachevsky and others, after which he committed suicide.

Liushkov's *Kaizo* Article As Propaganda

Coox discovered that during August 1938, only two months after his defection, Liushkov was transferred from the 5th, or Russia Section of the 2nd Bureau of the Japanese Army to "the 11th (Propaganda and Subversion) Subsection of the 8th (Psychological Warfare and Sabotage) Section". According to Coox's informants the Japanese felt that Liushkov's military knowledge had been exhausted. He was, after all, NKVD, not regular Soviet army.

> Yabe's successor Asada agrees that Lyushkov came to be viewed as possessing no further intelligence value for the 5th Section, which is why he was moved to the 8th Section to work in the area of propaganda and subversion, in anticipation of an ultimate outbreak of hostilities between Japan and the Soviet Union. (Coox 1, 179)

In addition to writing articles and an introduction to at least one anti-Soviet book Liushkov recorded "anti-Stalin speeches addressed to the Russian people in case of war" and wrote leaflets.

Liushkov related other facts to the Japanese that confirm Soviet accusations made at the time. For example, he cited many instances of genuine acts of sabotage. (Coox 2, 80, 81, 82, 83) Coox also recounts more of Liushkov's information about real military conspiracies in the Far East:

> Lyushkov's opinion that, with respect to the situation of the Red Army in Siberia, the influence of the 'anti'-group was great and discontent was pent up in the military. (Coox 2, 73)

Perhaps of most interest to historians of the USSR generally, as well as to our present study, is Liushkov's outline of the various conspiracies that existed within the Soviet military.

> Within the Soviet armed forces, elements hostile to the regime existed, universally hostile to Stalin but nurturing differing objectives. One group of commanders had been sincerely loyal to Trotsky; for example, V. K. Putna, V. M. Primakov, and others working in his favor. Another group of Soviet commanders of Polish, German, Lettish, and similar minority backgrounds were disappointed with the course of communism and had resurrected historic feelings; for example, A. I. Kork and R. P. Eideman. Still another grouping of commanders had served in the Tsarist Army, favored a military putsch, and had been prepared to cooperate with any other groups; e.g. Tukhachevsky, I. P. Uborevich, N. D. Kashirin, V. M. Orlov, etc. Others who were hostile to the regime and ready to work in opposition had included Gamarnik, I.Y. Yakir, Sangurski, Aronshtam, P.E. Dybenko, N. V. Kuibyshev, I. P. Belov, and M. K. Levandovsky. (Coox 2, 85)

This account shows some similarities to the description of the different groups of military conspirators that Ezhov gave after his arrest at his interrogation of April 26, 1939:

> After three or four days Egorov came to my place again and this time told me in detail about the existence in the WPRA[145] of a group of conspirators consisting of important military men and headed by himself, Egorov.

[145] *Raboche-Krest'ianskaia Krasnaia Armia,* "Workers and Peasants Red Army."

> Egorov further gave me the names of the participants of the conspiratorial group that he led: Budiennyi, Dybenko, Shaposhnikov, Kashirin, Fed'ko, the commander of the Transbaikal military district, and a number of other important commanders whose names I will remember and give in a supplement.
>
> Further Egorov said that in the WPRA there exist two more groups competing with each other: the Trotskyist group of Gamarnik, Iakir and Uborevich, and the officer-Bonapartist group of Tukhachevsky.[146]

Ezhov called the Gamarnik-Iakir group "Trotskyist". Putna and Primakov had been closely connected to Trotsky in the 1920s. Ezhov's "Bonapartist" group headed by Tukhachevsky corresponds to Liushkov's group that had been Tsarist officers and "favored a military putsch." Of interest as well is that both Liushkov and Ezhov described Marshal Semion Budiennyi as a conspirator. Liushkov informed the Japanese as follows:

> What was happening to Blyukher was happening to others at the top of the army. Thus Marshal S. M. Budennyi's difficulties were caused by his playing with various plotters. (Coox 2, 85)

In this second article Coox confirms that Liushkov was working "on anti-Stalinist strategy and propaganda" in late 1938. (Coox 2, 92)

The Importance of Liushkov's Testimony

Lenoe correctly notes that Liushkov had inside knowledge of the investigation of the Kirov assassination. He could have added: of the investigation of Zinov'ev and Kamenev, and of the Far Eastern Region as well. Lenoe also writes:

> Moreover, Liushkov gave his evidence outside the Soviet Union, free from the dictates of the party line, and under

---

[146] I have put an English translation of the complete text of Ezhov's confession of April 26, 1939 online at http://msuweb.montclair.edu/~furrg/research/ezhov042639eng.html The Russian original is also online at my site at http://msuweb.montclair.edu/~furrg/research/ezhovru.html

> the protection of the Japanese military police (after World War II Japanese officers who worked with Liushkov testified that he did fear a Soviet assassination attempt. (687)

Lenoe also draws upon Coox's important articles, to which he refers repeatedly (687 and 808 nn. 11, 13, 16, 17 and 18). Lenoe correctly points out that Liushkov's testimony about NKVD operations is consistent with other sources; that he told the truth about his private meeting with Stalin; that Liushkov's estimate of the numbers of arrests and executions is in line with what recent research has disclosed. (687-688)

But Lenoe neglects to mention the important information in Coox's article outlined above, although he obviously knew about it. Liushkov's confirmation to the Japanese of the existence of a number of important conspiracies, plus the knowledge that he deliberately concealed their existence in his public writings, undermines Lenoe's hypothesis about the Kirov case and the other conspiracies and trials of the 1930s.

To summarize:

* Coox showed that there is a big contradiction between what Liushkov said in his news conference and published articles, and what he privately told the Japanese.

* Liushkov informed the Japanese that real conspiracies did exist and were widespread in the USSR.

* Coox pointed out that Liushkov was explicitly working for Japanese military propaganda.

* Liushkov inculpated many of the military figures tried and executed as conspirators.

* Liushkov explicitly implicated Rykov. He told the Japanese:

> For a long time Deribas had been in contact with Rykov and was the latter's 'hidden conspirator.' (Coox 1, 156)
>
> Blyukher told Gulin that before the removal of Rykov he was in connection with him and had often written that the 'right wing' wished to see him at the head of the armed forces of the country. (Coox 1, 158)

These statements are broadly consistent with testimony at the March 1938 Moscow Trial, at which Rykov was a defendant. Rykov, Bukharin and others testified there about their contacts with conspirators in Siberia.

We also now have a few selections of interrogations of Bliukher in 1938. In one of them Bliukher explicitly mentions a letter from Rykov that stated exactly what Liushkov said.

> The beginning of my contact with the Rights took place in 1930... These political waverings and unsteadiness of mine became known to Rykov and permitted Rykov in 1930 to write to me an anti-Party and anti-Soviet letter, **which I hid from the Party, and in which he spoke of his desire to see me at the head of the military...**[147]

This agrees with Coox's account of what his Japanese informants told him about Liushkov's words, already quoted above:

> Blyukher told Gulin that before the removal of Rykov he was in connection with him and **had often written that the 'right wing' wished to see him at the head of the armed forces of the country.** (Coox 1, 158, emphasis added, GF)

Other snippets of interrogations of Bliukher implicate Deribas, Lavrent'ev, Pokus, Aronshtam, and other figures whom Liushkov identified as participants in the military conspiracy in the Far East. Liushkov's statements to the Japanese confirm them. By the same token, Liushkov's statements to the Japanese refute the notion that these statements were false, the result of torture, threat, or simple NKVD fabrication.

Lenoe's Hypothesis Refuted

Lenoe wrote that Liushkov's testimony "is in fact the most important in the case". (687) We can now see that Lenoe's statement, in the form he

---

147 Nikolai Velikanov. *Izmena Marshalov*. M.: Algoritm, 2008. Interrogation of Bliukher of November 6, 1938, p. 343. Emphasis added, GF.

meant it, is false – as referring to Liushkov's statements at the July 1938 press conference and his March 1939 *Kaizo* article.

Ironically, however, Lenoe's statement is true – but in a sense Lenoe did not intend. For the information Liushkov gave privately about the conspiracies to the Japanese military was indeed given "outside the Soviet Union, free from the dictates of the party line, and under the protection of the Japanese military police", as Lenoe stated.

Someone might object to this conclusion on the following grounds:

> "Thanks to Coox we know that Liushkov lied when he stated in pages 118-119 of his *Kaizo* article, quoted above, that "no conspiracy did or could exist." We know that because he privately informed the Japanese that serious conspiracies did indeed exist. So we know Liushkov lied about those conspiracies about which he told the Japanese.
>
> But Coox does not cite any evidence that Liushkov spoke to the Japanese privately about the Kirov assassination. Coox only records what Liushkov said publicly about the Kirov assassination, and publicly he said it was a frameup and that only Nikolaev was guilty (and, in an accessory capacity, perhaps Shatsky).
>
> No liar lies all the time. Any skilled liar must interweave his real lies with some truth, in order for the lies to be credible.
>
> Therefore it is possible that Liushkov, while lying about the other conspiracies, was telling the truth about the Kirov assassination in asserting that it was a frameup, though the other conspiracies which he also called frameups really were not."

To such an objection I would reply as follows: it is a principle of logic and of historiography that one can draw no conclusion *e silentio* – in this case, from Liushkov's silence.[148] The fact that, as far as Coox (and we)

[148] See, for example, the Wikipedia page: http://en.wikipedia.org/wiki/Argumentum_e_silentio

know, Liushkov *did not* tell the Japanese privately that the Kirov defendants (except for Nikolaev and Shatsky) were falsely accused or "framed" does not permit us to say anything about what he *might have* told them.

It's easy to imagine why Liushkov might well not have discussed this subject with the Japanese. They were military men, not historians. They were vitally interested in opposition movements against the Stalin regime and especially within the military. They would have had little interest in purely civilian conspiracies that had taken place years before. So either Liushkov did not tell them privately about the Kirov assassination, or they did not pay much attention and did not remember it when they spoke with Coox many years later.

But Liushkov confirmed to the Japanese that Rykov was a participant in the anti-Soviet conspiracy. One of Liushkov's two statements about Rykov agrees very closely with a statement in Marshal Bliukher's confession. Therefore, Liushkov's statements about Rykov partially corroborate not only Bliukher's confession but some of the testimony at the March 1938 Moscow trial. Lenoe failed to inform his readers about this very important information.

As we have shown in another chapter, Lenoe makes an attempt to dismiss the major testimony concerning the Kirov assassination made at this trial – that of Iagoda – and gets it wrong. Lenoe refuses to examine other evidence from the 1938 Moscow Trial. Likewise, he avoids any examination of the evidence given at the 1936 and 1937 Moscow Trials.

Therefore, Liushkov's failure to mention the Kirov assassination privately to the Japanese throws us back on the other evidence we have, and which we examine in other sections of the present study. Ironically, however, Lenoe's claim that Liushkov's testimony "is in fact the most important in the case" is true – but only if we "turn it around", apply it not to what Liushkov said or wrote publicly, as Lenoe does, but to Liushkov's private statements to the Japanese.

In his remarks about the military purge and particularly about Tukhachevskii's involvement in it, and about Rykov's role in the Right-Trotskyite conspiracy Liushkov provides us with something very rare. He gives us evidence from outside the Soviet Union that confirms the existence of real anti-Stalin and anti-Soviet conspiracies and the guilt of Rykov and Tukhachevskii.

But Rykov and Tukhachevskii implicated all the other major figures in the network of interlocking conspiracies alleged in the three public Moscow Trials and the Tukhachevsky Affair. In this way Liushkov's statements to the Japanese constitute strong evidence not only that the 1938 Moscow Trial was not a fabrication but that the previous Moscow Trials were not fabrications either.

At the 1938 trial Genrikh Iagoda testified about his role in the Kirov assassination and the conspiracy surrounding it. Iagoda testified about it in even more detail in pretrial interrogations first published in 1997. In confirming a number of the essential charges made in the 1938 trial Liushkov did indeed provide us with the strongest evidence we now have about the Kirov assassination: that it was carried out not, as Lenoe, Kirilina, and others would have it, by a "lone gunman", but as outlined in the Moscow trials. What Liushkov told the Japanese corroborates a huge amount of other evidence we have that Kirov was indeed murdered as the result of a conspiracy.

Lenoe himself reveals the basic flaws in his approach to the Kirov assassination. He comments that Liushkov

> confirms entirely the picture of the crime that emerges from documents of the 1934-1935 investigation (discounting of course the Stalinist accusations against the Zinovievites). (688)

Again, this statement is true – and again ironically, in precisely the opposite sense from what Lenoe intends. Lenoe misreads the evidence we have and that he cites and then claims that it proves the defendants (other than Nikolaev himself) were "framed." Elsewhere in this study we have shown that in fact there is no evidence that Nikolaev acted alone or that any of the defendants was "framed", and a great deal of evidence to the contrary. Far from shaking that conclusion, Liushkov's statements to the Japanese corroborate it.

Lenoe also states:

> Liushkov knew nothing of any conspiracy to murder Kirov. His evidence invalidates the Yagoda-Zaporozhets version of the killing put forward at the March 1938 show trial. (688)

Here too Lenoe is entirely mistaken. Liushkov's public statement and articles were anti-Soviet propaganda. But Liushkov directly contradicted his *public* statements in his *private* statements to the Japanese. In his private statements Liushkov confirms some of the accusations and confessions made at the Moscow Trials – not only the March 1938 trial but, indirectly, at others as well.

We don't know why Lenoe did not inform his readers of this vital evidence. What are the alternatives to the hypothesis that Lenoe realized all this and deliberately deceived his readers by hiding it from them? If we set aside the hypothesis that Lenoe deliberately lied, then we are forced to conclude that he did not understand Coox's articles at all; that he failed to read them properly. At best Lenoe has once again committed some serious errors in his assessment of the evidence provided about Liushkov by the full text of the March 1939 *Kaizo* article and Coox's research. As we demonstrate in the present study Lenoe made similar errors throughout his book.

How could this have happened? I can think of only two explanations. Lenoe may not have read the whole of the *Kaizo* article. He may have studied only that part that is translated in his book, that deals directly with the Kirov assassination. Certainly he shows no evidence that he has read the rest of it!

But even if that be so, I believe that another explanation is more probable: that Lenoe never really set out to investigate the Kirov murder objectively in the first place. Acting under the influence of what is acceptable to "mainstream" anticommunist Soviet historiography Lenoe began with the preconceived idea that it must be a frameup. Lenoe confined his attention to the only real question in his book, and probably in his own mind: "Did Stalin mastermind Kirov's assassination, or did he simply make opportunistic use of it to frame real or imagined political enemies?"

Since there is no evidence that Stalin was behind Kirov's assassination Lenoe draws the latter conclusion: "[H]e used it." (689) Lenoe never really considers the hypothesis which is supported by not most, but *all* of the evidence we possess: that the Kirov assassination was carried out by conspirators much as was gradually revealed in the Kirov investigation and the subsequent Moscow Trials of 1936, 1937 and 1938.

Lenoe was determined from the start to see only what he wanted to see. If we discount deliberate falsification on Lenoe's part, this is the only explanation consistent with his reasoning and conclusions.

Chapter 18.
Enukidze and the "Lone Gunman" Story

Long thought to have an obvious solution, the Kirov murder has been made into a mystery which half a dozen Soviet commissions and a considerable number of professional scholars have endeavored to "solve". The "mystery" was created when Khrushchev and his people made the decision to reject the validity of the December 1934 trial of the Kirov defendants and of all the subsequent trials of oppositionists. Since Khrushchev's day only two hypotheses have been entertained by politicians and scholars alike. One was that Stalin had had Kirov killed; the other, that Nikolaev acted alone, for personal reasons.

The original conclusion – that Kirov was murdered by decision of a bloc of oppositionist groups – was long ago "ruled out of bounds", considered unfit for serious consideration. But it is the only conclusion that satisfies the evidence. Nevertheless, it is not acceptable to most researchers, just as it was unacceptable to the Khrushchev and Gorbachev regimes and remains unacceptable to the Russian government today. This conclusion is routinely, almost reflexively, dismissed – but not on evidentiary grounds. We believe it is dismissed because it disrupts, in fact refutes, the prevailing paradigm of Soviet history during the Stalin period.

Any honest study of the Kirov murder has at least two tasks. First, it must solve the Kirov murder in a manner that satisfies all the evidence available at the time. Second, it must consider the implications of its solution for our understanding of Soviet history after 1934. That is what we shall try to do in this and the concluding chapters.

There can be no doubt that Kirov was murdered by Leonid Nikolaev acting on behalf of a conspiracy by a clandestine illegal Zinovievite organization. We have a large amount of evidence supporting this conclusion, while no evidence whatever supports any other conclusion. This is the more striking since the Russian government continues to withhold much of the relevant evidence, though we do not know how much. It is hardly possible that they would have wanted to withhold any evidence that would point towards Nikolaev's having been a "lone gunman". That is the official viewpoint of the Russian government and its predecessor, the Gorbachev-led Soviet government.

It was also the official position of the Khrushchev regime. Khrushchev's men devoted the work of several commissions and, one must suppose, of many researchers and archivists, to finding some other explanation of the Kirov assassination than the original "Stalinist" one. The Khrushchev, Gorbachev, and Russian regimes would have widely publicized any evidence that supported either the version that Khrushchev originally tried to support – that Stalin masterminded Kirov's murder – or the "lone gunman" conclusion. Any evidence that supported either of these scenarios would surely have been made public in Khrushchev's or in Gorbachev's time. But there is none.

Likewise there is no evidence to dispute the conclusion that Nikolaev was indeed the instrument of a Zinovievite conspiracy. There is no evidence of a "frameup" of innocent men. Lenoe tries twice to make a case for such a frameup. He suggests that Nikolaev confessed to being part of a conspiracy, and that some of the others made similar confessions, due to compulsion of some kind: threats, promises, and/or torture. Lenoe does not explicitly test, much less abandon, this hypothesis. But he is unable to cite any evidence whatsoever in support of it.

Lenoe also claims that Stalin gave an order to "target the Zinovievites", thus ordering his NKVD men to frame them. We have examined the evidence Lenoe puts forward in support of both of these "frameup" hypotheses. In each case the supposed evidence cannot withstand any critical scrutiny. Both of Lenoe's hypotheses utterly fail the evidentiary test.

The "Lone Gunman" Version

The only evidence for the "lone gunman" hypothesis is the early interrogations of Nikolaev. As we have demonstrated in this study, we do not have a reliable text of Nikolaev's first confession. Nor do we have a complete text of any subsequent confession by Nikolaev. From the evidence now available we can tell that by December 4 Nikolaev had already begun to abandon his claim that he acted completely alone. In a passage Lenoe excised from his partial translation of the Prosecutor's indictment, by the middle of December Nikolaev was confessing that his early claim to have acted alone had been worked out in advance in order to shield his confederates.

But even if we did have reliable texts of Nikolaev's early confessions, and even if in them Nikolaev did claim to have acted completely on his own as the "lone gunman" hypothesis demands, that evidence would fail in the face of his subsequent confessions. Nikolaev tried to kill himself within seconds of killing Kirov. This means that in effect Nikolaev's plan was to assume sole responsibility for Kirov's murder. Such a hypothesis would also explain his wife Mil'da Draule's initial statements. They would have served as well or better if Nikolaev had been dead by his own hand. When Nikolaev failed to kill himself he at first tried to adhere to his original plan of shielding his fellow conspirators. He seems to have suffered some kind of temporary breakdown or anxiety attack. This is understandable – he had not expected to be in this situation and was unprepared for it. Nikolaev then began to insist that he had acted alone. But his story quickly broke down after only a few days.

We have demonstrated in this study that the text of Nikolaev's first confession is in doubt. Two versions have been published: one by Kirilina, the second by Lenoe, and they contain important differences. This first confession of Nikolaev's is the main evidence that supports the "lone gunman" hypothesis, which Lenoe shares with Kirilina. Lenoe does not mention these differences, although he wrote after Kirilina and acknowledges his debt to her study. Whatever the reason for this omission of Lenoe's, the doubtful nature of this first confession undermines one of the only two pieces of evidence that support the hypothesis that Nikolaev acted alone.

Nikolaev was the first to claim that he had acted alone, though he abandoned this story within days of the murder. The NKVD never believed him and they were proven correct. But the "lone gunman" hypothesis continued to circulate.

Avel' Enukidze

According to a document partially printed by Lenoe that purports to be the report of an NKVD man of September 1936 but concerning events of December 1934 and January 1935, Avel' Enukidze, secretary of the Presidium of the Central Executive Committee, the highest executive body of the Soviet state, spread the story that Kirov was killed by Nikolaev because Kirov had been "courting" Nikolaev's wife. (502-503) The anonymous NKVD informant was right to think this behavior on Enukidze's part was more than strange. Enukidze would have had access to high-level, inside knowledge about the investigation. He would have known at least as much as, and almost certainly much more than, we do today.

There is no evidence for the story that Enukidze was spreading. If any existed, we would know about it – the Khrushchev and Gorbachev commissions searched very hard for exactly this kind of evidence. Therefore Enukidze's version came from somewhere other than suppressed evidence, and certainly other than the evidence available to NKVD investigators and high-level Party members. We have good reason to believe that it formed part of the plot from the beginning. Nikolaev had tried to commit suicide immediately after shooting Kirov, but later confessed that he had a plan to claim that he was the "lone gunman" in order to shield his confederates. Enukidze had participated in the decision of the conspiracy center to authorize Kirov's assassination. Like Iagoda, Enukidze had agreed only reluctantly. Claiming it was an individual act could have been one way of trying to limit the investigation so that it would not lead to the discovery of, first, the Leningrad Zinovievite group, and then, gradually, all the other conspiracies related to it. This is the only explanation for Enukidze's version that makes sense. It is also consistent with what Iagoda told NKVD investigators in 1937.

The "lone gunman" theory was spread by rumor through the Kremlin library among persons to whom Enukidze had access. On March 1, 1935 P.I. Gordeeva, senior librarian, was interrogated concerning rumors she and others had been spreading.

> Question: Who told you the slander connected with the murder of com. KIROV?
>
> Answer: After the publication of the first government communication about the murder of com. KIROV the secretary of the consultative part of the secretariat of the CEC Vera Aleksandrovna EL'CHANINOVA, member of the Komsomol, came to me in the library. She told me that the murder of com. KIROV had no political character but was the result of personal revenge. EL'CHANINOVA explained that the information transmitted to her was trustworthy and was being kept in the greatest secrecy…

> Question: What kinds of conversations connected with the murder of com. KIROV were there in the government library?
>
> Answer: Among the library staff there was talk that the murder of com. KIROV was completely a matter of personal accounts...
>
> Question: Which precisely of the library staff were spreading provocational fabrications about the murder of com. KIROV?
>
> Answer: KONOVA told me that among the library staff there were conversations of this kind but she did not name the persons. I personally observed that ROZENFEL'D and RAEVSKAIA were gloating over the murder of com. KIROV.
>
> Question: How, concretely, did this express itself?
>
> Answer: The whole period of time from the moment of the murder of com. KIROV till the publication of the announcement of the uncovering of the "Leningrad center" of the Zinovievite organization ROZENFEL'D was in a very upbeat and joyful state, one that was normally quite uncharacteristic of her. ROZENFEL'D was always whispering with BURAGO and DAVIDOVA, and they, right after a talk with ROZENFEL'D went off to NELIDOVA and PETROVA, the staff members who give out the books. But after the publication of the announcement about the uncovering of the "Leningrad center" ROZENFEL'D"s mood changed sharply and her former joy and upbeat demeanor disappeared.
>
> - Lubianka 1922-1936, 618-619.

On March 8, 1935 K.K. Mukhanov was interrogated. His sister, Ekaterina K. Mukhanova, an employee of the government library, had been arrested in connection with the investigation of a terrorist conspiracy that later became known as the "Kremlin Affair."

> Question: What did Ekaterina tell you about the murder of com. KIROV?

Answer: Ekaterina did not say anything about this to me. Someone told me that the murder of KIROV was done by NIKOLAEV for personal reason and that it had no political character. I can't remember from whom I heard this.

[...]

Question: Your sister Ekaterina MUKHAKOVA has systematically expressed counterrevolutionary views. Tell the investigation everything you know about this.

Answer: I admit that my sister Ekaterina MUKHANOVA is a supporter of the bourgeois system and in conversations with me has consistently expressed anti-Soviet views, and has shown a hostile attitude towards Soviet power.

As far as the politics of Soviet power, E. MUKHANOVA has stated that collectivization is leading to hunger and the dying out of the peasantry, to the doom of agriculture, that the intelligentsia who have no special knowledge is fated to a pauper's existence, and a part of the engineering and technical intelligentsia are being thrown into prison despite their innocence.

Arguing that Soviet power is having recourse to massive terror against the peasantry and intelligentsia MUKHANOVA has declared that the majority of the population, mainly the peasantry and also a part of the workers, are hostile towards Soviet power and in the event of a war not only will not defend this power but will come out against it with weapons in hand and will organize uprisings in the rear of the Red Army.

In the period 1931-33 MUKHANOVA stated that the policy of the Soviet power was directed against the interests of the overwhelming majority of the population and drew from this the conclusion that the country is going to its ruin.

- Lubianka 1922-1936, 627.

On March 11, 1935 the NKVD interrogated B.N. Rozenfel'd, a nephew of Lev B. Kamenev (his brother's son). A 19-year old in 1927, Rozenfel'd had been expelled from the Komsomol for belonging to the Trotskyite opposition. His mother N.A. Rozenfel'd had already been arrested in connection with the "Kremlin Affair." He was questioned about the Kirov assassination.

> Question: Did you know F.I. MUZYKA, the secretary of L.B. Kamenev?
>
> Answer: I know him. N.B. ROZENFEL'D [his father] has often spoken about him as a person with whom he has good relations. The last time I saw MUZYKA after the murder of com. Kirov, was at the high-pressure hot water power plant, where he was doing his practicum and I was working as an engineer. MUZYKA told me Kamenev and Zinoviev were being hounded, pointing to an article in Pravda. I answered him that the murder of Kirov was a suitable excuse for Stalin to organize the hounding against Zinoviev and Kamenev. He agreed with me.
>
> [...]
>
> Answer: I remember that N.B. ROZENFEL'D told me that MUZYKA was a desperate man and is capable of extreme actions when in an excited state.
>
> Question: What was the context in which N.B. ROZENFEL'D said to you that MUZYKA is capable of extreme actions?
>
> Answer: I was telling N.B. ROZENFEL'D about my talk with MUZYKA and expressed the conjecture that MUZYKA would be arrested. I said this because MUZYKA was informed about Kamenev's counterrevolutionary activity. From my father's statement about MUZYKA's personal "qualities" it became clear to me that he was a terrorist by conviction.
>
> - Lubianka 1922-1936, 630.

Young Rozenfel'd had more to say about terrorist conspiracies.

> Question: At the interrogation of March 2 you confessed that M.V. KOROL'KOV took part in counterrevolutionary conversations that took place in your apartment. What more do you know about this?
>
> Answer: We cannot speak about M.V. KOROL'KOV only in connection with counterrevolutionary conversations at our apartment.
>
> In reality the situation is as follows:
>
> M.V. KOROL'KOV is a hard-core counterrevolutionary and has close relations with M.N. PROKHOROV, who owned some kind of business before the revolution and is a notorious Black Hundreds and White Guardsman; with POPOV, the son of a tea merchant; with V.I. INKIZHIKOV, a film actor who has fled the country. Since we were aware of of KOROL'KOV'S political feelings we had complete confidence in him.
>
> KOROL'KOV shared the terrorist views of N.B. and N.A. ROZENFEL'D [i.e. his own father and mother], of MUKHANOV, and my own.
>
> - Lubianka 1922-1936, 631.

On the same day, March 11, 1935, the aforenamed M.V. Korol'kov was interrogated as well. He was questioned not only about the rumors concerning Kirov's assassination but also about the other terrorist views and plans that had emerged as a result of the investigation. Like all of those in the "Kremlin Affair" the whole interrogation is of interest. We will just quote those passages that illustrate how investigation of the rumors that Nikolaev was a "lone gunman" who killed Kirov for personal reasons also led to uncovering other conspiracies.

> Question: What slanderous rumors did N.A. ROZENFEL'D spread about the leaders of the Party and government and who took part with her in the spreading of these rumors?
>
> Answer: N.A. ROZENFEL'D said in my presence and in that of my wife that ALLILUEVA died an unnatural death and that STALIN was responsible for her death.

> She told us also that the men who occupy high positions have mistresses.
>
> About com. KIROV she said that he was killed for personal reasons, because of NIKOLAEV'S wife, and that NIKOLAEV'S wife, in her words, is a beauty who after KIROV'S murder remained living in Leningrad and was not repressed. I also heard from N.A. ROZENFEL'D and from N.B. ROZENFEL'D that the latter likes to draw counterrevolutionary lampoons of com. STALIN, among other lampoons, in a Zinovievite-Trotskyite spirit.
>
> Question: You have confessed that the ROZENFEL'DS carried out counterrevolutionary work and were preparing the murder of com. STALIN. Do you confess to being their accomplice?
>
> Answer: I was not their accomplice, but I admit that I am guilty in that I did not inform the organs of power that the ROZENFEL'DS have a very counterrevolutionary attitude and hate STALIN to the extent that they raise the question of his murder.
>
> - Lubianka 1922-1936, 635.

On March 17, 1935 I.V. Bol'shikh was interrogated. She had been working as a supervisor in the Secretariat of the Presidium of the Central Executive Committee of the USSR – that is, directly under Enukidze, who was Secretary of the Presidium of the CEC. In addition to much else of interest she also repeated the "Enukidze" rumor concerning Kirov and Nikolaev's wife.

> Question: What counterrevolutionary slander were you spreading?
>
> Answer: Right after the murder of S.M. KIROV, F.C. AGRANOVICH told me that the murder was carried out by NIKOLAEV for personal reasons, since KIROV had been close to NIKOLAEV'S wife, and the latter killed him out of jealousy, but the government announcement was untrue.
>
> Question: To whom did you pass on this slander?

> Answer: I passed this slander on to my sister Elena Vasil'evna KUR'EVA, who as I have already stated, works in the Council of People's Commissars of the RSFSR [i.e. for the executive branch of the government of the Russian Republic – GF]
>
> Question: You are not telling us everything. The investigation insists that you say everything connected with the spreading by you of slander against the leadership of the AUCP(b).
>
> Answer: I have not told you everything. I do not remember from whom among the employees of the Kremlin I heard that N.S. ALLILUEVA supposedly died an unnatural death, and committed suicide because STALIN drove her to it. I told F.C. AGRANOVICH and my sister Elena about this.
>
> - Lubianka 1922-1936, 648.

As the chief of the CEC Enukidze was a likely source for this rumor, all the more since we know, thanks to the NKVD report that Lenoe cites, he was saying the same thing at the same time, in December 1934.

On March 20, 1935 Lev B. Kamenev, the former member of the Politburo and ally of Grigory Zinoviev's, was interrogated. Among other matters the investigators inquired about the fact that his brother, N.B. Rozenfel'd, had confessed to involvement in a plot to assassinate Stalin. Kamenev denied knowing about any such plot but admitted that Rozenfel'd had been present during some "counterrevolutionary talks" he, Kamenev, had had with Zinoviev, during which Zinoviev had said that he approved of some of the views about the Party and the situation in the country expressed by Trotsky in his *Bulletin of the Opposition.*

> Question: Your brother, N.B. ROZENFEL'D, has been arrested by us for terrorist activity. During the investigation he has admitted that he took part in preparation to murder com. STALIN, and confessed that his terrorist intentions were formed under your influence.
>
> What can you tell us about this matter?

Answer: I did not know that N.B. ROZENFEL'D took part in the preparation to murder STALIN. ROZENFEL'D has been at my home from time to time, and I have helped him materially. While at my home he was present at conversations that took place at my apartment and at my dacha at Il'inskoe. These conversations were mainly with ZINOVIEV. In these conversations with ZINOVIEV we criticized the activities of the Party, the Central Committee, and permitted ourselves attacks on STALIN. At different times, with more or less sharpness, we talked with ZINOVIEV about our situation and expressed the conviction that we will not be permitted to return to active political life. In a few cases we reacted to the hopelessness of our situation with hostile attacks on STALIN.

The counterrevolutionary conversations that we had with ZINOVIEV in the presence of N.B. ROZENFEL'D caused the latter to become an enemy of Soviet power and of the Party and incited in him bitterness against STALIN. I concede that N.B. ROZENFEL'D, who was embittered by my exile to Minusinsk and reacted to this in an extremely painful manner, affected by the counterrevolutionary conversations that I later had with ZINOVIEV, in particular about STALIN, could have extended to terrorist intentions.

Question: What talks did you have with ZINOVIEV in connection with the counterrevolutionary documents published by Trotsky abroad?

Answer: ZINOVIEV has become familiar with the so-called bulletins of the opposition at the Lenin Institute. He informed me about the contents of these counterrevolutionary documents of Trotsky's and has expressed his positive attitude towards certain questions of the evaluation by Trotsky of the situation in the Party and in the USSR. I did not protest to ZINOVIEV and

> did not tell anyone about his counterrevolutionary views on this question right up to my arrest.
>
> - Lubianka 1922-1936, 649-650.

On May 12 Kamenev was bound over for trial on the grounds that he was an organizer of the plot to kill Stalin. Genrikh Iagoda, head of the NKVD, recommended that N.A. and N.B. Rozenfel'd, his sister-in-law and brother, be sentenced to 10 years in prison. Iagoda also recommended that six persons in this case be sentenced to death. On July 17, 1935 the Politburo reduced the sentence of five of the six and recommended that Kamenev be resentenced to 10 years in prison instead of the five years he had been sentenced to at the January 1935 trial. (Lubianka 1922-1936, 681)

> No. 535
>
> DECREE OF THE POLITBURO OF THE CC AUCP(b)
>
> CONCERNING THE MEASURES OF PUNISHMENT IN THE KREMLIN CASE
>
> 17 July 1935
>
> No. 30, p. 82 – Matter for the NKVD.
>
> [...]
>
> 6. L.B. Kamenev – sentence to 10 years in prison.
>
> (Lubianka 1922-1936, 681)

This represents a lessening of Iagoda's recommendation as well, since Iagoda had recommended that Kamenev stand trial on a capital offense that could have brought the death penalty.[149]

Enukidze's insistence on spreading the rumor that Lenoe had acted alone out of personal motives appears to have been a futile attempt to deflect attention away from the search for a conspiracy. According to Iagoda's

---

[149] According to Zhukov (p. 105) the Military Collegium of the Supreme Court sentenced two people, Sinelobov and Cherniavskii, to death. Zhukov states that this was down from 25, though I can't find the document he refers to.

testimony both he and Enukidze had opposed the assassination from the beginning on the sensible grounds that it would endanger both the conspiracy itself and Iagoda's position as head of the NKVD and thus the person ultimately responsible for organizing protection for Party leaders like Kirov. But the united leadership of the conspiracy voted to go ahead with the assassination anyway.

Though Iagoda does not say so in those interrogations of his which have now been published there must have been a decision to portray the assassination as a lone act. An assassin had to be found who was dedicated enough to kill Kirov and then immediately kill himself. Under those circumstances the hypothesis of a "lone gunman" acting from personal motives would have been a plausible one. At the very least it would have been difficult to disprove, had Nikolaev's suicide attempt been successful.

During the first few days after the murder Nikolaev attempted to portray himself in just that way. But the "lone gunman" story quickly broke down under interrogation. Enukidze must have known about this. But the evidence cited by Lenoe shows that he refused to adopt the official, and quite correct, version of a conspiracy (Lenoe 502-505). This was bound to appear suspicious, and it would have been natural for the NKVD to wonder why one of the highest political figures in the land and a longtime comrade and friend of Stalin's would be behaving that way. Moreover, it seems to have led directly to the "Kremlin Affair", which in turn pointed the way to a gradual unraveling of the entire conspiracy. One consequence was that Enukidze lost control over the Kremlin guard – the force that was to be used to kill or arrest the Party leadership in what the conspirators called the "palace coup" plan.

In 2000 Russian historian IUrii N. Zhukov published the only serious study devoted to the Kremlin Affair that has yet appeared. Zhukov had access to archival documents that have still not been declassified. His conclusion is that, on the evidence, the "Kremlin Affair" was not a fabrication, but the uncovering of a real conspiracy.

> Therefore, at the present time – until there is a substantial widening of the evidentiary base, until the declassification of the materials in the Central Archive of the FSB, we just consider the following to be beyond doubt. Of all the possible hypotheses that can be

> formulated to explain both the "Kremlin Affair" and the Enukidze case, the only one that can account for all the known facts without exception is that which assumes that the conspiracy against Stalin and his group really existed.[150]

Evidence

Zhukov cites powerful evidence in support of his hypothesis, and all of it is circumstantial. In this connection Zhukov has some important things to say about evidence generally that is relevant to our purposes.

> It goes without saying that in this hypothesis the lack of evidence should make us wary – either direct or indirect evidence, but indisputable evidence. And for this we must decide the question as to whether evidence is to be expected in general in such cases. Could such evidence be found in the investigation of the "Kremlin affair" and if so, what kind of evidence? Plans for the arrest of the members of the "narrow leadership"? A list of the future Politburo and government, or something similar. Or lists of conspirators, perhaps confirmed by their signatures? Or, perhaps, declarations, decrees, orders intended for publication immediately after the seizure of power and prepared in advance? **Hardly, because any normal conspirator who was also preparing a coup d'état would do everything possible to be certain that no evidence of this kind existed.**
>
> It would be just as futile to hope to find while searching the homes of the conspirators, let us say, plans of the Kremlin, on which were noted the apartments and offices of Stalin, Molotov, and others, the routes of their usual walks. The conspirators – if they were indeed such – would not need them either. Both Peterson and Enukidze, who had lived and worked in the Kremlin, would have long known these things.

---

[150] IU. N. Zhukov, "Tainy 'Kremlevskogo dela' 1935 goda i sud'ba Avelia Enukidze" (The Secrets of the 'Kremlin Affair' of 1935 and the fate of Avel' Enukidze). *Voprosy Istorii* No. 9 (2000), 83-113, at p. 109.

> We could not expect to find evidence of any other kind that definitively reflected the criminal plots that have been uncovered. Unless the conspirators suffered from dementia, they would never commit their plans to paper. Everything, absolutely everything, would be only in their heads. (Zhukov 110-111; emphasis added GF)

Zhukov cites an example of the kind of evidence that he finds convincing and reasonable to expect.

> Now let us consider an alternative hypothesis, the most paradoxical one. Let us suppose that the conspiracy really existed. Are there any facts to confirm this? Yes, although they appeared only two years later, and also are of a very specific and unconvincing character – only confessions of suspects at interrogation. On the day of the arrests of Enukidze, February 11 [1937] in Khar'kov, and of Peterson, April 27 [1937] in Kiev they gave to different investigators confessions of guilt that are identical down to the details. They related how they were preparing a coup and the arrest or murder in the Kremlin of Stalin, Molotov, Kaganovich, Voroshilov and Ordzhonikidze.[151] (108)

Zhukov goes on to cite pretrial confessions by Iagoda published in 1997 in the same collection we have used earlier in the present study.

---

[151] Zhukov has discussed these specific confessions and the conclusions he draws from them in more detail in a meeting with Vladimir L. Bobrov on December 6 2002. (Email letter LETTER_V3o.doc, rec'd 12.08.02 doc from Vladimir L. Bobrov to Grover Furr.)

Chapter 19.

Osmund Egge

In December 2011, after the present book was largely completed and being translated into Russian, I learned about a book on the Kirov murder that had just appeared in Russia. "Zagadka Kirova: ubiystvo, razviazavshee stalinskii terror" (The Kirov Mystery: the Murder that Unleashed Stalin's Terror) is a translation into Russian of the book *Kirovgåten. Mordet som utløste Stalins terror*, published in 2009 in Norwegian by University of Oslo professor Åsmund Egge (in Russian: "Osmund Egge"). Son of the former prominent Norwegian communist and anti-Nazi resistance fighter Ørnulf Egge, Åsmund Egge was himself a prominent communist and then leftist for many years, before resigning and then becoming a professor.

Egge's book is published by the ROSSPEN publishing house, in its series "The History of Stalinism" (*Istoriia Stalinizma*). This series of what is to be 100 books was launched in order to combat the popularity of Stalin among the Russian population and is funded by the Boris N. Eltsin foundation.[152] Only anti-Stalin and anticommunist books are considered for this prestigious series. Under such conditions, when historical works have to conform to a certain tendentious paradigm instead of the discovery of the truth, historical objectivity is impossible. Rather than history, such works are "propaganda with footnotes". Sadly, Egge's book is no exception.

In this study we use the Russian translation of Egge's book. Egge certainly scrutinized it so we can be sure it reflects what he thinks. Not many people read Norwgian, the language Egge wrote his book in – and we cannot read it either, or at least not well. Surely the vast majority of people who read Egge's book at all will read it in Russian.

---

[152] See the series description at the ROSSPEN page http://www.rosspen.su/ru/catalog/.list/id/56/

There are a few things of interest in Egge's book – not in his conclusions, but surrounding his research. Egge's main archival sources are from Fond 617 of the Russian State Archiv of Social-Political History, or RGASPI. This is Nikolai Ezhov's *fond* (archival collection) and much of it, though by no means all of it, has been declassified.

From this *fond* Egge cites a number of December 1934 interrogations from the NKVD investigation of Kirov's murder that are not mentioned by either Kirilina or Lenoe. Kirilina wrote before this *fond* had been declassified. But Lenoe claims that he consulted it (xix). Perhaps Lenoe did not bother to check this *fond* carefully. Or perhaps he did check it and found, as Egge did, that none of the additional investigative materials would help prove his predetermined conclusion that Nikolaev was a "lone gunman" and that Stalin "framed" all the other defendants.

Like Kirilina and Lenoe, Egge does not try to solve the Kirov murder. Rather, like them Egge simply *assumes* that Nikolaev was a "lone gunman" and then proceeds to ignore or dismiss any evidence that tends to contradict this predetermined conclusion. Since Egge is not trying to discover the truth – as we'll see, he literally thinks it is "obvious", without any evidence at all – there's no reason for him to be careful in his research. Consequently, he isn't careful. We'll give some examples here before examining in detail Egge's chapter on the evidence: the interrogations of the defendants carried out in December, 1934.

> * Egge cites Genrikh Liushkov's remarks about the Kirov murder. He even quotes parts of Liushkov's April 1939 *Kaizo* article. This means that he may have had it translated. But, like Lenoe, Egge assumes Liushkov is telling "the truth". Egge "believes" Liushkov, who was specifically writing propaganda for the Japanese army, while "disbelieving" the many texts of NKVD interrogations of the men Nikolaev had named as his associates. Egge ignores Alvin Coox's articles of the late 1990s in which Coox shows that Liushkov privately confirmed to the Japanese the existence of a number of the conspiracies whose existence he denied in the *Kaizo* article. (For more details see our separate chapter on Liushkov.)

> * Egge takes on faith any statements made by the Gorbachev commissions, such as the "Reply to Iakovlev". For example, he accepts the claim that Lobov killed Sokol'nikov in prison at Beria's orders (Egge 259; RKEB 3, 468) without any attempt to verify it.

We have refuted this story in a separate article to appear shortly. Like Lenoe, who also refers to it in passing, Egge could have done this too – tried to verify it. Instead, he just "accepts" it. This illustrates his attitude towards evidence: he simply "accepts" statements from highly anti-Stalin sources, presumably because they support his preconceived bias.

* In Chapter 5 Egge puts scare quotes around the word "bloc":

> ...Zinoviev, Kamenev, and two other men who had gone through the January trial a year earlier, G.E. Evdokimov and I.P. Bakaev, were now accused not only of knowing about the terrorist goals of their counterparts in Leningrad but also that they had directly taken part in organizing Kirov's murder. They were also accused of forming a "bloc" with the Trotskyites and with Trotsky himself. (68)

As we have discussed in the present work, the existence of this bloc has been proven since 1980 from documents in the Harvard Trotsky archive. There is no excuse for Egge, a professional historian of the USSR, not to know about this – or, if he does know about it, there is no excuse for his putting scare quotes around the word "bloc," thereby giving his readers the impression that the bloc's real existence is in doubt.

* This means that Egge's discussion of Trotsky's "version" is wrong. Trotsky repeatedly denied the existence of the bloc. Of course he had to do this in order to preserve conspiratorial secrecy. But that also means that Trotsky's whole discussion of the Kirov murder is a deliberate falsification on Trotsky's part. Since he did not want to admit that a real bloc of Zinovievites, Trotskyites, and other oppositionists existed, Trotsky had to fabricate a story that it was Stalin who was supposedly "fabricating" here!

* Egge accepts as unproblematically true the testimony allegedly given during Khrushchev's studies of the Kirov murder. Lenoe demonstrates in his book that Khrushchev was out to *pretend* to prove Stalin had Kirov killed. Lenoe also adduces the evidence that memories of long-past events are often, if not usually, faulty – even if we assume that those who testified to Khrushchev's men in the '60s were actually remembering, rather than just telling Khrush-

> chev's men what they wanted to hear, a more likely scenario. In effect Egge has made the assumption that testimony given during the Stalin period is false, even when there is no evidence that it is false, while assuming the testimony given during Khrushchev's time is true, even when there's no evidence to confirm that. That is, Egge decided before writing his book that he would not solve the Kirov murder on the basis of the evidence. This means his conclusion is predetermined by his assumptions. Egge's work is an extended example of the fallacy of "begging the question."

Egge spends a great deal of space on unimportant, even trivial, matters. Chapter 6 summarizes "rumors and guesses". In fact, as I argue in another chapter, the rumor that Nikolaev killed Kirov out of "jealousy" or for "personal reasons" originated with the conspirators themselves, as shown by the fact that it can be traced to Avel' Enukidze. Egge falsely claims that the rumor that Nikolaev's wife Mil'da Draule was involved with Kirov "had appeared in the city in the summer of 1933". His reference is to Kirilina, but Kirilina cites no evidence whatever that this is so. Otherwise, however, "rumors" are irrelevant to the historical question of who killed Kirov and why.

Egge also spends many pages exploring the death of Borisov, Kirov's bodyguard. But it only makes sense to do this in the context of trying to solve Kirov's murder – and Egge ignores all the evidence we have that any conspiracy was involved. If you insist, as Egge does, that Nikolaev acted alone and from personal motives, there's no reason whatever to question Borisov's death.

> * Egge cites the important work *Genrikh Iagoda* three times, but always on inconsequential matters. As we have discussed extensively in the chapter on Iagoda, this source of Iagoda's pretrial interrogations has been recognized as genuine by anticommunist scholars, and gives primary evidence of first-rate importance on the conspiracy against Kirov. Egge never mentions these vital documents, which sharply contradict his theory that Nikolaev was a "lone gunman".

Egge does note some useful facts in his book, though he does not really make use of them as they do not help to prove his preconceived thesis. We'll review them here.

* Egge notes that Nikolaev held 13 jobs in 15 years, the last several of which were very good jobs at high pay. This strongly suggests that Nikolaev had friends in high places in the Leningrad party who obtained such jobs for him. The leaders of the underground Zinovievite group were just such men.

* He notes that Nikolaev and his family had a three-room apartment in a new building. This was very privileged housing in Leningrad at the time, but Nikolaev was far from a prominent person. This too suggests he had *blat* – connections, pull among influential people.

* Egge notes that Nikolaev lied in his early confession and in letters to Party officials such as Kirov.

> + In his first interrogation on December 1 Nikolaev said that the idea for the assassination had come to him at the beginning of November. Later he said it was September. (53)
>
> + In his letter to Kirov Nikolaev complained that his children were "starving". (56) He also complained that he could not find work, and that a job was "essential". (54) Yet Egge also documents that Nikolaev had turned down all offers of work. (48)

* Egge notes that Nikolaev's relatives were unanimous that the family was not in need. Yet in his "diary" – Egge correctly remarks that these documents are much more than just a diary and encompass other kinds of writing too – Nikolaev complained about poverty and hunger.

It seems undeniable that Nikolaev was lying in these "private" writings. Egge notes the facts but never points out the conclusion: that Nikolaev wrote these false accounts for some ulterior purpose. Much less does Egge ask why Nikolaev would have done such a thing. We know, however, that Nikolaev later testified that he had faked these accounts in advance in order to strengthen the appearance that he had murdered Kirov for personal reasons. Egge must know this too – after all, it is in the Prosecutor's Indictment. But Egge does not tell his readers that Nikolaev had said this. We have discussed Nikolaev's confession about this fact in another chapter of the present work.

Egge's Account of the Investigation

The central chapter in Egge's book is Chapter 8, titled "The 'investigation' and terror". The scare quotes around the first word are no doubt intended to convey Egge's opinion that the investigation was faked to conform to a supposedly predetermined conclusion, and that all the defendants, save Nikolaev, were innocent men whom the NKVD had "framed". In fact this is the central conclusion of this chapter and of Egge's book as a whole. As we shall see, Egge fails to cite any evidence whatever to support this hypothesis.

In the beginning of this chapter Egge reports rumors, and then notes that they are unsubstantiated. For example Egge reports, from Roi Medvedev, that at the Leningrad railway station Stalin slapped Leningrad NKVD head Medved' across the face – and then notes that Stalin's bodyguard Vlasik later denied that Medved' had been present at all. Egge reports another rumor – that Iagoda had ordered everyone at Smolny to stand at attention facing the wall as Stalin entered – but cites only Bastrykin and Gromtseva's lurid pot-boiler as a source. Bastrykin's evidence for this statement is his conversations with Tammi and Rosliakov, who reported this and other details. Egge, however, doesn't even tell us that fact. This is a good example of a serious failing by Egge. Sometimes he evaluates his sources, but at other times he does not bother.

Egge spends several pages reporting rumors – from Amy Knight, from Alexander Orlov, from Medvedev again, again from Bastrykin and Gromtseva, and from Nikita Khrushchev – before conceding that rumors are not history:

> But some historians continue to believe these rumors, and some of them even consider them almost as proven facts. (156)

A little further on Egge cites Rosliakov concerning what happened during Stalin's questioning of Nikolaev – and then notes that Rosliakov was not present at the interview but was only in the same building at the same time! So this is yet another rumor. Moreover, it exposes the worthlessness of Rosliakov's account.

Egge falsely reports Molotov's statements to Feliks Chuev that he believed the Zinovievites "used" Nikolaev. But then Egge claims that Molotov contradicted himself:

> According to Molotov Nikolaev stated that the murder was ideologically motivated, since he was a supporter of Zinoviev. Nevertheless this story of Molotov's about Nikolaev does not fully correspond to other accounts by Molotov. He also said that Nikolaev was probably not a true Zinovievite nor a true Trotskyite, but that the Zinovievites used him. (158)

Later, Egge claims Molotov said Nikolaev acted alone:

> During the talks with Chuev Molotov said that Nikolaev had acted alone. (191)

But this statement of Egge's is not true. According to Chuev's account, this is what Molotov actually said:

> That same evening we travelled to Leningrad – Stalin, Voroshilov, and I. We spoke with Nikolaev, the murderer of Kirov.
>
> An ordinary type, expelled from the Party. He said that he killed consciously, on an ideological basis. A Zinovievite. I think that women have nothing to do with this. Stalin interrogated Nikolaev in the Smolny.
>
> – How did Nikolaev appear to you?
>
> – An ordinary person. A white-collar worker. Of medium height. Rather thin. I think that he had obviously become embittered about something, expelled from the Party, a person who felt offended. And the Zinovievites used him. Probably he was neither a real Zinovievite nor a real Trotskyite.
>
> — Not just Nikolaev, but a whole list of men were condemned, – I say.
>
> The fact is that they were not condemned for the murder but because they participated in the Zinovievite organization. But as far as I remember, there was no

> specific document that this was done by decision of the Zinovievite group.
>
> Therefore he acted as if separately, but by his past he was a Zinovievite.[153]

So Molotov's opinion is, in fact, clear: he believed Nikolaev had acted "as if separately", but not separately in fact. In other words, Molotov confirmed the version of the Soviet government in the 1930s. Therefore Egge seriously distorted Molotov's words.

But in any case Molotov's opinion, given over 40 years later, is not evidence at all. Egge recognizes this himself (Chapter 8 at note 39). Molotov was not involved in the investigation and had no detailed knowledge about it. Like the rest of the Politburo, and like Stalin himself, Molotov was plenty busy with other things to do. So why does Egge record it – what's more, record it inaccurately? Evidently he does so because that inaccurate account supports his preconceived idea: that Nikolaev was a "lone gunman."

Egge begins to discuss the problem of using interrogations as evidence, but then makes the following statement:

> It is obvious that the transcripts of the interrogations of the Kirov murder case do not give the full picture of what took place during these interrogations. This became especially clear after Stalin decided precisely who he should make the scapegoats. It is clear that after this the transcripts of interrogations distorted the real state of affairs. Those who were partly guilty were forced to give confessions that corresponded to a scenario created by the investigators. (169)

Egge's use of the words "it is obvious that", "especially clear", and "it is clear that", are the certain sign that he has no evidence. Of course none of these statements is at all "clear" or "obvious." Elsewhere in this book we have shown that Stalin directed the investigators' attention towards the Zinovievites long after Zinoviev's and Kamenev's names had come

---

153 Feliks I Chuev. *Molotov: Poluderzhavnyi Vlastelin.* Moscow: OLMA-PRESS, 1999, 376.

up in the interrogations. Either Egge does not realize this or he has hidden it from his readers.

Egge then says:

> However there is every reason to suppose that the earlier transcripts, despite all their omissions, were less tendentious and worthy of more trust than those that were compiled in order to drive the suspects into a corner. (170)

These are mere assertions by Egge, aimed at discrediting the later interrogations in the minds of his readers without any evidence. Egge does not tell his readers what "every reason" is[154] and gives no evidence that the interrogations were "composed in order to drive the suspects into a corner" – whatever that means. In general, no investigator ever believes that a suspect's earliest statements are the most truthful. The normal thing for a guilty person to do is to deny at first, and then gradually divulge more and more information. This was the case with Nikolaev's confessions, as we demonstrate in the present work.

Although he repeatedly attempts to discredit the evidence of a conspiracy Egge apparently cannot even convince himself. For example, he states:

> However, Katsafa's confessions about how he heard Nikolaev talking in his sleep are not sufficiently reliable. Probably Katsafa was asked to make this claim in order to give the investigators a pretext to arrest Shatskii and Kotolynov. (170)

Egge does not say what is "not sufficiently reliable" about Katsafa's statement – much less what his criteria are to distinguish "reliable" from "not sufficiently reliable" statements.

Then he concedes that his own explanation cannot be true:

> But why then did Agranov on the very same day speak about them [Shatskii and Kotolynov] in a report to Stalin as "Trotskyist" and "Anarchist"? (170-171)

---

[154] The original Russian is "vse osnovaniia", literally "all the bases". This is not idiomatic in English so I have translated it as "every reason."

Egge tries to discredit the December 6 interrogation, in which Nikolaev named some of his Zinovievite confederates by claiming that he should have had "concrete evidence":

> But Nikolaev could not present any concrete proof for such accusations. (172)

This is nonsense, a particularly desperate move by Egge. For what can he possibly mean by "concrete evidence"? Does Egge expect all "real" conspirators to carry around "material evidence" with them – say, a list of their fellow conspirators and plans for their activities? Therefore this remark is another "tell" – an admission that he has no way to discredit the confessions by the Zinovievite conspirators.[155]

Egge continues with the story that Nikolaev declared a hunger strike, twice tried to kill himself, and claimed he was being "tormented" (*menia muchaiut*). However Egge fails to inform his readers that all these details come from Iurii Sedov, one of Gorbachev's investigators, and that Sedov gives no source, no "concrete evidence" – to use Egge's own words – that Nikolaev ever even uttered these words. Much less has any evidence ever been presented to prove that these words, purportedly of Nikolaev's, are true, for the fact that someone claims he is being "tormented" does not mean he really is. Also, Sedov is a dishonest witness, some of whose falsifications we have examined in an earlier chapter.

On the following page we reach the central falsehood in Egge's book. He writes:

> The transcripts of Nikolaev's confession reflect two possible scenarios of the investigators. The result of the first is the preliminary insistence by Nikolaev that he alone carried out the murder, which could indicate his intention to conceal the guilt of other persons involved in the crime. After they gave him good conditions in the prison and promised to spare his life, and this did not yield the desired result, they applied harsh pressure against him (possibly, even torture). As a result he was

155 Elsewhere in this study we have quoted the cogent words of Russian historian IUrii Zhukov, who sensibly points out that no sane conspirator would keep evidence of a conspiracy anywhere except in his head.

> broken and confessed to the existence of a conspiracy with the participation of a "Leningrad center." This interpretation corresponds to the Stalinist version of the murder. Otherwise, we must concede that Nikolaev was telling the truth when he denied having any accomplices. However gradually, under the pressures of promises and threats, he confessed to the participation in the conspiracy of the former Zinovievites, and this corresponded to the wishes of the Moscow investigators (after they had assumed control of the investigation). **From what we know today there can be no doubt that this second interpretation is the true one. It is obvious**, that the reason for Nikolaev's hunger strike and attempts to kill himself were the torments of conscience he experienced after implicating innocent people. (173-174; emphasis added GF)

Here Egge finally admits that he has no evidence whatsoever that Nikolaev's confessions were false. Once again we perceive that phrases like "there can be no doubt" and "it is obvious" are Egge's substitute for evidence – because he does not have any. And Egge has to go much further than this. He also has to "assume" that it is "obvious" that all the other defendants' confessions are false as well, as we shall see.

This is as clear an admission as we could wish for that *Egge has no evidence at all* to support his hypothesis that Nikolaev was a "lone gunman" and all the rest of the defendants were innocent, "framed". If Egge is going to "assume away" all the evidence we have, why bother to look at the evidence at all? In fact, why write the book in the first place if you're going to ignore all the evidence – unless your only real goal is to make anti-Stalin propaganda?

Egge is either simply lying about Latvian consul Bissenieks, or – possibly -- has just not done the research:

> The Latvian consul Georg Bisseneks denied any contact with Nikolaev and Kotolynov. A verification of the archives of the Ministry of Foreign Affairs of Latvia also did not reveal anything… It appears that Nikolaev was strongly pressured to admit to that which the

> investigators demanded from him. All this looks like a complete falsification. (175-176)

Lenoe, who would also like to dismiss any charges against Bissenieks, admits that the Latvian consulate was a source of anti-Soviet propaganda, that Nikolaev was right about the layout of the Latvian consulate, and that he accurately picked Bissenieks out of a photo lineup (Lenoe 299-300). But Egge claims:

> …there is no evidence of such "contacts" and the "consul affair" appears improbable. (176)

In fact Lenoe cites good evidence in support of Nikolaev's allegations against Bissenieks (Lenoe 384). Egge does not mention any of this. Maybe he didn't have access to it? But then Egge, like Kirilina, should have admitted to their readers that they did not have access to all the investigative materials – something that, to his credit, Lenoe does admit – and then taken this fact into account in his research and in drawing his conclusions. Egge fails his readers in this regard.

Egge makes an interesting admission concerning the indictment:

> Kirilina asserts that the indictment was fabricated. However, it did reflect to a significant degree the contents of the interrogation transcripts. (184)

Though reluctant to say that Kirilina is wrong Egge in effect suggests that she is lying here by confirming that the indictment does indeed reflect the interrogation transcripts. But then Egge commits his own falsification:

> But we must take into consideration that these transcripts reflect only crudely and tendentiously the confessions obtained during interrogation. Meetings of old comrades, probably devoid of any political content, were changed into meetings of the members of a counterrevolutionary organization. (184)

Egge has absolutely no evidence to support any of these statements. He simply decides to declare all the evidence falsified! He has no evidence that this is so. This is yet another "tell" on Egge's part – he has decided to ignore all the evidence and invent his conclusions out of thin air because he possesses no evidence to support his hypothesis.

Egge describes the following incident as though it actually occurred during the trial:

> When Nikolaev was called into the courtroom he at first retracted his confessions at interrogation and asserted that he alone had planned the murder of Kirov. (185)

Lenoe (359) notes that Agranov's letter to Stalin does not record "this embarrassing moment", which of course is not reflected in the trial transcript either. But Lenoe also discloses that this detail only emerged in 1956, when Khrushchev's men, led by Pospelov and Serov, were trying hard to overturn the "conspiracy" version of the 1930s and were both destroying evidence (the file "Svoaki") and withholding other evidence even from Presidium members whom, like Molotov, Khrushchev did not trust.

Lenoe also fails to point out the fact that Khrushchev had taken terrible revenge upon some who did not tell the lies that he wanted them to tell,[156] and this was well known, especially to persons involved in the former NKVD and later MGB/MVD. So anyone questioned by Khrushchev's men had good reason to tell any story he wanted them to tell!

Even setting that aside, there is still the matter of source criticism. Here Egge abandons his responsibility. We have no reason to doubt the confessions of the 1934 defendants, while we have good reason to question anything Khrushchev's men produced since we know they were lying and destroying evidence, as Lenoe admits. This is an important and interesting issue – one which Egge had the responsibility to lay before his readers but does not.

So Egge is correct, as far as it goes, when he writes:

---

[156] In his memoirs Pavel Sudoplatov relates how he was arrested after refusing to fabricate stories against Beria. Sudoplatov might have ended up in Khrushchev's December 1956 "kangaroo court" being tried and executed as Beria's "accomplice" along with Kobulov, Dekanozov, Merkulov, Meshik, Volodzimirskii, and Goglidze. None of the supposed "crimes" Beria was charged with have ever been proven – good evidence that they did not exist. Sudoplatov also relates the story of how General Maslennikov killed himself rather than either fabricate a story against Beria or face trumped-up charges of helping Beria in the latter's supposed coup attempt. Evidently Sudoplatov gets the date of Maslennikov's suicide wrong – it was March 16, 1954, not August 1953. But in other respects his account agrees with other versions of Maslennikov's suicide.

> Neither Nikolaev's reactions nor his statement that he had acted alone went into the transcript of the trial. (185)

Small wonder! Egge has no evidence that Nikolaev made such statements. There's no good reason to think he did. Although even if Nikolaev did try to revert to his initial story that he had acted alone – and we do not know that he did – it would have made no difference. There was plenty of evidence against him from the testimony of his confederates.

Egge is guilty of blatantly lying when he writes that all the defendants (except for Nikolaev) denied knowing about the plan to kill Kirov:

> In addition they all denied that they had anything to do with the murder or knew about plans for the murder. (186)

Egge's footnote here is to the "Reply to Iakovlev" and to Iurii Sedov's article in *Trud* of December 1990. But Egge has also studied Kirilina's book and cites it frequently. Yet Kirilina states that Sokolov admitted he knew that Nikolaev intended to kill Kirov but still tried to get him a ticket to the Smol'nyi (Kirilina 286; 299). Again, according to Kirilina:

> During the investigation and at first at the trial Antonov, IUskin, Zvezdov, and Sokolov admitted their participation in the terrorist group and the preparations for the murder of Kirov and gave similar confessions against other defendants at the trial. (Kirilina 301)

Since Egge studied and refers to Kirilina's book it appears as though Egge may have suppressed this evidence. It is logical to suppose he did so because this evidence supports the hypothesis that Nikolaev acted for a clandestine Zinovievite conspiracy and so does not fit Egge's preconceived idea that Nikolaev was a "lone gunman." Similarly, Egge accepts Katsafa's 1950s testimony about Kotolynov's "last words" in which he supposedly said that all the defendants were innocent except for Nikolaev. We should recall that even Lenoe does not believe Katsafa's story. (Lenoe 370-1).

Egge simply rejects evidence that is inconvenient for his conclusion. For example, he states:

> Many of the interrogation transcripts were falsified, and those who were interrogated did not sign them. (188)

But he presents no evidence at all that even a single one of the interrogation transcripts were falsified. Nor does he identify any that were not signed.

(Parenthetically, this last point of Egge's is interesting, for at least two reasons. First, Egge quotes from Ezhov's *fond* (archival collection). It is probable that the interrogation transcripts in this *fond* were copies, not originals. Certainly multiple copies were made – for the Prosecutor, for the interrogators themselves, and probably for Stalin. Only the original would be signed. Yet Egge does not address this issue at all.

Furthermore if, as Egge assumes without any evidence, Nikolaev was tortured or threatened with torture, what would have stopped the NKVD from doing the same to other defendants and thereby forcing them to do whatever the investigators wanted: sign false transcripts, confess to taking part in Kirov's murder, etc.?

Therefore, even if the defendants had refused to sign the interrogation transcripts – and Egge does not establish this – that would be just as likely to suggest that they were *not* fabricated, as to suggest the opposite.)

Again, Egge states:

> In the interrogations Nikolaev is practically never mentioned as a participant in the "Leningrad center", however at Stalin's insistence he was included among its members. (189)

Once again Egge presents no evidence whatsoever to support this statement – and, by the way, this is a claim that neither Lenoe nor Kirilina made. On the contrary: as we have seen in a previous chapter, Zvezdov specifically named Nikolaev as a member of the Zinovievite group, and Lenoe reproduces his statement to this effect (Lenoe 310-311).

Concerning the Leningrad center Egge falsifies yet again. He writes:

> The indictment was based exclusively on the confessions of the accused, who asserted that such a center did exist and who named names of its supposed members. No one ever mentioned again that this center carried out any activity at all. (189)

This is false. Earlier in this book we quoted from Nikolaev's testimony that Kotolynov personally helped train him, and several other defendants helped him monitor Kirov's movements. Several defendants named Rumiantsev as a leader of the center, which also kept touch with the Moscow center.

Egge quotes the 1961 testimony of Makarov that the interrogators used "provocational methods" – what are those? – and "moral and physical pressure" to force them to sign the transcripts. Lenoe demonstrated that Khrushchev was trying to "frame" Stalin and falsified materials, and we have shown elsewhere in this book that Makarov was seriously wrong about another detail in his testimony. His testimony is not a reliable primary source.

Egge lies again concerning Nikolaev's "diary". He states:

> As already stated in Chapter 4, these notes bear witness to the fact that the motives for the murder were of a purely personal nature. However the investigators attributed another meaning to these notes. Nikolaev had supposedly maintained his diary in order to deceive the investigation. In their opinion the diary represented a sophisticated trap which was aimed to deflect suspicious away from the Zinovievites who had planned the terrorist act with political aims. (190)

But Egge conceals from his readers the fact that Nikolaev himself had admitted that, as the following passage from the Indictment shows:

> Here we must note that with the aim of concealing the traces of the crime and of his accomplices, and also of disguising the real motives of the murder of com. Kirov, the accused L. Nikolaev prepared a series of documents (a diary, statements addressed to different institutions, etc.) in which he attempted to describe his crime as an act of personal despair and dissatisfaction due to his supposed difficult material situation, and as a protest against "unjust treatment towards a living human being on the part of certain government figures."
>
> - vol. 1, l.d. 6
>
> The accused L. Nikolaev himself admitted the falseness and invented nature of versions of this kind and explained that he created this version after preliminary

> agreement among the members of the terrorist group, which had decided to depict the murder of com. Kirov as an individual act and by so doing to conceal the real motives of this crime.
>
> In his confession of December 13 of this year L. Nikolaev states this directly:
>
> > "I was supposed to depict the murder of Kirov as an individual act in order to conceal the participation in it of the Zinovievite group.
> >
> > Vol. 1, l.d. 266.
>
> This situation is also confirmed in that, as has been exhaustively established during the investigation, the accused L. Nikolaev determinedly and systematically rejected any offers to arrange a job for him, referring now to the weak state of his health and the necessity to recover, now to some other circumstances that supposedly prevented him from working.[157]

The section of Nikolaev's December 13 interrogation referred to in this excerpt from the Indictment has been published in the original and is translated by Lenoe, so we can be reasonably assured that the Indictment is honest here – and, if genuine here, the probability is high that it is also honest in other respects.[158] Yet Egge simply declares Nikolaev's testimony "obviously absurd" (190)[159] This appears to be simply an evasion on Egge's part, an attempt to cover up the fact that all the evidence supports the hypothesis that Nikolaev acted on behalf of the underground Zinovievite conspiratorial center, and that he has no evidence at all to refute this hypothesis. This is the fallacy of "begging the question" with a vengeance! If Egge is going to just "assume away" all the evidence that is inconvenient to his hypothesis, why bother to write the book in the first place?

---

[157] I have put the original Russian text of the Indictment online at http://msuweb.montclair.edu/~furrg/research/obvin_zak_dec34.html

[158] Lubianka 1922-1936 No. 482, pp. 578-579; Lenoe 316-317.

[159] "Absurdnost' etikh utverzhdenii ochevidna."

Like Lenoe, Egge quotes Liushkov's article in *Kaizo* of April 1939 but fails to contextualize it – Liushkov's job was to write propaganda for the Japanese Army – or to point out that Liushkov told his Japanese handlers the opposite of what he stated in this article. (190-191)

There is no limit to Egge's "begging the question"! He states:

> There is not a shadow of a doubt remaining that the others accused in the case of the murder of Kirov were innocent, and that the whole story of the "Leningrad center" was invented in order to strike a blow at the opposition. (191)

Another bluff, or "tell"! Egge realizes that he has no evidence whatever to support his view that Nikolaev was a "lone gunman". So he is reduced to assuring us that there is "not the shadow of a doubt." This is "begging the question" with a vengeance.

On page 130 Egge tries to explain away testimony inconvenient to his hypothesis with references to "brainwashing", "party loyalty", and "the Stockholm syndrome." But does he have even a shred of evidence for any of these things? No, he does not. Again, Egge states:

> In the first case the investigators were able to find only a pair of defendants who supported Nikolaev's lie. (192)

As we have seen, Kirilina says that not a "pair", but *four* of the defendants confessed! But the real point here is the phrase "Nikolaev's lie" – Egge *assumes* Nikolaev is lying! He has no evidence to back up this statement. When a researcher simply "assumes" that which is to be proven – commits the fallacy of "begging the question" – then the text of his book becomes not scholarship but merely a smokescreen to hide something. Egge wants to smuggle in his preconceived ideas under the disguise of "research."

Egge states:

> It was Stalin himself who ordered the investigation to concentrate their attention on the Zinovievites. (193)

No one denies this. The question is: What does it mean? We have discussed this question in detail in our discussion of Lenoe's book. There we have shown that Stalin did not do this until there was already plenty of testimony about the Zinovievites from Nikolaev and other defendants.

Concerning the January 1935 trial of other Zinovievites, Egge states:

> As has already been stated in Chapter 5, the press disclosed the arrest of these well-known Zinovievites, but they were not brought to trial yet because of the lack of evidence. (194-195)

Obviously if Stalin had wanted to "frame" – falsely accuse – these people he could have done so at any time. Therefore, he did not want to do so. If Stalin had wanted to falsify interrogations of these defendants, that could have been done as well. But it was not done. Instead, the public was told that there was "insufficient evidence." *Clearly Stalin and the Soviet government were more interested in evidence than Egge is today!*

Egge states:

> That same day, January 16 [1935], 77 persons of the 137 were sentenced by the Special Commission (*osoboe soveshchanie*) to sentences in a camp or to exile of 4 to 5 years. They were accused of membership in a "counterrevolutionary Zinovievite group" in Leningrad led by Safarov, Zalutskii, and others. Among those convicted were Nikolaev's mother, his sisters, and several other relatives, one of Nikolaev's neighbors, and also Anna, IUskin's wife. (195)

We have no reason – that is, no evidence – to suppose that Nikolaev's relatives were unjustly treated here. We know Nikolaev had explicitly implicated his sisters, as well as his brother (who had also confessed) and his brother-in-law. Of course, we do not have all the investigative materials either.

Despite the fact that we have a lot of testimony about them Egge calls the Leningrad and Moscow centers "mythical":

> In addition, the trials in the case of the mythical members of the "Leningrad and Moscow centers…" (196)

Egge continues:

> However, the executions of some of those arrested began quickly. Mil'da Draule, Nikolaev's wife, her sister Ol'ga and Ol'ga's husband Roman Kulisher, were

> sentenced to death by the Military Collegium of the Supreme Court of the USSR, that is by the same organ that had passed sentence upon Nikolaev and his partners (*soobshchniki*). (196)

...and...

> Nikolaev's step-brother Petr was also shot. On January 16 [1935] Nikolaev's older sister Ekaterina Rogacheva was sentenced to five years in a camp. Three years later the "troika" sentenced her to execution. Such "troikas" were usually comprised of two NKVD men and a judge; after meeting for 10-15 minutes they announced their sentence on a case or on a group of cases. (197)

Egge does not trouble himself to ask the only relevant question: What was the evidence against these defendants? Only have a few quotations from a few of the interrogations of Mil'da Draule have been made public, but from them we know that she implicated herself and other members of her family. Lenoe himself shows that Piotr Nikolaev confessed to helping Nikolaev.

Evidently Egge wants to create the impression that all these people were "innocent". He does this in part by concealing the evidence that we know existed against them. As for Rogacheva's execution three years later, we have just a little bit of information about it. Egge too could have revealed it to his readers instead of, as he does, withholding it:

On a "Memorial Society" web page we read the following:

> Rogacheva Ekaterina Vasil'evna
>
> Born 1899, Russian, born in the village of Mel'goshchina, Gvozd' region, Leningrad oblast'; member of the AUCP(b) 1918-1934; chair of the Profkom of the bath and ironing trust.
>
> ("Natural sister of Nikolaev, who committed the savage murder of S.M. Kirov.")
>
> Lived in Leningrad.
>
> Arrested December 1, 1934.

> Sentenced: by the Special Commission of the NKVD of the USSR on January 16, 1935, for "active participation in a counterrevolutionary Zinovievite group."
>
> Sentence: 5 years in a concentration camp.
>
> Source: *Leningradskii martirolog*, vol. 8 (in press).
>
> Rogacheva Ekaterina Vasil'evna
>
> Born 1899, Russian,
>
> born in the village of Mel'goshchina, Gvozd' region, Leningrad oblast'; member of the AUCP(b) 1918-1934; place of imprisonment: Solovki.
>
> Sentenced: By the special troika of the UNKVD of the Leningrad Oblast' on February 14, 1938, for "counterrevolutionary Trotskyite agitation among the prisoners".
>
> Sentence: Death. Shot February 17 1938. Place of burial: Solovki.
>
> Source: *Leningradskii martirolog*, vol. 8 (in press).

Rogacheva was one of the 77 persons convicted on January 16 as mentioned by Egge. She was executed in 1938 for something entirely different – Trotskyite agitation. Was she innocent? Guilty? In order to determine that we would need to study her investigative file. Did Egge ask to see it? Was he refused? He doesn't tell us. But without it, on what grounds can we decide whether the charges against her were supported by good evidence or not, her conviction and subsequent execution just or unjust?

Of the other defendants Egge writes: "Afterwards many of these defendants were arrested again and shot." How does he know this? What is his evidence? There's not even a footnote. It's reasonable to assume that once again Egge has no evidence and is "talking through his hat" here too.

Conclusion

Egge reveals that there are other, perhaps many other, interrogations that are available to scholars, since they were available to him. But in other respects Egge's work is similar to those by Kirilina and Lenoe. However, it is useful – but in a negative sense, in that it confirms what we already knew: that there is no primary-source evidence that can impugn the investigation of December 1934 or the conclusion that the defendants at that trial were guilty.

Chapter 20.

Conclusion: The Logic of the Evidence

There are two possible hypotheses to explain the immense amount of evidence we now have confirming the guilt of the Kirov murder defendants and their accomplices:

Hypothesis #1: All the evidence attesting to the existence of the conspiracy has been fabricated by one means or another. Investigators lied; defendants were forced to give false testimony under some kind of threat or inducement; documents (where there are any) have been forged.

Hypothesis #2: The conspiracy did exist, as attested by the evidence.

Like all hypotheses, the first one must be supported by evidence in order to stand. Hypothesis #1 presupposes a "conspiracy" too – a conspiracy to falsify evidence. If there were some evidence of such a conspiracy – evidence that these investigative materials had been falsified or the defendants forced to lie – we could study it. Although one or two pieces of such evidence would not invalidate everything, they might well invalidate certain specific pieces of evidence.

But there is no evidence of any such conspiracy. No matter how "deep" into the archives the investigators go they have never found any indication of such a conspiracy, or of any fabrication of evidence. On the evidence, therefore, any objective scholar is forced to abandon Hypothesis #1 for lack of evidence, and decide in favor of the second hypothesis.

Accordingly, we can confidently state that the defendants in the Kirov trial of December 1934 were guilty as charged. There is a great deal of evidence against them. There is no evidence whatsoever to exculpate any of them. In light of these facts any objective student is forced to conclude that the trial was fair and the verdict just. Moreover, subsequent to the trial further evidence came to light of the conspiracy. We have examined it as well. It confirms the guilt of the Kirov trial defendants.

Like Iurii Zhukov, we too have discussed the kind of evidence that can be reasonably expected to exist in the case of conspiracies. We have had the advantage of writing years after this article of Zhukov's and now have far more documentary evidence than Zhukov had in the late 1990s. To any objective student, as to Zhukov, the evidence of these conspiracies is overwhelming.

Most of the primary documents in the cases of the conspiracies of the 1930s are still classified top-secret in Russia today. A very few privileged researchers have evidently been permitted to see some of it. But other evidence is off-limits even to them. All the evidence from these archives that has been published has, obviously, either been official or semi-official – that is, it could not have been published without the permission of one or another official body. The fact that different archives are under the control of different agencies may account for the publication of documents such as the striking pretrial confessions of Genrikh Iagoda and others published in a tiny press run of 200 copies in 1997. Even this volume, however, was supervised by mainstream, highly anticommunist historians.

We also have the two Shvernik Commission reports done for Khrushchev in the early 1960s, the "Zapiska" and the "Spravka". We have the volumes of official documents, including the "rehabilitation reports", of the Gorbachev years, and many other documents in official collections. All of this material has been published by scholars with a strong anti-communist and anti-Stalin bias. Yet the result is always the same. All the primary source evidence confirms that the conspiracies of the 1930s did take place.

The only unofficial source of publication of still-secret documents from former Soviet Archives that have direct bearing on the conspiracies of the 1930s is the Volkogonov Archive. Dmitrii Volkogonov was ferociously anti-Stalin and on very good terms with both Gorbachev and El'tsin. It can be assumed that his research assistants would have brought out any documents that tended to support their boss's views. But all the documents in this archive that bear upon the conspiracies of the 1930s tend to confirm, not to dispute, the existence of the conspiracies and the guilt of the accused. We have mined this archive for several confessions from the December 1934 investigation of the Kirov murder and cited them here.

We do have some non-Soviet evidence attesting to the existence of these conspiracies: that of Liushkov, made when he was beyond the reach of the Soviets, and Valentin Astrov's confirmation in 1993 of his 1937 confessions. This evidence is not only interesting in itself. By attesting to the conspiracies, it also corroborates the evidence of the Soviet investigations, including pre-trial interrogations and trial testimony.

The Coverup

Despite the attempts to make it into one the Kirov murder is not a mystery. Nor has it ever been one. The claim that it is a mystery is part of a web of falsehoods spun around this event almost from the day Kirov was killed.

Trotsky's Coverup

It was Leon Trotsky who, as early as December 1934, was the first person of note to claim that the assassination was a mystery.

> The assassination of Kirov has remained a complete mystery for several weeks…
>
> It was clear, however, that this information relating to the "Zinoviev group" was not issued by accident; it could imply nothing else but the preparation of a jural "amalgam", that is to say, a consciously false attempt to implicate in the assassination of Kirov individuals and groups who did not and could not have anything in common with the terrorist act. ...
>
> Nicolaiev becomes the terrorist agent of an internal opposition to the party, at the head of which there were to be found the former Chairman of the Communist International, Zinoviev, and the former Chairman of the Political Bureau, Kamenev, both of them Stalin's colleagues in the "troika". It is clearly to be seen why we

> have called the dispatch of the TASS a colossal sensation. We can now also call it a colossal lie.[160]

This article comprised the whole of issue #41 of Trotsky's *Bulletin of the Opposition* of January 1935.[161] Throughout this lengthy article Trotsky repeats over and over again that the indictment was a lie, the defendants arrested on false charges. Moreover, Trotsky predicts that Trotskyism, and he himself, will be accused of involvement in the Kirov assassination:

> ... At that moment, in a conversation with a friend (I apologize for these personal details, but they are necessary for the understanding of the psychological undercurrents in the case), I said, "The matter will not rest long on this plane, tomorrow they will bring Trotskyism to the fore."

In an appendix Trotsky notes that he is named in the indictment.

Trotsky described his alleged motive for writing the article:

> There is only one way to forestall en route the amalgams that are in preparation: *Expose the scheme in advance.*

Trotsky claimed that Zinoviev, Kamenev and the rest must be innocent because, like him, they were Marxists who disavowed individual terrorism:

> They could not suddenly turn to a belief in the utility of individual terror for changing the social régime...

In this study we have examined the evidence that Trotsky's son Sedov did not disavow but instead embraced terrorism. Sedov's logic was the same as that voiced by Kamenev, Zinoviev, and other defendants: violence was the only way that the Stalin leadership could be removed. We

---

160 Leon Trotsky. "The Stalinist Bureaucracy and the Assassination of Kirov. A Reply to Friends in America." *Bulletin of the Opposition* No. 41 (January, 1935). Translated in Trotsky, "On the Kirov Assassination" (December 1934). At http://www.marxists.org/archive/trotsky/1934/12/kirov.htm

161 The Trotskyist editors of Marxists.org claim that this was published as a pamphlet. The *Biulleten'* version, in Russian, is at http://www.mit.edu/people/fjk/BO/BO-41.html (M.I.T., Boston USA) and at http://www.1917.com/Marxism/Trotsky/BO/BO_No_41/Main.html (Russia)

noted that in his published work Sedov also rejected "terror" in the strongest possible terms, and that Sedov had no political program separate from his father's. Other scholars have shown that Trotsky didn't hesitate to lie in his writings for political gain.

But we also know more: that Trotsky was deliberately lying in this specific article. From the Harvard Trotsky Archive we know that in 1932 the Soviet Trotskyists, including I.N. Smirnov, had formed a bloc with, among others, Kamenev and Zinoviev, with Safarov soon to enter it.

Trotskyist scholar Pierre Broué claimed, without any evidence, that this bloc was an "ephemeral" one that did not outlast the year it was formed. But even Broué knew that was not true. In his 1993 biography of Leon Sedov Broué wrote:

> Liova est dans son élément. Il écrira plus tard au secretariat international cette phrase à la fois modeste et triomphante:
>
> > "I.N. Smirnov et d'autres qui nous ont quittés dans le temps sont revenus."
>
> Liova [the diminutive of "Lev", Russian version of "Leon"] was in his element. He wrote later to the International Secretariat [of the 4th International] this phrase, at once modest and triumphant:
>
> > "I.N. Smirnov and others who left us in time came back."

Broué dates this remark to May, 1934:

> L. Sedov. "La situation de l'"opposition de gauche en URSS" [nd, mai 1934], rapport au SI. Archives J. Rous et Tamiment Library, New York.[162]

By May 1934 I.N. Smirnov had long been under arrest – an arrest that had been foreseen by the 1932 letter of Sedov to Trotsky. But among the "others who had left [who] had returned" were, certainly, Radek,

---

[162] Pierre Broué, *Léon Sedov. Fils de Trotsky. Victime de Staline* (Paris: Éditions Ouvrires, 1993), 79.

Sokol'nikov, and Piatakov. We know of Trotsky's letter to Radek, and we know from Sedov's "slip of the tongue" in January 1937, as well as from his exchange of letters with his father of 1932, that they had been in touch with Zinoviev and Kamenev as well as Radek.

Therefore, Trotsky was already lying in this December 1934 article about the Kirov murder. As Arch Getty has written,

> The point here is that Trotsky lied... he had good reasons to lie. But what he said was not the truth. It was not "objective." (H-RUSSIA November 24, 1998)

In our capacity as historians we cannot blame Trotsky for lying. Indeed, no underground conspiratorial network can exist without lying. *But this also means we cannot accept what he wrote for public consumption as a true representation of what he thought and believed.* According to the evidence Trotsky was indirectly involved in the Kirov assassination through his supporters, to whom he sent his orders. The fact that Trotsky denied this should not distract us from the evidence, since we know that Trotsky lied when he found it to his advantage.

It was in Trotsky's interest to portray the Kirov murder as a mystery in order to anticipate and try to refute in advance the accusations against himself which he must have known would inevitably come if the conspiracy unraveled. In light of later testimony it seems clear that Trotsky suspected his own role in this bloc might well be exposed sooner or later. This is likely the reason for him to, as he put it, "expose the scheme in advance" – reveal that the NKVD would be accusing him soon.

Khrushchev

But Trotsky's opinions were mainly influential only among his own followers – and he had only a very small following. Few people paid much attention to what Trotsky wrote until Nikita Khrushchev delivered his infamous "Secret Speech" to the 20th Party Congress in February 1956 in which Khrushchev savagely attacked Stalin (and Lavrentii Beria). In that speech Khrushchev too declared the Kirov murder a "mystery":

> It must be asserted that to this day the circumstances surrounding Kirov's murder hide many things which are inexplicable and mysterious and demand a most careful examination. There are reasons for the suspicion that the killer of Kirov, Nikolayev, was assisted by someone from

> among the people whose duty it was to protect the person of Kirov.
>
> A month and a half before the killing, Nikolayev was arrested on the grounds of suspicious behavior but he was released and not even searched. It is an unusually suspicious circumstance that when the Chekist assigned to protect Kirov was being brought for an interrogation, on December 2, 1934, he was killed in a car "accident" in which no other occupants of the car were harmed. After the murder of Kirov, top functionaries of the Leningrad NKVD were given very light sentences, but in 1937 they were shot. We can assume that they were shot in order to cover the traces of the organizers of Kirov's killing.

Even before Khrushchev gave this speech he had managed to force a reconsideration of the Kirov murder through the Presidium (the new name of the Politburo as of October 1952). In determining that Nikolaev's act was of a "political character" and asking for information about the activities of the various conspiratorial groups in Leningrad at the time the "Molotov commission" on April 23, 1956 basically reasserted the conclusion of December 1934.[163]

But Khrushchev's men, including KGB chief Ivan Serov and Prosecutor Roman Rudenko, issued a report at about the same time that set for the "new line": that Nikolaev had been a "lone gunman." This became the basic position during the Khrushchev years, as Lenoe's book amply documents.

The Wider Implications of the Kirov Murder

In a passage we have quoted elsewhere in this study Lenoe recognizes the implications of Khrushchev's "rewriting" of the Kirov assassination in this way:

> If the official charges in the first two trials – that former Zinoviev supporters / 592 / had conspired to murder Kirov – were entirely bogus, then the indictments in all

[163] Lenoe 577-8; Russian original in RKEB 2, 73-74.

> of the succeeding show trials collapsed. … But if there was some truth to the charge that Zinovievites conspired to kill Kirov, then that preserved the possibility of arguing that the latter charges were also valid, at least in part. Therefore Serov and Rudenko … chose to make a clear-cut argument that Nikolaev had had no relationship at all with the ex-Zinoviev supporters convicted in the trial of the "Leningrad Center. (591-2)

Lenoe goes on to examine Khrushchev's "coverup" – a conscious plan to fabricate a false version of the Kirov assassination, which included destroying some evidence and concealing other evidence from the Molotov commission, which had been formed supposedly to resolve the "mystery" of the Kirov assassination.

We agree with Lenoe's analysis this far. Khrushchev's men did not want to know the truth about the Kirov assassination – or, perhaps more accurately, they did not want anyone else to know the truth about it. They wanted to perpetrate a fraud for political purposes. This preconceived purpose fatally compromised Khrushchev's investigation from the very beginning, as it was intended to do. Lenoe recognizes this, but he fails to perceive its implications. For having proven that Khrushchev's investigation was fraudulent, Lenoe then embraces the conclusion of this same investigation, the "lone gunman" hypothesis.

Can Lenoe possibly believe that Khrushchev's inquiry, which abandoned objectivity and pursued a preconceived conclusion from the outset, nevertheless somehow stumbled upon the truth despite itself? Evidently he does. Lenoe is extremely contradictory concerning Khrushchev and everything he did. Having proven to his readers that the Khrushchev-sponsored study of the Kirov assassination was dishonest from the beginning, Lenoe nevertheless assures us that it arrived at the truth. Lenoe then makes the further assumption that the *other* research Khrushchev's men did – the research that, supposedly, established Stalin's "heinous crimes" and the "collaboration ... in mass murder" of his principal associates – *that* research was, somehow, honest.

For example, after examining in some detail the way in which Khrushchev's men biased the Kirov inquiry Lenoe says the following:

> No one was "covering" for Stalin at this moment – the Khrushchevites revealed many of his most heinous

> crimes, as well as the collaboration of Molotov, Kaganovich, Malenkov, Beria, and others in mass murder. (604)

Khrushchev Lied

Lenoe should have known better. To this point not a single one of the accusations of Khrushchev and his men of criminal behavior or mass murder against Stalin and his associates has been verified. For example, every single one of the accusations Khrushchev made against Stalin and Beria in the "Secret Speech" is false. Every allegation against Stalin made by Aleksandr Shelepin in his speech to the 22nd Party Congress is false. Marshal Zhukov was provided with dishonestly edited documents to read aloud at the June 1957 Central Committee Plenum at which Khrushchev ousted Stalin supporters Malenkov, Molotov, Kaganovich, and Shepilov.

Khrushchev never stated outright his real reasons for his mendacious attack on Stalin and others. Nor, of course, did Khrushchev ever publish the evidence to support his claims, while the little documentation he did cite has since been proven to have been falsified. Once we recognize this immense deception for what it is the question returns with even greater force: Why did Khrushchev do this?

A generation later Mikhail Gorbachev carried out an essentially similar attack on Stalin but with a much more overt motive: to justify capitalist-style market economics into the Soviet system and, ultimately, to do away with its socialist aspects altogether. Gorbachev's actions suggest that Khrushchev may have been up to something similar but at an earlier stage of the process. Other, or additional, explanations are possible. Some have suggested that Khrushchev may have wanted to stop the erosion of power away from Party First Secretaries towards the Soviet government.

Thought somewhat suspicious of Khrushchev Lenoe accepts the Gorbachev-era studies completely. This means that he also accepts the Khrushchev-era conclusions despite his inconsistent expressions of distrust of them. He embraces Kirilina's book, which bases itself upon Gorbachev-era materials. Kirilina also proceeds from the preconceived idea that Nikolaev was a "lone gunman", without even the pretense that she is trying to resolve a question that has not been previously answered.

Her whole book is an exercise in "assuming that which ought to be proven."

Lenoe claims to be trying to solve the Kirov murder "mystery". But in fact Lenoe did not approach the Kirov assassination as a crime to be solved or a problem to which the solution is not known. Instead Lenoe wrote his book to present the best possible case for a preconceived idea: the "lone gunman" hypothesis. He ignores almost all of the evidence that is incompatible with this hypothesis. He twists the evidence he does deal with to try to force that evidence to appear compatible with the "lone gunman" hypothesis. In the end Lenoe utterly fails to find any evidence that supports this hypothesis, yet he still concludes it is correct. This means Lenoe had decided what his conclusion *must* be before he did his research.

The Kirov case opened the door to the rest of the high politics of the 1930s. NKVD investigators kept "pulling at loose ends", as Iagoda put it, and kept uncovering more and more conspirators, and conspiracies. We can trace this process in a general way despite the continued refusal of Russian authorities to release the documentation. Meanwhile more than the statutory 75 years have passed since the Kirov murder and trial, the period after which such materials are, apparently, supposed to be declassified in today's Russia. Yet the Russian authorities continue to keep many of the Kirov assassination materials secret. Although we do not know why, one possible explanation is that the evidence, once made public, would definitively disprove the "lone gunman" hypothesis.

In the previous chapter we gave a brief account of how the "Kremlin Affair" evolved from the Kirov case and how it began to lead to what was to become the First Moscow Trial of August 1936. In pretrial interrogations and at the August 1936 Trial Sokol'nikov was named, along with some Trotskyite military figures. That led investigators to the January 1937 Trial, at which yet more figures were named, and that led to the Tukhachevsky Affair of May-June 1937 and ultimately to the 1938 Moscow Trial. Meanwhile all of these events, but especially the Tukhachevsky Affair, led directly to the "Ezhovshchina", or "Great Terror", of July 1937 to November, 1938. That ended only when Ezhov himself was persuaded to resign from his post as Commissar of the NKVD – in effect, when he gave up on the chances that his own bloody conspiracy would succeed.

The Big Coverup of Soviet History

When Khrushchev assumed power in 1953 the revolution of 1917 was 36 years old. Kirov's murder had occurred only 19 years earlier, the Moscow Trials and Ezhovshchina more recently still. Khrushchev undertook the incredibly bold task of completely rewriting a history that was very recent and known to tens of millions of people. And his "rewriting" was a drastic one. Stalin had been touted as a hero by tens of millions of people within the USSR, to say nothing of hundreds of millions around the world. Khrushchev did not go half-way – he made a frontal assault on Stalin, and thereby on recent Soviet history.

In 1961 Khrushchev masterminded a second attack on Stalin at the 22nd Party Congress. This attack was, if anything, sharper than the one he had proposed five and one-half years earlier. This time it was followed by a veritable flood of officially-sponsored historical works in which Khrushchev's reversal of historical assessments was elaborated. This wealth of material became the source for anticommunist historiography for the next quarter-century and more, until Gorbachev sponsored an even more extensive and still sharper attack on Soviet history. Gorbachev went further in that he included Khrushchev and his contemporaries, the "anti-Stalinists" of a generation before, as secondary villains.

The "Gorbachev" paradigm of Soviet history is a version of the "Khrushchev" paradigm, which was the version of Soviet history almost universal outside the USSR and communist bloc during and after Khrushchev's day. This paradigm of Soviet history – elsewhere I have called it, for the sake of brevity, the "anti-Stalin" paradigm – remains the "mainstream" model today. Most research is done in such a matter as to fit more or less seamlessly into this paradigm. This paradigm is rarely challenged in academic journals and books. Both Lenoe and Kirilina tailor their arguments and conclusions to fit comfortably within this paradigm. The only "left" version of Soviet history permitted in mainstream historiography is the Trotskyite version, which privileges Leon Trotsky to an absurd degree but otherwise partakes of all the anti-Stalin myths of the mainstream anticommunist paradigm.

But this mainstream "Khrushchev – Cold War – Gorbachev – Trotskyite – anti-Stalin" paradigm fares very poorly when the evidence for it is carefully examined. It is made up of a number of assertions none of which can be demonstrated by the evidence available now. This is the Soviet history of the Stalin period that is widely "known" and widely taught, and that provides the framework for most of the research on Soviet history that is done today.

The Kirov murder is a foundational part of this paradigm. As Lenoe noted with respect to Khrushchev's men: if Nikolaev and the other men convicted with him really were part of a clandestine terrorist Zinovievite conspiracy, then the possibility exists that the rest of the alleged conspiracies of the 1930s were true, more or less as they were described at the time. That would not only necessitate a rewriting of Soviet history of the 1930s. It would mean throwing out the whole "anti-Stalin" paradigm that has structured Soviet historiography in the West for 50 years, and that in the late USSR and Russia for more than 20 years.

There is a huge individual and institutional "investment" in this historical paradigm. It is fundamental to the careers of a great many historians. It is a component, even an essential, part of the Cold War narrative of communism. It is part of the foundational historical mythology of all the post-Soviet states. A paradigm such as this one serves powerful capitalist interests, which are always eager to embrace arguments that the exploitation of man by man cannot be ended, that attempts to end it lead to even greater horrors, that those who want to change the world through communist revolution are really the enemies of mankind because they can only bring out greater suffering and destruction. Thus the "anti-Stalin" paradigm performs a great service for the cause of exploitation and inequality.

Like all historical paradigms the "anti-Stalin" paradigm is relatively impervious to refutation by research. No single piece of research can overturn a paradigm. At the same time the paradigm acts to contain research. Research results that do not fit within the paradigm are likely to be simply ignored or, at best, considered marginal by professional historians within the institutional structure of knowledge production – universities and other research institutes generally.

The present work, like the work we have published previously and the work of a few other researchers, constitutes a frontal challenge to and rejection of this mainstream "anti-Stalin" paradigm. We predict it will be ignored by some and marginalized by others. But it will also be welcomed – by those who are looking not for an elaboration of the mainstream an-

anticommunist paradigm, but for the truth. It is to those readers we look for comment and criticism.

Appendix One – The Issue of Torture

In the opening pages of his book Lenoe refers to what he terms "layers of evidence in the assassination case, the most important of which are:

> 1. Pre-murder documents related to the lives of Kirov and Nikolaev.
>
> 2. The materials of the December 1934 – January 1935 investigation of the killing [of Kirov].
>
> 3. Documents from the renewed "investigation" of the Great Terror years (1936-1938), many of which are witness statements given under torture or the threat of same. (8)

Lenoe uses no quotation marks around the word "investigation" in reference to the December 1934 – January 1935 investigation, but does use them in reference to the 1936-1938 investigation. He does not explain this variation. Likewise Lenoe does not allege "torture or the threat of torture" in the case of the 1934-35 investigation, but does so in the case of that of 1936-1938.

The reader of Lenoe's book will discover that Lenoe does examine a lot of the evidence of the December 1934 investigation. Lenoe suggests that some of the confessions made by suspects in December 1934 might have been due to torture, though he presents no evidence that any of them were.

The confessions of a number of the defendants at the December 1934 Kirov trial are disconcerting to Lenoe. If they were genuine, then Lenoe's entire thesis – that Nikolaev was a "lone gunman" – falls to the ground. Yet Lenoe can produce no evidence that they are *not* genuine – for example, that they were false and either "scripted" or otherwise forced from the defendants by "torture or the threat of same" (Lenoe 8), by threats against family members, or by some other means. In a classic example of "begging the question" Lenoe simply *assumes* that the confessions of the December 1934 defendants were false. Lenoe never examines any – not a single one – of the many documents from 1936 – 1938 that bear on the Kirov murder. To any objective reader who has even a passing familiarity with the Kirov assassination this is an astonishing omission, one that demands an explanation.

We suggest that Lenoe uses the allegation of torture to avoid examining a great deal of evidence that would, if examined, disprove the thesis of his book that Nikolaev was a "lone gunman" and that all the rest of those convicted of participation in Kirov's murder were innocent, "framed" by Stalin and/or the NKVD. That is to say, Lenoe employs "torture" as a "smokescreen" or a "bogeyman", either to obscure the fact that Lenoe has avoided examining huge amounts of important evidence, or to "frighten" the reader into acquiescing with Lenoe's decision to assume all this material was "fabricated" or forced unwillingly from the defendants, without Lenoe's having to give any argument or evidence at all that this was the case.

The bogeyman of "torture" has been employed before this by those who write about the history of the USSR during the 1930s. We believe Lenoe is doing just that in this book. In order to dispel the fog of confusion surrounding the concept of "torture" we need to examine it more closely.

Torture and the Historical Problems Related To It[164]

From Stalin's day on no one has denied that many prisoners arrested on political charges during the period that Nikolai Ezhov was head (People's Commissar) of the NKVD, particularly in the period 1937-1938, were tortured. "Rehabilitation" courts in Khrushchev and post-Khrushchev times have often "rehabilitated" defendants on the basis that they were tortured. Normally this took the form of declaring their convictions invalid. In a judicial procedure, even in the USSR during Stalin's time, evidence obtained from a defendant by torture was invalid and could not legally be used at trial.

The fact that a defendant was tortured does not mean that defendant was innocent. It is not evidence that the defendant was innocent. But it is

[164] The following paragraphs are taken from Grover Furr, *Khrushchev Lied* 151-3. See also the section "The Charge of 'Torture' As A Smokescreen" in Furr, "Evidence of Leon Trotsky's Collaboration with Germany and Japan", *Cultural Logic* 2009, 151-153. At http://clogic.eserver.org/2009/Furr.pdf

often erroneously assumed to be. In reality, there are many different possibilities:

* A person may be guilty, be tortured, and confess;

* A person may be guilty, be tortured, and not confess;

* A person may be innocent, be tortured, and confess (e.g. in order to stop the torture);

* A person may be innocent, be tortured, and still not confess.

* A person may be innocent, not be tortured, and still confess guilt to another crime. (Examples of this occur in the Rehabilitation documents).

* A person may have been tortured, but be found guilty by other evidence, such as testimony of other defendants or physical evidence. Other testimony, from other individuals, and other evidence, usually come into play.

In addition, it is important to bear in mind that any "confession" may be honest – i.e. the person confessing is trying to tell the truth as he remembers it – or dishonest (the person confessing is deliberately lying).

Any confession may be truthful or untruthful: the fact that someone tells the truth as he remembers it does not mean that what he says really is truthful. An example of this is Bulanov's confession at the March 1938 Moscow Trial concerning the death of Borisov. Bulanov thought he remembered that Iagoda was involved in arranging for Borisov to be killed. But in the archival, i.e. original, version Bulanov admits that his memory is "rather confused" *(dovol'no sumburnyi)*. And sure enough, Bulanov remembered incorrectly.

Establishing the fact that someone really has been tortured is not always easy. The mere fact that someone claims he confessed because he was tortured is hardly foolproof. There are many reasons why people might want to retract a confession of guilt. Claiming one was tortured is a way of doing this while preserving some dignity. To be reasonably certain a person was tortured we need further evidence of the fact, such as a statement or confession by a person who actually did the torturing, a corroborating witness, or physical injuries consistent with torture.

When there is no evidence at all that a defendant was tortured objective scholars have no business concluding that he was tortured. This obvious point is often overlooked, probably because a "paradigm" that everybody was tortured, and thus that everybody was innocent, acts powerfully on the minds of both researchers and readers.

For our purposes all this should just serve to remind us of the need for evidence.

> * We can't assume a person was tortured without evidence that he was.
>
> * We can't assume a person was guilty or innocent just because he was tortured, much less on the basis of a mere allegation that he was tortured.

Most important, we can't assume that testimony was obtained through torture because that testimony is inconvenient for us or contradicts our own hypothesis. This is in fact what Lenoe and Egge do, time and again. Rather than consider each piece of evidence, including the evidence, if any, that it was obtained by torture or threat, Lenoe refuses to examine any of the pretrial or trial evidence of the three Moscow Trials of August 1936, January 1937, and March 1938. In effect, he simply rejects this evidence out of hand. A great deal of this evidence directly concerns the assassination of Kirov but all of it tends to disprove Lenoe's hypothesis that Nikolaev was a "lone gunman."

On page 9, Lenoe writes:

> During the Great Terror NKVD officers tortured witnesses until they provided testimony supporting fantastic charges of conspiracy against former party leaders. This highly unreliable and self-contradictory body of testimony muddied the waters of the Kirov case…

Lenoe displays a lack of objectivity here. For example, he employs the word "fantastic" applied to the charges against the Moscow Trial defendants and others in a subjective manner. This is the logical fallacy known as the "argument from incredulity", which takes the following form:

> P is too incredible (or I cannot imagine how P could possibly be true); therefore P must be false.[165]

This is a form of the argument from ignorance. The truth or falsehood of a hypothesis or proposition must be demonstrated by evidence. It cannot depend upon whether a given individual can "believe" it or not for, to quote Hamlet, "There are more things in heaven and earth, Horatio, / Than are dreamt of in your philosophy." There is nothing objectively "fantastic" about the confessions. The word "fantastic" is a statement about the person who is using it, not about the testimony itself.

It appears that Lenoe is attempting, through the use of rhetorical language, to persuade his reader to allow him to conjure away his obligation to examine all the evidence. His use of the words "highly unreliable" and "self-contradictory" are also indicative of deception. Lenoe does not inform us by what measure he has gauged the degree of "reliability" – whatever that means – of testimony. Of course, he has not done so. Lenoe is also guilty of the opposite fallacy: declaring someone's work "reliable" because it is convenient for his, Lenoe's, hypothesis (see the chapter "Iurii Sedov – "reliable researcher").

As we show elsewhere in this study the evidence about the Kirov assassination that we find in the transcripts of the three Moscow Trials is damning to Lenoe's hypothesis that Nikolaev was a "lone gunman." Rather than examine this evidence carefully and try to assess its strengths and weaknesses, Lenoe prefers to simply dismiss it with words like "tortured", "fantastic", "unreliable", and "self-contradictory."

The term "self-contradictory" hides a fallacy too. For we ought to suspect forgery if statements by different conspirators about the same events were identical in detail – that is, if they did *not* exhibit contradictions. This adjective, along with "unconvincing", occur in Khrushchev- and Gorbachev-era "rehabilitation" reports, in which the goal was to declare former oppositionists "innocent" without evidence. The same is true about testimony by a single suspect. If a suspect at first denies his guilt and then proceeds to admit guilt gradually – a common practice – then of course his later confessions will "contradict" his earlier confessions, and his con-

---

165 See for example, the discussion of the Argument from incredulity at http://rationalwiki.org/wiki/Argument_from_incredulity

fessions as a whole will be "self-contradictory." In reality, "self-contradiction" of this kind is to be expected, and it would in fact be more suspicious if none were observed.

Lenoe's use of the word "torture" here represents the first example of a practice which we call "the use of torture as a smokescreen". Nowhere does Lenoe even attempt to demonstrate that testimony obtained through torture was material, much less crucial, in the prosecutions against former party leaders in the matter of Kirov's murder. We shall examine some more instances of Lenoe's allegations of torture as a "smokescreen" behind which to obscure his refusal to study evidence highly relevant to Kirov's murder but fatal to his own hypothesis that Nikolaev acted alone.

On page 17, discussing the Bush administration's use of torture in 2009, Lenoe refers to

> ...the use of torture by Stalin and his secret police to extract false but politically useful 'confessions' of terrorist conspiracies.

It is incorrect to refer to the NKVD as "his" – meaning Stalin's – NKVD, as Lenoe does here. To date scholarship has uncovered no evidence whatever – not a single example – that Stalin or those loyal to him used torture "to extract false but politically useful 'confessions' of terrorist activity". Lenoe's use of the word "his" here is an attempt to imply that Stalin ordered that innocent persons be tortured into giving false confessions when – to repeat – no scholar, no matter how anticommunist or anti-Stalin, has ever uncovered a shred of evidence to support that charge.

Moreover, if we did have some examples that would not mean that "everyone was tortured". Much less would it mean that "everyone whose testimony contradicts Lenoe's hypothesis gave that testimony 'under torture or the threat of same.'"

It is certainly true that the NKVD under Ezhov used torture widely to get innocent people to sign scripted confessions of guilt. We have a lot of evidence of this now in the form of testimony by former NKVD men themselves, those who tortured or who witnessed torture. All of this evidence is from the post-Ezhov period when, under Beria as Commissar of the NKVD, Ezhov's horrifying practices were being examined, NKVD men arrested, tried, and convicted, and cases of condemned people being reviewed. That is, much of what we know about the torture of suspects in the Soviet Union during the 1930s comes from Beria's investigations which were, of course, supported by Stalin. Ezhov was involved in a conspiracy to overthrow Stalin and the Party and government leadership and also to assassinate Stalin. I have collected all the texts of Ezhov's confessions that have been published in various sources so the readers can study them for themselves.[166]

Lenoe fails to cite a single instance of the use of torture to "extract false confessions" of Moscow Trial defendants material to the Kirov murder case. This is another example of "torture as smokescreen." Lenoe assumes all of this testimony is false without studying any of it. He employs the unsupported allegation of torture as a smokescreen behind which Lenoe disposes of all the post-1934 evidence that contradicts his hypothesis.

Lenoe's allegations of torture to avoid discussion of the Moscow Trial evidence is also a "tell" – a tacit admission that he recognizes the contradiction between this evidence and his preconceived idea that Nikolaev was a "lone gunman" and that no opposition conspiracies took place. In this section we will examine a number of instances of this practice of Lenoe's.

On page 313 Lenoe asks: "Why did Zvezdov and other purported members of the 'Leningrad Center' confess?" and continues:

> Then there was physical abuse. Beatings and other direct physical torture were not officially permitted by the NKVD leadership at this time, but they **undoubtedly** occurred. Interrogators **certainly** used other forms of torture… (emphasis added, GF)

Lenoe tries to use this allegation of torture to cast doubt upon the confessions of Zvezdov and other defendants solely because those confessions are fatal for his "lone gunman" hypothesis. Lenoe should have informed his readers at this point that he has found no evidence at all that torture was used against them. Instead he goes on to use the words "un-

---

166 The original Russian texts are at http://msuweb.montclair.edu/~furrg/research/ezhovpokazaniia.html (English translations at http://msuweb.montclair.edu/~furrg/research/ezhovinterrogs.html)

doubtedly" and "certainly" without any justification whatever. Lenoe fails to even consider the possibility that Zvezdov was telling the truth.

There is no evidence of torture used against Moscow Trial defendants. We have pointed out elsewhere with reference to the case of Valentin Astrov, a follower of Bukharin's who was interrogated about Bukharin and who confessed against him. In articles written after the end of the USSR, at a time when he was free to say anything at all, an aged Astrov insistently denied that he was tortured by the NKVD. Indeed, Astrov asserted that the NKVD investigators were respectful and never even called him "ty".

On page 369 Lenoe quotes, from an archival document, defendant Mandel'shtam's explanation, given during the December 28-29 1934 trial, for retracting part of a confession of December 19. Mandel'shtam allegedly said: "On December 19 I was in such a condition that I would have signed anything." Lenoe then writes: "The implication would seem to be that he had been tortured."

In fact, it is next to impossible that he had been tortured. He would have certainly said that to the court, since it would be the strongest and most convincing reason for retracting one's confession. During 1937-1938 a great many persons testified at their trials that they had been tortured. This testimony is recorded in the transcripts, portions of which have been quoted in the works of a few privileged researchers who have had access to them.[167]

It is common for people under intense interrogation to confess to things that they later wish to retract. For example: elsewhere in this study we examine Iagoda's testimony at the 1938 Moscow Trial. It seems clear from the published transcript that under intense interrogation Iagoda momentarily agreed that he was an "accomplice" in Kirov's murder. But

---

[167] So what else could Mandel'shtam have meant? In the first place, it meant that he was withdrawing the confession in question. In Soviet law the defendant had to confirm any confessions made before trial, or that evidence could not be used against him at trial. This does not mean that the confession was either true or false, only that the defendant wished to withdraw it. That would force the prosecution either to get him to retract his withdrawal or to rely upon other evidence – for example, the testimony of his co-conspirators.

later in the transcript he repeatedly and insistently denies his complicity, as he also had done during pretrial interrogations published in 1997.

On page 468 Lenoe writes "Tukhachevsky and his fellows were tortured and shot." This is simply false. Lenoe cites no evidence that the marshal was tortured because none exists.[168]

On page 573 Lenoe refers to "evidence" (in scare quotes) that was "extracted under torture in the process of fabricating a case against arrested NKVD chief Yagoda." Lenoe never even identifies, much less examines, a single piece of such "evidence". Nor does Lenoe provide any evidence whatsoever of torture. More importantly, he ignores all the evidence in the confessions by Iagoda himself, refusing even to tell his readers that it exists. We examine that evidence in a separate chapter.

On page 601 Lenoe writes:

> ...the 1937 testimony of the driver and guards who accompanied Borisov on December 2 was extracted under torture, and was therefore untrustworthy.

Lenoe provides no evidence to support this statement (and even if he had, it would not prove that the testimony was false). But in any case the issue is whether Iagoda and the bloc of Rights, Zinovievites, and Trotskyites conspired in Kirov's murder. The issue of Borisov is a detail that is irrelevant in this context. Whether Borisov was or was not a part of the conspiracy to kill Kirov – and no one today thinks that he was – does not bear on the issue of whether the conspiracy existed.

"Torture" and evidence

It is indicative of Lenoe's use of the torture issue to confuse matters that he states that "testimony ... extracted under torture ... was therefore untrustworthy." Lenoe should know, and convey to his readers, that ALL testimony is "untrustworthy" in that no testimony should be simply "trusted". All testimony, like all evidence of any kind, has to be carefully studied.

---

[168] Moreover, there is a great deal of evidence that they were guilty, including evidence from outside the USSR.

Moreover, it is not the case that testimony *not* given under torture is "more trustworthy" than testimony given under torture. People who are tortured may be lying – but people who are not tortured may also be lying. Simply knowing whether someone was "tortured" or not does not help us determine whether the testimony they gave was truthful or not.

On page 610 Lenoe is discomfited by the fact that in January 1961 Karl Ivanov, "an officer who sometimes guarded Kirov in the early 1930s" reconfirmed his testimony from the 1930s. Lenoe comments:

> Obviously Shatunovskaya's practice of asking witnesses to confirm their testimony from the Terror years led to the perpetuation of falsehoods extracted under torture.

This is far from "obvious", as Lenoe would have it. Lenoe does not know that the 1930s testimony in question was obtained "under torture" or not, nor does he suggest that Ivanov's 1961 testimony was obtained "under torture." This would appear to be simply a chance for Lenoe to gratuitously raise the "torture bogeyman" again. He cites no evidence at all that Ivanov had been tortured, or that people were confirming testimony in the post-Stalin years that they had only made because of torture in the 1930s.

On page 622 Lenoe writes:

> [Klimov] made extensive use of 1937-1938 depositions from Gubin, Zaporozhets, other Leningrad NKVD officers, Yagoda, and Yagoda's former deputy Bulanov, extracted under torture and used to incriminate Yagoda at the March 1938 trial.

Lenoe cites no evidence that Iagoda or Bulanov were tortured because there is none. On the contrary, as he did during the March 1938 Moscow Trial Iagoda made a differentiated confession – he confessed to some crimes during his pretrial interrogations but stoutly refused to confess to others, despite the efforts of his interrogators. This behavior is not consistent with a hypothesis that Iagoda was tortured.

Lenoe ignores the very extensive pretrial confessions of Iagoda that bear directly on the Kirov murder case, and of course ignores the testimony at the March 1938 trial as well. As for "depositions" of Gubin and Zaporozhets, none of them has been published and Lenoe does not quote any of them. But whether they were "tortured" or not is irrelevant. Iagoda's

Iagoda's testimony implicates both of them directly. We examine Iagoda's testimony in a separate section.

Evidence that torture was *not* used

The *only* piece of evidence that supports Lenoe's hypothesis and conclusion that Nikolaev acted alone are the texts of his early interrogations. These texts present significant problems that Lenoe hides from his readers; we examine them elsewhere in this study.

On page 289 Lenoe writes the following, referring to December 7 and 8 1934:

> He [Nikolaev] declared a hunger strike, and resisted leaving his cell. To get him to interrogations the guards had to put him in a straitjacket and carry him down the hall while he struggled and shouted, "It is I, Nikolaev, they're torturing me, remember me!"

This is an important moment for Lenoe's hypothesis, since it is the *only* reference to torture in his examination of the December 1934 investigation of Kirov's murder. By December 6 Nikolaev had already renounced his early confessions that he acted alone. Now he was confessing to being a part of an underground terrorist Zinovievite conspiracy. Since Nikolaev's early confessions constitute the sole evidence that supports the "lone gunman" hypothesis it is vital for the "lone gunman" theory that Nikolaev's later confessions be discredited.

Lenoe's source for Nikolaev's words about torture is an article in the popular magazine *Trud* of December 4, 1990 by IUrii Sedov.[169] However, Sedov gives no source for Nikolaev's words. We do not know whether they are from an official report by NKVD investigators or represent only a rumor – a fact Lenoe fails to tell his readers. Even if we knew and had access to the source, a study of that source would be essential before we could state it as a fact that this incident had occurred. Even if it did happen, that does not mean that Nikolaev was actually "tortured". There is no other evidence that Nikolaev was tortured, and Lenoe does not repeat the allegation.

---

169 We examine Lenoe's further use of Sedov elsewhere in this study.

And we must remember that even if it were proven that Nikolaev was tortured – whatever that term means – this would not prove that he did not tell the truth. As we pointed out above, there is no correlation between torture / lack of torture and falsehood / truth. A person may be tortured and still tell the truth; a person who is not tortured may lie; and so on.

Lenoe repeats much later allegations that Nikolaev had been promised lenient treatment for himself and/or his family. Lenoe claims that these promises were "in exchange for giving the testimony they [the NKVD interrogators] desired". (288) But Lenoe is making this up. He has no evidence whatsoever to support these statements. He does not cite any testimony that the investigators demanded *false* confessions from Nikolaev. In any case it is legal even in the United States today for investigators to lie to suspects, give them better food or treatment, etc., in order to elicit information. This is not a form of compulsion, much less of "torture."

Lenoe reproduces on page 343 (Document #70) a note of December 21, 1934 from Lev G. Mironov, an NKVD chief, to investigator Genrikh S. Liushkov asking that he try to ascertain certain facts about Nikolaev. It is important to note – though Lenoe does not – that these are not "leading questions", but requests for facts.

On page 378 Lenoe admits that, on February 3, 1935 Agranov, chief of the now-concluded Kirov murder investigation, said "we were not able to prove that the 'Moscow Center' knew about the preparations for a terrorist attack on Comrade Kirov."[170] This constitutes additional evidence that no torture was used, since presumably at least one of the January 1935 defendants would have "cracked" under torture. It is, therefore, strong evidence that the defendants in the December 1934 Kirov trial testified voluntarily. A number of them confessed fully, as we discuss elsewhere in this study.

Though he does not discuss the Moscow Trial testimony concerning Kirov's murder Lenoe does note that Bukharin and Rykov, while admitting their guilt to many capital offenses, vigorously denied any part in Kirov's

[170] Kirilina, 366, cites the original Russian text of Agranov's words.

assassination. (479) He does not seem to realize that this in fact constitutes evidence that they were not tortured or threatened.

Appendix Two – Texts of Primary Documents Ignored by All Previous Writers

This section will contain the following documents that are relevant to the December 1936 Kirov trial and have not been published before anywhere. All translations are my own.

NOTE: For English pages choose Character Encoding Western (ISO-8859-1). For Russian page choose Character Encoding Cyrillic (Windows-1251)

- Kotolynov interrogation of December 12 1934 (English)

    http://tinyurl.com/kotolyn121234

- Tsar'kov interrogation of December 13, 1934 (English)

    http://tinyurl.com/tsar-kov121334

- Kotolynov interrogation of December 19, 1934 (English)

    http://tinyurl.com/kotolyn121934

- Gorshenin interrogation of December 21, 1934 (English)

    http://tinyurl.com/gorshenin122134

In addition, I include the following three documents. All are previously unpublished and all contain material references to the Kirov murder.

- Zinoviev interrogation of July 28, 1936

    http://tinyurl.com/zinoviev28jul36 (in Russian)

    http://tinyurl.com/zinoviev072836 (in English)

- Kamenev interrogation of August 10, 1936

    http://tinyurl.com/kamenev10aug36 (in Russian)

    http://tinyurl.com/kamenev081036 (in English)

- Zinoviev interrogation of August ?, 1936 (date not readable)

  http://tinyurl.com/zinovievaug36 (in Russian)

  http://tinyurl.com/zinoviev0836 (in English)

I have put the following documents on the Internet because they are important and hard to obtain:

* Nikolaev's First Confession, as in Kirilina's book;

  - http://tinyurl.com/nikolaev120134kirilina (in Russian)

* Nikolaev's First Confession, as in Lenoe's book;

  - http://tinyurl.com/nikolaev120134lenoe (in English – not available in Russian)

* The "Indictment" (Обвинительное заключение).

  - http://tinyurl.com/indictment-russ (in Russian)

Bibliography and Sources

Many primary and secondary sources were consulted in preparing this book. Most are in Russian only; as of the date of publication very few are available in English. This is one reason for the many quotations from primary and secondary sources in the text. All translations are by the author unless otherwise noted in the text.

Editor

The Bibliography has been put online in order to reduce the length, and the cost, of this book. It may be found at

http://msuweb.montclair.edu/~furrg/research/kirov_bibl.html

The significant errors in the first two printings, may be found at

http://msuweb.montclair.edu/~furrg/research/errata&addenda.html

Index